All the best
Nitin seth

WINNING IN
THE DIGITAL AGE

NEW EDITION

Celebrating 35 Years of
Penguin Random House India

PERSPECTIVES FROM INDUSTRY LEADERS
ON *WINNING IN THE DIGITAL AGE*

This is a practitioner's book. With the advent of digital technologies, traditional non-tech enterprises in particular, struggle with where and how to begin their digital journey. Nitin, with his hands-on experience and deep understanding of organizational dynamics, has created this comprehensive handbook precisely to address this need. The focus, rightly so, is on leveraging new digital technologies rather than on technology itself. It very well addresses the softer behavioural issues related to change management. A very timely book.

Som Mittal
Former Chairman and President, NASSCOM

In a very lucid style, Nitin Seth shares the key elements of success in any digital transformation effort. He explains very clearly why this amounts to a fundamental and multi-dimensional organizational transformation rather than a mere technology initiative. His insights are distilled from a wealth of personal experience spanning over twenty years in multiple organizations with roles encompassing consultancy, entrepreneurship, knowledge management, investment management and e-commerce, and culminating in his work at Incedo that involves handholding end-to-end digital transformation initiatives across multiple companies and sectors . . . By laying out seven key building blocks for successful digital transformation, Nitin has very elegantly and eloquently laid out an easy path to accomplish a complex task. A must-read for anyone driving or even contemplating digital transformation.

R. Chandrashekhar
Former President, NASSCOM;
Former Telecom Secretary, Government of India

Seth has meticulously crafted an invaluable handbook for those who wish to structure their thinking and action on a digital transformation programme . . . Seth has witnessed success and failure, entrepreneurial and institutional cultures, local and global applications and understands how digital can transform and disrupt. The entire expanse of the digital journey across strategy, technology, organization and leadership are explored and lessons are shared in a usable manner. He brings this to bear in a patient, well-structured discussion, sharing lessons learnt from failing well, yet being resilient enough to persevere. A rewarding read.

Leo Puri
Former Managing Director, UTI Asset Management Company;
Chairman Designate, J.P. Morgan South and South East Asia

The book demystifies everything related to digital transformation very well—it provides the big picture as also the deep dives on all critical aspects for successfully driving it . . . Nitin's unique combination of experiences with McKinsey, Fidelity, Flipkart and now Incedo, provide a very compelling view of the digital world . . . These experiences are directly applicable in many of the situations where enterprises are challenged in their digital journeys and can resort to success recipes which Nitin has laid out very well. I thoroughly enjoyed reading it and would recommend this book to all business leaders and young professionals!

Raman Roy
Chairman and MD, Quattro;
Former Chairman, NASSCOM

Nitin's timely book focuses on the most critical issue facing companies today: how to survive and thrive in the digital age. As investors, we have seen billions of dollars squandered on technology by companies without implementing the fundamental retooling required by the organization. Nitin's recommendations will increase the probability of success, reduce wasteful spending, enhance growth and improve the return on investment of these efforts. I am sure both business leaders and investors will greatly benefit from Nitin's insights as they support their operating management and companies on this journey.

David Cohen
Retired partner, Farallon Capital;
Chairman and Founder, Simcah Holdings

Winning in the Digital Age is a timely book that captures insights obtained from working with a wide range of businesses. While the book covers a vast array of topics, it dives deep into the most important facets to provide practical insights, learnings and visual frameworks. Drawn from Nitin Seth's personal experience, the book includes practical examples of how value creation continues to change in a knowledge-based world . . . I have personally experienced many of these industry transitions and was able to find new concepts and ideas that prove to be valuable to entrepreneurs starting off as well as successful business executives. *Winning in the Digital Age* provides valuable insights that will be relevant for many years to come.

Dhrupad Trivedi
CEO, A10 Networks Inc.

Fluent in the languages and skills of both a consultant and a practitioner, Nitin brings together a vast range of information and insights in his new book, *Winning in the Digital Age*, and makes them easy to digest by providing a framework for survival and growth in what he calls the VUCA world. I recommend this book as important reading for students, entrepreneurs and managers seeking to better understand how to build and execute a sustainable digital transformation strategy.

Dr. Ashish Chand,
President & CEO, Belden Inc.

Winning in the Digital Age is a practitioner's tried-and-true framework for digital transformation that acknowledges common pitfalls and offers a guidebook for the key components of a successful programme. Incorporated are critical areas of focus to steer new graduates and early career professionals towards leveraging the abundant opportunities to thrive in the digital age. A must-read for leaders in firms that are facing digital disruption, either by design or competitive dynamics.

Mukesh Mehta
EVP and CIO, AssetMark

In the tradition of the great Indian gurus, Nitin transcends the ephemeral mantras of typical management books by embracing the contradictions and conflicting priorities of the new digital world engulfing the old. He expertly takes the reader on a whirlwind tour of the value drivers of digital transformation, their illustration in specific industries and the technologies underneath, and practically describes which questions to ask, which insights to seek and which actions to take to ace a digital transformation. Most passionately, though, he discusses the human side—be it with his enlightened counsel for leaders on how to avoid burnout and anxiety in the VUCA world, or his advice for young people. A profoundly useful book!

Dr Tobias Baer
Former Partner, McKinsey & Company;
Senior Advisor at various fintechs
Author of *Understand, Manage, and Prevent Algorithmic
Bias: A Guide for Business Users and Data Scientists*

Nitin has written a rare book that blends the strategic imperative with the real executional unlocks on digital transformation. Nitin has distilled his twenty-five years of transformational experience as an advisor, a leader in the trenches and a CEO, into this book. A nifty collection of practical wisdom and inspiration for anyone interested in embarking on digital transformation.

Dinesh Khanna
Global Chair—People Team, Boston Consulting Group

I have known Nitin for nearly two decades and he has effectively captured and brought to life key lessons for what is, undoubtedly, one of the core business imperatives of today. There is not a company that would not benefit from the lessons articulated in this book.

Pradip Patiath
Senior Partner, McKinsey & Company

The steps from digitization of records to digitization of processes, to a digitally transformed system of work and life, have created many opportunities and uncertainties. What is very clear, as Nitin Seth clearly articulates, is that there are new forces at play that must be understood. As always, Nitin distils these complex topics into a simple set of building blocks that the reader can use to construct their own strategy towards winning in the digital age . . . Simply put, if you are looking for 'fundas' on how to orient yourself in a volatile, uncertain, complex and ambiguous digital world, you will find them here.

Dr Anurag Agrawal Director,
Dean, Biosciences and Health Research
Trivedi School of Biosciences, Ashoka University;
Principal Scientist, Institute of Genomics and Bioinformatics, CSIR

Nitin Seth writes with the confidence of a battle-hardened general and the clarity of a veteran observer. His leadership positions in leading firms gives him the kind of perspective that an academic or journalist can never get. And then he uses his training as a McKinsey consultant to put together frameworks to think through the most massive changes as digital transforms everything. I personally enjoyed reading and thinking about the two-speed execution, leadership in VUCA times and real-time audit. You may be a digital native yourself or trying to fend off one—either way, this book will help you think it through comprehensively.

Sandeep Tyagi
Chairman, Estee Capital

We are indeed living in the digital age, with technology transforming businesses, experiences and our lives. Nitin has come up with a comprehensive framework to play offence when it comes to digital transformation; he connects the dots beautifully and is able to differentiate the true signals from all the noise around us. This book is a must-read for all business and tech leaders.

Puneet Chandok
President, AWS India and South Asia

If you are in the digital function at a company or in the leadership team looking to understand how to harness digital, *Winning in the Digital Age* is a highly pragmatic book written by a practitioner, not a theorist. Whether it is the seven building blocks of successful digital transformation that Nitin outlines or the industry-specific examples that he cites, the first-hand experience and authenticity of his message rings true. Nitin does a great job dispensing practical information on key technologies and how to put these in context of organization and business practices. I wish I had had this book handy when I had to grapple with these issues.

Abhi Ingle
COO, Qualtrics

This book is a must-read for any world-class business leader who demands nothing but excellence. Digital disruption is the single greatest opportunity and threat for every company on this planet. Without equivocation, I can say that *Winning in the Digital Age* is the roadmap to success. Nitin Seth is a truly extraordinary, once-in-generation CEO.

Chatri Sityodtong
Chairman & CEO, One Championship

Winning in the Digital Age presents a comprehensive yet simple approach to thinking about digital disruption. Nitin's wide range of experiences from consulting to running operations and from large companies to start-ups, covers a whole spectrum of real-life learnings presented beautifully. This book is a must-read for all entrepreneurs, especially those running family businesses as they reinvent themselves in a new world full of opportunities and threats.

Puneet Dalmia
MD Dalmia Bharat Ltd.

Rarely do you find a book which is as relevant for the new intern as it is for the CEO. Nitin has managed to string his years of experience working at the intersection of technology and strategy to craft a framework which is equally relevant for a CEO wrestling with a long-term business plan as for a new intern creating a roadmap for a thirty-year career.

Amit Lodha
Fund Manager, Fidelity Investments

Covid-19 has put digital transformations into overdrive, with legacy enterprises (irrespective of the sector) scrambling to figure out how to adapt their business models and compete more effectively with their cloud-borne rivals. This is not just about buying cloud-based software, but re-engineering end-to-end processes . . . Overall, Nitin's book provides a solid framework, key building blocks and a comprehensive roadmap for the incumbents that are trying to reinvent themselves.

Anurag Rana
Senior Technology Analyst, Bloomberg Intelligence

I have now known Nitin for twenty-five years and have always been super impressed by his ability to crystal gaze new trends. His new book is a pathbreaker and a must-read for everyone—students, academicians and business leaders included.

Atul Khosla
Founder and Pro-Vice Chancellor, Shoolini University

WINNING IN THE DIGITAL AGE

SEVEN BUILDING BLOCKS OF SUCCESSFUL DIGITAL TRANSFORMATION

NEW EDITION

NITIN SETH

Co-Founder & CEO of Incedo Inc.

PENGUIN
ENTERPRISE

An imprint of Penguin Random House

PENGUIN ENTERPRISE

USA | Canada | UK | Ireland | Australia
New Zealand | India | South Africa | China | Singapore

Penguin Enterprise is part of the Penguin Random House group of companies
whose addresses can be found at global.penguinrandomhouse.com

Published by Penguin Random House India Pvt. Ltd
4th Floor, Capital Tower 1, MG Road,
Gurugram 122 002, Haryana, India

First published in Penguin Enterprise by Penguin Random House India 2020
This edition published in Penguin Enterprise by Penguin Random House India 2023

ISBN 9780670095421

Typeset in Adobe Caslon Pro
Printed at Replika Press Pvt. Ltd, India

www.penguin.co.in

To all my teachers, especially to my mother
and sister, who were my first teachers.

To the pillar of my life, my wife Arpna and my wonderful family
who provide me with the balance to do my best in this crazy digital age.

To all my colleagues for the fun, the learning
and the amazing journeys together.

Contents

SECTION 3: TECHNOLOGY BUILDING BLOCKS OF DIGITAL TRANSFORMATION

SECTION 4: LEVERAGING THE GLOBAL ADVANTAGE

SECTION 5: TRANSFORMING THE ORGANIZATION TO WIN IN THE DIGITAL AGE

SECTION 6: LEADERSHIP IN THE DIGITAL AGE

SECTION 7: ADVICE TO YOUNG PROFESSIONALS

Introduction to the New Edition

When *Winning in the Digital Age* (*WITDA*) was published in 2021, I scarcely imagined the overwhelming positive response it would get. I feel humbled that WITDA has received the support of both critics and readers—it has won five Best Business Book awards and has been on the bestseller lists consistently for the past two years.

I believe the success of *WITDA* is owed to the relevance of the topic, the digital age. It is the overwhelming megatrend of our times and impacts all workers, not just 'techies' and business professionals. Now the digital age is not static, but a highly dynamic amalgam of multiple technology and business forces at work. For example, in the past two years, many of the trends we had talked about in the original edition of *WITDA* have become mainstream. For example, cloud implementation is becoming pervasive across most industries, data explosion is continuing to gather remarkable momentum, AI adoption has gone mainstream. Generative AI, in particular—in the form of its popular application, a chatbot called ChatGPT—has caught public attention. While most digital technologies are scaling up, there have been some notable reality checks as well. As I had indicated in *WITDA*, the hype around Bitcoin and other cryptocurrencies has dampened, while their underlying technology, the blockchain, continues to make steady progress.

It is this quality of continuous evolution of the digital age which was an indication for me that its story and success mantras need to be chronicled and updated constantly, and it prompted me to pen this new edition of *WITDA*. In this edition, I have made the following notable changes to the first edition.

- Substantially restructuring and supplementation of the first section, 'New Rules of Business'. I have added a new chapter, 'Everyone Is Going Digital (and Most Fail!)', which offers a description of the digital phenomenon. I felt this introduction was especially important for readers who might not have had significant exposure to digital. I have also tried to bring greater clarity to the concept of 'VUCA' and the six fundamentals driving the digital revolution.
- In Section 3, 'Technology Building Blocks of Digital Transformation', I have included two introductory chapters that outline why problems with digital technology investments are persisting, and then go on to provide a framework for maximizing returns from them. These two chapters provide helpful context for the seven digital technologies that I then go on to explore in this section.
- In Section 5, 'Transforming the Organization to Win in the Digital Age', I have enhanced the chapter on the Future of Work – Unlocking the Potential of the Workforce through AI. This is particularly timely, given the ongoing mainstreaming of AI in many industries and organizations.
- Finally, towards the end, I have added a new chapter on how digital provides India a remarkable opportunity for breakthrough growth. I call it India's 'Second Independence opportunity'. History has demonstrated that during every industrial revolution, there is a reshuffling of global superpowers. I strongly believe that the digital age, which is the Fourth Industrial Revolution, will instigate a shift in the global order and India will emerge as one of the digital superpowers.

I continue to be super excited about the potential of the digital age and have thoroughly been enjoying studying continuously and chronicling the amazing developments that are unfolding. I hope you enjoy reading the new edition of *WITDA* and appreciate the ways in which it is an improvement over the first edition of the book.

Introduction

Seven Building Blocks of
Successful Digital Transformation

To accomplish a difficult task, one must first make it easy.

Marty Rubin, Author

Digital transformation is one of the most significant megatrends of our generation, one which is continuing to grow in scope and scale. Digital started as a new channel for engaging customers, for digitizing back-end processes and was largely the domain of the technology function. Today, digital has become all-pervasive and it is not an exaggeration to say that we are living in a digital age. Digital is touching every aspect of our lives as consumers, is impacting every industry, and is totally transforming not just products and processes but entire business models. This change is not just a technology change, but something that is impacting every part of the business and the organization. It is redefining what business companies are, forcing a shift in long-held organizational principles and practices, and it is changing expectations from leaders and young professionals alike.

For the enterprise and its leaders, the digital age is a roller-coaster ride with more than its fair share of thrills and spills. It presents them with great opportunities to leapfrog and grow. However, success is not easy in the digital age. I characterize the digital age as the VUCA world—Volatile, Uncertain, Complex and Ambiguous. Competing in the digital age requires you to make changes at multiple levels—in business strategy, products/service offerings, technology, processes, organization, talent, culture—which is not easy at the best of times. The complexity of the VUCA world makes it very difficult to establish both what should be done and how it should be done, resulting in a lot of confusion at the enterprise leadership level. That is why despite significant investments in digital transformation initiatives, its impact has been underwhelming.

In this book, I have attempted to synthesize the learnings from my past twenty years of experience in digital—both whilst leading various organizations as well as a consultant serving other organizations—to bring clarity to the complex topic of digital transformation and share best practices and practical insights. My digital experience has been both at large legacy enterprises and younger digital natives, and the contrast in their approaches has provided many interesting learnings. While I have attempted to take a broad and holistic approach to digital in this book, I do not claim to be comprehensive. Digital is such a vast and dynamic topic that it is impossible to capture all aspects of it in a single book. I have taken a practitioner's perspective and attempted to bring together a range of best practices and insights that will be most relevant and helpful for both business leaders and young professionals.

My digital journey

I have been fortunate that my professional journey coincided with the growth of the digital age, which has given me the opportunity to experience its many aspects first-hand.

My early exposure to e-business building in McKinsey

My first exposure to digital was at McKinsey in the late 1990s. We were serving one of the largest banks in India and I was part of the assignment, developing an e-broking business for them. The learnings we had from that project more than twenty years back, involving this new e-business, hold true even today. The project presented us with an opportunity to create a new product that cut across three different divisions and technology stacks of the bank. This was a technology integration challenge, but even more so a challenge of coordination across different divisions. I think the most important action we took was to structure this new e-broking business as a separate organization to ensure it was not caught in the legacy organizational issues. I find it remarkable that more than twenty years later, when I look at large enterprises setting up new digital businesses, the **key issues are still organizational—** should a new capability be established as a new organization or as part of the existing organization? What should be the nature of its relationship with other parts of the organization? How do you handle cannibalization, and so on . . .

My own start-up in the 'dotcom bubble'

I ended up doing more 'e-business' and technology-related projects at McKinsey, which got me very excited about the potential of the 'dotcom' business models that were beginning to get very popular in the late 1990s. I left McKinsey in early 2000 to establish ActiveKarma with a couple of colleagues from McKinsey and friends from IIT Delhi, my alma mater. ActiveKarma's focus was on leveraging the internet to facilitate active and healthy lifestyles for executives. Our journey with ActiveKarma reflected the progression of the 'dotcom bubble' in many ways. We started with a bang, building a great team and working hard to launch a pretty extensive internet-based offering. We quickly attracted a lot of investor interest too.

However, the fall was also rapid. The market demand for internet-based health services was not large enough at that point. We were probably well ahead of the times; we struggled to build a feasible business model and the funding dried up quickly as the 'dotcom bubble' crashed. We wound up ActiveKarma after two years, but my first foray into entrepreneurship taught me many invaluable lessons such as the importance of anchoring the business in a solid customer proposition, going slow to go far, managing cash flows, and so on. I was reflecting on how this 'dotcom bubble' that many of us lived through has been such an important milestone in the evolution of the digital age we see today and still holds many important lessons for enterprises and entrepreneurs. It showed the disruptive growth opportunity of internet-based businesses; it also showed how dangerous it can be when business models and enterprise valuations are **not anchored in cash flows** but on speculation. The 'dotcom bubble' burst in a couple of years and it took Nasdaq fifteen years to regain its dotcom peak.

My wonderful journey of transforming McKinsey knowledge centre into an innovation centre

After ActiveKarma, I rejoined McKinsey where I led the fledgling Knowledge Centre (McKC) the firm was building in Gurgaon. What followed was a fascinating journey of eight years that taught me a lot of what I know about building businesses in the digital age. McKC started as a back-office to provide overnight research support to consulting teams based in North America. Its concept soon extended beyond this to provide leverage to research teams based in McKinsey offices across the world. These humble beginnings snowballed into a fascinating journey. We ended up building arguably the largest knowledge centre of its type in the world, a powerful innovation hub that transformed McKinsey's client and knowledge capabilities in significant ways. We built deep expertise and research capabilities across all industries and functional areas, conceiving and setting up analytics as a global service line, and leveraging McKinsey's knowledge assets to create new product-based client offerings.

There is so much to talk about the McKC story and the learnings from it that it would merit a separate book. But at this stage, the main learning I want to highlight is the amazing potential of the global delivery model. McKC was created to drive cost efficiencies and increase productivity. However, when we added high-quality talent to the mix and gave them an entrepreneurial culture to flourish in, the impact was explosive. We brought talent at McKC with significantly higher capabilities than what we traditionally had in the research function at McKinsey. It took some time for this talent to build domain understanding and grow in maturity, but when that happened, it changed the scope of McKC dramatically. It evolved into an innovation centre and allowed McKinsey to experiment with and build new capabilities, which it could not have otherwise. This ability to **increase innovation capacity leveraging the global delivery model** is a great opportunity for enterprises in the digital age.

My part in the digital transformation at Fidelity

From McKinsey, I moved to Fidelity, one of the largest investment management firms in the world, to head the India and Tunisia operations for their international business, which housed a large proportion of the firm's technology and business operations. My role soon expanded to driving strategy for the business. Fidelity's international business was going through a transformation, with the distribution business, which was a technology platform-driven business, becoming more important. So, a significant part of my strategy role was to plan this transformation from an investment management-driven business to a more technology-driven business model. It is at Fidelity that I learnt how intertwined business strategy and technology strategy were and understood the challenges of driving transformation in a large enterprise with a lot of legacy. The legacy technology stack and **'tech debt' can slow down well-**

meaning digital transformation programmes, restricting a large enterprise's ability to compete with younger, nimbler competitors.

My stint at Flipkart in the VUCA world

Driving strategy and transformation at Fidelity showed me how technology was transforming business and how legacy businesses were facing structural challenges in competing in the new environment. It became clear to me that if both enterprises and leaders did not change their game, they would find it difficult to stay relevant. I felt I had to work in a 'digital native' to experience the cutting edge of technology. This motivation took me to Flipkart, India's largest e-commerce company. I have mentioned the VUCA world earlier in this introduction. It was at Flipkart that I truly came in direct and fierce contact with the VUCA world. E-commerce is a high-velocity business, especially so in a rapidly growing market like India. In addition to the natural dynamics of the e-commerce business, there were other forces at work in Flipkart. We were locked in fierce competition with a rival like Amazon, we had negative cash flows, and the organization was struggling to move ahead on the maturity curve. All this made for a unique set of challenges.

It was at Flipkart that I realized that methods and practices which work in traditional enterprises do not work in high-velocity and volatile businesses that are typical of the digital age, and that you **need new rules of business**. I also learnt how 'digital natives' like Flipkart were **able to do many things better than traditional companies.** They had a technology-first mindset and attracted high-quality tech talent. They practised rapid experimentation (A/B testing) with a focus on analytics and data-driven decision-making. They had the ability to execute with amazing speed, and were imbued with a spirit of audacity (thinking big and not being afraid), to name a few of their attributes. At the same time, I also saw the challenges young companies like Flipkart faced—organizational maturity struggling to keep pace with business growth, culture lacking a strong anchoring in values, and process and governance gaps. Entrepreneurial culture was the root of Flipkart's success but that also became a challenge in some senses. A key question for young companies like Flipkart is how to build structures and processes that will allow them to realize their scale-up potential while retaining their entrepreneurial core. This is an important dilemma that many companies need to resolve in the digital age.

My work at Incedo on end-to-end digital transformation across industries

All of my experiences above have culminated in my strategy for Incedo—driving digital transformation end-to-end, from strategy to execution, bringing the best from digital natives to more traditional industries, focusing on analytics and data as the 'secret sauce' and leveraging the global advantage. At Incedo, I have worked closely with a number of Fortune 100 companies on their digital transformation priorities. This has given me a ringside view of the nuances of digital transformation across many industries—banking, wealth management, telecom and media, life sciences and healthcare, and enterprise products. It is fascinating that while each industry is at a different stage on the **digital maturity curve**, there are many common characteristics among them too. Some form of disintermediation is happening in most industries, impacting value chains and business models; customer expectations are rising across the board, technology function's role is becoming more pivotal, and lines between business and technology are blurring. While many successful companies often see their situation as unique, it is interesting that when you step back, you can see many common patterns across them.

I have tried to distil the experiences from my digital journey, and in particular, my experiences at Incedo, into a framework of seven building blocks, which I believe are necessary for successful digital transformation.

The seven building blocks

Digital transformation is multi-dimensional, complex and has many interconnected parts. Therefore, it is not easy to establish the strategy and execution approach for it. The resulting confusion and lack of clarity are the bane of digital transformation. To bring clarity to this important topic, I have designed seven building blocks on which executives need to focus their attention as well as actions for successful digital transformation. As the quote at the beginning of this chapter says, 'to accomplish a difficult task, one must first make it easy', similarly, my intent with this book is to **bring clarity** to a complex topic like digital transformation and **make it easy** for executives to identify actions that will make the most difference and execute them with conviction.

This book is structured into seven sections, each section illustrates the challenges of each building block and provides best practices for each.

Building block 1: New rules of business

While digital is such a pervasive trend impacting every industry, and while most enterprises are committing significant investments to digital transformation, the impact of these investments has fallen short of expectations in many cases. Why is that? The failures I see are both those of strategy and execution. However, there is something more fundamental at work here. My assessment is that most traditional companies underachieve at digital because they fail to recognize that many of the fundamentals of business have changed in this VUCA world. Customers are very demanding, data is exploding in volume, variety and velocity, technology is becoming mission critical, the pace of change is very high, and business/product cycles are getting crunched, to name just a few of the fundamental shifts. Despite these changes, many enterprises' approach to digital lies in extending what has worked in their traditional business to digital. Such an approach is doomed to fail. Every enterprise needs to understand how the fundamentals of their business are changing and based on that, define their 'new rules of business' for application to both strategy and execution to drive a successful digital transformation. In section one, I elaborate on the above challenges and share my perspectives on the 'new rules' at three different levels:

- The general level of the VUCA world and overall implications for business
- The digital transformation level
- The level of specific technology elements of digital

Building block 2: Industry maturity curves

Digital transformation is resulting in radical shifts across industries. Customer expectations of experience are rising, there is disintermediation, direct channels are becoming more important, new competitors are emerging, and boundaries across industries are blurring. Such radical shifts are both a threat and an opportunity. For enterprises to emerge as winners in the digital age, it is critical that they form a forward-looking picture of how their industry is likely to evolve, so they can anchor their business and technology strategies accordingly. This anchoring of digital transformation programmes in outside-in industry changes is extremely critical to realizing the full potential of digital. However, this is not an easy exercise. While there are a number of common characteristics in the shifts happening across industries, their specifics and degree of development vary significantly. It is not easy to predict the nature and speed of evolution in each industry. While deep industry-specific context and insight is of course important, I believe there is a lot of value in observing patterns from other industries and trying to develop foresight as to how they might impact your business.

Now, the interesting thing is that the industry maturity curve is not a given; enterprises can shape it based on their efforts. This is one of the distinguishing features of the digital age—you have the ability to shape your own future!

In section 2, I have shared my perspectives—both insights and foresights—on what digital means for specific industries, where Incedo has deep experience. These industries are banking, wealth management, payments, telecom, enterprise product business and life sciences. In many places in section 2, I have also shared how the Covid-19 pandemic is impacting digital priorities in these industries. Generally, I have observed that the protracted work-from-home situation resulting from the pandemic has given a significant boost to digital penetration in every industry that we are operating in.

Building block 3: Digital technologies

While I have mentioned earlier that digital transformation is now much bigger than just technology change, technology continues to be the heart of any digital transformation programme. There are seven key technologies that play a critical role in the execution of digital transformation—design/customer experience, analytics/data science, automation/operations transformation, artificial intelligence (AI), data infrastructure, blockchain and cloud. The most important aspect of these digital technologies is that they are **not independent but interconnected**. Enterprises realize transformative value from them when these digital technology building blocks are connected end to end. These technologies represent different layers of the technology stack; connecting them tightly creates a virtuous cycle. To illustrate: customer experience and design are typically the starting points of digital initiatives, and personalization of experience is often a key value driver. Personalization is driven by data science, and AI/machine learning (ML) are further taking it to the next level of impact. Both data science and AI are dependent on data depth and quality. At the same time, data is exploding in the digital world. This digital data deluge itself can create tremendous customer and business value for enterprises. In my experience, **data is the fulcrum for digital**. Data can trigger a virtuous cycle; equally, data challenges can quickly escalate into a vicious cycle. Given the pace at which data is continuing to grow, most enterprises tend to be in a catch-up mode on data infrastructure. That is where the cloud comes in. Cloud, which started as an infrastructure solution, continues to grow in scope and has become a key enabler for transformation in the digital stack. In particular, cloud can provide effective solutions to the host of data challenges that have been a particular thorn for CIOs in the digital age.

Hopefully, you could see from the above illustration how various digital technologies are interconnected and why it is so important to take an end-to-end approach. In section 3, I explore the end-end digital stack and also dwell on the role of each of these technologies, the challenges in leveraging them, and their future possibilities.

Building block 4: Global delivery model

Every enterprise in the digital age has to be a global enterprise. In particular, it needs to have an effective global delivery model to make progress on the ambitious technology and operations agenda, which most firms tend to have in the digital age. Enterprises can develop this global footprint either by partnering with service companies or by establishing their own dedicated technology and operations centres in emerging economies. In section 4, I have used the term global delivery centre or GDC to cover both types of entities.

While GDCs have existed for many years, their proposition and operating model needs to change significantly if they are to meet the new expectations of the digital age. Enterprises are facing the dual challenge of protecting their existing revenue streams while investing for future growth. This implies CIOs and COOs have to reduce costs while simultaneously increasing the velocity of transformation/innovation as well as addressing the skill gaps required for building cutting-edge capabilities. Only a global delivery model that taps into the large, high-quality yet lower-cost talent pool in emerging economies like India and Eastern Europe, can achieve these seemingly contradictory objectives.

Historically, GDCs have been seen as cost and execution centres. This needs to change and they have to become revenue and innovation centres. This is a fascinating opportunity for them. Enterprises that are able to make this transformation and leverage global delivery effectively stand to gain a competitive advantage in the digital age.

Building block 5: Organizational transformation

I have made the point earlier that for digital transformation to be successful it has to be end-to-end. Digital is about a new way of doing things. You need to move with speed, execute iteratively rather than sequentially, put more focus on experimentation and innovation, 'fail fast', and take a lot more risks. In addition, technology has to become a core part of your DNA, whichever industry you are in. These changes cannot be sustained without rewiring the organizational culture. Change in the **organizational culture is probably the most important enabler of digital transformation**, allowing the enterprise to go beyond individual programmes and affect a more pervasive shift in its organizational DNA. I believe that in addition to culture, there are at least seven organizational capabilities that are keys to sustained success in the digital age. These are proprietary knowledge building and sharing, innovation, agility, learning, diversity, change management and enabling functions like HR and finance.

In section 5, I share my perspectives on expectations and best practices in the matter of organizational culture and these seven key organizational capabilities. I conclude by sharing my perspective on how AI is likely to impact the future of work—the impact will be significant, but it is likely to be about man and machine, not man or machine. Enterprises and leaders need to understand the impact of

AI for their specific industries and functions and take proactive steps to redesign jobs accordingly to benefit from this expected evolution in the nature of work.

Building block 6: Entrepreneurial leadership

This digital age and VUCA world are a great test for leaders. In an era of unprecedented uncertainty and change, traditional tools of management like structure, strategy, planning and policies do not just lose their effectiveness but can become a roadblock. Instead, you need vision, inspiration, intuition, collaboration and the ability to constantly adapt. This requires a shift in expectations of executives, from their being efficient managers to becoming entrepreneurial leaders. 'Managers to Leaders' is an often-repeated cliché in management. It has become an absolute imperative in the digital age.

Management of duality is another important requirement in the digital age. There are contradictions that leaders need to respond to—growth versus profitability, short term versus long term, and many more. It is not enough to find the trade-offs on these complementary values, leaders need to find win-win solutions. Finally, balance and sustainability are also critical topics for leaders to address. The breathtaking pace of activity is a defining feature of the digital age, but it is also one of its biggest challenges. Individuals are at greater risk of burnout, anxiety and depression. At the societal level, the obsession with growth is resulting in irreparable damage to the environment and grave socio-economic issues. Leaders in the digital age have a responsibility not just towards their enterprises, but also towards society as a whole. They need to find balance within themselves. I believe spiritual practices and meditation can help leaders centre themselves and find peace within. In addition, they need to consider how they can build an ethical foundation for their organizations and make a broader contribution to society.

Building block 7: Next-generation talent

The unprecedented disruption we are seeing in the digital age requires a significant step up from talent across the organization. I believe this change offers amazing opportunities to young professionals. This technology-based disruption is a great equalizer. Prior experience and successful track records are less relevant than before because you need to unlearn the old and learn the new rules of the game. In fact, the fresh perspective that young professionals bring to the enterprise is an advantage to it. They are 'digital natives', more intuitively able to understand new technologies and how new businesses can be built using digital technologies.

So, how should a young professional prepare to win in the digital age? Many of the desirable competencies and mindsets for enterprises and leaders that we have talked about earlier are also relevant for young professionals. Prominent among these requirements are continuous learning, creativity and innovation, tech DNA, agility, management of duality, and spiritual and ethical balance. In addition to these six competencies and mindsets, there are six more points of advice I have for young professionals to win in the digital age: find and live the unique purpose of your life, be an entrepreneur, don't be afraid to be a maverick, stay the course, build strong problem-solving and decision-making skills, take personal responsibility and drive change around you.

It has been an amazing learning opportunity for me to bring together all my experiences in digital transformation over the past twenty years into this book. So much change has already happened in the digital age, but there is so much more yet to come. This unprecedented change creates fascinating opportunities at all levels. Throughout the book, I have shared insights and best practices across the seven building blocks that can help unlock the tremendous potential of digital. These insights are not theoretical but based on what I have observed and practised working with some of the best companies

Seven Building Blocks of Successful Digital Transformation

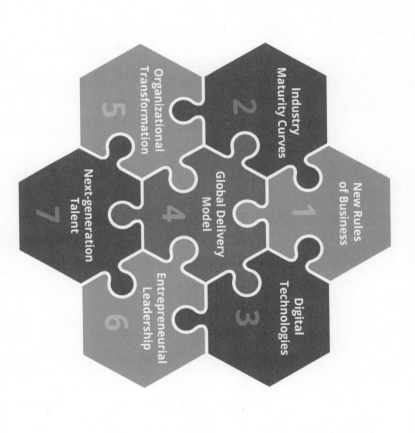

Industry Maturity Curves — 2

New Rules of Business — 1

Organizational Transformation — 5

Global Delivery Model — 4

Next-generation Talent — 7

Entrepreneurial Leadership — 6

Digital Technologies — 3

in the world. I hope the insights in this book will bring clarity to a complex and vast topic like digital transformation and help you make better decisions and execute effectively; moreover, prepare you to lead effectively in this digital age, and thus help both you and your organization step up and realize your infinite potential.

Happy reading!

SECTION 1

NEW RULES OF BUSINESS

Introduction: New Rules of Business

The First Industrial Revolution used water and steam power to mechanize production. The Second used electric power to create mass production. The Third used electronics and information technology to automate production. Now a Fourth Industrial Revolution is building on the Third, the digital revolution that has been occurring since the middle of the last century. It is characterized by a fusion of technologies that is blurring the lines between the physical, digital, and biological spheres. These include artificial intelligence, robotics, the Internet of Things, autonomous vehicles, 3-D printing, nanotechnology, biotechnology, materials science, energy storage, and quantum computing. This technological revolution will fundamentally alter the way we live, work, and relate to one another. In its scale, scope, and complexity, the transformation will be unlike anything humankind has experienced before.

Klaus Schwab, World Economic Forum

I have found the above excerpt to be prophetic and, therefore, wanted to use it to set the stage for section 1 of this book and establish a connection with what's playing out in front of and all around us. It is important to understand that the velocity and magnitude of change we see in this digital age are unprecedented. I like to use the term VUCA to describe this changing world around us. VUCA captures the essence of the digital age, and I have often used these two terms interchangeably throughout the book.

To win any game, it is important first to understand and master the rules of the game. It is the same in business. My proposition is that the VUCA world or the digital age is very different from the world we have seen so far, and thus we need new rules of business to succeed. Therefore, I call the first six chapters of the book the new rules of business. Here, the focus is to understand what is different in this VUCA world/digital age, why enterprises are facing challenges to adapt, and what new principles and approaches they should consider.

Some of the factors that have led to this unprecedented velocity of change in the VUCA world include: changing expectations of **customers** who are younger, digitally savvy and demand high-quality experiences and solutions; **technology** disruption where every company needs to develop a technology DNA; a dramatic increase in **velocity** of change where industry structures are shifting and new competitors and new industries are rapidly emerging; an explosion of **data** from multiple touchpoints as the volume, velocity and variety of data is growing at an unprecedented rate; digital is a constantly moving target requiring an **iterative** approach; in today's digital businesses, the problem is not simply about marketing, finance, operations or technology—digital problems are **interdisciplinary** and require greater organizational collaboration to solve customer problems. With all of these change factors, it is important to realize that incremental thinking no longer works; if you don't think differently, someone else will cannibalize you.

Fortunately, most enterprises have embarked on some variation of digital transformation programmes. However, the impact of these programs often falls short of expectations. There are many reasons for this, which we will explore further in section 1, but the core issue is that enterprises have not recognized how much business fundamentals have changed in the digital age. They continue to take their existing business models, infrastructure and approaches and apply them to digital age problems and opportunities. It is clear if you apply old world formulas to new world situations, your outcomes will be sub-optimal.

In section 1, I present the logical thread of how these basic business fundamentals are changing, what are the challenges being faced and what should be the new principles and approaches at two different levels. First, the general nature of the VUCA world and overall implications for business, which include my *New Rules of Business*. Second, getting down to what is digital transformation and my recommended approaches for success.

Across these changing basic business fundamentals, I see some common themes that are important to consider while driving action and transformation in the digital age:

1. **It has to be an end-to-end transformation:** While technology is the key driver of digital, it is only one of the pieces of the puzzle. Enterprises encounter success or failure often because the other factors are missed. Strategy, organizational structures, processes, talent, etc., have an equal and often more important role to play. End-to-end transformation can often be a cliché, but in this case, it is very appropriate.

2. **Strategy-to-execution boundaries are getting blurred:** The pace of change in every aspect of the digital age, whether customer expectations, competition or technology, is very high. Therefore, the traditional lines between 'the what and the how' are blurring at all levels, whether in terms of business strategy or technology execution. This change from sequential to iterative feedback loops is a fundamental one. Every aspect of execution, from organizational structures to processes, infrastructure and leadership mindsets, need to reflect that.

3. **Two-speed execution is essential:** Speed and experimentation are key characteristics of the digital age. It puts a huge focus on execution and short-term impact. At the same time, the need to place long-term bets does not go away. You have to think big and bold and not be stuck in the incremental. So, you need both short-term execution and long-term bets. I call this two-speed execution, and managing this duality across levels is essential for success in the digital age.

4. **Learning from digital natives:** Born in the digital age, companies such as Google, Amazon, Apple and others, have been remarkably successful. Their success is not just founded on technology but a new way of doing business. While every start-up is not a success and every legacy enterprise is not doomed to fail, I believe there is a lot legacy companies can learn from the digital natives.

I have tried to reflect on these common themes across the following chapters. So, let's quickly summarize what we will talk about in the rest of section 1.

Chapter 1: Everyone Is Going Digital (and Most Fail!)

In this chapter, I lay the foundation for what digital is and how pervasive it is. We also discuss the winners and losers of the digital age, the huge investments made by enterprises and yet the high failure rate of achieving their vision.

Chapter 2: It's a VUCA World: The New Fundamentals

As we move to the next stage, we dive deeper into the VUCA model and the implications of a VUCA world. I share my observations on the fact that a digital age business is fundamentally different from traditional business as usual in at least six ways: the customer is younger and more demanding; technology is not a support function, it's at the core; the velocity of change is unprecedented; there is an explosion of data; a 'right the first time' approach does not work, it must be iterative; and lastly, digital problems are highly interdisciplinary.

Chapter 3: Introducing the Eight New Rules of Business

Here, I present the eight new rules of business, which I believe are essential for every enterprise and leader (or aspiring leader) to internalize and adopt. If you absorb only one chapter of the book— this is it.

Chapter 4: Introduction to Digital Transformation in Business

In this chapter, I provide a better understanding of the key aspects of digital transformation. It operates at two levels, changing how a business interacts with customers using technology and leveraging technology to automate or digitize operational processes to drive greater efficiencies and reduce turnaround time. I also introduce the core steps of a digital transformation journey and the technology building blocks involved.

Chapter 5: Five Rules for a Successful Digital Transformation

I propose that having recognized that drivers of digital are different, individuals and enterprises need a new mindset and approach to succeed. I recommend a five-point action plan: rethinking the business model and adapting to the needs of a digitally savvy customer, anchoring digital programs on business KPIs, harnessing the power of data, taking an integrated end-to-end approach and implementing a two-speed model (here I'll also explain my two-speed model).

Chapter 6: Building Scalable Models in the VUCA World: The CIO View

In my final chapter in section 1, I bring key insights from my extensive conversations with leading CIOs across industries and around the globe. Most industry leaders realize that the VUCA environment is here to stay and that it has far-reaching implications across three dimensions: people, processes and technology. Digital transformation is an unavoidable organizational imperative in such an environment, so much so that **technology strategy has now become 'the strategy'** for enterprises. The only way to win in this VUCA world is to build a customer-centric organization with leaders as the change agents and an agile architecture that delivers high-quality experience to the end customer.

Section 1: The New Rules of Business is a clarion call for all of us to understand the impact of the VUCA world and digital age. We need to recognize the fact that time-tested business strategies and assumptions need to be questioned, and we need new principles and approaches to be successful. Let's get started!

1

Everyone Is Going Digital (and Most Fail!)

No product is made today, no person moves today, nothing is collected, analyzed or communicated without some 'digital technology' being an integral part of it. That, in itself speaks to the overwhelming value of digital technology.

Louis Rossetto, Founder and
Former Editor-in-Chief of Wired Magazine

Let me first set a firm foundation for what I mean when I use the word digital. Simply put, digital is the wide-ranging set of technology trends that are impacting every aspect of life and business for the last fifty years. It is also *continually expanding and growing* in capabilities and influence in ways unimagined by previous generations.

Digital really took off in the 1970's with the explosive growth of computers and compute power availability moving the world from **physical to digital**. From there, it was the **advent of the internet** in the late 1990's that drove the next major wave, **the dotcom boom** that turned to a bust in the early 2000's. From that trough, the latter 2000's saw the explosion of **Social, Mobile, Analytics, Cloud** (SMAC) wave, followed by the amazing wave of **digital ecosystems**. In the early

2020's, we are riding another huge wave driven by **new technologies** (including technology that has not been invented yet, by you, because the idea that you can be a world changing entrepreneur is just getting planted in your mind as you read this book). Each wave pushes the impact and power of digital further out in an ever-expanding sphere.

Each of these areas and technologies have birthed amazing changes while being interconnected in many ways and leading to a madcap virtuous cycle—from computers, internet, browsers, search engines, and mobile devices, to e-commerce, advertising, commercial cloud, internet of things (IoT) devices and on and on it goes. Digital is all-pervasive and will continue changing our lives in ways beyond our imagination.

Win big or lose unrecoverable ground

With these amazing and dramatic changes, many enterprises are struggling to cope with the digital disruption happening in their industries. Digital disruption is one of the megatrends of our time, but it is a difficult challenge to master. Many different forces have come together in the VUCA world, where it is difficult to predict the winners. But it is precisely for this reason that the VUCA world also presents a huge opportunity for enterprises and individuals: those who are able to figure out the new rules of the game and transform themselves, stand to win big.

The opportunity to win big or lose unrecoverable ground is unavoidable. No organization can choose to not make a decision and stand still. As an example of winning big, note the market capitalization (shares of a company multiplied by their market price) of Amazon and Apple combined is more than **3 trillion dollars** which is greater than the economies of all but four nations in the world.[1] Or look at the market capitalization of Tesla which **exceeds the market capitalization of top ten automobile companies combined**!

It would not be an overstatement to say that the divergence between winners and losers is dramatic and is accelerating,

What is Digital?

Wide ranging set of technology trends that are impacting every aspect of life and business

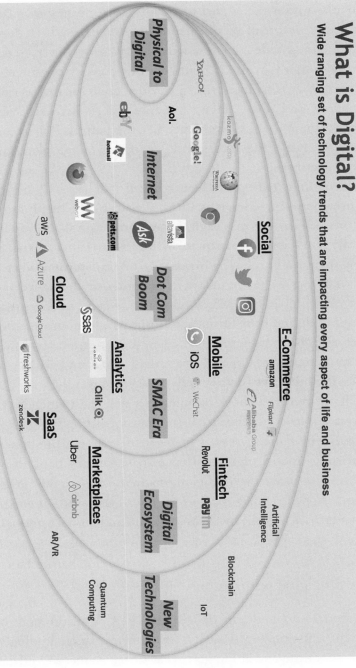

particularly after the impact of Covid-19. For example, recall that before the outbreak of the pandemic, WebEx was a dominant player among video conferencing services, however, seemingly overnight after Covid-19, Zoom became the service of choice—to the point that it replaced the term video conferencing as everyone frequently said 'Let's set up a Zoom call'. There are countless other examples of the divergence but the pattern is clear—across industries, rapid and accelerating change is taking place and you cannot stand still.

Thankfully, enterprises have realized that digital is imperative, and everyone is investing in it. Over 77 per cent of Chief Information Officers (CIOs) say that **digital transformation is the top budget priority** for their organization to drive growth. Almost 40 per cent of global organizations **have a formal digital transformation strategy**, while another 31 per cent are in planning or the active research stage.[2] From 2020 to 2023, enterprises are expected **to invest $6.8 trillion in digital transformation initiatives** to improve efficiency, increase customer value and create new monetization opportunities.[3] The most amazing fact of all this activity and spend? **70 per cent of the digital initiatives do not deliver targeted results!**[4]

70 per cent is a shocking number given the tremendous time, effort and intellect applied to digital transformation projects. This is precisely why *Winning in the Digital Age* is so timely. By applying the frameworks, models and knowledge shared in this book, if we can increase the success rate of digital programs by just a few percentage points (I hope for much more as we spread the word), it will unlock huge returns across the business spectrum and propel careers. Given the high stakes of the game, let's take a deeper look.

Why do digital programmes fail?

I learned about and experienced the VUCA world in two very different situations—at Fidelity, an eminent market-leading global investment firm, and at Flipkart, a classic tech 'unicorn' and a poster

In the Digital Age, Either You Win Big or Lose Unrecoverable Ground

Winners have applied New Rules of Business

Apple
amazon.com
TESLA
zoom

While Laggards have lost significantly

BlackBerry
NOKIA
SEARS
kmart
gm
COMPAQ

Covid-19 has further accelerated the Digital Transformation

child of the e-commerce revolution in India. Subsequently, I have had the opportunity, through Incedo, to observe and work with many Fortune 100 companies that are facing digital disruption head-on. Let's take a closer look at the reasons why they fail.

There are two primary reasons that I've uncovered behind why organizations fail to achieve their digital initiative objectives. The first reason is **failure of vision**—not seeing the world for what it is or not pushing the thinking far enough. The second reason is a **failure of execution**—this is where ambition meets reality and technology plus people and organizational dynamics slow and derail progress.

Looking closer at **failure of vision**, there are several recurring issues I've found:

1. **Too incremental:** The initiative is safe and achievable with limited risk and as a result does not have the impact to be sustainable and successful, or the necessary solution is being parsed into separate incremental pieces that are rendered ineffective when implemented individually.
2. **Offline to online:** Here, leaders believe they can simply take real-world offerings and processes and recreate them in the digital realm.
3. **'New' customer:** The vision is off the mark due to a lack of understanding of the 'new' customer in the digital realm, created by changes brought about by digital—expectations of faster responses, 24/7/365 access, etc.
4. **Risk averse:** This is marked by an attitude of avoiding difficult and painful changes to the business model or products/services— particularly cannibalizing existing business, products or services.

With respect to **failure of execution**, I believe there are five key items:

1. **Technology stack:** Here, the constraint is the inability to scale the traditional technology stack to support the digital programs, whether it is modernization of legacy systems or new tech

... But Majority Fail - 70%+ of Digital Initiatives do not deliver target impact!!!

Failure of Vision

- Too Incremental
- Just taking offline offering & processes online
- Lack of understanding of the "new customer"
- Risk averse – esp. to self-cannibalize

Failure of Execution

- Not able to scale up tech stack
- Lack of required talent
- Too slow
- Inability to break organizational silos
- Trying to go "Big Bang"

integration. The dramatic demise of the traditional retail giants like Sears and JCPenney in the US are good illustrations of this. They were not able to anticipate the e-commerce onslaught and build the technological capabilities required to compete in the industry.

2. **Lack of talent:** Technology expertise is expensive and difficult to acquire in the highly competitive digital age. Given the enormous demand for talent, it is difficult to hire and retain the needed digital technology and product experts to architect, build and support digital programs, particularly in industries that are perceived as traditional.

3. **Too slow:** Failure here is driven by over-analysis, over-managing or other corporate culture constraints that keep the programme from moving at digital speed—always on and always moving forward.

4. **Silos:** Organizations frequently have departments, divisions, etc., that can be separate and siloed, creating transformation-killing friction in communications, cooperation, data exchange, technology integration, etc.

5. **'Big Bang':** Leadership in this case pushes for a dramatic shift, a 'Big Bang' where new technology, systems, processes, etc., supersede the prior. This frequently leads to spiralling costs and unmanageable programs as complexity expands in the execution phase.

At Fidelity, I experienced these challenges head-on at a traditional, successful company. It is a very profitable business and a great company, but with the industry going through significant disruptions, the company required major changes in strategy. Some of the significant changes that were implemented were:

• **Shift in market structures:** The rise of passive/index funds (versus actively managed funds), increasing regulation, aging population and plateauing of growth in the core markets.

- **Consequent shift in the business model:** The shift was from product-centric to customer-centric, while building of the enterprise's own distribution network and the resultant focus on technological and operational efficiencies. This required a very different DNA from that of investment management expertise and 'alpha generation', which had taken years to build and was thus not an easy change.

Clearly, **traditional organizations** are struggling to adapt to the pace of change in the digital age. Clayton Christensen articulated it brilliantly in his seminal book, *The Innovator's Dilemma: New Disruptive Technologies Cause Great Firms to Fail.* The same practices that had led the businesses to success in the first place can also result in their eventual demise!

While you would expect traditional organizations to struggle in the VUCA world, it is not that new-age companies are necessarily set up for success either. **New-age companies have high mortality**. I saw this first-hand at Flipkart, and my experiences with the start-up ecosystem in India made me realize that many are not mature enough to negotiate their way ahead in this new world and only a few are able to scale up. The following situations or weaknesses are hurdles in their path to sustained success:

- **Being in constant war mode:** They are quick to market but not able to build long-term capabilities.
- **Lack of experienced talent:** Their leadership does not always have the resilience to battle through the ups and downs of a business cycle.
- **Weak foundational capabilities and practices:** Their enabling functions such as HR and finance, for example, have not kept pace with the business.
- **Fragile values and culture:** These are key factors contributing to a lack of organizational resilience and longevity.

However, I want to reiterate that it is not all doom and gloom for enterprises—disruption also presents breakthrough opportunities:

- Companies that master the art of leading in a VUCA world can create breakthrough businesses (and significant value) through disruption.
- The growth of tech-driven companies such as Facebook, Uber, Airbnb and Tesla over the past ten years is illustrative of this. Each of these has offered a new customer proposition, built a new industry and created huge shareholder value in the process.
- In India, Flipkart and Paytm are great examples of firms benefitting from disruption, as is the e-commerce industry as a whole.

As we see, the unfolding of the digital age is an exciting time with an abundance of opportunity. Enterprises have discovered via huge investments of money, time and effort that the digital age risks are high, but so are the rewards. With this foundation in place, in the next chapter, I am excited to go deeper and discuss the dynamics of VUCA.

Summary

- Digital is the wide-ranging set of technology trends that are impacting every aspect of life and business for the last fifty years. It is also *continually expanding and growing* in capabilities and influence in ways unimagined by previous generations.
- From 2020 to 2023, enterprises are expected to invest $6.8 trillion in digital transformation initiatives.
- 70 per cent of digital initiatives do not deliver targeted results.

- Why organizations fail to achieve their digital initiative objectives:
  - o *Failure of vision*—Not seeing the world for what it is or not pushing the thinking far enough.
  - o *Failure of execution*—Technology plus people and organizational dynamics slow and derail progress.

- Clearly, traditional organizations are struggling to adapt to the pace of change in the digital age; however, it is not that new-age companies are necessarily set up for success either.

2

It's a VUCA World: The New Fundamentals

Change is the law of life and those who look only to the past or present are certain to miss the future.

John F. Kennedy, Former US President

In a world of constant and extensive technology disruption where organizations are engaged in a battle for survival, the urgency to digitally transform is well understood by almost every large enterprise. In the last five years, most of these companies have embarked on large-scale transformation programmes. However, despite pumping tremendous amounts of manpower and resources into these exercises, the actual business impact of these initiatives has been underwhelming and far less effective than expected. Many executives have been left wondering why this is so.

Many business leaders are not recognizing that the world has dramatically changed due to the arrival of the digital. Along with it, the underlying fundamentals that support traditional business models have changed, rendering old models ineffective. What worked in the past is not working today or is quickly diminishing in its returns. This change in fundamentals requires a new framework for the digital age.

One of the best frameworks for encapsulating the multivariate dynamics of the digital age is the VUCA model that I have already referenced many times. This model best captures 'the spirit of the age' while allowing for practical application. Let's examine some of the components of the framework:

- **V: Volatility** – High degree and speed of change
- **U: Uncertainty** – *Lack of predictability* and a prospect of *surprise*
- **C: Complexity** – *Multiplex of forces*, the confounding nature of issues, absence of cause-and-effect chains and the confusion that generally surrounds the organization today
- **A: Ambiguity** – *Haziness of reality*, the potential for being misread, the mixed meanings of conditions and cause-and-effect confusion

What I have seen first-hand is that legacy enterprises have embarked on their digital journeys without recognizing the full implications of the VUCA world we are in. The underlying business and organizational drivers of a digital business are fundamentally different from those of a traditional business. By continuing to apply legacy management and organizational principles to their digital programmes, enterprises are not only limiting the true potential of a digital business to deliver but also experiencing frustrating failure most of the time. Let's explore what is really different about a digital business and the new fundamentals:

1. **Customers:** Today's digital customers are younger, fickler, and typically in the eighteen-to-thirty-five 'millennial' demographic. They are not only active on social media but also greatly influenced by their peers and the brands they follow across various platforms such as Twitter, Facebook, Instagram and Snapchat. 86 per cent of millennials say they use social media, compared with smaller shares among older generations.[6] Because of this, they are not as brand loyal as the older generations and are extremely price

sensitive. At the same time, they are more demanding and expect high-quality digital experiences. These customers also have two attributes that I want to call out:

o *Differentiated expectations*: Different sets of customers can have very different expectations from the same experience. For example, customer expectations from the digital experience with an e-commerce company might be very different across segments, ranging from convenience for the top-tier to value-seeking for the mid-tier segments. It is important to understand this and to design targeted customer offerings accordingly. Additionally, it must be remembered that it is not just customer segmentation but personalization too that is becoming increasingly important.

o *Information transparency*: Digital is leading to greater information transparency for customers, on matters ranging from composition and manufacturing details of food products to pricing in insurance. In many cases, transparency is leading to downward pressure on pricing.

2. **Technology:** Technology started off as a support function that ran company servers and data centres. Over the past decade or so, it has progressed to becoming an enabler that builds and maintains the applications that run businesses. Today, technology is front and centre—in the sense that every business today is a technology business. To succeed in this new digital reality, every company needs to reinvent itself and build a technology DNA. If organizational leaders do not truly understand the power of technology and what it can do for their company, their business will not succeed. Equally, the capabilities and profile of the technology function need to be significantly upgraded as we now need the technology leaders to be transformational leaders. Moreover, it must be recognized that technology changes are a great equalizer: large organizations that are not nimble are often at a disadvantage in leveraging technology changes. Smart

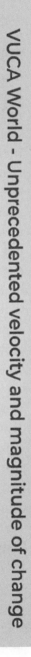

VUCA World - Unprecedented velocity and magnitude of change

Volatility
Nature and speed of change

Uncertainty
Lack of predictability

Complexity
Multiplex of forces

Ambiguity
Haziness of reality

entrepreneurs and young companies are often best placed to experiment with and leverage new technologies.

3. **Velocity:** The velocity of change has increased on all fronts. Technologies from a few years ago, such as cloud and mobile, have become commonplace and have been replaced by newer technologies such as AI, the internet of things and blockchain, which are driving current conversations. In a couple of years, these technologies will also be replaced by something else. The velocity of change is equally rapid on the business front. Industry structures are shifting and new competitors are emerging as a result. Here's a hypothetical example: Let's say you run a large global bank and you are introducing a digital strategy. You are not only concerned about what your competitor bank is doing but also now waiting to see how a disruptor like Amazon is breaking into the financial services world. Another reality is that your traditional markets probably do not offer you the same opportunities they did earlier; new markets with much higher growth rates are constantly emerging. Also, along with the rapid technology changes and hyper-competition, product and business cycles are shrinking dramatically. It does not take very long for the hunter to become the hunted. Take the example of the Indian IT industry. They created the global outsourcing industry, which has disrupted a number of traditional operational processes and delivery models over the last twenty years. However, this industry is now facing growth challenges and is being forced to reinvent itself or risk getting disrupted.

4. **Data:** The volume, velocity and variety of data that we are seeing today are unprecedented and will continue to grow exponentially, especially for digital businesses. Research by DataReportal[8] has shown that more than half of the world's population now uses social media. This enormous amount of data gives businesses a phenomenal opportunity to understand

Winning in the Digital Age is not an Easy Formula, many of the Fundamentals are Different

Volatility

Uncertainty

Complexity

Ambiguity

Customers

Technology

Velocity

Data

Iterative

Inter-Disciplinary

customers deeply and offer them more personalized experiences. This is becoming the norm and is now generally expected by most of the customers, prospects and peers we interact with today. On the flipside, data can also become quicksand, in the sense that if an organization does not harness it for the customer and organizational benefit efficiently, it can suck the firm into a never-ending investment cycle.

5. **Iterative:** There are three themes working in conjunction to make digital transformation a continuously moving target requiring an iterative approach. First, customers have ever-evolving needs. Second, there is an explosion of data and constant improvement in analytics capabilities that allow one to continually gain superior insights. Third, rapidly maturing digital technologies enable continuous deployment, taking away the need for big-bang implementations.

   As a result, 'right the first time' does not exist; your whole approach has to become iterative. Continuous experimentation and learning are key. You execute, 'fail fast', get new insights, tweak, improve, then re-execute.

6. **Interdisciplinary:** When it comes to building a digital business, the problem is not simply about marketing, finance, operations or technology; digital problems are interdisciplinary. Thus, it is about how all of these different functions come together in a cross-functional setup to develop a solution to customer problems. In my experience, this requires greater organizational collaboration and multiple functions that work seamlessly. Digital natives tend to be more successful in accomplishing this collaboration, while legacy enterprises tend to struggle to go beyond their embedded organizational structures.

   The bottom line is that the fundamental nature of a digital business is very different from that of a traditional business. Until big enterprises understand this, I believe they will struggle to get digital right. Expecting to build a successful digital business without changing the organizational fundamentals is a futile pursuit. It is not about building a digital business but about an end-to-end business transformation.

Summary

- We live in a VUCA world characterized by:
  - Volatility
  - Uncertainty
  - Complexity
  - Ambiguity

- Digital transformation has not been successfully executed because traditional enterprises have not completely understood how the fundamentals of business are changing dramatically in the VUCA world.
- Digital businesses are different because of younger, more demanding target **customers** with expectations of differentiated experiences and information transparency.
- **Technology** needs to be at the core of all business processes. Technology changes are also a great equalizer as nimble smaller organizations have an advantage over larger enterprises.
- The **velocity** of change has increased on all fronts. Industry structures are shifting, and new competitors are emerging as a result while product and business cycles are shrinking.
- The volume, velocity and variety of **data** that we are seeing today are unprecedented and will continue to grow exponentially.
- There is a need for an **iterative** rather than a 'right the first time approach'.
- Digital problems are **interdisciplinary**. Therefore, it is about how various functions come together in a cross-functional setup to develop solutions to customer problems.

3

Introducing the Eight New Rules of Business

If no mistake you have made, yet losing you are . . . a different game you should play.

Master Yoda, *Star Wars*

As we have discussed, the digital age is changing everything. When our world is changing so fundamentally, old rules of management are just not going to work. We need new rules to win in this new VUCA world that we just discussed in the previous chapter. Based on my experience across digital natives such as Flipkart and the more traditional companies such as Fidelity, and from leading transformation projects at many other Fortune 100 enterprises across the globe, I propose eight new rules of management to win in the VUCA world.

As we dive into the eight new rules of business, it is important to note that this set of new rules is the first and most important component of the seven building blocks of digital transformation that are the core foundation of 'winning in the digital age'. This first block requires a significant shift in mindset and approach towards business and as such is a meta theme or overarching influence throughout the seven building blocks. With this knowledge, let's begin with rule 1:

Rule 1: Innovate and shape the future

Typically, companies use historical performance trends to define their future plans. That counts for little in the VUCA world. The e-commerce industry is a good example of this. Historical trends will not help predict market evolution; instead, *you* have to shape the markets. *You* have to be audacious, think big and constantly innovate. In that process, do not be afraid to cannibalize your own systems, processes, products or ideas. If you do not, somebody else will! The great Steve Jobs famously said, 'Those who are crazy enough to believe that they can change the world are the ones who actually do so.' That is the first management rule in the VUCA world!

Rule 2: Strategy lies in connecting the dots

Strategy is the starting point for most businesses. However, the best plans have not been able to survive the reality of the VUCA world. Mike Tyson said it well, 'Everyone has a plan until they get punched in the mouth.' And in the VUCA world, you are getting punched all the time!

So, how do you approach business in the digital age? Now, you do need to have clarity about your purpose and long-term bets, but the strategy for getting there cannot be cast in stone. It has to be light and agile. Rather than strategy, execution is more important—getting runs on the board and failing fast. Successful execution can help you discover your strategy by connecting the dots across what works and what does not. Therefore, the strategy-to-execution cycle has changed from what has been traditionally practised. Strategy now lies not in looking forward but in looking back from execution.

Rule 3: Co-create with customers

Most companies talk about 'customer first' but very few live it. In corporate and executive action, there is sometimes conflict between what we think is right for the customer and what is right for the business (in the short term). These boundaries need to break in the VUCA world. 'Customer-centricity' and 'customer-first' can no longer be mere slogans but have to be taken to a totally different level for a firm to succeed in the VUCA world. You will not have the time for long feedback loops. Therefore, you have to co-create with your customer: the relationship has to move, with your customer not as a client but as a partner. Working relationships will become iterative, with multiple checkpoints and points of interaction. The good news is that this real-time and iterative mode of working can be enabled by technology.

For those in the business to customer (B2C) industry, personalization will become more and more important. Until recently, we were talking about customer segmentation, but technology allows you to understand and reach out to every individual customer. Your ability to manage the huge quantum of customer data that you now generate and draw sharp insights from it, will become key differentiators.

Rule 4: Every company has to become a technology company

Traditionally, companies have focused on the core functional capabilities of their industry and have seen technology as a support function. However, in an era of constant technology disruption, technology has to be a core competence, irrespective of the industry in which one is operating. It has to move from being an enabler to a core source of ideation, strategy and competitive advantage for your business. Business and technology have to connect deeply, but often there is a gap in understanding on both sides. Building a technology DNA for your company is probably the most important step you can take to future-proof your business.

I must warn you that this is not an easy journey. It is not just about building new capabilities but also about evolving your culture. This journey can take many years. However, it is a journey you have to embark on *now*. If there is one action point you take away from this chapter, please see this as the most important one.

Rule 5: Simplify organizational structure and processes

To handle the constant change and uncertainty of VUCA world, you have to rethink your organizational structure and processes. Traditionally, the foundation of organizational structure and processes has been risk management: this means putting in place enough controls to ensure that nothing goes wrong. Over time, as the business and organization grow, the layers increase and processes become complex, slowing speed of execution. This runs contrary to the key requirements for competing in the VUCA world.

These three principles are important as you redesign your organizational structure and processes:

- Speed over risk management
- Simplicity over perfection
- Empowerment over control

These principles imply a flatter organizational structure and a likely shift from vertical to more horizontal structures, both of which facilitate cross-functional collaboration. In addition, you will most certainly need to simplify your internal processes and reduce controls, keeping in mind that both customers and employees are now equally your primary focus.

Rule 6: Build a learning and knowledge-sharing organization

Continuous learning is the key to survive in the VUCA world—both for the organization and the individual. The good news is that technology has democratized access to knowledge and learning. For example, massive open online courses (MOOCs) make it easy for people to access world-class educational content. However, a significant proportion of knowledge is still tacit (not codified, residing in the minds of people). This proprietary knowledge is an important source of competitive advantage in a world where information is easily available. Organizations need to invest in codifying and leveraging their proprietary knowledge. For this, building a knowledge-sharing culture is key, and leaders need to lead by example.

Rule 7: Build an open organization and web of partnerships

Nobody can win it alone in the VUCA world—collaboration is key. There is a host of new players emerging; see them as an opportunity. Build and/or leverage open innovation platforms for collaboration. In addition, scan the value chain of your industry and look for partnership and/or acquisition opportunities on a continual basis. You need to have a dynamic approach towards this because the boundaries between partner and competitor are very fluid now, and either can metamorphose into the other very quickly. 'Coopetition' (collaboration between business competitors) will increasingly become the norm.

Another aspect of an open organization and web of partnerships is the importance of leveraging the global advantage. The VUCA world is truly boundary-less. So, do not be stuck in a silo and think global, both from a markets and delivery capabilities perspective.

Rule 8: Foster entrepreneurial leaders and culture

With the rules of management changing, expectations from talent will also change. Clearly, 'what got them here will not get them there' is a cliché but one that is very true. Companies will need more leaders, not managers. This will require managers to unlearn and relearn. It will be a big challenge for successful managers who are well set in their ways.

Building Block 1: Eight New Rules of Business

Unlearn the Old Rules and Learn the New Rules or Lose Unrecoverable Ground

Innovate and Shape the Future

Strategy lies in Connecting the Dots

Co-create with Customers

Every Company has to become a Technology Company

Simplify Organisation Structure and Processes

Build a Learning and Knowledge Sharing Organisation

Build an Open Organisation and a Web of Partnerships

Foster Entrepreneurial Leaders and Culture

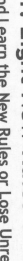

Companies will need to build a more entrepreneurial culture, one that is more aligned to a tech DNA. There are at least four important changes that both enterprise and individuals need to make:

- Build a higher tolerance of chaos and acceptance of failure.
- Inculcate a learning culture—encourage brutal honesty and humility over hubris.
- Ability to manage duality—deal with seemingly conflicting objectives such as short-term and long-term as well as speed and thoughtfulness at the same time.
- Build resilience, as whatever you do, you will face knocks and need to bounce back.

We are living in very exciting times. Change is a constant. It can be thought of as a huge challenge or an enormous opportunity, depending on your approach. Transforming the enterprise to win in the VUCA world entails **deep surgery**, requiring an extensive change in both organizational and individual principles and priorities. It might seem like a daunting journey, but the rewards are high.

I have talked about the eight new rules of management to win in the VUCA world. But if there is one, I recommend that enterprises focus on first, it would be building a deep tech DNA and capabilities. Tech disruption is the most fundamental of the disruptive forces at work in the VUCA world. Tech disruption is not a one-off but a fundamental feature of the times we are in. Therefore, enterprises have no option but to build a **strong tech DNA to future-proof themselves**. It is a difficult transformation to make but an absolutely essential one. To build and sustain a tech DNA, the **organizational culture will need to evolve significantly**. This, clearly, is not a 'quick fix' but requires a comprehensive effort that has to be blessed from the top and sustained over a period of time. So, with this quiver of eight new rules of business established, let's build a common understanding of digital transformation in the next chapter.

Summary

- The digital age is changing everything so fundamentally that *the old rules of management do not work and we need new rules to win* in a VUCA world.
- The *eight new rules of business are the first and most important component of the seven building blocks of digital transformation and require a new mindset and approach* to business:
  - **Rule 1: Innovate and shape the future**—In the VUCA world, history does not define future plans, *you* have to shape markets and constantly innovate.
  - **Rule 2: Strategy lies in connecting the dots**—Strategy lies not in looking forward, but in *looking back from execution*.
  - **Rule 3: Co-create with customers**—The customer relationship changes from a client to a trusted partner, with rapid iteration supported by technology.
  - **Rule 4: Every company has to become a technology company**—Technology has to be a core competency, regardless of a company's industry, moving from an enabler to a source of competitive advantage.
  - **Rule 5: Simplify organizational structure and processes**—Traditional organizational structure and processes slow execution, requiring a redesign with a focus on speed over risk management, simplicity over perfection and empowerment over control.
  - **Rule 6: Build a learning and knowledge-sharing organization**—Organizations must invest in proprietary knowledge and a knowledge-sharing culture led by leadership.
  - **Rule 7: Build an open organization and web of partnerships**—Collaboration is key where boundaries

between partners and competitors are fluid and 'coopetition' is increasingly the norm.

o **Rule 8: Foster entrepreneurial leaders and culture—** Companies need more entrepreneurial leaders, not managers, requiring them to unlearn and relearn, build tolerance of chaos and acceptance of failure, value honesty and humility over hubris, and cultivate the ability to manage duality and resilience.

4

Introduction to Digital Transformation in Business

At least 40 per cent of all businesses will die in the next ten years . . . If they don't figure out how to change their entire company to accommodate new technologies.

John Chambers, Former Executive Chairman, CISCO Systems

I now introduce the key aspects of digital transformation for your business—the challenges, the technologies and above all, how to succeed. Given the recent coronavirus pandemic, it has never been more important to get this right.

What is digital transformation in business?

Digital transformation is a very broad topic, and it covers a number of different types of initiatives. But what it boils down to is changing how a business interacts with customers using technology, and how its internal processes can be significantly improved by using technology.

So, digital transformation in business has two aspects: customer-facing and internal. With respect to customers, an enterprise must provide a range of technology-based channels for engagement, sales, service and other interaction needs. Internally, there is a need to digitize or automate processes that can substantially improve both efficiency and response time. This dual nature of digital makes it truly transformative—it can dramatically improve access and experience for customers while reducing response time and costs of delivery for enterprises. Thus, digital transformation also creates the opportunity to create new business models, which can open new markets and customers and be a source of breakthrough innovation.

Getting off the starting block

To be successful with digital transformation, the starting point has to be the customer. Digital transformation starts with knowing who your customer is, how their needs are changing and what you need to offer to them.

Let's look at the example of the investment management industry to understand this better. Historically, an investment management company would sell its investment products through advisers. But now, in the digital economy, there is an opportunity to sell to the investor (the consumer, directly), bypassing the adviser. This is a good example of a shift that the digital economy can cause.

Five steps for digital transformation

Step 1: Understanding how your industry value chain is changing

A key component of a digital business is understanding who your customer is and what you are offering to them. In the example above, the customer is changing from the intermediary—that is, the adviser—to the direct consumer. That is what businesses, in this case, investment management firms, need to think about: how do I directly engage with the consumer, what are their needs and what is it that I can offer them?

Step 2: Anchoring the digital transformation in business key performance indicators

Digitization is all-pervasive, and that is a huge opportunity as well as a problem. It is very easy to get lost in digital transformation because of the multi-functionality and complexity of these initiatives. It is necessary, therefore, to anchor these initiatives by defining clear business key performance indicators (KPIs). Is it about revenue growth? Is it about higher customer engagement? Is it about customer retention? Is it about product up-selling? Having numbers with which you can anchor the digital journey will keep you focused, otherwise, it is easy to lose focus in a digital transformation initiative.

Step 3: Recognizing data as the secret sauce of the digital world

Digital channels generate massive new volumes and variety of data about customers. This data provides a great opportunity for personalization—for each customer, you can optimize offerings and interactions appropriately. I asked one of my clients, one of the largest telecom companies in the US, how they looked at segmentation.

The response was, 'We now have 130 million segments'— because each customer was now well identified.

'You can identify every one of your customers and customize your offerings for each too. That's the great possibility with digital, and that is really made possible through data. That's the third step: clarifying and specifying the customer problem to be solved, identifying what data is needed to solve that problem, and how do you make that data available.'

Step 4: Understanding the implications for organizational structures

By its very nature, digitization tends to be cross-functional; it is not just about IT or marketing, it is about many of these functions coming together. The question is: how do you organize your business so that you are able to act on these cross-functional projects?

And finally, you execute on digital transformation initiatives with:

Step 5: The Two-speed strategy

If you implement digital projects with a big bang effort, chances of failure are high. While the promise of digital is high, the success rate is not very high. The best way to execute digital projects is using what I call 'the two-speed strategy', which is to stay focused on specific use cases within an organization (small wins). Do not make it all-pervasive. Focus on simple but targeted use cases, leverage these quick wins as a pilot or foundational platform and build on them, as opposed to trying to do it all or launching a project across the whole organization.

To summarize: to begin a digital transformation project, start by identifying customer problems; define business KPIs; figure out what data is required; bring different functions across the organization together; and start with very specific use cases.

Who should lead digital transformation?

Before addressing how digital transformation must be led, it is important to understand who should lead it in the enterprise, because this is becoming an awkward problem in many organizations.

Should the CEO, CMO or CIO/CTO lead the change, or should a new role be created? This is a tough choice, one that often creates friction. The answer is, no one person can really lead

What is Digital Transformation?

Comprehensive set of External and Internal changes to adapt and realize the tremendous opportunities of Digital Age

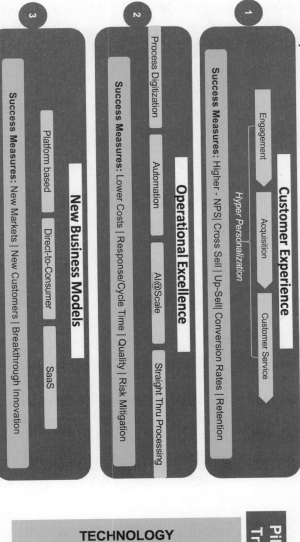

1

Success Measures: Higher - NPS| Cross Sell | Up-Sell| Conversion Rates | Retention

Customer Experience

Engagement → Acquisition → Customer Service

Hyper Personalization

2

Success Measures: Lower Costs | Response/Cycle Time | Quality | Risk Mitigation

Operational Excellence

Process Digitization | Automation | AI@Scale | Straight Thru Processing

3

Success Measures: New Markets | New Customers | Breakthrough Innovation

New Business Models

Platform based | Direct-to-Consumer | SaaS

Pillars of Digital Transformation

| TECHNOLOGY | DATA | ORGANIZATION | TALENT |

digital transformation completely, because digitization cuts across marketing, technology, operations and finance. As I said earlier, it is pervasive, and one person trying to lead an enterprise's digital transformation is a recipe for disaster.

Creation of new roles does not wholly address the challenge either. For example, the role of a chief digital officer is emerging, but it is often difficult to fully empower this role. The CIO and the CMO roles still exist, so the chief digital officer would still need to depend on them, and so it ends up being an almost superficial role. Those approaching the issue of digital transformation leadership should look towards the digital natives such as Google, Facebook and Amazon, and learn how they have done it.

These digital natives would never say that they are going through a digital transformation journey and that their CIO or CMO is leading it. The entire company is organized around delivering on customer problems. The product manager would be the one leading specific initiatives for different customer problems. At Google, you will see hundreds of product initiatives and hundreds of product managers. Its organization is structured around customer problems.

I strongly believe that is the way to go; that is the way legacy enterprises can really succeed in the digital world. The heart of their problem with digital lies in their organizational structure. Enterprises need to reorganize themselves into this product-based structure, which is a cross-functional structure organized around customer problems. This is how the digital natives have done it, and I think the time has come for legacy enterprises to adopt the same philosophy.

How to lead digital transformation

There are a number of key attributes that leaders (or product managers) need to possess to make a success out of digital transformation. Here are two.

The first is **deep customer insight.** In any business, the customer is king. In the digital economy, this philosophy becomes even more critical. A deep understanding of the customer—what customers need now and what they will need in the future—is the most important starting point for leading digital transformation.

The second is the ability **to understand both technology and business**. This will require a new breed of leaders or managers who are equally comfortable with technology and business. This tends to be an issue in large legacy enterprises where the IT function does not necessarily understand the business well, and business functions do not understand IT.

Managerial ability to bridge these two worlds is essential and it is becoming a prerequisite for roles such as the CIO, CTO and product manager. There are more aspects to this, but deep customer understanding and the ability to bridge both IT and business must be the key attributes of product managers leading digital transformation.

The technologies enabling digital transformation

There are four key technologies enabling digital transformation: data science, AI and machine learning, automation and cloud. These are the four pillars of digital and each has a certain role to play in an enterprise's digital transformation.

- **Data science is at the heart of digitization**. Data science is what makes optimization of specific customer journeys and internal processes possible.
- **The power of AI and machine learning** is at the core of personalization, necessary for enhancing customer experience at the individual level. With machine learning, the role of data is moving from one of insight to action.
- **Automation** brings a lot more efficiency to internal processes. As mentioned earlier, digital transformation for the business as a whole has implications for internal as well as external processes. Optimization of internal processes is where automation

technologies such as Robotic Process Automation (RPA) and intelligent automation are making a big difference.

- Finally, the **cloud enables digital transformation.** Initially the cloud's role was more on the infrastructure side. Embracing cloud makes the entire organizational infrastructure and all its applications a lot more scalable. With digital, your demand could grow significantly, and cloud provides a scalable and efficient way of building infrastructure. Cloud's role is now expanding beyond infrastructure, and it is becoming a key enabler of transformation across the technology stack.

Digital transformation: Succeed or perish

Digital transformation should be a strategic priority. In the digital economy, customers are getting a very different value proposition from what they did before. If businesses do not shape themselves up in keeping with these changes, their own survival comes into question. Possible extinction is looming large for many businesses, especially given the current situation, with the coronavirus pandemic having forced businesses to embrace digital alternatives to their usual physical operations.

We have seen it play out vividly in the retail industry when the likes of Kmart, Walmart and others all over the world were severely challenged by Amazon. That was the trailer of the movie that is likely to play out in industry after industry, simply because the customer is getting a value proposition from these digital natives which is of an order of magnitude superior, lower cost, and of higher convenience and better customer service than from their old-world counterparts. If, as a legacy enterprise, you do not embrace digital transformation, both externally for your customers and internally for optimizing your processes, you will be dead.

One of the key ways for legacy enterprises to ensure success in digital transformation is to connect strategy and execution. Service companies providing digital transformation services either strategy consulting capabilities or specialize as IT execution shops under current structures. This is the problem. Digital is a space where, if strategy and execution are not integrated or connected, chances of execution failure are very high!

Summary

- Digital transformation has both customer facing and internal aspects.
- Digital transformation should begin by understanding how the industry value chain is changing, anchoring on business KPIs, leveraging the power of the digital data deluge, defining implications for organizational structure and executing using a two-speed implementation strategy.
- The four technology pillars of digital transformation are data science, AI and machine learning, automation and cloud.
- Digital transformation is by nature cross-functional, and initiatives should be led by product managers bringing together cross-functional teams.

5

Five Rules for Successful Digital Transformation

It is our choices, that show what we truly are, far more than our abilities.

Albus Dumbledore, *Harry Potter and the Chamber of Secrets*

That everyone is trying to go digital, we established in chapter 1. Yet, organizations continue to grapple with achieving breakthrough business impact from digital transformation programmes—failure rates on these programmes can be 70 per cent or even higher. In chapter 2, we saw that a digital business is fundamentally different from a traditional one: the customer is younger and more demanding; there is an explosion of data; velocity of change is unprecedented; technology is not a support function, it is at the core; a 'right the first time' approach does not work; and lastly, digital problems are highly interdisciplinary.

The inability to recognize this difference leads to both the failure of vision and execution in digital transformation programmes. It is imperative that enterprises recognize that they need a new mindset and approach to succeed in the digitally disrupted world, or as I have said earlier, they risk losing unrecoverable ground to digital-native companies.

The following are the five action points for achieving transformative success in your digital journey.

1. Rethink the business model

Industry value chains are becoming disintermediated. The end customer, who was once a few steps removed, now interacts with your enterprise directly. So, the first question to ask is: who is your customer and how are their expectations changing? You need to rethink your business model to benefit from disintermediation in value chains and to engage with this younger, digitally savvy customer. You also need to rethink your products, pricing, customer touchpoints, service delivery models, etc. As you evolve the business models, you cannot be afraid of cannibalizing some of your existing activities or business. Business model decisions are often limited by the worry that some of your revenue from an existing channel or service line might be impacted. This incremental thinking does not work in the digital age. If you are not ready to cannibalize a portion of your business for your own long-term and larger benefit, someone else will come past and cannibalize you.

2. Focus obsessively on business and customer outcomes

Digital transformation initiatives can end up becoming massive, never-ending projects and it is easy to lose sight of what one set out to achieve. In my experience, the ideal way to start is with sharply defined KPIs that will have the most material impact on your business. Once the business KPIs are defined, they should become the anchor for the entire transformation programme. Business KPIs should flow from your strategic priorities, such as increasing the digital channel mix, increasing cross-selling or up-selling or improving customer retention. Once you have chosen the business KPIs as a starting point, the next step is to identify and solve the customer pain points that will move these business KPIs. A sharp eye on business and customer outcomes will help you keep your focus and ensure that you are solving the right problems.

3. Harness the power of data

In the previous chapter, I spoke about the phenomenal opportunity for businesses to harness available data to understand customers deeply and offer them more personalized experiences. The key to successful optimization, whether of a customer journey or internal process, consists in analytically sound data-driven decisions. Research by Gartner projects that by 2024, 75 per cent of organizations will have established a centralized data and analytics (D&A) centre of excellence to support federated D&A initiatives.[9] Effective use of data science is truly the 'secret sauce' in digital optimization. Algorithmic decision-making based on data wins over human discretion. However, 90 per cent or more of the focus in data initiatives, both in terms of time and money, is usually on getting the data prepared and bringing it together in a data lake and less so on utilizing data for drawing out insights and for decision-making. Reverse the approach: first, figure out the decision you want to make, then go about collecting data for it. As you anchor around the problem you are trying to solve (driven by your business KPIs), you will realize that your data management efforts will also become more focused and manageable.

4. Adopt an integrated, end-to-end approach

Large enterprises are shackled in siloed structures that are a function of their legacy businesses.

This becomes a huge challenge when they embark on digital programmes, as digital by its very nature is interdisciplinary. You need to put in place new organizational structures that allow simplified cross-functional collaboration, swift decision-making and an integrated approach. Your operating model needs to enable

Five rules for successful digital transformation

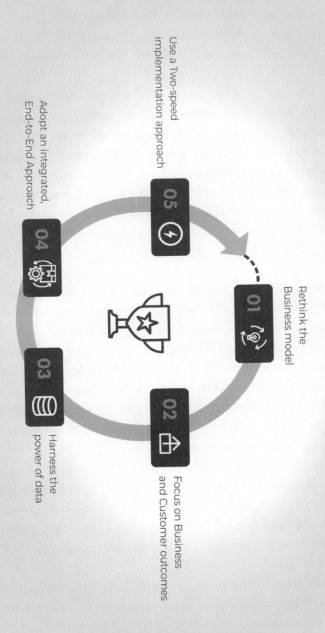

Rethink the
Business model

Focus on Business
and Customer outcomes

Harness the
power of data

Adopt an integrated,
End-to-End Approach

Use a Two-speed
implementation approach

01

02

03

04

05

'aligned autonomy', ensuring that end-to-end capabilities are brought together and each team is empowered and vested with ownership of the outcomes. At the same time, there needs to be clarity and alignment across teams on the business outcomes to be achieved.

Many consumer internet companies have solved this difficulty by empowering business success managers or product managers who have end-to-end ownership of and accountability for initiatives. The product manager plays the role of an integrator who takes a customer-centric view, understands both business and technology and works as a connector, bringing together the different capabilities and initiatives required to achieve the desired outcomes.

5. Use a two-speed implementation approach

Going 'Big Bang' is, in my experience, a recipe for disaster given the iterative nature of digital. At the same time, focusing on narrow, ad hoc use cases has limited impact. I strongly advocate the adoption of a 'two-speed' approach—focusing on high-impact use cases that will really move the needle to begin the journey while also leveraging the successes to build up your data and technology platform. Over successive agile implementation cycles, a two-speed strategy will allow you to solve the most pressing business problems while developing a scalable platform.

Two-speed implementation is relevant not just for technology programmes but also for business strategies. Adopting multi-year, fixed business strategies is a kiss of death in a world where customer needs and available technologies are both changing very rapidly. In this paradigm, business strategy should be agile and driven by your execution experience.

Organizations will achieve success in their digital transformation journey only if they recognize that digital businesses are fundamentally different from traditional ones and need a different response. A digital business requires end-to-end business transformation,

Two speed implementation drives successful execution

SPEED 1 - Deliver business value use-case by use-case

SPRINT-1

- Use case prioritization
- Product + UX Design
- Leveraging Data, AI/ML
- Tech + Process implementation

SPRINT-2

SPRINT-N

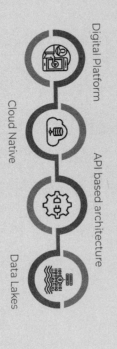

SPEED 2 – Build a scalable infrastructure overtime that is evolving continuously

Digital Platform

Cloud Native

API based architecture

Data Lakes

starting with a compelling vision, followed by smart ways of ensuring successful execution. Merely approaching digital transformation as a technology project will yield only limited results.

Summary

Five-point action plan to succeed in digital transformation programme includes:

- Rethinking the business model to adapt to the needs of younger, digitally savvy customers.
- Focusing obsessively on business and customer outcomes by anchoring success on KPIs.
- Harnessing the power of data to draw out insights and facilitate fact-based decision-making.
- Adopting an integrated, end-to-end approach to allow simplified cross-functional collaboration and swift decision-making.
- A two-speed implementation approach that focuses on high-impact use cases that will really move the needle.

6

Building Scalable Models in the VUCA World: The CIO View

In today's era of volatility, there is no other way but to re-invent. The only sustainable advantage you can have over others is agility, that's it. Because nothing else is sustainable, everything else you create, somebody else will replicate.

Jeff Bezos, Founder of Amazon

In this chapter, I will be sharing the key insights I have gleaned from my many interviews and discussions with CIOs across various industry verticals. Most industry leaders realize that the VUCA environment is here to stay and that it has far-reaching implications across three dimensions: people, processes and technology. Digital transformation is an unavoidable organizational imperative in such an environment, so much so that technology strategy has become *the strategy* for enterprises. 78 per cent of respondents in a recent study revealed that a company's survival depended on its digital transformation capabilities.[20]

On the ground though, change is not happening fast enough. Enterprises are plagued by concerns about the effectiveness of their digital efforts. Despite investing significantly in new technologies, high performance and breakthroughs in business impact typically do not live up to the expectations. It is vital that companies find ways to bridge this gap between the massive potential of digital and the current reality of its sub-par impact.

In this chapter, I have summarized the feedback I have received from CIOs into three dimensions:

1. What VUCA means for CIOs
2. Key priorities for digital strategy in the VUCA world
3. Challenges in implementing digital strategy

I will discuss each of these in detail below.

What VUCA means for CIOs

Disruption is happening across industries because of multiple factors, both internal and external. Enterprises are in a constant state of flux owing to the pace of change in the technology landscape, ever-increasing customer expectations, new competitors causing industry disruption and rapidly changing talent requirements. The revenue models and oftentimes entire business models, are rapidly evolving. In addition, companies need to grapple with the frequent regulatory changes introduced by governments globally. This has led to the emergence of the VUCA era, where organizations are forced to adapt to an unprecedented velocity and variety of change.

These rapid adaptations are occurring at multiple levels. Companies have to revamp products to cater to more digitally savvy customers and create their branding in the digital space. This typically requires a new type of talent. Dynamic strategies and dynamic resource allocation have become the norm and are the cornerstones of sustained success for any enterprise.

In as much, 'big is *no more* beautiful' which necessitates micro approaches that evolve fast with disruptions—an all-too-common VUCA feature.

Key priorities for digital strategy in a VUCA world

Digital is much less of a thing than it is a way of doing things. A digital strategy lays the foundation for delivering the right experience based on real-time intelligence.

The three impact areas around which companies can knit together their digital strategy and drive outcomes are:

1. **Customer experience:** Digital transformation gives the enterprise the opportunity to move away from creating various siloed customer experiences to a unified, customer-centric approach. With the ever-increasing number of options available for doing this and the accompanying digital clutter, enterprises need to provide frictionless and intuitive customer experience. Otherwise, they risk customer churn. The key factors enterprises need to focus on are delivery of digitally empowered simple solutions, ensuring immediate and real-time resolution, consistent omni-channel experience and continuous reinvention. To do this, a cross-functional approach is needed, which can ensure speed, efficiency and agility in action.

   Ensuring a seamless, well-integrated and omni-channel communication strategy is an important dimension of enhancing customer experience. Often, customer experiences are determined by how your brand communicates with the customer. When customers call, email, or use social media to communicate with enterprises, the company's response system could make or break the relationship. For instance, if a customer first emails a query to a company and subsequently follows it up with a call, they expect the company representative to be aware of the conversation history across all the digital platforms and respond accordingly. This calls for unifying communication across different product lines and businesses.

2. **Acceleration:** One of the biggest opportunities with digital technology and the accompanying business models is scalability.

They allow you to both build and scale up a new business rapidly. However, for that you need to find the right product-market fit, develop the right business model, make intelligent technology choices and leverage the ecosystem smartly. This is where a dynamic strategy, broken down to a micro-level, becomes crucial for success. One has to bear in mind that there is no end state. It is a continual change process.

3. **Insights:** The velocity, volume and variety of data that are now available present tremendous opportunities, such as one-on-one personalization for your customers at one level and helping enterprises improve the quality of their decision-making at another level. On top of this are the massive opportunities brought by AI and machine learning. The opportunities provided by data are unprecedented. Perhaps, it is fair to even suggest that digital strategy is really a data strategy!

Digital is not only about the 'what'; it is increasingly about the 'how'. Digital strategy demands a mindset shift while the organization is moving from legacy to digital. It is an overall strategy, not just a strategy pertaining to certain operations or departments. It is a complete shake-up of the status quo. It is cross-functional. It is interdisciplinary.

While strategy in the VUCA world needs to be holistic, there is also a need to fundamentally rethink one's approach to strategy. The traditional flow of action from strategy to execution does not work and can even be counterproductive, given the dynamic environment of the VUCA world. It requires a more dynamic approach to strategy, which is more real-time and adaptive, where you make many changes as you are executing. A good analogy is how ailerons on airplane wings adjust the flight path of the craft thousands of times every minute!

Strategy in a VUCA world is messy; **you can even say that VUCA is the end of strategy!** What we can certainly say is that VUCA requires a more dynamic approach to strategy, with dynamic

Three building blocks of Digital Strategy

Delightful customer experience: with a customer-centric approach and well integrated omni-channel strategy

Dynamic Strategy: broken down to a micro-level; Drive continual change

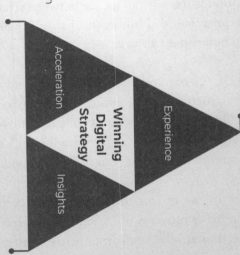

Acceleration

Winning Digital Strategy

Experience

Insights

Data- Velocity, Volume and Variety: personalization for customers; enhance quality of internal decision making resource allocation. Here, the traditional strategy-to-execution cycle is reversed. A clear picture of your strategy emerges only upon looking back and connecting the dots.

This leads us to the final topic of discussion in this chapter.

Challenges in implementing digital strategy

Organizations often struggle to meet the challenges of digital disruption in the VUCA world. There are typically five challenges that enterprises face in the execution of their digital strategies. These challenges are the reason for the big gap we see between strategy and execution in the enterprise world. How each of these challenges is met will determine an enterprise's future.

1. **Architecture:** VUCA requires companies to move from large, monolithic structures to a more micro-services-based agile architecture. Increasingly, the approach has moved from defining an 'end-state architecture' to working on an 'emergent architecture', an architecture that can be integrated and is extensible.

   Architecture is no more something you solve completely, but something you make progress on. Cloud, virtualization and API-based architecture are the key components of a company's dynamic architecture. The customer lifecycle view should form the basis of any IT transformation initiative. Making the IT environment agile, which also helps enable seamless integration of the enterprise's IT environment with that of its partners, is another critical dimension.

2. **Organizational structure:** Traditional organizations typically operate in silos in the form of business units, functions, geographies and the like. This is a major hindrance to digital transformation, which is inherently cross-functional. Digital typically needs different units to work in unison to solve customer

Five challenges in executing Digital Strategy

Architecture:
Moving from Monolithic
to Micro-services based

Organization Structure:
Siloed to cross-functional

Talent:
Development, adoption
and retention

Culture:
Organizational structure,
processes and mindsets

Leadership:
Vision of the new-gen
leaders

01

02

03

04

05

Successful
Execution of
Digital
Strategy

problems. A borderless organization that is customer-centric brings the best out of the organization and gives it the velocity and agility to deliver in the VUCA world. That is the need of the hour.

3. **Talent:** Finding talent which can adapt to this dynamic world is a challenge. Do you try re-skilling existing talent or just hire fresh talent? Creating a small but distinctly upgraded talent pool can be a huge positive multiplier and create a pull for the rest of the talent. However, getting talent in a hot talent market is just the beginning; you still need to plan for their development, adoption into the organization, and their retention. At the same time, digital is also a great opportunity to focus on the 'skills of the future' to unlearn, learn, up-skill and re-skill. If harnessed well, digital can bring new meaning and purpose to talent and to the organization as a whole.

4. **Culture:** While digital is seen to be about technology, the most fundamental roadblock preventing its realization is not technology (or even strategy) but organizational structure, processes and mindsets that are rooted in an enterprise culture. Culture is 'the way we do things here'—something deeply embedded in the organizational psyche and difficult to change. An illustration of this is moving to daily release cycles, which can be a huge challenge in legacy enterprises. It is not just about implementing agile but about building organizational agility. This is a massive change management process and requires taking the entire organization along.

5. **Leadership:** So how do you change a complex thing like culture? Our panel of CIOs strongly felt that leadership is the starting point for this change. Digital transformation has completely changed the nature and dynamics of leadership. Companies need a new generation of leaders who are technology natives and have

the foresight and vision to proactively develop strategies so that the enterprise may benefit from the tectonic technological shifts. But most importantly, they need to be change agents, customer-obsessed organization builders, and must have the resilience to absorb and learn from the many shocks that will invariably come in the VUCA world.

To sum it up, VUCA is real, and we are already in the middle of massive digital transformations and disruptions. Enterprises have the opportunity to scale up and leapfrog competition by adopting ambitious digital strategies. However, there are many challenges due to which we see a big gap between the potential and current impact of digital. Technology is only one part of it; the issues that are more fundamental are rooted in the organizational design, culture and leadership of the enterprise. Enterprises and leaders need to drive organizational transformation at multiple levels to bridge this strategy-to-execution gap in digital. It is not easy, but those who succeed will win big!

Summary

- Customer experience, business strategy acceleration and data-driven insights are three key impact areas to which companies can anchor their digital strategy and drive outcomes.
- The five challenges in executing digital strategy include:
    o **Architecture:** Moving to a more micro-services-based agile architecture
    o **Organizational structure:** Having a borderless customer-centric organization
    o **Talent:** Creating a distinctly upgraded talent pool
    o **Culture:** Developing an agile culture
    o **Leadership:** Developing customer-obsessed leaders who can act as change agents

SECTION 2

DIGITAL TRANSFORMATION ACROSS INDUSTRIES

Introduction: Digital Transformation across Industries

In the previous section, we saw that VUCA is defining new rules of business and that successful digital transformation is the key to winning. Digital transformation presents enterprises with significant opportunities for value creation to benefit from the radical shifts that are being observed across industries. While there are nuances in these shifts across industries, I see some common characteristics in them, having been able to observe these shifts across industries first-hand, as Incedo serves many Fortune 500 clients across multiple verticals. Based on my experience with them, I see at least **six common shifts** resulting from digital disruption across industries.

1. ***Customer expectations are rising for a better experience,* necessitating a radical relook at the existing offerings and processes that serve them:** FAANGs (Facebook, Amazon, Apple, Netflix and Alphabet) have completely changed consumers' experience, whose expectations from other industries have also changed as a result. In a McKinsey survey, 80 per cent of customers said that they want a Netflix-style experience everywhere.[1]

2. *Disintermediation* **in industries as** *direct channels to end customers* **(D2C) are gaining higher share:** We have already seen the biggest shift in the media and entertainment, and retail sectors with Netflix and Amazon, respectively. Many other sectors are also experiencing such disintermediation; for instance, the payments, travel and hospitality sectors. The Direct-to-Consumer Purchase Intent Index has forecast that more than 80 per cent of end consumers are expected to make at least one purchase through a D2C brand within the next five years.[2]

3. *Value chains across industries* **are also changing as** *boundaries are blurring*: Digital giants like Google and Tencent today have multiple businesses spanning several verticals. They have been able to enter many new areas because of their customer access and/or data and technology capabilities. This is forcing traditional enterprises to defend their businesses very well and also to invest in new ventures to retain their customers and grow their wallet share.

4. *New competitors are emerging*: 50 per cent of S&P 500 companies will be replaced in the next decade, says Innosight Research.[3] New-age companies are solving customer problems that have not been addressed by traditional enterprises all these years. Additionally, they are leveraging emerging technologies like cloud, AI and automation, to deliver a seamless customer experience that helps them win over traditional enterprises.

5. *Consumers have wider choice* **as there is a** *proliferation of products*, **leading to relatively shorter cycles:** Businesses today move through their life cycles twice as quickly as they did thirty years ago. Enterprises that deploy data science and build infrastructure to seamlessly integrate their business functions are able to realize the maximum lifetime value (LTV) from customers.

6. *Pricing pressures* **are mounting on businesses as both customers and regulators are asking for more transparency:** This is further accentuated by the increased proliferation of products and shorter business cycles in the digital age. A McKinsey report

There are some common themes across industries in digital transformation

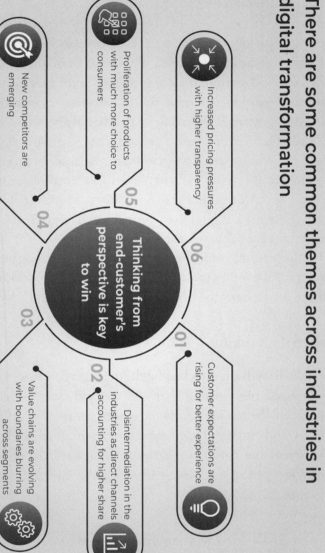

Increased pricing pressures with higher transparency

Proliferation of products with much more choice to consumers

New competitors are emerging

Thinking from end-customer's perspective is key to win

05

04

06

03

02

01

Customer expectations are rising for better experience

Disintermediation in the industries as direct channels accounting for higher share

Value chains are evolving with boundaries blurring across segments

says the bottom quartile of players who do not respond to digital natives in their industries face ~3x higher reduction in revenues than the top quartile.[4]

As a result of these shifts, **every business is now becoming a direct-to-consumer business**. Thinking from the end-customer perspective is, therefore, the key to success. I see this shift happening in the most traditional of industries. **'Customer-centricity'** is perhaps the most important implication of the digital age across industries.

While there are common characteristics in what digital means to different industries, there are many specific nuances. Different industries are at varying levels of maturity in terms of digital adoption and their speed of digital transformation. However, for sure, this maturity curve of digital transformation has accelerated in every industry because of the Covid-19 pandemic.

In this section, I share some observations and insights as to what digital transformation means—the key challenges, priorities, etc.,—for some select verticals, based on Incedo's work in these areas:

Chapter 1: Banking

- Banks have been attacked by digital natives. However, they still command high market share driven by customer stickiness.
- Most of the banks' efforts have been centered on digitizing the front-end and developing a better system of engagement.
- Whereas the core issues of their legacy system of records and business processes—which are stuck in a 'control' mindset—still persist.

Chapter 2: Wealth Management Industry

- Digital transformation has been a topic of management discussion ever since robo-advisors attacked the market. However, little has changed on the ground.

- The Covid-19 pandemic was a real stress-test of the industry for its work-from-home readiness. Despite initial concerns, the industry has, on the whole, successfully passed the test. Still, a lot of work needs to be done on cybersecurity and adherence to the wave of regulations that has happened globally.
- We will see an acceleration of digital transformation in the industry, with themes like advisor personalization, intelligent automation of the mid-back office and harnessing the full potential of data with cloud.

Chapter 3: Payments

- Payments has been at the forefront of digital transformation, and already FAANGs and the Chinese Big Three (Alibaba, Baidu and Tencent) have attacked this space.
- One can expect some big moves in this space as it will see disruption happening at a rapid pace.
- The enterprise payments space will see a change similar to what has already been observed in the consumer-to-consumer segment.

Chapter 4: Telecom

- Telcos have been investing a lot in digital infrastructure as the industry progressed from 2G to 5G. However, they have not realized the desired value from these investments.
- Instead, OTTs have won the game of content, leveraging the infrastructure that telcos had primarily invested in.
- Now, 5G presents telcos a breakthrough opportunity. But to realize gains from it, they will need to reshape their offerings, their business models and internal processes.

Chapter 5: Enterprise Product Business

- This industry is one of my favourites and stands to gain the most from digital and leapfrog ahead, leveraging cloud-led 'saasification'.
- To play offence and emerge as a winner, it is critical that product businesses first play defence well.
- There are six themes that leaders of product businesses must emphasize and re-evaluate to bring about change. These include protecting revenues from existing clients, opportunities to grow in white spaces between existing products, stepping up leveraging of global delivery model and innovative partnerships for go-to-market (GTM).

Chapter 6: Life Sciences

- Life sciences has been one of the laggards but is now at a tipping point for digital transformation.
- To win, players must consider a fundamental shift in the business model by putting the patient at the centre. Historically, it is the clinician that has been the customer in this industry.
- Four imperatives to drive successful execution in this industry are: cloud, automation, a partnering ecosystem and driving open innovation.

It is fascinating for me to observe closely the fundamental shifts that are happening across industries because of digital disruption and also to compare and contrast the specific nuances that I see. These industry shifts are creating amazing growth opportunities for incumbents and digital natives alike. I hope the insights in this section help spark some positive ideas and actions!

Industries are at varied stages on their Digital maturity - presenting different challenges to the players

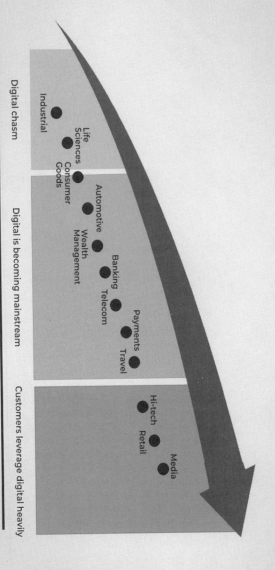

1

Digital Banking 2.0

What we don't know is what usually gets us killed.

Petyr Baelish, *Game of Thrones*

Digital innovation in the banking industry has, to date, largely focused on the transactional side of money management—the key priorities being enabling customers to manage and transact on their accounts, digital payments, and some rudimentary analysis tools. Peel the onion a layer or two, and it becomes apparent that not much has changed substantially; product choices available to customers are more or less the same; customer-bank relationships haven't strengthened; and the operating cost structure of banks hasn't changed dramatically over the last few years (the average ROE for US banks has fallen from 12–15 per cent in the early 2000s to 8–11 per cent in 2012–20).[5]

Most customers still continue to think about banks as a 'utility'—where cash can be stored, moved and monitored—and not much else. This is the reason why banks are vulnerable to attacks from fintechs and digital-only banks, which continue to chip away at their customer base with their specialized solutions. For instance,

Nubank, a digital bank in Brazil, came in as the top-ranked bank in Brazil in a Forbes study.[6] In 2019, the bank saw its customer base grow from 9 million to over 20 million. And that trend continues to accelerate. In 2020, with the onset of the Covid-19 pandemic, the bank has reportedly expanded its user base to include older demographic segments that are switching over from traditional banks.

The message is loud and clear: it is time that financial institutions rethink their digital strategies to go beyond functioning as a mere utility for transactions and payments and learn how to build deeper customer relationships from the digital natives. For this, they have to rethink their operating models, leveraging data and investing in technology in a meaningful way.

Digital transformation 2.0: key building blocks

Traditionally, banks have focused on building trust and security with their distribution network of branches. They have, by and large, not been able to keep pace with the improvements in customer experience observed across other consumer businesses. As Nubank has shown in Brazil, banks need to fundamentally rethink what it will take to pivot to a more customer-centric business model, aggressively go beyond their branch-based distribution networks, and at least invest in operations transformation which can bring back the returns to scale. This will require a tremendous shift in focus from strategy to execution across all dimensions—of people, processes and technology.

I believe the Digital Banking 2.0 playbook must include the following objectives:

1. **Rethinking of the product and service engagement models** to move away from product-centric silos to a more holistic customer-centric approach.
2. **Creation of personalized customer experiences** by servicing customers in the channel of their choice in a truly multichannel world.

3. **Re-imagining of operations** to create simpler, agile processes that are able to adapt to rapidly evolving customer engagement needs.

Data and technology will undoubtedly be the backbone on which these objectives will hinge while the execution process is on.

A comprehensive technology strategy for a bank must include the following:

- Enterprise AI to design, train and deploy the next generation of analytical models.
- Data infrastructure to power the AI models.
- Core banking modernization to not just enable process automation but also to drive actions based on AI model recommendations.

Product and services engagement

In most banks, products and services are designed and executed along functional product lines. While this drives a product-centric efficiency mindset, it misses out on a crucial factor: customers do not always think of their financial journeys as falling into such well-defined brackets. For instance, a family might have to make a choice between home improvement and college tuition, both of which are driven by a combination of factors related to the customer's life journey. In this scenario, in all likelihood, two different functions within the bank would individually design offers and target the family, not factoring in the trade-offs that the family needs to make in choosing either option. This comes with another paradox. The biggest competitors for banks today, the fintechs, usually offer specific products. The bank would, in all likelihood, be competing with two different fintechs— one in home equity and another in education loans.

Today, banks can convert this challenge into an opportunity: what if the bank takes a complete lifecycle-journey view of the customer and uses that to define bundled product offerings that can combine the home improvement and education loans? A data-driven approach would look something like this:

- Leverage AI-based choice modelling to predict customer responses to different offerings, standalone and bundled.
- Use scenario modelling to quantify the value and cost trade-offs, both for the bank and the customer base.
- Tailor offerings specific to customer micro-segments to drive maximum economic value.

These data-driven recommendations could then serve as the basis for customer relationship managers to have a truly deep and meaningful engagement with their customers. This cross-product, customer-centric approach has the potential to create a competitive advantage for banks over the product-specific fintechs.

A leading Cleveland-based bank introduced three new banking products: no-fee overdraft protection, a 2 per cent cashback credit card, and a debit-linked savings programme, all bundled together as a solution to reward customers for working towards their financial goals. Danske Bank, a northern European bank, has gone a step further and offers a housing app to its customers to help them navigate the house-buying process, including the loan applications, approval and disbursement process. It goes even further, offering customers home equity loans to finance the purchase of appliances, etc.

In both these examples, the banks decided to step out of their traditional product mindset to look at the overall customer journey and design customer-centric solutions. I expect to see many more such examples of product bundles from banks, tailored to customer-journey needs.

Personalized customer experiences

Two of the biggest demographic trends in consumer banking in recent times have been:

- **Slowing down of new customer acquisitions:** In mature economies like the US, the deposit base has levelled off over the last several years. This, in turn, has meant that banks have to rely on their existing customer base to deliver growth.
- **Channel preference by age group:** While the baby boomers have not wholeheartedly adopted digital banking (although that is changing in the post-pandemic world), millennials and the subsequent generations, by and large, prefer to almost exclusively bank digitally.

Both these secular trends have meant that a key growth driver for banks is going to be increasing revenue per customer—which is why cross-selling and up-selling are becoming key elements of customer engagement. As more and more customer interactions shift to digital channels, there is an opportunity for traditional firms to learn from tech firms. For instance, Amazon attributes 35 per cent of its sales to cross-selling[7]—it has achieved this by creating hyper-personalized customer experiences on the back of data and AI. Taking a leaf from their playbook, here is how a bank might want to approach the personalization challenge:

- FAANGs pioneered the idea of **'Segment of 1'**—intending to move away from the traditional idea of broad segments, which limited personalization—to develop micro-segments with a two-pronged strategy. This strategy enabled them to engage with customers with a high degree of precision, which in turn has significantly expanded the customer relationship and share of wallet for them:
  - o Identify transactional and behavioural attributes that help define customer characteristics to a high degree of personalization. For a bank, this would be along the multiple dimensions of wealth and income, financial acumen and digital sophistication.
  - o Approach segmentation as dynamic. Over a customer's life journey, the need states and capabilities (especially financial

status), and hence behaviours, continue to evolve all the time. And with that, the segments will need to be refined with ever-increasing frequency.

- As banks' understanding of customers deepens with micro-segmentation, it becomes possible for them to design **personalized offers** tailored to specific customer micro-segments and layered with customer-need states. For a bank facing limited net growth in new customers, it is critical to design and offer products and services which cut across product lines. Personalized engagement needs to be addressed in the following dimensions:
  - o What is the most relevant product/service?
  - o What is the right channel? A bank would need to factor in the possibility that customers can switch channels within specific interactions. For example, a customer might respond to a digital offer by calling into the call centre and/or walking into a branch. The bank needs to have the capability to provide a seamless experience to the customer through these channel hops.
  - o What is the right engagement frequency? Unlike in retail shopping, customer interactions with banks are relatively low-frequency, with a high-value transaction happening only once in a while. This requires the bank to be able to drive the right frequency of engagement across its channels to be able to truly capture the customer's attention at the right time with the right product/service.

- And last but not least, the traditional notion of customer lifetime value (CLV) was pioneered in the retail industry and embraced by banks over the last two decades as an underpinning for loyalty programmes. As loyalty, especially among Gen Zs, wanes, it is time for banks to start moving away from attempting to predict the total lifetime value of customers and instead focus on the 'next best action'. The goal is to predict immediate actions that are likely to have the highest customer impact and hence maximum response rates.

- This is becoming even more important in the highly volatile and uncertain economic environment that we have today. For instance, in the current sluggish economy, a bank should focus on protecting its credit customers by driving actions sensitive to their need states. A proactive adjustment offer of loan refinancing with the focus on the customer's current situation, as opposed to a reflexive reaction to an eroding CLV, for example, could go a long way in building customer loyalty.

Operations

Digital banks have exposed two main operational gaps in traditional banks:

- From back-end centralized processes (e.g. loan processing) to distributed processes (e.g. account opening at a branch), everything continues to be largely manual. And whatever automation does exist is typically at the task level; the processes themselves haven't changed over all these years. Digital banks, meanwhile, have shown that vastly simplified processes are possible.
- The scale advantage that larger retail banks enjoyed over the years, with their shared overheads for IT, infrastructure, etc., may not exist for too long. Digital banks have shown that productivity improvements led by technology (not just RPA, but cognitive AI too) are possible across a bank's processes.

Together, these two factors are not just impacting the cost structure of banks, but also creating vastly superior customer experiences. I see three big areas of opportunity for transforming banking operations:

1. **Self-service and straight-through processing:** Processes were defined with a 'risk and control' mindset that focused on

minimizing operational risk at the cost of speed and flexibility. As the digital natives from banking to retail have demonstrated, it is possible to reimagine the processes with customer experience as the primary goal, and then define technology-enabled risk guard-rails for exception processing. This is possible, especially because customers increasingly prefer digital self-service options.

One success story here is that of cheque deposits: this process has moved from being a manual, in-branch activity to a near-flawless straight-through processing experience. Many more such opportunities do exist—it will take a rigorous approach to identify them, define the SLAs that could be impacted, and drive the solutions to enable them.

2. **Intelligent automation:** Task automation through RPA (e.g. bots that auto-populate forms) has, by and large, run its course and delivered point efficiency gains. The next wave of automation is a combination of AI-enabled intelligent task automation (e.g. document scanning to extract data for a variety of document verification activities) and workflow-enabled end-to-end process automation (e.g. customer onboarding, verification and disbursement of consumer loans). These not only create great customer experiences by reducing the time and effort required but can also free up time for relationship managers to engage with their customers in deeper and more meaningful ways.

3. **Redefinition of operating processes:** This would be to take a more dynamic and flexible approach in response to a rapidly changing macro-environment and its impact on the customer base, as evidenced by the events of 2020. A leading consumer bank is relooking its consumer portfolio-level risk assessment in light of the economic chaos triggered by the Covid-19 pandemic. Instead of relying on payment history alone to assess risk of default, the bank is looking to glean underlying behavioural factors from data points like contact history—not just at the number of contacts and contact channels, but also the contact sequences—to assess the default risk scores on a daily basis. This

not only requires building AI models that can supplement the risk-scoring models but also means suggesting interventions for the field agents.

I believe the Digital Transformation 2.0 journey has just begun. Over the next few years, I expect to see a dramatic change in digital retail banking. In much the same way that computing technology with algorithmic trading and automation helped drive radical change in banking capital markets, technology, I believe, will be a key enabler in driving transformation in consumer banking too.

Technology

Banks have traditionally been big technology spenders. Some of the biggest banks have spent billions of dollars on digital transformation initiatives. The results have been less than stellar. In a recent survey, 75 per cent of investors who were asked, 'How confident are you that banks' digital transformation strategies will be effective?' replied with either 'skeptical' or 'too soon to tell'. On the other hand, these very banks have, on average, spent close to 5 per cent of their revenues on transformation programmes, which amounts to hundreds of millions of dollars.[8] It feels like a digital technology trap—lots of investments with little to show by way of outcomes. And, as expected, technology spending varies across banks. While the biggest banks spend around 0.4 per cent of their asset base on technology (that alone is a whopping $11.4bn for JP Morgan Chase), the mid-tier banks (with assets of between $500m and $5b) clock in at 0.22 per cent, or about half the proportion of asset base the big banks put in. Generally speaking, while the big banks are struggling to show results from their tech investments, the smaller banks are, in all likelihood, not spending quite enough.[9]

Suffice it to say that big or small, banks need to think hard and drive the right set of technology priorities to stay ahead in their digital transformation journey. This they must do by pushing on the key building blocks outlined above. And, in my experience, any digital technology strategy must include meaningful investments in three areas: infrastructure modernization (table stakes), enterprise AI, and data.

Infrastructure modernization

The banking industry was among the first to drive large-scale investments in IT infrastructure. And, as it often happens, being the first mover is both an asset and a liability. While it has served to drive productivity improvements over the years for the banks, aging technology and rigid infrastructure have become more of a liability for them in recent years. This has spurred the banks to invest in complete technology infrastructure upgrades. While this is certainly necessary, it is not sufficient to drive competitive advantage, especially when the competition consists of fintechs and digital banks.

Infrastructure modernization is underway and is likely to be a big investment area for banks for several years to come.

Some of the key factors that will determine the long-term success of their core infrastructure modernization are:

1. **Cloud first:** Most CIOs have accepted the fact that managing IT infrastructure is not a bank's core competency and that cloud migration and enablement is the most important imperative for banks to be able to modernize their technology infrastructure.
2. **Cloud security:** The rush to cloud migration needs to be balanced with the right cloud security, especially given the sensitivity of data banks have to handle (banks continue to remain the favourite target of malicious hackers). Most banks are opting, rightfully so, for a hybrid cloud infrastructure.
3. **Modernization is a journey:** Banks are saddled with multiple systems, starting with the core banking platform and layers of other applications. This has created a patchwork of data sharing

and integration built over years. Starting with core banking, upgrading all of the systems to a modern cloud infrastructure is a multi-year journey. Through these phased, multi-year migration programmes, it would be necessary to go through phases of data duplication across the legacy (on-premise) and modern (on-cloud) systems. This forced inefficiency needs to be managed well with integration governance.

4. **Interoperability:** One of the key—if not the most important—elements of a modern, distributed application ecosystem is the definition and adoption of architecture and interoperability standards built on modular architecture elements and well-established protocols for data sharing through APIs.

Enterprise AI

Organizations have run AI projects for several years now. But they are mostly isolated examples in the areas of marketing and risk management. These projects were typically limited by data and compute constraints and are nowhere near to the large, sophisticated AI engines that power the fintechs and bigtechs today. Banks can no longer afford to remain at the level of piecemeal projects, at least if they hope to stay relevant and compete against the digital natives in the coming years.

It is essential that banks today invest in enterprise AI with the following clear capabilities to support a wide range of use cases across products and services, customer engagement and operations:

1. An enterprise AI platform that can support some of the latest in AI techniques, all the way to deep learning. More importantly, the platform should have the ability to incorporate the latest advances that are coming out of academia, open-sourced from FAANGs, etc.

2. AI is compute-resource hungry, and nothing can be more frustrating than a constraint on resources. To deliver on scale

and performance, it is inevitable that the enterprise AI platform should be cloud-based.

3. It is always worth remembering that AI is not for AI's sake—the goal is to deliver business outcomes. And for that to happen, there needs to be a clear way of taking AI recommendations and using them to drive business processes. This requires the enterprise AI platform to:

   a. Operationalize the AI models, starting with the data pipelines, training, deployment of models and ongoing monitoring of the models.

   b. Integrate the model outputs with operational systems to integrate seamlessly into the overall decision-making process.

4. There needs to be recognition of the fact that AI has its roots in the open-source industry, from shared datasets to shared algorithms. A robust AI ecosystem in the enterprise must be able to replicate this democratization across functional silos. That is critical to enable a culture of reuse and sharing of best practices; and perhaps, more altruistically, to build and foster a learning ecosystem with the enterprise data science community.

5. And last but not least, the need for strong AI governance cannot be understated. One of the biggest challenges of AI relates to its ethics. Enterprise AI needs to take ownership of the following ethical dimensions:

   a. **Data privacy and security**: Access to data must be balanced with the enterprise security guidelines, especially when it comes to customer-sensitive data.

   b. **Algorithm bias**: Consumer banking is especially sensitive to this—particularly when it has material implications for specific population segments. There needs to be constant monitoring of algorithms to guard against bias.

Data

Data may or may not be the oil of the twenty-first century, but it certainly is the fuel that powers AI. And yet, organizations have failed to devote the necessary attention and resources to build data as a strategic asset. And if there is a single reason why AI has not delivered the promised value, it is this myopic view of data. For the longest time, organizations have treated data as an afterthought: the recent excitement about data lakes and the investments in them haven't yielded much either.

The situation with banks is no different. If there is one (more) lesson to take from the tech firms, it is that for data to truly generate economic value for the firm, it has to be treated as front and centre of the business and operating model. As banks, big and small, are finding out, this is easier said than done. The biggest constraint is legacy. The current data infrastructure and data models have evolved through functional silos, archaic systems and decades of accumulation of disparate systems through mergers and acquisitions. To add to that, organizational data fiefdoms have resulted in patchy (at best) progress in standing up a data ecosystem that can support AI to drive digital transformation.

This is why I believe that data must be one of the top organizational priorities for banks if they expect to survive and thrive in the fintech onslaught. Some of the key data priorities that banks need to embrace right now are:

1. **Cloud data platform:** The last decade saw organizations splurge millions on Hadoop systems, swept by the 'big data' narrative. That is unravelling rapidly, as the on-premise Hadoop infrastructure is unable to scale, both in performance and costs. It is time to move away to the cloud, and not just from the cost and scalability points of view. The cloud also offers enterprises the ability to innovate, especially with event logs and streaming

data, which are the backbone driving real-time digital customer engagement.

2. **Data pipelines:** Any data infrastructure is only as good as the data. It may sound obvious, but the reality is that most banks have not done enough at all to move data from multiple legacy systems to a centralized source. Banks have (and continue) to burn millions of dollars on building enterprise data lakes with the promise of creating a curated, centralized data repository for all analytical needs. Clearly, this has not happened with any degree of success (not just in banks, but across industries)—largely because the time, effort and focus required are just not available in most organizations. Eventually, the result is less of a clean data lake and more of a muddy data swamp. In any case, it is important to invest in building and maintaining the flow of data into the cloud-based centralized repository for it to be even useful.

3. **Data harmonization:** This involves more than just transfer of data; it needs a complete integration and harmonization roadmap across disparate systems. In a typical bank, customer data is sourced from multiple systems—many organic (e.g. account transactions, loan origination, customer care) and many inorganic (systems acquired from bank mergers and acquisitions). Integration across these systems to create a complete data view is necessary. This is perhaps the hardest challenge to surmount, less from a technical perspective, but more from an organizational process perspective.

4. **Data quality:** The garbage in garbage out (GIGO) principle has never been truer than in the digital world. Much like data harmonization, this is a tough problem, and yet a necessary one to solve. In a not-too-distant future, when the banks will need to drive personalized engagement with customers and automate operations internally, good-quality data will be key to ensuring that these processes drive the expected value.

5. **Data for AI:** AI feeds on data, and good AI is one that learns and keeps getting smarter over time. To make this happen,

Digital Bank 2.0 - Digitization goes beyond the front-office

**Objectives:
Digital Banking
2.0 Playbook**

01 Re-think the product and service
engagement models

02 Create personalized customer
experiences

03 Re-imagine Operations to
create simpler, agile processes

Harness the power
of Technology and Data

Enterprise AI to be the source
of competitive advantage

Data Infrastructure moving
away from siloes

Core banking modernization
to drive a complete overhaul of
processes and be digital-first

well-documented and reliable training and validation datasets need to be created. They must not just be comprehensive but also have guards against reinforcing algorithmic bias.

6. **Data governance:** None of the above is remotely possible without strong data governance that operates at the bank-level (not functional group-level) and takes responsibility for:

   a. Breaking down the trust barriers to share data across groups,

   b. Establishing a data ethics framework to protect against bias,

   c. Advancing the cause of a centralized, shared data ecosystem with the right security and regulatory compliance.

It is obvious but worth repeating that these technology investments in infrastructure modernization, enterprise AI and data are not to be treated as sequential. The real competitive advantage for banks is in the how: the ability to execute on all three fronts, even as they are continuously evolving with and learning from the market dynamics and other macroeconomic factors.

Conclusion

Digital transformation in retail banking is at an inflexion point, and we can also expect this to accelerate significantly in the coming years, even as the industry is going through profound changes triggered by the economic uncertainty arising from the coronavirus pandemic. Success in this difficult environment will require clarity in strategic direction, the ability to make the right bets in technology and people, and, above all, speed and agility in execution. One thing, though, is increasingly certain: the banks of tomorrow will look a lot less like the branch-based networks we have been used to and ever more digital, with a limited physical footprint, offering customers a truly seamless multi-channel experience at every stage of their financial journey.

Summary

- Banks have been under threat by digital natives, however, they still command high market share driven by customers' stickiness. While banks have centered efforts around digitizing the front-end and developing a better system of engagement, they will need to significantly step up their efforts to compete in the digital disruption happening in the industry.

- Three key imperatives for banks in their digital transformation journey are:
  - Rethink product and service engagement models by leveraging AI-based interventions for customers and stepping outside traditional product mindsets.
  - Create personalized customer experience: Think about the 'segment of 1' and the 'next best action' to maximize impact.
  - Reimagine operations: Deploy 'self-service', RPA+AI+ Cognitive, redefine processes.

- They must harness the power of technology and data, upgrade their legacy systems and move away from siloed data infrastructure. Banks must consider prudently leveraging 'hybrid' cloud while enterprise AI becomes the source of competitive advantage.

2

Digital Transformation in the Wealth Management Industry

Every minute the future is becoming the past.

Thor, Marvel Comics

Digital transformation in wealth management has been an important theme for a long time but the industry has been relatively slow in adopting digital technologies. The wealth management industry has been dealing with challenges in the form of changing business models, disintermediation and disruption from fintechs, increasing client expectations, revenue pressures due to zero commissions and alternate fee models. Wealth management was front and centre of the volatility in the aftermath of the Covid-19 pandemic. The disruption caused by the pandemic has further accentuated the VUCA environment, and the need and push for digitization have become more and more important.

I have both observed and participated in the digital transformation that has been happening in this industry over the past decade, initially helping drive strategy and transformation for Fidelity's international business. Over the last three years, at Incedo, I have been working with some of the leading players across the wealth management industry value chain. Based on these experiences, I have identified ten priorities for digital transformation in the wealth management industry, especially in the wake of the Covid-19 pandemic:

1. **Advisor enablement is key:** The financial advisory industry has been rapidly pivoting from a transaction-led model to a more relationship-based model. The financial advisor is expected to provide holistic goal-based financial planning to his clients, and here the role of technology in delivering tools and capabilities becomes paramount. Digitization has been at the forefront of the evolution of the advice-centric model for the industry. Client expectations are increasing; customers expect more personalized services and specialized advice tailored to their goals and life events. Financial advisors are therefore demanding tools and insights to offer hyper-personalization, get a 360-degree view of the client and efficiently service them at scale. The advisors want a unified experience and functionalities such as account aggregation, client portal, online document storage, CRM and client-servicing tools. The role of digital tools has become more important in the wake of the Covid-19 pandemic, so wealth management firms should double down on their investments here.

2. **Improving scale through seamless processing and omni-channel servicing:** Wealth managers want to focus more of their time on delivering value for their clients, and a lot of attention has been paid to digitizing time-consuming and error-prone activities. Digitizing activities such as account opening, account transitioning, document delivery and e-signatures has helped in reducing errors and NIGOs (not in good order), and in improving the operational scale for wealth managers. During the pandemic, adoption of these technologies received a tremendous boost, with both clients and advisors calling for straight-through processing using workflow-based digital tools. At the same

time, due to the volatility and uncertainty in the markets, the need for investment information and client servicing increased dramatically. The investments made by wealth management firms to provide an omni-channel experience to their advisors and clients via multiple channels really paid off, helping the firms service their respective stakeholders effectively.

3. **Digital collaboration has helped manage fears of disruption:** Wealth management has traditionally been an extremely high-touch industry with in-person servicing expectations. But during the pandemic, the tools and technologies available for digital collaboration have really helped the industry manage its fear of disruption and put its clients at ease. We expect these digital collaboration channels to further evolve via integration with tools such as financial planning and CRM. Wealth managers who fail to adopt such technologies stand to lose their clients to their more digitally savvy counterparts.

4. **AI/ML usage will increase in tandem with data availability:** AI/ML in wealth management is gradually shifting from drawing boards to practical usage, but use cases are still limited. Robo-advisory continues to be the most notable use of AI/ML, and firms have rolled out these tools to advisors to attract a newer generation of investors. Lately, firms have also started to use AI/ML in other areas, such as in tracking and modelling events for lead management and to ensure that more quality leads are converted. Some wealth management firms are also using OCR and character recognition techniques to improve the speed and accuracy of unstructured data ingestion.

The buy-side firms have for long used AI/ML for algorithmic trading using proprietary quant models, but its use in long-term financial planning is still limited. As the data ecosystem becomes more mature and the ability to consume and interpret alternate unstructured data increases, usage of AI/ML will broaden. In the future, AI/ML usage will further expand to use cases such as the 'next best' action, chatbots, stock analytics, ranking (already underway), price prediction and generation of the alpha. It will greatly complement the work of wealth managers in scaling and improving their client servicing and investment decision-making.

5. **Operations transformation:** While many client-facing initiatives get attention in conversations on digital transformation, digitization has been having a massive impact on improving operations. Many wealth management firms grapple with the inefficiencies introduced by their legacy platforms and the workarounds and customizations built for supporting their business. The dilemma faced by technology leaders is whether to build focused point automation or whether to go in for a bigger transformation. The success of any operations transformation initiative requires the firms to also redesign their legacy processes to cut down inefficient and non-value adding activities. Without a parallel effort to apply digital design principles, the results of any transformation can be underwhelming.

6. **Central role of data:** Data is the anchor and will play a central role in the execution of all of the initiatives above, whether it is providing more high-touch services, operational transformation to increase scale, or using AI/ML to drive client servicing and investment decisions. Harnessing data, especially in the digital world, to derive insights for clients, advisors and other stakeholders and offer them personalized services, will remain a key priority for wealth managers. This becomes even more important as business models evolve, regulatory pressure continues to increase and sources and volume of data explode. Dealing with data growth, ensuring data quality and integrity, harmonizing disparate data sources and putting good data governance practices in place should be the top priorities for wealth management firms. This will ensure that their data lakes

do not turn to data swamps and are able to generate actionable insights for decision-makers.

7. **Cloud adoption:** A majority of the wealth management firms is already on its cloud adoption journey. This was primarily driven by the desire for flexibility, scalability, resilience, and for reducing infrastructure complexity. As the firms modernize their technology stack, many new tools are getting built and deployed on the cloud directly. The pandemic did not impact the firms' cloud strategy, but given how the industry was able to effectively deal with increased trading, volatility and application usage, it served as a good validation of the resiliency and scalability offered by cloud.

8. **Cybersecurity in the remote working environment:** The wealth management industry is among the most regulated industries, one subject to frequent audits and reporting. Due to the nature of the clients and investment data the firms deal with, cybersecurity has been inherently built into the DNA of most large wealth management firms. However, the Covid-19 pandemic has presented its unique set of challenges, with most of the staff moving to remote working. The industry now requires to invest in additional security initiatives and has to conduct more regular internal audits to ensure that data security is not compromised.

9. **Impact of fintechs and fear of disruption from FAANGs:** Fintechs have played an important role in expanding the technology choices available to advisors and wealth management firms. Tools introduced by the fintechs have also helped push the digital agenda forward, leading to refinement of the usability and interactive aspects of the tools available to advisors. The industry is also witnessing overlapping of services offered by various players in the wealth management value chain. This is

Key enablers for driving digital transformation in Wealth Management

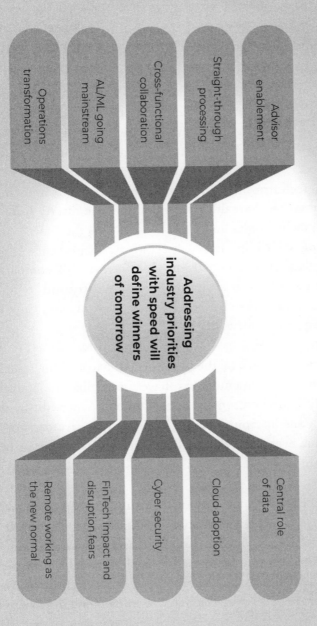

Advisor enablement

Straight-through processing

Cross-functional collaboration

AL/ML going mainstream

Operations transformation

Addressing industry priorities with speed will define winners of tomorrow

Central role of data

Cloud adoption

Cyber security

FinTech impact and disruption fears

Remote working as the new normal

a result of wealth management firms seeking to capture greater customer wallet share and to see industry consolidation.

We see broker-dealers increasingly focusing on expanding their registered investment advisor (RIA) channels. Schwab and Vanguard have started offering automated planning and advisory solutions. Morgan Stanley and Goldman Sachs made a push for the retail pie with their takeover of E-Trade and United Capital, respectively. Similarly, Empower, a retirement record keeper, will start offering financial planning services with its acquisition of Personal Capital. I see, as a continuation of this trend, bigtech firms like Facebook, Apple, Amazon and Google making forays into wealth management in the future. Adoption of digital technologies and harnessing data as the central theme for driving such initiatives will stand the incumbents in good stead against such competition. In the end, all competition and new ideas lead to evolution of the industry and its service models. New players challenging the status quo will only help the industry move forward.

10. **Remote working will be the new normal:** Most of the functions of wealth management firms have been able to transition seamlessly to remote environments, and productivity in most cases has gone up from previous levels. I expect remote working to continue even after the pandemic subsides. In-person office visits might be limited to requirements such as joint ideation.

Overall, the wealth management industry has been able to adapt very well to the Covid-19 disruption. Digital transformation was a trend already underway in the wealth management space, and the pandemic simply gave a push to the implementation efforts and adoption of such initiatives. The success of digital transformation is as much a factor of successful technology implementation as it is of orienting the organization towards a digital mindset. How wealth management firms shape their organizational culture will determine the success or failure of their transformation initiatives.

Summary

- Digital transformation has been a topic of discussion ever since robo-advisors attacked the market. However, little has changed on the ground.
- Digital transformation has been accelerated by the Covid-19 pandemic, leading to work shifting out of the office space and to less in-person servicing.
- A key theme for digital is to drive personalization for advisors so they can engage better with clients.
- AI/ML will see new use cases beyond robo-advisory.
- Cloud adoption will increase, and cybersecurity will be augmented. Future-proofing against the entry of FAANGs into the industry is necessary:
  - Improving scale through seamless processing and omni-channel servicing,
  - Redesign processes such that it simplifies processes end to end and not just incremental point automation,
  - Continued investment in data infrastructure as the core anchor to aid transformation initiatives and generate insights leveraging the digital data deluge.

3

How Digital Is Disrupting Payments

I could either watch it happen or be a part of it.

Elon Musk

To say the payments industry is going through disruption is certainly not a hyperbole these days. The fundamental shifts in how commerce gets done have begun to impact the way payments have been done all these years. On one side, the payments industry has seen the entry of diverse fintech players, including giants like Facebook and Tencent, in addition to the start-ups that are presenting increased competition for banks and corporations. On the other, the threat from fintechs is being further fuelled by rapidly evolving customer expectations, which continue to push the boundaries for the industry as a whole. It is increasingly apparent that the payments marketplace will look fundamentally different a decade from now. There will be new form factors, real-time infrastructure, greater levels of integration with social media and e-commerce, to name a few of the changes. In effect, the revolution that has completely disrupted the consumer payments industry over the last decade or so is finally coming to take into its fold the corporate payments industry, too.

I see three big trends that are likely to shake up this segment, which is at half a trillion dollars a year, and growing:

1. **Direct-to-consumer models:** As firms across industries move to direct engagement with their customers, it is becoming increasingly necessary to deliver them the same level of digital experiences as the consumer payments industry does.

2. **Global payment flows:** Cross-border payments now make up over 11 per cent of all corporate payments, and they are growing.[11] These flows are almost always digital in nature, with the added complexity of regulatory compliance and risk management.

3. **Data monetization:** Bank treasury services have had the advantage of managing and servicing fund flows between their corporate clients. And as these fund flows become increasingly digital, they have enabled banks to build a data goldmine. Banks are now actively looking to leverage this data to deepen their service offerings.

Banks and corporations have started responding to the call of digital and the payments processing industry is currently going through a wave of infrastructure modernization. I see significant technology investments by CIOs across firms that are setting the stage for the next wave of digital transformation. The payments industry will look fundamentally different, a few years from now. By adopting digital channels, embracing automation, adopting open standards and making smart bets in technology, banks and corporations can emerge as winners in the payments marketplace.

Making digital transformation happen

As digital transformation initiatives in payments pick up steam, there are four main areas of focus, each of which is important to ensure not just a solid foundation for a digital payments ecosystem, but also to ensure the groundwork for unlocking the revenue potential from treasury and payment operations. This is something yet to be tapped in most organizations:

1. **Enabling of digital channels:** Buoyed by the consumer payments industry, there is a rapidly growing array of digital payment channels that need to be integrated into the digital payments service offerings.
2. **Process automation:** Payment processes typically span across entities (bank-corporation-consumer) and integration across disparate systems will make for a critical foundation to enable scalable implementations.
3. **Payment analytics:** Payment processes have always been data-rich, and even more so when digital channels continue to grow. Effective use of the data to make better decisions (e.g. manage risk, prevent fraud) and furthermore, explore data monetization opportunities, are becoming important.
4. **Adoption of standards:** For any multi-entity ecosystem with entities across the globe to scale with technology, it is essential to establish standards. Adoption of open banking standards is essential for digital payments to succeed—and we are at an inflexion point, given the increasing adoption of these standards.

Digital channels

The ubiquitous cheque has been the staple in corporate payments for years now. Despite being the most expensive payment instrument, the cheque has dominated the corporate payment world for decades. It is not just the processing cost of the paper cheque that makes it a burden for banks. It is also a security headache. It is well known that paper cheques are the largest vehicle of payment fraud.

All that is changing. And, as it usually happens, this started with the consumer payments business. As the direct-to-consumer models continue to evolve, the B2C payments business is growing rapidly (annual growth rate of 15 per cent led by digital e-commerce).[6] The digital payment technologies that are coming out of the consumer payments industry (Zelle, Paypal, digital wallets, et al) offer a rich choice for banks and corporates to offer digital experiences to their customers:

- **Disbursement of funds:** Transfer volumes of Medicare/Medicaid funds by healthcare providers to their members continue to rise and should, by and large, be digital.
- **Refund management:** In a direct-to-consumer world, corporations need to manage refunds to customers from excess payments and product returns. Customers used to instant digital payments from the e-commerce world are expecting a similar experience everywhere.
- **Loyalty/reward disbursements:** As corporations build deep relationships with their customers, they continue to adopt customer engagement strategies from e-commerce retailers. These include cashback payments and encashing of loyalty points, which need to be executed through digital channels.

A similar revolution is around the corner in B2B payments with the expansion of consumer-like payment rails, such as digital wallets, in addition to the existing ones like ACH, Wire, virtual cards, etc. We believe the convenience of digital payments is only a starting point. There is so much more to it by way of benefits:

- **Streamlining of payment processes** has a direct impact on working capital management. Trade finance is key to enabling global supply chains, and fintechs are coming up with specific solutions.
- **Cross-border payments to suppliers and subsidiaries** need to stand up to heavy regulatory requirements in addition to managing the risk of fraud. Digital payments are increasingly the safest alternative. In addition to enforcing compliance, digital channels can ensure transparency of global fund flows.

- Of late, *acquiring a deeper understanding of the supplier ecosystem* has become an important factor (see the section on payment analytics below).

Automation

70 per cent of corporate treasury and payments professionals list manual and inefficient processes among their top challenges. In addition to their high costs, manual processes are also error-prone, difficult to scale in response to variable volumes, and increasingly susceptible to fraud.

Process simplification and automation opportunities extend across the value chain—from establishing the payment exchange with suppliers (B2B) and consumers (B2C) to creating a variety of services around three-way (PO, invoice and receipt) matching, and all the way to the disbursement of funds through different digital payment channels. Several fintechs see this as a big area of opportunity and are building to this end auxiliary platforms that can integrate with corporate systems and automate the end-to-end processes.

Bank treasury services offer a slew of products and services— from cheque processing to Automated clearing house (ACH)/ wire—to their corporate clients. For instance, a large bank helps one of the largest healthcare providers in the US process over 4 million transactions on an annual basis, covering their entire value chain, from providers—corporate hospitals (B2B) and individual doctors (B2C)—to pharmaceuticals (B2B).

- There is a clear opportunity to digitally onboard these entities onto the payments network in a rapid, secure manner using DIY portals as well as create an 'omni-channel' like experience that minimizes onboarding friction.
- Automating a payment network of this size and complexity is undoubtedly an integration challenge, given the multiple legacy systems at enterprises and, increasingly, enterpise resource

planning (ERP) systems. With the increasing adoption of application programming interface (API)-based data exchanges, end-to-end automation with multiple payment rails is a necessary building block for digital payments.

Data and analytics

Payment processing through digital channels is data-rich: strategies and execution led by analytics on the transaction data can help in a variety of ways—improving revenues, cutting operating costs, detect fraud and other anomalous behaviour.

Risk and fraud analytics: As payments migrate to digital platforms, it is almost inevitable that fraud becomes more sophisticated too. And, as the volume and complexity of payments grow, fraud is becoming just as hard to track, identify and prevent. Fraud prevention will have to move beyond transaction-centric assessment to leveraging AI for detection and prevention of emerging fraud. Broadly speaking, organizations need to think of payments fraud at two levels:

- *Account fraud*: Digital identity theft is a leading cause of fraud. Methods like account takeover (ATO) and synthetic identity creation can be used to gain access to accounts and siphon funds. Tracking and preventing this requires going beyond the traditional knowledge-based authentication methods to monitor authentication journeys, looking for anomalous patterns.
- *Phantom payments*: Businesses lose significant amounts to fraudulent payments, triggered both by employees (e.g. initiating a phantom payment) or payees (e.g. creating double invoices). Monitoring and flagging them requires a range of methods, starting from rule-based systems (e.g. proximity of transaction requests) to more sophisticated machine learning methods (e.g. payee behaviour risk-scoring and setting of guard-rails sensitive to each risk segment).

Data monetization: A bank managing the payment flows between its corporate clients and their network of suppliers and customers has the unique ability to understand the financial behaviour of all the firms in this network. This can be a powerful tool for the bank to develop targeted strategies to drive superior experience and value for its clients:

- *Working capital optimization*: Banks can help their clients optimize their working capital by forecasting fund flows and using that to transfer the optimal funds into their payment accounts.
- *Service bundling*: Using a combination of behavioural and transactional patterns, banks can help define optimal service bundles for their clients. For example, corporate payments that span multiple countries can be optimized with a combination of exchange-rate hedging and currency-float solutions.

Adoption of standards

Open banking

Starting in 2015, when the European Parliament adopted open banking standards (PSD2), there has been a growing momentum in adoption of standards. And, as it happens with standards, this can catalyse innovation and efficiency across the world of payments once they reach a critical mass of adoption. Open banking regulations require banks to open up their systems and data to third-party providers through secure channels. This has the potential to accelerate:

1. Seamless transfer of funds between banks, using standards as opposed to relying on the current custom of point-to-point software integrations.

Payments - Disrupt or get disrupted!

Key Trends shaping Payments Industry

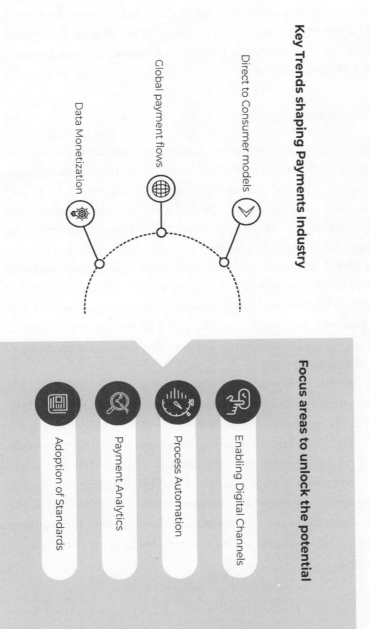

Direct to Consumer models

Global payment flows

Data Monetization

Focus areas to unlock the potential

Adoption of Standards

Payment Analytics

Process Automation

Enabling Digital Channels

2. The capability of corporations with multiple bank accounts across currencies to efficiently aggregate bank account data into a single accounting portal for automated reconciliation, mitigating issues in one of the most complex of payment transactions—cross-border payments.

Blockchain technology

Several financial services firms are increasingly looking to blockchain technology to mitigate the risk of fraud. The three fundamental underpinnings of the technology are distributed ledger and immutable and permissioned access. Taken together to underpin a payment processing service, they make it possible to trace the entire sequence of wire transfers. Visa launched its B2B Connect Platform based on a private blockchain with the aim of enabling faster cross-border payments. Similarly, a host of banks, including HSBC, BNP Paribas and ING, launched Contour, a blockchain-inspired platform designed to make the $18-trillion trade finance market more efficient and secure. I expect this space to see a lot more action in the coming years.

After decades of plodding along with archaic systems, the $2 trillion behemoth that is the global payments industry, is waking up, shaken up by the fintechs (a revolution of sorts that PayPal ignited).[12] And, as it often happens, innovation in one sector rapidly spills over to adjacent areas; the dramatic change that started in consumer payments created the technology building blocks for digital disruption in corporate payments too. Combined with the adoption of standards and, most notably, the maturity of blockchain technologies, the corporate payments industry is primed for a burst of innovation.

Summary

- Payments has been at the forefront of digital transformation, and already FAANGs, Chinese Big 3 (Alibaba, Baidu and Tencent) have attacked this space.
- Big moves can be expected in this space. Enterprise payments will go the consumer payments way.
- Winning moves for enterprises would be: enabling of digital payment channels for corporate clients, payment automation and analytics, and adoption of open banking standards.

4

How Telecom Players Can
Win in the Digital Age

Good companies will meet customer needs, great companies will create new
markets.

Philip Kotler

The telecommunications industry has evolved around technology advancements in the communications space. The industry has developed from being a provider of landline services to delivering high-speed broadband services with ubiquitous mobility.

The telco industry today is certainly at a point of inflexion and in order to remain relevant in the rapidly changing marketplace, its long-standing aspiration of evolving from the legacy of providing connectivity services to a more value-added provider of content, applications and data services, has to be accomplished. In fact, the rapid adoption of digital transformation by enterprises is a great opportunity for telcos globally. For telcos, it's not just about the digital transformation that they are themselves undergoing, it is also about their being the digital enablers for other enterprises and sectors. GSMA has projected that the number of connected devices will grow from 7 billion in 2018 to 24 billion in 2025;[13] and telecom operators are in a unique position to capitalize on this by providing innovative digital connectivity solutions that will form the backbone of the globally connected digital world in the near future.

In this chapter, I will share my perspectives on the key challenges facing the telecom industry, how 5G can be a game-changer and actions telcos will need to take to realize value from the 5G opportunity. My perspectives are based on my experiences with telco majors in North America; however, I believe these insights should be relevant to other parts of the world as well.

Four key challenges for the telecom industry

1. **Despite growing data consumption, telcos have been losing the content and application battle to OTT (over-the-top) players, leading to flat-line/shrinking revenues.**

   In general business terms, increasing customer demand leads to an increase in revenues, but for telecom operators, data usage has increased exponentially while revenues at best have remained flatlined. Capex investments made by telcos in 3G and 4G in the last decade have led to a major technological shift in the form of high-speed global mobile networks. Most of these investments have enabled entry to OTT players who offer consumers innovative services. While OTT players who fully leverage the connectivity infrastructure provided by telecom operators have grown their revenues exponentially over the past decade, the telecom operators haven't been able to monetize this phenomenon and bite into any incremental revenues for themselves.

2. **Massive investments are being made in 5G infrastructure; however, monetization through IoT solutions and the ability of telcos to create new revenue streams is unclear.**

   When it comes to new revenues streams for telecom operators, IoT is high on the list. After all, IoT is the big phenomenon which is likely to create billions of connected devices across the world powered by these telecom operators. While there is no doubt about the potential of the 5G + IoT combination, the big question is, how are the telcos going to capitalize on this and generate revenues for themselves. Despite a number of trials and pilot implementations, it is not clear what role the telco can play or what business model it can have beyond that of a connectivity provider.

3. **Digital channels have not yielded the desired results; digital contributes less than 15 per cent of total sales and services for many leading telcos.**

Telcos have made very significant investments in digital transformation over the last five to seven years. However, these investments have not yielded the desired outcomes and customers continue to rely heavily on stores and call centres for their needs. The main reason for this is that telcos have not adapted their products and services for digital channels. In this industry, policies, the fine print and pricing continue to be complex, necessitating the need for assisted sales. Moreover, the telcos' digital journeys have mirrored physical journeys, making them long and cumbersome.

Another challenge the telcos face is that while they generate huge amounts of data on customer usage, the systems of insights to convert this data to create personalized experiences for the consumer have not evolved at the required pace.

4. **Keeping up with cybersecurity, regulatory and government policy changes.**

The focus of regulators is increasingly turning towards areas such as general data protection regulation (GDPR), while legacy issues such as wholesale pricing and VoIP interconnection regulations are easing. But other areas of regulation are changing very fast, and we have spectrum release roadmaps, data protection frameworks and accounting rules, all in ever-evolving states.

Monitoring call and communication quality is crucial for ensuring that customers get the kind of telecom experience they deserve. Tracking and understanding their communication life cycle will be essential for telecom companies for another reason too—which is to do with data and privacy. Customers are terrified at the possibility of identity theft and financial loss. As a result, customers are demanding the same level of control over their personal data as they have over passwords to their bank accounts and email addresses. Telcos will need to work harder to create environments where people can feel safe.

Telco operators are working towards providing personalized experiences leveraging AI/ML and digital analytics capabilities, which, from a customer-centric point of view, is the right thing to do. However, customers don't want to compromise on how their data is protected and stored. Telcos will need to ensure that their networks can protect consumer data in line with industry standards and to the satisfaction of their customers.

While there are headwinds, and given that the telecom industry is at a point of inflexion, telcos have inherent strengths that they can use to turn the tables to their advantage. Telecom players have huge physical assets that act as entry barriers; they generate massive amounts of customer data, given the 'always on' nature of customer usage, and provide a service that has become essential in many aspects of life. These advantages, coupled with what is perhaps the most significant technology change for the industry—5G—can prove to be a force multiplier. While the telecom industry has undergone many technology upgrades, each more significant than the previous, 5G has everyone in the industry excited like never before. And there is a good reason for it.

Why are telecom operators obsessed with deployment of 5G?

- Capex investments made by telcos in 3G and 4G in the last decade have provided a major technological shift in the form of high-speed global mobile networks. We have already discussed how this has allowed the entry of OTT players who, leveraging the connectivity infrastructure of the telco operators, have grown revenues exponentially over the past decade, while telecom operators themselves haven't profited in any substantial way from this.

- 5G, quite like its predecessors, is a huge leap forward in terms of speed, capacity and latency. But when combined with the distributed architecture and real-time edge computing capability, this technology is unmatched. The edge computing infrastructure allows telcos to shift the data processing and application deployment to devices *they* control, thus changing their equation with OTT providers.

- The connectivity needs of enterprises are rapidly evolving. Enterprises are no longer interested in static services; what they want is the ability to subscribe to varying speeds based on differentiated quality of experience (QoE), or the ability to use varying network capacity/slices, with the option to enhance or downsize network resources dynamically. The real power of 5G technology lies in its capability to enable and provide such transformational services for enterprises and industrial customers.

- However, for telcos to win in this scenario they will need to leapfrog in terms of product design to deliver world-class experience, including IoT devices and applications, to their customers. This will require innovative collaboration with original equipment manufacturers (OEM), building a thriving ecosystem of tech start-ups to build pointed applications, and upgradation of their own product development and GTM infrastructure to stitch all these elements into compelling solutions for different industry-based enterprise customers and end consumers.

5G will mean a massive investment on the part of telecom players. The reason they are so excited about this is because it can potentially

Telecom at crossroads - Addressing key challenges to grab the opportunity

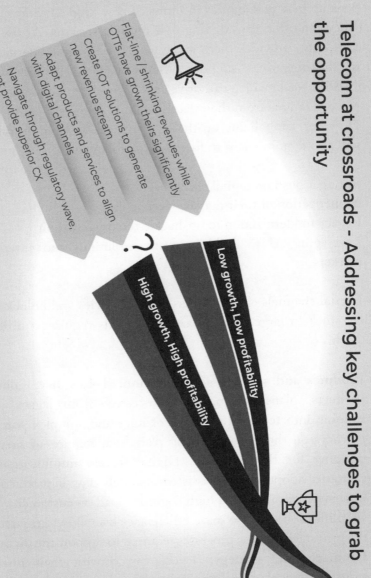

Flat-line / shrinking revenues while OTTs have grown theirs significantly

Create IOT solutions to generate new revenue stream

Adapt products and services to align with digital channels

Navigate through regulatory wave, yet provide superior CX

High growth, High profitability

Low growth, Low profitability

tilt the scales back in their favour on the customer's share of wallet. It opens up new possibilities in terms of new products and services that they can offer, thus driving new revenue streams. At the same time, 5G also provides them a way to drive legacy modernization across the operations support systems/business support systems (OSS/BSS) stack, which can drive cost optimization and unshackle their organizations from their decades-old systems and processes.

However, capitalizing on these advantages and the promise of 5G will also require telcos to focus on the following:

- Stronger push on digital channels
- Monetization of their massive data assets
- Legacy modernization to unshackle the organization
- Leveraging AI to build innovative solutions and enter new markets

Digital channels can drive massive efficiencies and unlock huge dollars stuck in large physical assets, but this requires a different approach:

- **Products and services simplification:** Telcos have complex products, plans, pricing and processes—from legacy plans running into tens of thousands of lines and complex purchase journeys on the web to pricing plans that require an agent to decipher for the customer. Digital forces simplification, as customer adoption of unassisted channels dips if products are non-intuitive and puts a high cognitive load on customers. This simplification can also drive efficiencies overall by rationalizing the tech stack and the processes required to support the products.
- **Omni-channel strategy:** Telcos can convert their physical stores into enablers of digital sales through mechanisms like in-store/kerb-side pick-up, local delivery (from store), etc. This will also require a redesign of incentives such that channels are not competing with but complementing each other. Disney, Target,

Starbucks, Walgreens, etc. are good examples of traditional brick-and-mortar businesses that have successfully transformed into omni-channel experiences for the consumer and are fighting the e-commerce threat.

- **Customer service:** This is another area where digital transformation can unlock immense value. Digital natives like Amazon, Uber, etc. drive over 90 per cent of their customer service through digital self-serve mechanisms and are constantly pushing the boundaries on use of AI/ML to predict and prevent customer service issues. Telcos, on the other hand, lie at the other end of the spectrum, with assisted customer service being a large cost head on their P&Ls.

Telcos generate a huge amount of data; conversion of this data into powerful insights can allow them to build collaborative domain-specific solutions.

- Telcos, thanks to their unique positioning in the ICT (information and communications technology) value chain, have access to the deepest and richest insights into customer behaviour and usage. Telcos are also now able to serve these insights on a real-time and targeted basis using advanced AI/ML technologies for multiple use cases that extend beyond the telecom industry.
- To capitalize on this capability, telcos are developing external partnership models to leverage data for creating innovative products and services in digital ecosystems. Examples of this include:
  o Footfall analytics for more effective marketing
  o Credit scoring as a service
  o Health analytics using wearable technology, powering healthcare and insurance applications

- To fully unleash the potential of data, telcos will need to build more entrepreneurial culture and mechanisms. They will need to transcend their functional silos to build cross-functional PODs that are empowered to take product design and GTM decisions, and at the same time be accountable for the commercial success of these solutions.

Modernization of the legacy OSS/BSS infrastructure is a key enabler for telecom operators.

Failing to modernize OSS/BSS could result in an immediate and negative impact on revenue, with up to 67 per cent of potential revenue at risk[14]

—TM Forum

Telecom operators are desperately looking to create new revenue streams, and with the advent of 5G, newer technical capabilities like network virtualization and network slicing will create possibilities for telcos to develop innovative digital connectivity solutions. However, unless the traditional OSS/BSS systems and applications are modernized to handle operations and billing at these newer revenue-generating services, telecom operators will not be able to obtain the desired revenue growth.

Traditionally, these OSS/BSS systems and applications have been operating in silos with static and manual workflows. It is imperative for telcos to modernize the decades-old OSS legacy infrastructure. This will allow them to dynamically allocate network resources for their customers on a real-time basis. This capability will help them create new service offerings for existing and new customers. Along with OSS modernization, modernization of the billing stacks is also necessary so that these dynamically provisioned self-services, at a massive scale (connecting billions of devices), can also be billed to customers in accordance with the Service Level Agreement (SLA) commitments.

Most of the new service offerings from telecom operators to enterprise customers ask for planning, provisioning and operating in a real-time scenario. This implies the following requirements:

Focus areas for capitalizing in 5G world

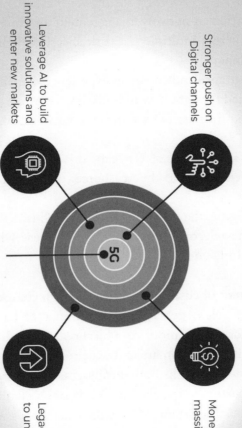

Stronger push on
Digital channels

Leverage AI to build
innovative solutions and
enter new markets

**Value creation
through 5G**

Monetizing the
massive data assets

Legacy modernization
to unshackle the organization

1. Modernization of network planning and optimization function.
2. Fundamental shifts in service provisioning and fulfilment applications for handling of real-time service offerings to customers.
3. Reimagination of network management and billing systems for operating across multiple network slices, both in physical and virtual domains.
4. Service assurance and customer experience management systems to be readied for data flow in both directions, i.e., from network to users and from users back into the network.

Artificial intelligence (AI) can drive efficiencies, improve customer experience and be a source of product and service innovation.

AI is changing the way the world does business, and it is no different in the telecom industry. The key areas where telcos are investing in AI include:

- **Improvement of customer service through chatbots and virtual assistants:** Telcos get a massive number of customer service requests for installation, troubleshooting and maintenance. Virtual assistants automate and scale responses to these requests at high speeds, which dramatically cuts business expenses and improves customer satisfaction. Vodafone's chatbot TOBi and Nokia's virtual assistant MIKA or Telefonica's Aura are good examples of telcos leveraging chatbots and VAs to deliver superior customer experience at lower costs.
- **Network quality improvement using predictive maintenance and self-organizing networks (SON):** Prevention of outages using AI/ML predictive models can enhance customer experience while delivering huge cost savings by preventing costly support calls and reactive truck rolls.
- **Fraud detection and prevention:** Fraud is a big driver of costs and bad customer experience. To prevent fraud, telcos end

up putting restrictive policies, checks and balances that make life difficult even for their genuine customers. AI/ML allows companies to leapfrog in their ability to predict and detect fraud using the sophisticated models and massive data at their disposal. They can now implement more nuanced controls that are razor-focused on fraudulent activity.

- **Personalized recommendations:** As telcos shift more of their business to digital channels, AI-based predictive models allow them to build more personalized offers and purchase journeys, thereby improving overall adoption of digital channels and improving KPIs like revenue, cross-selling/up-selling, etc.

5G is certainly a game-changer for telecom operators because it has the ability to open new revenue fronts, at the same time also shifting the balance of customer ownership in their favour from the OTT players. However, in order to capitalize on this opportunity, telcos will have to ensure timely modernization of legacy infrastructure, develop digital channels more effectively and adopt emerging technologies like AI and ML to deliver world-class customer experience.

Summary

- Telcos have been investing a lot in digital infrastructure as the industry progressed from 2G to 5G. However, they have not realized the desired impact.
- Instead, OTTs have won the game of content, leveraging the infrastructure that telcos invested in over the years.
- Now, 5G presents opportunities for telcos to emerge as winners in the market if they take the following steps:
  - **Embrace the digital-native approach** which encompasses product simplification, omni-channel strategy and self-service,

- o **Build domain-specific solutions** that leverage deep insights from customer data,
- o **Legacy modernization** of operational support system (OSS) and business support system (BSS) infrastructure,
- o **Drive innovation,** leveraging AI, which leads to efficiencies and enhanced customer experience.

5

Driving Enterprise Product Business in Uncertain Times

We're here to put a dent in the Universe, otherwise why else even be here?

Steve Jobs

With the pandemic bringing unprecedented difficulties in the way of businesses globally, what strategies can software product companies deploy to win?

Massive lockdowns, whole industries coming to a complete standstill and volatile global financial markets, the Covid-19 pandemic has led to severe disruption in almost every sphere of activity across the globe. Volatility, Uncertainty, Complexity and Ambiguity (VUCA) have amplified manifold. As businesses come to terms with the new market realities, they are being forced to rethink their business strategies, growth plans and, most pertinent of all, drive acceleration of digital and tech adoption.

The pandemic has given way to a 'new normal', throwing up new trends and opportunities. For many traditional businesses, digital transformation has progressed from something that was nice-to-have to something that calls for accelerated adoption cycles. This has created tremendous potential for tech innovation, in particular for software product companies who can take advantage of this shift.

Takeaways from business leaders on the frontline

I have spoken with many business and engineering leaders from market-leading software product companies to understand how they are navigating the crisis. Should organizations play defence or offence—should they concentrate on consolidation and protection of their existing businesses or should they adopt a more aggressive approach for growth and expansion? How quickly can they reorganize themselves to take advantage of the situation?

Six key insights emerged from our conversations, as to what the industry players should do:

1. **Preserve existing revenues by taking care of your client needs**
   We learned from publicly listed product companies that 60 per cent of them faced revenue compression in one of the preceding three years. Further, the impact of the ongoing coronavirus pandemic is widely visible and has significantly impacted a number of industries: airlines, hotels, leisure and hospitality, automotive, oil and gas, to name a few. As a software product provider, it is very important to evaluate the impact of Covid-19. Executives and business leaders of many such companies have set up war rooms to preserve and protect their existing revenues and revalidate their forecasts for the rest of 2020, simply because the original revenue forecasts are no longer credible under the unusual circumstances.

   Most of the leaders have proactively started reviewing the changing spend patterns of clients with an intent to capitalize on newer areas of opportunity and to be able to hedge the overall revenue decline. Although customer retention has always been an integral part of most business strategies, the need to strengthen and maintain relationships has become even more pronounced today. With newer relationships getting difficult to build, retaining current long-term relationships and expanding them has become critical.

2. **Find opportunities for growth in the white spaces between existing product offerings**

    It is apparent that business leaders in software product companies have dual tasks at hand. First, they have to look to survive the crisis and protect their turf. Second, as the new normal becomes more and more real, they have to invest in new areas of opportunities to be able to win the race. According to BCG research, it takes 2x investment into R&D to go beyond one's core products,[15] so it is clear that investing in completely new product areas is not an easy game to play.

    The economic scenarios that will emerge over the next few years will differ widely by country and industry, depending on the local impact of the coronavirus epidemic, government stimulus packages, and other factors. It is important to keep looking out for leading indicators and rapidly move forward with execution. As the market demand evolves, it might be interesting to find adjacencies to existing products and solution offerings and determine customer needs by segmentation. In some cases, it could mean addition of new products/offerings to existing roadmaps, and in others, pursuit of a different customer segment altogether.

3. **Reprioritize and refocus product roadmaps**

    Volatile and uncertain market scenarios are forcing organizations to reprioritize their plans. Business and engineering leaders at software product companies are also actively considering changes in their product roadmap priorities, reducing or reallocating budgets. Agile planning, rapid reprioritization and high-speed execution are the key success mantras, given today's realities. It is time to embrace a more flexible product portfolio to be able to continually iterate based on evolving client needs. After possible growth areas have been identified, it is imperative to reassess product roadmaps and re-baseline priorities in alignment with one's strategic goals, financial constraints, resource capability and capacity.

4. **Leverage global delivery model to drive consolidation and build new offerings**

   In order to effectively tackle uncertainty and change, every business needs to be more agile and adaptable. The companies that can optimize their expenditures to build greater resilience and responsiveness are the ones that are more likely to be successful in this VUCA phase. Therefore, almost everyone is trying to cut down operational costs and improve cash flows to weather the storm. For software product companies, it is also important to keep investing in R&D activities for accelerating growth. In our conversations, it was apparent that while executives and business leaders are exploring means to maximize returns on R&D investments, they are also equally concerned about the speed of execution, leveraging emerging tech capabilities. Leveraging a global delivery model becomes even more critical to meet these diverse and often conflicting objectives.

5. **Adopt new-age business models to accelerate reach and penetration**

   The shift in customer buying patterns has also accelerated growth in some areas that were already on the radar of software product companies even before the Covid-19 phase. For instance, a sudden spurt in digital activities had led to an increase in spending on cybersecurity and cloud-based products across different industries. Apart from increasing digital opportunities, demand for better communication and operational infrastructure has also escalated. Therefore, companies focused on these domains are looking to quickly expand their offerings in these specific

Enterprise Products - Play good defense to win through the pandemic

Preserve existing revenues

Leveraging Global Delivery model

Finding whitespaces opportunities for growth

Adopt new – age business models that are built on strategic partnerships

Reprioritize & Refocus Product Roadmaps

Consider M&As

areas. Many software product companies are evaluating the expansion of their partner ecosystem, both from the perspective of enhancing the product offerings and also for widening the go-to-market. In order to create end-to-end solutions focused on changing customer needs and to quickly address high-growth markets, many product companies are forging new partnerships, both in sell-with and sell-through business models.

6. **Mergers and acquisitions: A polarization of winners**

To many this may sound like a rather aggressive and overly optimistic approach, especially during a pandemic situation. But mergers and acquisitions are a fast way to expand portfolios and build new capabilities to align with the new market situation. Therefore, many companies are seriously looking at strategic acquisitions and partnerships to broaden their presence in certain key areas. The bigger companies can afford to expand by investing in acquisitions. For smaller niche businesses, acquisition may prove to be an effective survival strategy. Successful, cash-rich software product companies are looking to seize the opportunity by acquiring key capabilities to expand their horizons, both from the present and future business standpoints. At the same time, companies that are struggling for growth and cash flows are finding an amicable exit path. In many ways, we are observing a 'polarization of winners' in this market.

Even as the new normal throws up some new opportunities for software product companies, many are still treading cautiously and taking the defensive route to consolidate their businesses. Many believe that initially playing defence helps build resilience and creates a strong foundation, which in turn will enable them to adopt an offensive strategy when the market is ready. So offence is possible, but the path to doing that is through great defence. Ultimately, how an organization balances the two will determine its ability to survive and thrive in the long run.

Summary

- The software products industry is one of favourites standing to gain the most from digital and to leapfrog, leveraging cloud-led 'saasification'.
- To play offence and emerge as a winner, it is critical that product businesses defend well.
- There are six themes that leaders of product businesses must emphasize and re-evaluate to win:
  o Preserving existing revenues by taking care of client needs,
  o Finding white spaces/adjacent opportunities for growth in their markets,
  o Reprioritizing and refocusing the product roadmaps to align with emerging needs,
  o Leveraging global delivery model to drive consolidation and build new offerings,
  o Adopting new-age partnership models to accelerate reach,
  o Exploring mergers and acquisitions.

6

Digital in Life Sciences

Longevity in business is about the ability to reinvent yourself or invent the future.

Satya Nadella

'What business are you in?'—This question, raised by Professor Theodore Levitt in a *Harvard Business Review* (2006) article, is a fundamental one that life sciences manufacturers are faced with.[16] It lies at the heart of the digital transformation taking place in this industry. Pharmaceutical manufacturers have traditionally built businesses focused on product superiority, targeting clinicians (their 'customer') who have patients (the end consumers of their products). With digital becoming all-pervasive and with the industry moving towards specialty and personalized treatments, understanding the needs of the end consumer has never been more essential, in the process leading to a redefinition of who their end customer should be—the patient!

New and non-traditional entrants in the life sciences industry, many of whom are digital-native companies, add another dimension of disruptive forces at work, driving the need for digital transformation to be the centerpiece of a pharmaceutical company's future-state strategy. The pharmaceutical industry, unlike other sectors, has historically been a laggard in digital adoption. A 2018 *Deloitte–MIT Sloan Review* study found that less than 20 per cent of pharmaceutical companies had currently taken decisive and bold moves to take advantage of digital capabilities[17]. Together, these developments present a tremendous opportunity for forward-looking companies to shape their digital agenda to address their primary concern of serving patients better.

Digital presents new ways to these companies to provide value to customers (patients) and create a competitive advantage for themselves. Harnessing data and leveraging cloud-based technologies, combined with a deep understanding of customers and their unmet needs, offer new possibilities for innovation in R&D and delivery of differentiated multi-channel patient engagement programmes for improving patient outcomes.

Reimagining innovation in R&D

- **Linear methods of clinical research and discovery for new therapies** face the continuing pressure of increasing R&D costs and shorter product ('medicine') lifecycles.

  While placebo-controlled clinical trials remain the gold standard, synthetic control arms offer new ways of assessing new treatment interventions. The US Food and Drug Administration's (FDA) approval of Brineura from Biomarin for Batten disease, based on a synthetic control study and its accelerated approval of Alecensa from Roche for a specific form of lung cancer give new hope and possibilities for sustained innovation in this space.

  This method of clinical trial represents a notable shift toward the use of real-world evidence (RWE). Instead of using conventional data collection methods using patients in a trial, synthetic control arms model those comparators using real-world data. The use of real-world data from sources—including electronic health records of patients, patient-generated data from medical equipment, patient registries and historical trial data—makes possible equivalent and useful comparisons.

When combined with advanced analytics, including machine learning and natural language processing (NLP), equivalent and useful trial insights become available, accelerating the pace of clinical trials while reducing costs.

Connecting with the customer—Rise of digital patient engagement models

The retail world is full of examples illustrating the importance of embedding technology that fuses a consumer's physical and digital experiences. At the centre of creating such a composite experience is the ability to leverage data and the right digital channels to personalize, target and tailor a customized experience for each consumer.

For pharmaceutical brands, an urgent need to uncover the consumer's (patient's) unmet needs and effectively partner with the stakeholders in the healthcare system (clinicians, nurses, payers, patient advocates) to deliver a similar patient-at-the-centre experience is an enabler for differentiated service models.

Take, for instance, the market access programmes for patients. As the touchpoints between patients and the partners supporting the patient's care become digital and come through multiple sources, it results in an inconsistent, high-friction, disconnected and burdensome experience for patients engaging with a brand for their needs. The problems include repeating, confusing interactions for the patient as a result of lack of coordination among the touchpoints (HCP/practice, access, contact centres, insurance) and lack of a feedback loop, and the poorly understood patient journey leads to disconnects in service interactions. When one combines the scale of such operations that can typically include 500,000 or more patients on a programme—involving multiple touchpoints that include a 1,000+ person contact centre—across brands and therapeutic areas, the problem quickly becomes very complex.

The need and opportunity for pharmaceutical brands lie in solving this problem and, in the process, gaining competitive advantage using an integrated framework that combines data science to surface new insights from service interactions. They can then go on to redesign the patient experience, effectively incorporating desirable changes in the patient's journey.

The execution difference

For the life sciences business and technology executives, digital presents a distinctive set of new capabilities and differentiation opportunities for the future. But the secret to success lies in the approaches they take for execution within their organizations.

Successful digital transformations in the industry will mean a thoughtful approach and method of execution:

1. **Embracing a cloud-first strategy:** Pharmaceutical companies have until recently been slow to adopt cloud-based solutions as a mainstream strategy, often handicapped by the risks associated with the industry's regulatory implications. Unlike before, leading cloud providers, including Amazon AWS, Microsoft Azure and Google's GCP, have built-in clinical and healthcare assets that encompass machine learning models, integrations with clinical workflows and application domain-ready data models. A cloud-first approach as central to the technology strategy enables the enterprise to rapidly develop, test and deploy production-grade applications in service of end consumer ('patient') outcomes.

2. **Automating core business processes and improving decision-making with AI:** A pharmaceutical company's core business processes by design operate in an environment to increase regulatory compliance and reduce risk. However, the downside

of this legacy is that it drastically retards the speed with which companies begin to realize the value of their digital transformation initiatives. By embracing a thoughtful automation strategy using robotics process automation (RPA) platforms like Ui Path, Blue Prism, or Automation Anywhere, technology executives can eliminate inefficiencies and simplify their core processes.

Automating using RPA, however, is only half the answer. The other half lies in data science. By applying machine learning and NLP techniques, automated business processes become intelligent and significantly improve decision-making.

3. **Do-it-yourself versus partner model:** While gone are the days for pharmaceutical technology executives to decide between a buy versus build, the choice between doing it all themselves versus selecting a digital technology partner for execution remains.

The decision framework involves addressing a few questions, which include:

- *Source of differentiation*: What type of intellectual property (IP) is meaningful for a pharmaceutical company to build, and how closely will it align to the primary goal of improving patient outcomes?
- *Extent of experimentation*: Does the right approach lie in tackling every problem from scratch or in taking advantage of partner solutions, using accelerators that have done the hard work before? Patient data hubs, pre-configured clinical workflows, patient journey models and pre-configured machine learning models for specific applications, to name a few.

4. **Open innovation and collaboration:** Life sciences executives, particularly in R&D, leverage external partner ecosystems to accelerate their research pipeline. A similar opportunity extends to the execution of digital transformation in these organizations,

Life Sciences - Shifting Paradigm from Clinician to Patient

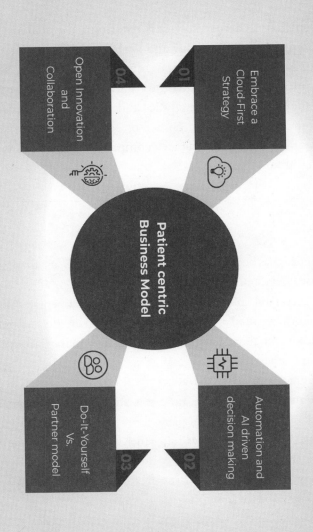

where they go beyond traditional technology partner models to develop a collaborative open innovation ecosystem for joint development of new solutions at low cost.

Patient-centricity is here to stay. It is redefining the business that life sciences companies are in today and with digital transformation in these organizations, will bring new meaning to who they serve, delivering improved patient outcomes and gaining competitive advantage in the process. Data, analytics and a cloud-first execution strategy combined with the right choice of partnership models will place the forward-looking life sciences companies well ahead in the race to win in digital.

Summary

- Life sciences has been one of the laggards but is now at a tipping point for digital transformation.
- To be successful, players must consider a fundamental shift in the business model by putting the patient at the centre. Historically, the clinician has been the customer in the industry.
- Four imperatives to drive successful execution:
  - Embrace a cloud-first strategy
  - Automate core business processes and improve decision-making with AI
  - Make thoughtful choices to partner with or develop one's own critical capabilities
  - Adopt open innovation that calls for joint development of new solutions at low cost.

SECTION 3

TECHNOLOGY BUILDING BLOCKS OF DIGITAL TRANSFORMATION

Introduction: Technology Building Blocks of Digital Transformation

In the introduction to the book, I had mentioned that digital transformation is multi-dimensional, and to bring clarity, I had broken it into seven building blocks. In this section, I will focus on technology, which is at the heart of digital transformation.

The digital technology stack further has seven key building blocks. These are design/customer experience, analytics/data science, automation/operations transformation, AI, data infrastructure, blockchain and cloud. These play a critical role in the execution of digital transformation; they are the collective force behind successful digital programmes.

Digital transformation has to be end to end

The most important aspect of these technology building blocks is that they are not independent, but interconnected. Enterprises realize transformative value from them when they are connected end to end. These building blocks represent different layers of the technology stack; connecting them tightly creates a virtuous cycle.

It is also critical to lay a foundation before diving into the technology blocks for *maximizing returns on digital technology investments*. There are two parts to this maximization equation—*why* the tremendous investments in digital technology do not return the desired results, and *how* to address these issues. I will provide technology principles that provide a guiding north star as we move to where digital should start.

While defining strategy and customer experience, digital transformation must start with design thinking. The whole experience must be thought up from scratch and redesigned to deliver 'what it should be' rather than starting from 'what it is'. One of the distinctive aspects of the digital customer experience is that it can be highly personalized and targeted at the individual. This is enabled by analytics. Analytics also enable customer insights, analysis of sales performance and operational efficiencies, and inform other key business decisions that help drive the business.

The superior customer experience that digital enables has to be fulfilled by internal operations. Typically, digital requires significantly improved response time and this requires a redesign of processes, which is enabled by automation. AI can power enterprises to reach the next frontier of digital transformation. The self-learning ability that AI provides can sharply enhance both customer experience and operations efficiency over time.

The bedrock of everything we have talked about—design/customer experience, analytics/data science, automation/operations transformation, and AI—is data. All these technology building blocks require high-quality and deep data. Data is also where the recursive relationship or the virtuous cycle between the technology building blocks happens.

Digital is leading to a data explosion—in volume, variety, and velocity. However, to realize the full potential of this 'digital data deluge', enterprises have to upgrade and build scalable data infrastructure. This is easier said than done. Most enterprises struggle with getting high-quality, harmonized data together.

Cloud, which began as an infrastructure capability helping provide scalability and making costs variable, is now becoming a key enabler for transformation across the entire technology stack that we have mentioned. Cloud's scope and capabilities are increasing tremendously, and many enterprises are transitioning to a cloud-native architecture. It provides them a great opportunity to upgrade the various elements of the technology stack and, in particular, to address the data infrastructure and quality issues that we have talked about.

As you can see, the various technologies that are the building blocks of digital are similar to the parts of an orchestra. Each part needs to be very good, but only when they sync together can beautiful music be created. That beautiful music, in our case, is *realizing the full potential of digital transformation*!

In this section, first I lay the foundation, in two parts, of how to *maximize returns on digital technology investments*, delving into why there is a gap between the promise and returns, and my high-level technology principles on how to address these issues by playing offence, not defence. From there, I cover in detail the various technologies that are the building blocks for digital. I have shared the role of each of these technology building blocks, the challenges in leveraging them and their future possibilities. A lot of these perspectives are influenced by the work we have been doing at Incedo with our clients. Incedo's focus is on end-to-end digital transformation, and it has been fascinating to work on, and in the process observe and learn from, the digital transformation journeys of many marquee companies across industries.

Chapter 1: Maximizing Returns from Digital Technology Investments

Part One: Why the Problems Persist

In chapter 1 of two companion chapters on maximizing your returns on digital technology investments, I discuss why, despite the enormous resources that are being poured annually into digital technology initiatives, there continues to be a gap between the promise and impact of these initiatives. The primary reasons are legacy processes and IT infrastructure that are not agile and unable to handle big data or other expectations of the digital age. If the current technology infrastructure and processes don't get upgraded, firms will be stuck trying to catch up and thus playing defence.

Chapter 2: Maximizing Returns from Digital Technology Investments

Part Two: Playing Offence, not Defence

In chapter 2, I lay out the high-level technology principles to address the problems identified in chapter 1. To change the play from defence to offence and compete, legacy firms can learn from the digital natives. It should leverage the tremendous advancements in cloud technology and adopt a cloud-native architecture; build agile processes that enable experimentation, measurement and adaptation; and adopt a two-speed approach to implementation.

Chapter 3: Customer Experience Design—Starting Point of the Digital Transformation Journey

Web/mobile interactions are necessary but not sufficient by themselves to deliver the gold standard in customer experience. The digital journey must progress beyond the first touchpoint of the consumer to the entire life cycle of experiences. Digital natives have done this successfully in various industries; legacy enterprises are expected to achieve the same.

Customer experience (CX) is the new face/promise of brands that sets the winners apart from the losers. Driving higher customer loyalty is the key to generate shareholder value in the digital age.

Successful transformation programmes take a holistic approach—defining the experience (one that puts the consumer at the centre), rejigging the organizational processes to deliver the experience seamlessly and enabling end-to-end integration for consistently delivering high-quality experiences.

Chapter 4: Used Properly, Analytics Is a Source of Competitive Advantage

Digital experience and its promise of personalization can be delivered effectively only when analytics informs the 'human + machine' agents to engage with consumers proactively in the digital age.

So far, analytics has been deployed by traditional enterprises to add incremental value, as opposed to the way digital natives have deployed it, which is to truly make it a source of competitive advantage.

There is a wide gap between the promise and reality of analytics. This occurs due to six key reasons, which I outline in this chapter. These must be carefully addressed by enterprises to make analytics a source of competitive advantage for themselves in the digital age.

Chapter 5: Operations Transformation—The Key to Realizing the Full Potential of Digital Transformation

Delivering the promised customer experience typically requires an end-to-end overhaul of the business processes. Even today, many traditional enterprises are stuck with a control mindset and have cumbersome processes. This often leads to bureaucracy, slow speed, and thus friction for the customer.

Enterprises need to go beyond incremental approaches to operations and build confidence by embarking on more transformational and end-to-end change programmes. The changes should include data-driven measurement of operations, intelligent automation that goes beyond RPA and leveraging AI for self-learning of processes.

Chapter 6: AI—The Critical Tool to Reach the Next Frontier

AI is becoming mainstream, especially among digital natives. However, it has not yet reached scale in many traditional enterprises as it is embraced mostly as a 'feature' and not as an 'architecture'.

AI has the potential to drive the next frontier of digital transformation, both on customer experience and operations transformation. To make this happen, there are four key considerations that I have outlined in this chapter.

Chapter 7: Data—The Fulcrum of the Digital Technology Stack

Data is the centrepiece of digital transformation, enabling design, analytics, operations transformation and AI. Without data, digital strategy cannot be executed.

The exponential growth of data in volume and variety, and at unprecedented velocity, is the engine of success for the digital natives. At the same time, it is paralysing many traditional enterprises that have invested millions of dollars in it but have not realized the desired impact from it.

It is imperative that enterprises develop a digital data architecture that is fit-for-purpose and also change their operating processes to harness the power of data in the digital age.

Chapter 8: Blockchain—A New Infrastructure-related Capability

Many have read the hype around Bitcoin fading away as a failure of blockchain technology itself. That is untrue. Blockchain is a powerful technology that is just getting off the ground.

Blockchain offers a new infrastructure-related capability that provides transparency, thereby increasing trust in the system. It has the potential to transform the value chain in many industries. A good example of its usefulness is in payments in banks.

Blockchain is currently at a nascent stage, with many proofs of concept (POC) being tested across industries. The challenges that need to be resolved before it becomes a mainstream technology are outlined in this chapter.

Chapter 9: Cloud—Going beyond Infrastructure Scalability to Being an Enabler of Transformation

Cloud is increasingly becoming the backbone of the technology stack, knitting the whole digital transformation programme together. Earlier, enterprises looked at cloud as a low-hanging fruit for realizing cost take-out in infrastructure, but now the possibilities with cloud have grown significantly.

Both business units and CIO teams are now considering cloud for broader purposes than just making costs variable and infrastructure scalable.

Business leaders are realizing the value of cloud in reimagining CX and achieving reduced time-to-market as they take on new-age competitors, whereas CIOs are leveraging cloud for managing enterprise data better and scaling up AI across the enterprise.

All the above-mentioned technologies are the key building blocks necessary for driving a successful digital transformation programme. In many cases, enterprises tend to be lopsided in their investments into digital programmes, relying heavily on one particular technology and waiting for the desired impact. This often results in a gap between the realized impact and the promise of digital programmes. It is very important to recognize that success in digital is dependent on end-to-end transformations. Successful enterprises make balanced investments across these technology building blocks and implement a two-speed strategy to realize the full potential of their digital investments.

1

Maximizing Returns from Digital Technology Investments, Part One: Why the Problems Persist

Do . . . or do not. There is no try.

Master Yoda, *Star Wars*

In today's business world, digital has become mainstream. Digital transformation is one of the biggest trends of our generation, and *enormous resources* are being poured into it annually. However, when we look below the surface, we see that *70 per cent of digital initiatives fail*, according to *Harvard Business Review*.[11] Many firms see suboptimal return on investment (ROI) on their digital investments as the technology budget keeps increasing but results are not visible.

Overall, the rate of full digital adoption is fairly low. Based on my experience across key industries, the rate of full adoption has been only 5–10 per cent (though digital adoption got a sharp boost over the year 2020 because of the Covid-19 pandemic). For example, according to Celent (via The Financial Brand), only *11 per cent of banking institutions* are executing an omni-channel strategy,[12] while 50 per cent of banks are still only conducting research on omni-channel capability. Personalization, in many cases, is also extremely limited. While Red Point Global found that 63 per cent of customers today expect personalization,[13] BCG found that only 15 per cent of enterprises are true personalization leaders.[14] The rate of real-time data leverage is extremely low, with only 1 per cent of all data collected ever analysed and used,[15] and only 16 per cent of the brands are very effective at delivering real-time interactions.[16]

Why does such a gap between potential and impact exist, and how can companies narrow that gap? The biggest problem is that most businesses today are playing catch-up when it comes to digital transformation. Instead, companies should learn from the digital natives and play offence rather than defence. Full digital adopters are able to extract meaningful impact from their investments, such as a 25 per cent increase in productivity, twice improved customer retention rates and two to three times faster growth than their peers.

Why problems persist for companies embarking on digital transformation

When it comes to digital transformation, most executives in large enterprises are simply not getting to the root of their problems. In this chapter, I will focus on the technology root causes of failed digital initiatives. In my experience of working with large legacy enterprises, I have seen four common root causes.

- **Data infrastructure incapable of handling big data:** The existing data infrastructure has limitations when it comes to leveraging unstructured data to drive insights. Originally created to deal with structured data, this infrastructure was not prepared for the explosion of big data. The pieces are hard to change once defined, since the addition of new data dimensions requires expensive design and reprocessing effort. Moreover, legacy data infrastructure makes it very hard to get to a deeper level of

Four key reasons why Digital initiatives do not deliver to their promise

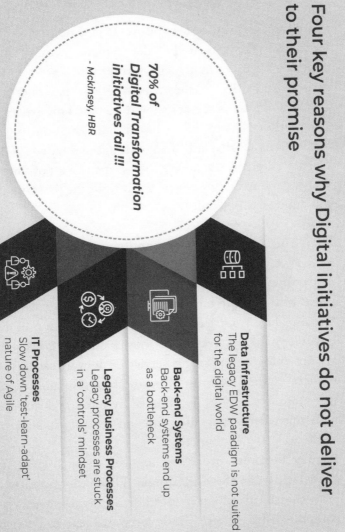

70% of Digital Transformation initiatives fail !!!

- Mckinsey, HBR

Data Infrastructure
The legacy EDW paradigm is not suited for the digital world

Back-end Systems
Back-end systems end up as a bottleneck

Legacy Business Processes
Legacy processes are stuck in a 'controls' mindset

IT Processes
Slow down 'test-learn-adapt' nature of Agile

granularity to draw insights. For example, when did you last see a bank as precise at personalization as Amazon?

- **IT processes do not support experimentation and agile methods:** Traditional IT deployment cycles, as they are currently set up in many legacy enterprises, are not designed to support and drive the 'test, learn, adapt' paradigm of modern analytics. These processes should be based on experimentation. If something has to fail, it has to fail fast. You try something, measure the results, fail, change things and try again. Instead, in a legacy enterprise, you have to first spend a lot of time doing the analysis and making sure you get it right the first time, because if you fail it may be fatal.

- **Back-end systems cannot handle real-time transactions:** In most legacy enterprises, these systems end up being a bottleneck. They simply are not designed to handle probabilistic choice-based workflows to enable real-time responsiveness to customer signals. Have you tried opening a bank account online? It is not possible, precisely because in most banks the back-end systems are not able to support this service or deliver real-time customer services online. As a result, businesses are unable to realize the true potential of tightly coupled systems and automation for real-time customer services and end-to-end transformation.

- **Legacy business processes are too slow for the changing expectations in the digital age:** The basic 'mindset' of these processes is all about control, risk management and being comprehensive. These processes were designed to get things right the first time without fail. As a result, businesses have built very complex processes to avoid failure. But, as with anything very complex, it is hard for it to be fast in real-time. The legacy mindset of the 'right-the-first-time' process design makes it difficult to drive iterative, experimentation-based improvements.

In other words, even if the technology works, business processes end up slowing things down.

Changing the game

In order to achieve lasting change, I believe legacy companies need to stop playing defence and start playing offence. They should take lessons from the digital-native companies that have leapfrogged them by reimagining these dimensions.

The main point is that digital initiatives themselves should be leading the strategy and not the other way around. This will allow businesses to drive speed to market, unlock ROI and—most importantly—change the game from one of defence to offence.

In the next chapter, we will dive deep into how enterprises can play offence.

Summary

- Digital transformation is one of the biggest trends of our generation, however 70 per cent of the transformation initiatives do not deliver the desired impact.
- Many enterprises are still playing defence with their digital technology investments. Digital adoption is as low as 5–10 per cent across industries with no clear plan to increase it substantially.
- The root causes of failed digital technology investments lie in data infrastructure, IT processes, back-end systems and legacy business processes.

2

Maximizing Returns from Digital Technology Investments, Part Two: Playing Offence, not Defence

Sometimes you've gotta run before you can walk.

Tony Stark, *Iron Man*

In the last chapter, we discussed how digital investments are not delivering the expected ROI for legacy enterprises and investigated some of the technology and process-related root causes for that. We also suggested that legacy enterprises need to change the game by learning from the digital natives. The central suggestion is that legacy enterprises need to play offence, not defence, when it comes to digital.

Here are some specific and actionable best practices from digital natives that can help legacy enterprises significantly increase ROI from their digital technology investments.

Cloud-native architecture

This architecture is an essential piece of the puzzle, and luckily for us, it is already here. In recent years, cloud strategy has moved from enabling computing resources to providing an integrated platform as a service (PaaS). Gartner says that by 2025, 85 per cent of enterprises will have a cloud-first principle and will not be able to fully execute their digital strategies without the use of cloud-native architectures and technologies.[18]

When fully realized, cloud standardizes technical skill sets, creating talent acquisition leverage and enabling improved development process, further accelerating time to market. Leveraging AWS, Azure and Google Cloud (GCP) provides the best-of-breed infrastructure, with the added advantage that these cloud providers continue to evolve and innovate at a rapid pace. That means enterprises can configure highly scalable end-to-end solutions quickly. So what businesses need to do is to develop comprehensive cloud applications and data migration strategies.

The best practices of a native cloud-based architecture would include the following five components:

Diagnostic pipelines

Business infrastructure must take a comprehensive approach to track, monitor, predict and experiment with elements such as end-to-end customer journeys, multi-channel funnel continuity, business process throughput, marketplace dynamics and data models.

This is important because engineering scalable, real-time data capture pipelines and integrating data capture into a data lake are critical for realizing business impact.

Integrated experimentation framework

Business infrastructure and applications need to support experimentation to enable an innovation cycle. That means establishing clear business baselines, measuring KPI movements in a statistically significant manner and integrating experimentation in the change management process to measure and validate impacts.

Operationalized data science cannot be enabled without a continuous experimentation cycle. So it is important to both embed experimentation into all layers of business infrastructure and develop an experiment-driven product management process.

Automated insights

Traditional analytics approaches have created significant 'dashboard fatigue' in organizations because of their non-scalable manual tooling and methodologies. Ad hoc analysis requires significant effort and often leads to new development efforts. Aggregate views tend to lead to an extremely rigid approach to analysis, limiting analytics approaches and thinking. New out-of-the-box analytics technologies often fail to live up to the hype because they lack business-specific models.

To overcome these challenges, processes that provide insights must be automated. That means applying a data science-driven analytics approach by leveraging KPI tree composition, insights tools and business-specific models. This will allow the organization to effectively automate key aspects of the insights process.

Recommendation applications

Recommendation engines (REs) drive real-time, autonomous decision-making for businesses. They have moved beyond customer personalization to enable automation across infrastructure. REs can factor in a broad set of features to drive business outcomes and customer experience.

A comprehensive data strategy—driven by KPI capture, experimentation, scalable data pipelines and business-focused data science—enables effective model embedding.

Playing offense calls for three critical shifts

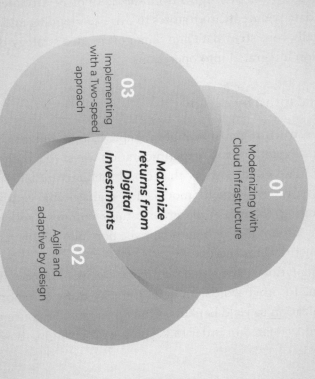

01 Modernizing with Cloud Infrastructure

02 Agile and adaptive by design

03 Implementing with a Two-speed approach

Maximize returns from Digital Investments

Data lake/feature store

A harmonized, consolidated data strategy is a critical requirement for operationalizing data science and evolving from the loose, semantic agreement of relational systems.

This strategy must include a consolidated view of structured and unstructured data types, semantic schema to enable federated cross-organization integration, insights from the sandbox environment for developing data science, feature stores to drive cataloguing and reuse of semantically consistent data and data governance strategy driven by automation integrated into operations.

Agile and adaptive by design

Modern infrastructures must be highly adaptive, agile and measured. Continuous adaptation and experimentation must be built into the strategy. The good news is that cloud architecture allows the creation of new development models for maintaining continuity while integrating change. Agile architectures compose and avoid system/team monoliths, while adaptive portfolio management processes are critical for success.

Experimentation and measurement drive impact-based prioritization. In other words, an agile mindset must be embraced by the organization to yield benefits. Outcomes must be continually measured and evaluated in order to keep up with changing business conditions.

Two-speed approach

So what is the best and most effective yet practical way for legacy enterprises to tackle digital initiatives? Despite my recommendation that enterprises should play offence and not defence, going all-out or adopting a 'Big Bang approach' might not be the right strategy in

Five extensions that drive speed-to-market and unlock ROI

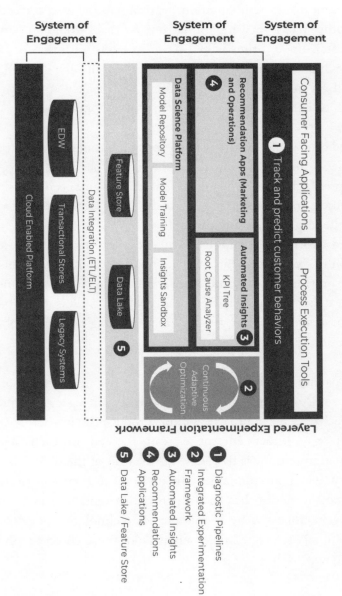

System of Engagement

System of Engagement

System of Engagement

Cloud Enabled Platform

EDW

Transactional Stores

Legacy Systems

Data Integration (ETL/ELT)

Data Science Platform

Model Repository

Model Training

Insights Sandbox

Feature Store

Data Lake

5

Recommendation Apps (Marketing and Operations)

4

Automated Insights

KPI Tree

Root Cause Analyzer

3

Continuous Adaptive Optimization

2

Consumer Facing Applications

Process Execution Tools

1 Track and predict customer behaviors

Layered Experimentation Framework

1 Diagnostic Pipelines

2 Integrated Experimentation Framework

3 Automated Insights

4 Recommendations Applications

5 Data Lake / Feature Store

most cases. This is because of the iterative nature of digital; you need to allow time for experimentation, learning and course correction. On the other hand, focusing on narrow use cases would amount to playing catch-up and thus would have little to no impact. So, it is critical to develop your 'offence' approach thoughtfully.

Based on my experience of working with legacy enterprises, I recommend that businesses adopt a two-speed approach.

- **Speed one** would involve solving specific business and customer problems and delivering direct impact. The specific projects and problems to solve would be based on your specific business priorities. Importantly, these projects have to be executed with an agile implementation mindset.
- **Speed two** means building a scalable platform and long-term capability enhancement. Here, businesses have to ensure collaborative discovery and reuse across projects, cross-business-unit cataloguing and sharing of artifacts, as well as adoption of common standards for various processes ranging from problem definition to solution deployment.

Approaching digital transformation as a one-off technology project is a waste of time and resources; this is what legacy enterprises have to realize. This approach will not produce the impact desired. The only way legacy enterprises can succeed in their digital transformation journey is by following the lead of the digital-native companies, which are fundamentally different in their constitution. Digital transformation has to happen end to end. It should start with a vision, followed by a smart set of technology choices, and then careful and strategic implementation of those choices with the two-speed approach.

Summary

Playing offence, not defence, with your digital technology investments calls for three critical shifts:

- Leveraging the tremendous advancements in cloud technology and adoption of cloud-native architecture. Such an architecture should include at least the following five best practices: diagnostic pipelines, integrated experimentation architecture, automated insights, recommendation applications and data lake/feature store.
- Building agile processes that enable experimentation, measurement and adaptation. Good news is that modern cloud infrastructure facilitates this agile approach.
- Two-speed approach to implementation by prioritizing high-impact use cases in speed one and building a scalable infrastructure in speed two by bringing together pieces already delivered via the former.

3

Customer Experience Design: Starting Point of the Digital Transformation Journey

You have to start with the customer experience and work backwards towards the technology and not the other way around.

Steve Jobs

Digital technology has transformed consumer habits and has caused a shift in customer expectations, resulting in a new kind of modern buyer. These buyers rate organizations on the basis of their customer experience and, increasingly, their digital customer experience first. And these digital experiences are no longer limited to interactions with the enterprise's website but have expanded in terms of channels and touchpoints to cover all aspects of the customer journey.

The benchmarks for these digital experiences are being set by the digital natives, including the FAANG companies. Customers are expecting similar or better experiences from all businesses they interact with. When they search for products or services, they want the search to be as intuitive as Google's; they want product recommendations as personalized as the ones Netflix offers; they want the checkout experience to be as effortless as on Amazon.

Since customers interact with these companies on a daily basis through their smartphones—and increasingly other devices—these expectations keep getting reinforced, and any company not meeting these standards is rejected quickly.

Given that experience design is the starting point, successful digital transformation initiatives need to include the following:

- Experiences designed to be intuitive and personalized, with the customer at the centre.
- Organizational processes aligned to deliver world-class experience—seamless integration of the enterprise processes like onboarding, billing, supply chain, customer service, etc., using technology and AI/ML.
- End-to-end integration with partners, suppliers and other ecosystem players so that high-quality experience is delivered across all touchpoints.

I believe customer experience designs will be shaped by the following trends over the next three to five years:

1. Companies that have simplified customer experience winning by a huge margin

- Customer attention spans have shrunk massively—they are looking for experiences that are simplified and transparent, and which do not hide policies and hidden charges behind fine print or have complex terms and conditions.
- According to a study by simplicityindex.com, the stock portfolio of companies that topped the customer experience simplification index (top 10) outperformed the major indices by 1,600 per cent between 2009 and 2021.[1]
- Simplification requires deep understanding of customer needs and personalizing experiences to those needs. To achieve this, companies need to:

a) Create a unified view of the customer across different touchpoints and businesses
b) Convert the huge amount of data they collect into meaningful insights
c) Integrate the insights with systems of engagement on a real-time basis.

2. Customers are looking for seamless omni-channel experiences

- Customers want end-to-end experiences that are unified. Individually optimized point-of-contact solutions (e.g. sales, billing, service, etc.) that are disconnected and require customers to hop across multiple systems/applications will not work. Unified solutions will require integration across the enterprise.
- This holds true regardless of how your customers choose to interact with your brand, be it via web, a mobile device, social media, IVR, a call centre, chat, or any other available channel.

3. Voice-first interactions are disrupting the customer experience

- Voice is a more effective way for humans to communicate instructions—voice commands are more efficient than navigation menus, allow for multi-tasking and with the help of advances in natural language-processing AI/ML, can work with less-than-precise instructions, making it more accessible to customers (e.g. there will be no abandoned searches only because the user is not able to spell the words correctly).
- However, in many situations, voice as an output mechanism is less efficient than screens. This is leading to convergence of pure voice-based systems (e.g. Amazon Echo or Google Home) and

screen-based outputs (e.g. Google Assistant) to hybrid solutions like Echo. Echo uses voice first and then GUI-based interaction sparingly when needed.

- Further convergence will focus on the right balance between voice- and screen-based interactions as companies experiment with and learn to use the right mix for different use cases and customer segments.

4. Virtual and augmented reality (VR and AR) are changing how customers engage with companies and employees perform their tasks

- VR and AR started more as a fad limited to gaming and video applications. However, with advances in the technology, companies are looking at reimagining processes and experience using VR and AR.
- Remote working, digital twins, paperless environments and hands-free working environments are just some of the applications that are transforming enterprises as both VR and AR hardware and software become more intelligent as well as more cost-effective.
- With increasing applications in corporate training, customer onboarding, warehouse operations, logistics, etc., companies are increasingly turning to augmented reality solutions to overcome cost and distance disadvantages. We expect these solutions to get an even bigger boost as a result of the constraints on human-to-human interactions on account of the Covid-19 pandemic.

5. Experience design is extending from B2C to B2B and also to enterprise use cases

- The bulk of customer experience design thought has so far been focused on consumer-led interactions and businesses. However, increasingly, companies are applying these design principles to B2B customers and also to internal enterprise processes and systems.

- There is a growing realization that customer experience is not just limited to website/app usage or interaction at a store point of sale (POS). Every function of an organization can impact customer experience, directly or indirectly. Designing effective enterprise processes that allow employees to perform their tasks in a timely and efficient manner can drive down costs and deliver better products and services to customers.

6. Intersection of data science, technology and UX design is key to designing world-class experiences

- The most effective experience designs emerge when left-brained and right-brained approaches come together to develop a well-rounded understanding of consumer behaviour, combining classical consumer research with advanced propensity models.
- Companies that test and refine their designs continuously perform better than companies that invest in massive design efforts upfront. Digital natives like Google, Facebook, Amazon, etc. invest heavily in their A/B testing infrastructure to run thousands of experience design tests simultaneously.

Customer experience will continue to be the key difference between winners and losers in this digital age. Digital transformation is one of the most powerful tools an organization has at its disposal to differentiate itself on the customer experience front. This will require elevating the role of customer experience design within the organization to make it a first-class citizen. Organizations that do this effectively will reap rich rewards in terms of customer loyalty and shareholder value.

Summary

The benchmarks for customer digital experience were initially set by the FAANG companies. Customers now expect similar experiences from other businesses too. Following trends are expected to shape design of digital experiences:

- Continued simplification of the customer experience
- Customers looking for seamless omni-channel experience
- As voice-first interactions are increasing, striking a balance between voice- and screen-based interaction has become important
- Processes and experiences are getting reimagined with the use of VR and AR
- Experience design is extending from B2C to B2B and also to enterprise use cases
- Intersection of data science, technology and UX design is key to designing world-class experiences.

4

Used Properly, Analytics Is a Source of Competitive Advantage

If you don't know where you want to go, then it doesn't matter which path you take

Cheshire Cat, *Alice in Wonderland*

Analytics is undoubtedly one of the pillars of the digital age. In an environment where data is exploding, it is logical to leverage analytics tools and techniques to develop data-based insights, use them for decision-making, constantly track the impact of the decisions and make continual course correction. This process of leveraging analytics to optimize performance has become the norm across businesses in the digital age, whether it is to personalize recommendations for shoppers in e-commerce, optimize operational controls in a chemical plant or design strategy in almost every sport.

I have been closely involved in analytics for the past twenty years and I am very happy to see it becoming a mainstream capability—an integral building block of any digital transformation. This was not always the case. I started my analytics journey at the McKinsey Knowledge Centre in 2002. When I moved from the consulting office to the knowledge centre, I was amazed to see how the combination of increasing data depth and analytical tools made possible analysis that was well beyond the scope of traditional consulting teams, even though the teams were staffed with talent of a very high calibre. I saw the possibility that analytics could become a core service line and potentially a source of competitive advantage for a consulting firm like McKinsey.

Evangelizing the potential of analytics at that stage was not easy. It was seen as a super-specialization, the domain of 'nerdy PhDs'. It took many years of sustained effort and internal selling to establish analytics as a full-fledged service line within McKinsey. It makes me happy that so many firms have embraced analytics as a core capability, and it has moved from the sidelines to centre stage. It has caught the imagination of enterprises and the public at large and is also becoming a source of significant job creation.

Analytics is changing dramatically, becoming an even more powerful tool

Analytics has grown tremendously in scope and scale over the past twenty years that I have been associated with it. However, I feel we are still seeing only the tip of the iceberg. With the continued explosion in data and rapid advancements in technology, multiple advancements are happening in analytics as well, which will take its impact to a totally different level, making it an even more effective enabler for digital transformation journeys of enterprises.

I want to call out four trends, in particular, that promise to significantly raise the impact of analytics:

1. **Prescriptive analytics:** Analytics has progressed from descriptive (what happened) and predictive (what will likely happen) to prescriptive (what should be done). This progresses analytics from insight to action, moving it from the realm of a support capability to a frontline capability. Machine learning is a key enabler in this progression of analytics from insight to action.

2. **Continuous analytics:** One of the biggest trends in data has been the explosion of real-time data. This is moving analytics from 'batch mode', where analysis was done offline, to continuous analytics and insights. This trend is mainstream in both consumer and industrial situations. IoT is a significant driver of this trend; it can produce millions of real-time signals, enabling dynamic tracking and optimization.

3. **Augmented analytics:** This approach combines analytics with AI and machine learning, automating tasks that might be traditionally done by a data scientist or a specialist analytics professional. One of the biggest leverages of augmented analytics is improvement of data quality. Often, more than 80 per cent of time and costs expended on analytics projects go into ensuring adequate data quality. AI and ML can play an important role in improving data quality, which can significantly improve both the effectiveness and efficiency of the analytics process.

4. **Cloud-based analytics:** Cloud is one of the biggest technology trends of our times and I believe it will have a profound impact on how analytics is done. Cloud platforms, of course, provide a scalable infrastructure for computing that can support and enable big data and real-time analytics. More than that, cloud platforms can help streamline the process of gathering, synthesizing and processing data. This can be a major productivity booster. Additionally, cloud providers like AWS, GCP and Azure are making tremendous strides in the capabilities of their analytics platforms. Many of the tasks historically done by the analytics specialist are in-built into these platforms. This is a fascinating development and will have far-reaching implications for analytics specialists, in terms of the roles and skills required of them.

Gap between promise and reality

Despite analytics being around for well over a decade and significant improvements to the tools and techniques being available, most organizations have still not figured out how analytics can play a transformational role within the enterprise. Considering the endless possibilities of analytics, application of analytics technology today is likely only at 5–10 per cent of its potential maturity, and even leading companies are still using analytics to drive decision-making in a very limited way.[3]

While analytics can be a source of competitive advantage if done correctly, there are six main reasons why most analytics initiatives fail to deliver the value they promise:

1. **Focusing on analytical rather than business problems first:** In most analytics projects, there tends to be a gap between understanding of the business context and its translation into the analytics problem that is being solved. Analytics projects tend to overly focus on solving an analytical problem very well, when instead they should focus on solving the business problem by understanding the linkage between business and functional drivers. In my experience, data scientists are often attracted to intellectually challenging problems and usage of the most sophisticated techniques. However, solving hard problems is much less relevant than solving problems that really matter.

    In the problem-solving process, problem discovery and scoping are a lot more relevant than analytics itself. Therefore, every analytics exercise must start with a sharply defined business problem based on specific use cases and business KPIs. This can be achieved by the upfront involvement of business teams in problem definition and solution design.

2. **Change not driven as end-to-end transformation:** There are four different layers in analytics. The first is the strategy layer, which is about identifying the core business problems; the second is model building, which hinges on choosing the right kind of data modelling for your specific problem; the

third is the actual data (access and collection), and the fourth is intelligent applications. Where many data analytics projects fall short is not recognizing that to achieve true business impact, change needs to be driven as an end-to-end transformation, where business-problem definition, analytics modelling, the data platform, technology and operations implementation are tightly integrated. A disproportionate focus is often placed on the outcomes of modelling and not enough attention is paid to the core building blocks to connect all the four layers.

I have seen many companies where analytics teams have hundreds of models but nobody is using them. Data scientists often derive great satisfaction from building great models, but a model by itself serves no purpose. It is only relevant when it is solving a clear business problem. What is more, even if the model is well connected to a business problem, you have to ensure that you can operationalize it and put it into production. Companies need to adopt an integrated approach towards building their solutions; only then can they derive significant advantage from their analytics investments.

3. **Embarking on Big-Bang implementation rather than starting small:** Analytics problem solving is inherently iterative. It needs a fair degree of experimentation to get right. You need to start small and then build up in a progressive manner. Starting with too large a problem makes specific actions, iterations and insights discovery difficult. As I have said earlier, there is no 'first time right' in analytical problem-solving. Trying to do a Big-Bang implementation with large data sets that have a cross-organizational impact is most certainly a recipe for disaster.

4. **Rigid structures inhibiting cross-functional collaboration:** Most organizations today are structured linearly, with negligible cross-functional collaboration. Successful analytics projects need cross-functional teams composed of data scientists, architects,

engineers and teams from business, operations and even finance, who can work through agile implementation cycles until they find the solution to meet their business needs. A mindset and culture that are not agile and structures that inhibit cross-functional collaboration are often the hidden causes of failure in analytics-driven transformations.

Moreover, placement of the analytics function within the organization itself can create challenges. I see different organizational models for placement of analytics—within a business unit, as a standalone shared service, placed with the technology function, etc. Each of these models has its issues. Analytics placed within the business has the benefit of proximity to the business context and to the problem to be solved, but typically, this position does not allow for scale to build depth and quality. Standalone analytics units often tend to be 'orphans' struggling for organizational prominence. Analytics units placed with technology have the benefit of being close to data but tend to get very distant from business context. Clearly, there is no perfect structural solution for analytics. Therefore, cross-functional teams and a culture that emphasizes the importance of analytics are key to success in the use of analytics.

5. **Data availability and quality are poor or non-existent:** Data is the lifeblood of analytics. Without the right type and quality of data, analytics is not possible. I have mentioned earlier that 80 per cent or more of time spent on analytics projects can go into getting the right quality of data together. In some enterprises, data can become an insurmountable challenge. Either data is just not there, or its quality is very poor, or it is very difficult to access using the technology systems. I have seen that many data scientists tend to get completely immobilized if there is no data. That is where it is very important for analytics professionals to develop not just the skills to work with data, but also problem-solving skills to be effective when data is not there or is limited!

6. **Analytics talent quality—inability to solve problems:** The last decade has seen a real explosion of jobs in the category of data scientist. However, there is huge variability in the skill profile and quality of data scientists. Analytics is a skill set where the gap between effectiveness of the top decile and the median can be massive. While analytics professionals tend to be very focused on analytical tools and techniques, my view is that the biggest driver of success would be their problem-solving skills. That is the biggest differentiator between top analytics professionals and average ones. Analytical tools and techniques applied mechanically and without sharp problem-solving rigour rarely gets you great outcomes. The challenge is that problem-solving skills are not easy to build in a programmatic fashion. These skills are built through coaching and nurturing, and require the right role models and enterprise culture.

Every legacy enterprise I know has ended up building analytics groups but is struggling to attract the right quality of analytics talent. This inability to attract talent is not because of their unwillingness to spend top dollars but because they struggle to build the culture that will attract the top talent. This talent issue has a huge impact on the output of the analytics function in legacy enterprises, where there is often a lot of analytics activity but not any corresponding high-quality output.

To sum up the challenges with respect to analytics, its implementation is not a silver bullet. Analytics projects are messy, complicated and iterative. Unless they are approached with an end-to-end business transformation mindset, they will fail to deliver the intended results.

Ability to connect the dots within analytics is not easy to come by. There are very few organizations who are currently able to manage each piece of the equation in unison to deliver true business impact.

What does the future of analytics look like?

Clearly, analytics is a critical building block not just for digital transformation but also for how business needs to be done in the digital age. Moreover, analytics capabilities continue to grow at a breathtaking pace with the explosion of data and advancements in technology, in particular, AI and cloud. However, we have also seen that there are many challenges in analytics execution currently, which has meant that organizations have not yet been able to harness the full potential of analytics.

So, what does the future of analytics look like? I have no doubt that analytics will continue to grow in importance and will assume a much larger role in both digital transformations and business in general. However, the shape of analytics will evolve significantly. I have three key hypotheses around what these changes will entail.

First, analytics will go mainstream and become all-pervasive and would potentially cease to exist as a standalone capability or function. Analytics capabilities as we know it, will split into two parts. First part will merge with business functions and analytical skills will become a core skill expectation for all business professionals across marketing, finance, operations, consulting or any other function. Second part of analytics will merge with the technology function. Picture data, AI and cloud as intersecting circles and what we know as analytics today will most likely get subsumed within these intersecting circles.

Second, the boundaries between services and platforms in analytics will blur. Analytics was initially more about services, involving deployment of high-quality talent with strong quantitative skills on data-intensive problems. Over the past few years, a host of analytics-based products and platforms have emerged. With the growth of cloud, these platforms have become more pervasive. And with AI, there is a growth in several point solutions. This growth in platforms and products will continue, blurring the lines between product and services. As a result, many of these platforms and products will work along with services.

Third, expectations from data scientists and analytics professionals will change significantly. So far, the main skill expected from them was statistical modelling. With the growth of analytical platforms, various aspects of modelling will get automated and simplified, and this will no longer be considered a core skill. My hypothesis is that we will see the emergence of two varieties of analytics professionals: those with deep domain knowledge and problem-solving skills, and others who have strong technology skills and work at the intersection of big data, AI and cloud.

I continue to find analytics to be a fascinating space. I am convinced that the best days of analytics are ahead of us and the scope of its role and impact will grow way beyond what we can see today. However, it is important to note that in the long term, its structure and form will be very different. This will have lots of implications, both for enterprises and for talent looking to make a career in analytics. There is a lot to look forward to in this space!

Summary

- An exponential rise in the data collected provides a unique opportunity for the enterprise to realize value through analytics.
- Further, the potential of analytics is growing rapidly with the explosion of data and the amazing growth in technology, in particular AI and cloud.
- However, the impact of analytics is well below its potential. There are six challenges that need to be overcome to realize value from analytics:
  o Gap in understanding the business context
  o Lack of end-to-end approach and disproportionate focus on modelling

- o   Adoption of Big-Bang implementation in spite of analytics initiatives being inherently iterative
- o   Lack of agile mindset and culture and limiting organizational models
- o   Problems in data availability and quality, and inability of analytics professionals to be effective in such situations
- o   Difficulties in attracting and nurturing high-quality analytics talent, and challenges in building problem-solving skills.

5

Operations Transformation: Necessary for Realizing the Full Benefit of Digital Transformation . . . and It Is Not Easy . . .

The revolution is not an apple that falls when it is ripe, you have to make it fall

Che Guevara, Argentine Revolutionary Leader and author

When operations transformation needs a complete overhaul

In every industry, the customer's digital expectations are rising, both directly for digital products and services, and indirectly for the speed, accuracy, productivity and convenience that digital makes possible. Organizations have realized that fulfilling these expectations takes a lot more than creating customer-facing digital properties: it requires a complete overhaul of end-to-end processes—from multi-channel fulfillment and customer support to billing and receivables. Amazon has upended the retail industry not by replicating the brick-and-mortar operating model but by reimagining the entire retail model with a digital-first mindset. While Amazon may have had the advantage of starting out as a digital-native business, Walmart and

Home Depot have successfully managed to integrate both their physical and digital channels to tremendous competitive advantage. One thing stands out for all the three firms: they approached the problem not in the narrow sense of digital customer experience but as a holistic end-to-end transformation, leading with operations as the main focus for driving their digital transformation. These firms realized early on that the traditional performance improvement initiatives—process re-engineering, cost reduction by piece-meal automation and outsourcing of operations—simply lack the required agility, flexibility and responsiveness to enable total transformation. In other words, operations transformation needed a complete overhaul.

The three trends that will drive the next wave of operations transformation

We have seen this repeat across industries—and it is now clear that to make digital transformation real and create true economic value, the playbook needs to have two key elements:

- Operations transformation must be integral to any digital transformation roadmap.
- Technology is a critical enabler to truly transform operations. While technology alone is not sufficient, what is clear is that without a strong technology focus, scaling operations in today's world is no longer possible.

And, as the retail e-commerce world has shown, the technology that powers operations, has been enabled by the trifecta of computing, data and artificial intelligence. We see three clear technology trends that are expected to drive the next wave of operations transformation:

1. **Data explosion,** which will help drive process design and optimization using data-driven methods.

2. **AI advances,** which will help design and implement self-learning processes which can adapt to changing business needs.
3. **Automation maturity,** which will help organizations go beyond task automation and enable cognitive technologies.

Research clearly suggests that the future belongs to organizations that can make the transition to intelligent operations that leverage data and AI to develop and manage flexible processes and infuse agility and responsiveness in them. It is estimated that by 2030, banking operations will look very different: 75–80 per cent of transactional operations (e.g. payments processing) and upto 40 per cent of more strategic activities (e.g. FP&A, treasury) are expected to be automated.[4] This is in addition to an even bigger structural transformation well underway: branch networks are shrinking at an ever faster rate; digital-only banks are jumping into the fray. The twin impact of these trends will mean that bank operations will be profoundly different from what they are today. And this makes it necessary for banks to address the operations transformation challenge on priority.

Data explosion: Diagnostics and optimization reimagined

Edward Deming, the doyen of TQM, was reported to have said, 'You cannot improve what you cannot measure'. In the pre-digital era, process monitoring involved laborious time and motion studies. Today, most organizations have systems (e.g. ERP, warehouse management systems [WMS] and other transaction processing applications) that measure the flow of information across the enterprise. This has enabled the creation of 'digital twins'—of existing processes and their modelling for analysis and simulation—through process mining.

Process mining has emerged as a key technology lever in business process transformation. Data mining algorithms are applied to event log data recorded by the transaction systems. This will identify trends and patterns related to process-time delays, throughput rates and shifting bottlenecks. There are distinct advantages in doing this:

1. **Discovery of issues in execution:**
   - Identification of shifting bottlenecks from activity-level event data logs.
   - Highlighting of quality issues and reworking in complex cross-functional processes.

2. **Improvement in process compliance and auditing:**
   - Process mining acts as a quality control mechanism and provides data-backed near-real-time evidence on process compliance for regulatory/auditory purposes.

3. **Assessing impact:**
   - It helps assess the dollar impact of an improvement action.
   - Provides granular visibility into process performance at both worker and session level.

4. **Identification of automation opportunities:**
   - Process mining uncovers specific opportunities for RPA and ML-based process automation.
   - Helps prioritize automation opportunities.

AI: Self-learning processes for exception handling

Google's AlphaGo defeated the world champion in the game Go, arguably the most complex game in the world. This was more than a research project: it has opened up the possibilities of leveraging deep-learning methods to build self-learning engines for designing and operating processes. This could have remarkable implications for business operations, where a key source of inefficiency is exception handling. In other words, the scope of 'straight-through processing' can be expanded to cover a wider array of scenarios that don't need to be defined upfront, but the process can adapt and learn as it keeps evolving with real-life scenarios.

We are already seeing artificial neural networks (ANNs) being applied to solve process optimization problems. Inspired by the structure of the human brain, neural networks have the ability to train themselves to learn from data. In other words, you no longer need to codify the entire set of operating rules upfront, but let the AI engine evolve the rules as it keeps learning from real-life scenarios. There are several potential applications across various operational processes that would otherwise require human intervention, and where decisions are often made on intuition. Some examples:

- **Logistics:** Risk management strategies across distribution channels, design and management of transport capacity,
- **Human resources:** Management of performance and human behaviour strategies at the individual level, sizing of personnel structure allocation at economic organization level,
- **Accounting:** Identification of financial frauds, audit procedures.

On the cusp of the third wave with intelligent automation, going beyond task automation

Automation has seen tremendous advancement in the last ten years. The first wave saw traditional automation that automated specific tasks (e.g. screen scraping to extract data, screen recorders, et al). These served to deliver incremental task-level efficiencies. We are currently in the second wave, where software bots, process design tools and workflow rule engines have helped automate specific tasks (e.g. auto-routing a customer care call to the right agent; rule-based PO-approval processes). These continue to drive efficiencies in processes that lend themselves to well-defined flows based on predefined rules.

I believe we are on the cusp of the third wave of 'intelligent automation', with the industrialization of NLP, voice-to-text and

Operations Transformation is a necessity to drive Digital Transformation

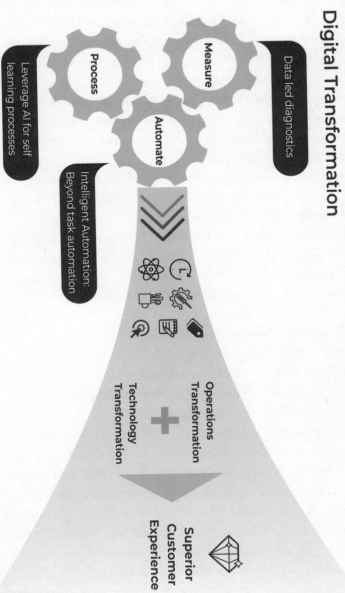

computer vision, which rely on sophisticated AI techniques to draw valuable information from hitherto unstructured data sources. A comprehensive intelligent automation strategy needs to be executed at a functional process level with a combination of complementary technologies:

1. **Task automation:** With tremendous advances in AI applications for processing unstructured data, there is opportunity to expand the scope of automation to include activities that were previously reliant on human agents:
   a. *Customer care*: Call transcription and classification can be done by a voice-to-text bot in real-time, leaving the agent to focus on customer interactions.
   b. *Account onboarding*: Document scanning and extraction of customer information, signature verification, etc., can be offloaded to computer vision bots, freeing up operations bandwidth to focus on customer engagement.

2. **Intelligent BPM:** Business workflows no longer need to be straight-jacketed process steps. AI expert systems offer a way to define a skeletal process workflow, and as the system learns from real-life experience, it continues to refine and evolve the workflow rules:
   a. *Audit process*: AI bots can evaluate journal entry submissions in real-time and based on contextual information (e.g. who, when, where, and how the entry is prepared and submitted) and flag them for appropriate review. The data associated with the entry may include emails and supporting documents in addition to the standard accounting rules. This has the potential to reimagine the audit process from a post-facto analysis to an in-process, real-time activity.
   b. *Dynamic inventory management*: The traditional method of safety stocks at each level in the supply chain has always been hugely inefficient. AI-enabled systems are already making a

big impact here by responding to signals across the supply chain in real-time and dynamically reallocating inventories to optimally manage service levels. These systems have the ability to learn and improve—and can further be tasked to optimize around specific goals (e.g. new product launch).

3. **Smart analytics:** As business complexity continues to grow, managers are expected to take decisions ever faster, often with limited information. Decision support engines—in the form of descriptive, diagnostic and predictive insights and recommendations—are proving to be invaluable in helping humans make better decisions. Increasingly, we see decision-makers augmenting their intuition and experience with machine-enabled recommendations:

    a. *Resource planning and allocation*: From capital resources (e.g. machinery, vehicle fleets, etc.) to human resources, analytics can help drive their optimal allocation across priority areas. This, combined with a performance tracking and monitoring system, can help identify potential hotspots and enable focus on specific areas requiring intervention.

    b. *Operational metrics*: Business operations teams are increasingly reliant on data-driven methods to define key operational parameters—from budgeting to daily operations monitoring in almost all functional areas. For instance, the customer onboarding team in a bank tracks 'speed to revenue' and subsequently, CSAT as a key metric to plan and execute the onboarding process.

It is clear that after the first wave of digital transformation of creating online and omni-channel customer experiences, the next wave of value is being created in operations transformation. And, as firms like Amazon, Walmart and Home Depot have shown, the truly successful organizations are the ones that are successful in integrating their front-end experiences with their back-end operations. To be sure, technology alone cannot be the answer—operations transformation will require significant focus on the overhauling of processes. Often, automating an inefficient process would be worse than leaving it alone. So it is just as important to invest in people; operations, more than any other part of the organization, needs a blend of human intuition and the power and scalability of machines, calling for changes from training personnel to rewriting job descriptions, and so on. In other words, operations transformation is not easy, but then again, it is apparent that not doing it is no longer a choice either.

Summary

- Digital transformation started with a focus on customer experience and front-end applications. However, focus of digital transformation now has to move to core operations as sustainable changes in customer experience cannot be delivered without substantial transformation of operations.
- Operations transformation is a significant yet under leveraged opportunity. Most efforts focus on incremental change while the need is to 're-imagine operations'.
- Three technology trends that are expected to drive operations transformation are:
  o Data explosion, which helps drive process mining and diagnostics,
  o AI advances, helping design and implementation of self-learning processes,
  o Automation maturity, helping organizations go beyond task automation and enabling cognitive technologies.

6

AI Powers the Forward March of Digital Transformation

AI is a core transformative way by which we are rethinking how we are doing everything

Sundar Pichai

Digital technologies and digitally driven business processes are reshaping and transforming industry after industry. There is widespread evidence to demonstrate how digital technologies have unlocked an unprecedented level of value for enterprises, giving rise to innovative products, business models and the reimagining of enterprise operating models.

Yes, we can debate that a large array of businesses which have embarked upon transformation journeys have found it difficult to realize the promised value. However, that has resulted more from their lack of clarity as to the meaning of digital for their businesses as well as from botched-up execution. This has not taken any of the lustre away from the bright light of digital technologies. The digital transformation march is moving ahead—faster, stronger and with more rigour than ever.

Now, as we have achieved early success from digital transformation initiatives, the question really is—**how do we take it to the next level?** One of the most important parts of the answer is **unleashing the power of artificial intelligence to reach the next frontier of digital transformation**.

The promise and impact of AI in driving digital transformation is already well established with a wide array of use cases around us—e.g. personalized offer recommendations to customers, image processing and facial recognition technologies, fraud detection, etc. However, we have just scratched the surface. We have been dabbling with this power so far, leveraging AI as an add-on to business processes and not really redesigning them into AI-enabled processes.

No doubt there have been hurdles in achieving AI's potential because of data and infrastructure limitations. With an exponential burst in digital data availability and the rapid rise of highly elastic cloud computing infrastructure, AI is set to fuel digital transformation journeys to the next frontier.

How can AI power digital transformation to reach the next level?

Over the last few years, AI capabilities have really come of age; AI has matured from an experimental topic to a mainstream technology delivering significant value. As confidence in AI-enabled digital processes grows, enterprises need to push the boundaries of AI application to bring it to the complex core of their business processes.

- **Hyper-personalization across all interactions**
  In today's environment of digital hyperactivity, customers are spoilt for choice in products, services and content. While this sounds like true nirvana, there is a major flipside to it too. Given too many choices and decisions to be made, customers often make poor choices and end up being less satisfied than they perhaps

were with fewer choices. And sometimes, being overwhelmed, they switch off completely when they have to make a choice.

Artificial intelligence-driven hyper-personalization, i.e., automatic curation of best choices for the customer, delivered in real-time across various channels of interaction, is the key to take digital customer engagement to the next level. For instance, as telecom customers look to take up new plans or upgrade their existing plan, they are presented with a seemingly infinite number of choices as to devices, plans, data plans, talk time, bundles, accessories, and so forth. It can be mind-boggling to really make a decision from among these choices. However, telecom service providers can leverage AI to analyse and uncover customer preferences, usage patterns and other key attributes to simplify the choices to top three. This not only makes it easy for the customer but fetches them customer delight too.

- **Automation really becomes intelligent**
  While the focus of the first wave of digital transformation has been on customer engagement, the real value of digitally transforming the enterprise's underlying business processes— such as customer service, supply chain, business operations— is yet to be realized. Significant progress has been made in leveraging technologies like robotic process automation to bring some degree of automation to mundane, standard and monolithic processes. However, these technologies have been largely insufficient, given the complex processes that require decision-making intelligence.

  Use of artificial intelligence to augment, automate and speed up decision-making in complex process journeys is a critical catalyst to really make automation intelligent and take it beyond the realm of simple process steps to automated complex decision-making.

  A case in point may be the back-office operations at any bank or wealth management organization, which are among the most critical and resource-intensive processes. The complexity of managing different types of documents and information makes it extremely difficult for any RPA technology to automate it. AI and NLP capabilities are really pushing the boundaries of automation with intelligent text data extraction and interpretation, enabling analysts to make faster, better decisions, hence reducing the average handling time (AHT) for each request. In several cases, AI-driven capabilities can achieve full decision-making ability, making straight-through processing a reality.

- **Opening new AI frontiers—AI not just *as* digital technology but also *for* digital technology**
  Digital transformation is really converting every business into a technology business. With new technology-centred products, services and business models growing, so is investment in digital technology to support them across all layers—infrastructure, data, applications and security. Technology has become the core of investment, operations focus and business value realization. The opportunity costs of disruption or downtime of IT infrastructure, erratic behaviour of applications, poor data quality or even data theft are way too high to be taken lightly.

  The potential to leverage AI to optimize the technology stack to best utilize precious resources, avoiding any downtime or disruption, and enhance the value realization, is very significant and real. The AI-driven approach is becoming key to efficient management of tech systems; e.g. automated monitoring and predictive maintenance of the digital infrastructure to ensure there is no disruption in the revenue-generating applications is as much a critical process as any other. AI algorithms can monitor the server logs, events, data traffic and other system parameters in real-time to automatically monitor the digital infrastructure—servers, devices, networks and applications—deliver early warning for proactive maintenance, and in some cases even auto-heal systems.

AI - Reach the next frontier of Digital Transformation

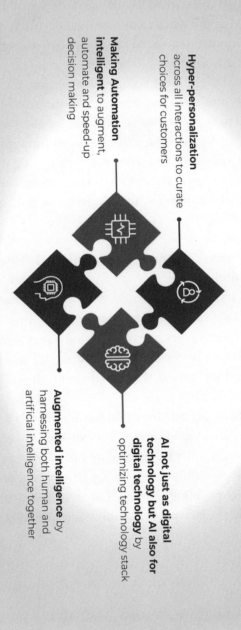

Hyper-personalization
across all interactions to curate choices for customers

Making Automation intelligent to augment, automate and speed-up decision making

AI not just as digital technology but AI also for digital technology by optimizing technology stack

Augmented intelligence by harnessing both human and artificial intelligence together

Similarly, while there is so much excitement around digital data, to really unlock its value, it needs to be of high quality. Leveraging AI approaches to uncover data quality issues such as hidden data anomalies and help rectify them, will really take the realizable value from digital data to the next level.

As data and digital technology have become the lifeblood of the enterprise, the need for strong cybersecurity capability has never been felt to be more critical. With the growing sophistication of cyber threats, AI-driven approaches to automatically decipher and ward off unauthorized access attempts and network and system vulnerabilities, and recommend or auto-fix security issues, can be extremely important to mitigate the risk of malicious attacks and data theft.

- **AI on the team—Human plus artificial intelligence = Augmented intelligence**
  As the digital transformation journey progresses, enterprises need to think about AI as *the core member of the team*. The debate of human intelligence versus artificial intelligence is irrelevant. In order to get deeper below the surface of digital transformation, enterprises need to harness the complementarity of human and artificial intelligence.

  As we rethink digital-driven operating models and business processes, artificial intelligence cannot be an afterthought anymore; rather, it must be at the core of it. The key is to think about how AI capabilities can be a performance enhancer for the employees, enabling better, faster decision-making and analysis of hidden data patterns which are humanly impossible to uncover.

AI-enabled digital transformation: Execution imperatives

AI technologies are going to fuel the next wave of digital transformation. The ability of enterprises to leverage AI as a core capability will differentiate the digital leaders from the laggards in their attainment of competitive advantage in the digital era. As enterprises progress further on this AI-enabled digital transformation journey, there are a few key imperatives to keep in mind:

- **Leveraging artificial intelligence across the business stack**

  Enterprises must think about leveraging AI capabilities across the business stack—customer experience, business operations as well as the technology ecosystem. As they reimagine digitally driven business processes, enterprises need to systematically curate opportunities across the business stack where AI can make a fundamental impact.

  The key lies in redesigning AI-enabled digital process maps, enabling better, real-time and autonomous decision-making, driven by insightful recommendations and automation. Prioritizing such opportunities and implementing them iteratively will propel enterprises to achieve the next level of digital transformation success.

- **Embracing 'AI as architecture' and not 'AI as a feature'**

  Artificial intelligence capabilities are no more to be thought of as augmentation to the existing technology stack, but rather, every component of the digital technology stack needs to be designed with the fundamental principle of AI-enabled real-time decision-making.

  This requires rethinking the technology and data strategy. The underlying technology and data architecture need to get aligned to the requirements of AI-enabled processes. For instance, AI algorithms need access to a wide array of diverse digital data points (multiple formats, sources, high speed, large volume), to uncover hidden patterns and to make the right decisions. The underlying data technology architecture needs to have the capability to handle such a complex data ecosystem and process it real-time to power AI algorithms. Similarly, the underlying compute capacity of the digital tech infrastructure should be able to respond in real-time to the demands of processing this data for the AI algorithms to work.

- **Investing in and experimenting with new AI technologies**
  AI technologies themselves are evolving very rapidly. New AI techniques like convolutional neural networks, self-learning algorithms like reinforcement learning, cognitive intelligence technologies such as computer vision, are all growing in capability and unleashing new possibilities of application across business processes.

  Enterprises need to systematically experiment with these new technologies, test them in their business processes to assess their potential impact, and scale the successful ones as mainstream AI capabilities.

  The culture of experimentation-driven innovation will help enterprises be at the forefront of leveraging AI to deliver consistent impact from digital transformation investments.

- **Rethinking the talent model in the AI-enabled world**
  As I have said earlier in this chapter, enterprises need to harness the complementarity of human and artificial intelligence. The manifestation of this complementarity is in the form of a talent model which will be relevant in the AI-enabled world. It requires skilling and training of employees to prepare and enable them to co-exist and grow with machines. The ability to work with or use AI is not just limited to highly skilled technology groups, it needs to become pervasive across all skill groups and levels in the enterprise. A customer service representative who can leverage AI-driven intelligence systems and its recommendations to resolve customer issues rapidly and to the customer's delight can make a far more significant impact in terms of business success. As the wave of digital transformation progresses, the ability of a company's employees to enhance their impact, by not just

designing AI systems but also by using them, will be one of the most critical assets for a successful digital business.

Digital technologies are all-pervasive and are rapidly pushing us forward on the digital transformation journey. We have just scratched the surface and tasted early success from it. Artificial intelligence capabilities will fuel the next wave of digital transformation, unleashing business value never seen before.

Summary

- Artificial intelligence as a technology is reaching a tipping point where it is now ready to power digital transformation for businesses to the next level.
- Artificial intelligence can enable hyper-personalization across all interactions, make automation more intelligent, aid in the deployment of other digital technologies, and augment human intelligence and decision-making.
- To leverage the most from artificial intelligence, it needs to be thought of as a core capability and embedded across the technology stack.

7

The Digital Data Deluge—Boon or Bane?

In God we trust, everybody else brings data

Edward W. Deming, Mathematical Physicist and
Founder of TQM Movement

Just when enterprises were starting to believe that they can handle their enterprise data and have the required management and governance ecosystem in place, they were hit by an unprecedented wave of technology-driven digital transformation. The new technology wave in the form of digitization has taken over the world, rendering carefully crafted data management frameworks obsolete. Suddenly, enterprises that were believed to have achieved data management maturity dropped down to the level of novices in their capability to handle digital data.

The digital wave, fuelled by massive volumes of complex, high-speed data—unstructured and uncurated—generated by mobile apps, social media, cloud and devices, has significantly impacted the enterprise's ability to manage and generate value from its data. The rise of the IoT, new technologies like artificial intelligence, genome sequencing and augmented reality have made the challenges even greater.

The implications? Enterprises face a new, dynamic and complex digital agenda that is disrupting their data management and curation capabilities. This disruption is making it critical for them to consider the opportunities presented by digital transformation so that they may manage the unprecedented and new risks of digital data, which is arriving in waves that their walls cannot contain and which they have no control over.

The opportunities and risk? Digital data is a potential gold mine, and digital natives like Google, Facebook and Amazon have already demonstrated the impact digital data intertwined with AI and machine learning technologies can have on creating digital businesses and value where none existed earlier. Several leading enterprises have even started applying these principles and artificial intelligence technologies to their B2B data, which too is expanding rapidly. On the flip side of the coin are the potential risks—privacy, security and much more—that digital data produces for enterprises if not handled well.

As enterprises navigate the digital age, leveraging digital technologies like AI, machine learning, automation and cloud to create new digital opportunities, they need to realize that **digital data is the fulcrum of the digital technology stack and the centrepiece of digital transformation**. Enterprises need to reimagine their data management approach—aligning people, processes and technology—creating an agile, scalable, secure and, above all, digital-ready enterprise data architecture.

The changing profile of data in the digital age

Much has been said and written about the trends of the digital age that are fundamentally changing the way businesses operate and the way consumers interact with them. These interactions and operating models are generating a very wide array of unprecedented data forms.

Examples include, but are not limited to:

- Connected medical devices, tele-health and consumer-driven healthcare.
- Genomic sequencing data and its use in precision and personalized medicine to make decisions about specific treatment paths that may be effective for the individual at hand.
- The internet of things, including machine-to-machine (M2M) integration and sensor technology in manufacturing, supply chain, telecom, oil and gas, and utilities, among other sectors.
- Omni-channel consumer choices in retail, consumer goods, banking and insurance transactions.
- Digital payments and transactions, among both enterprises and consumers, which are rapidly increasing across the world.
- Gamification—the introduction of game-like metrics such as rules, competition, prizes or points-earning—by an increasing number of banking, financial services and insurance companies.
- Enhanced, customized consumerism, such as use of facial recognition and biometrics, to create personalized experiences based on prior shopping behaviour and increasingly sophisticated predictive analytics.
- Digital marketing targeted at specific consumers based on their unique digital profiles and online behaviour.

The characteristics of these data forms are widely different from those of typical enterprise data like ERP, CRM, sales and finance, which enterprises and executives are familiar with. As we look closely at these digital data profiles, a few key themes emerge. It is very important to understand these digital data profiles and themes to be able to define and build data management frameworks for the digital age.

- **Variety—An uncharted world of unprecedented data formats**
  The rapid evolution of digital technologies is leading to exponential growth in new and unconventional data formats,

such as radio frequency identification (RFID) tags, smart metres, global positioning systems (GPS) and machine-to-machine. This is all in addition to the clickstream data produced by our interactions with websites, mobile apps and other platforms.

In the banking industry, as banks become more and more paperless, identity resolution will be achieved with retinal scans or image recognition rather than with documentation; physical signatures will be replaced by digital signatures; and paper cheques replaced by digitally signed e-cheques.

The data infrastructure must learn how to handle, store and process these digital data forms (such as images, fingerprints, retinal scans, digital signatures and social media data) that go beyond the conventional customer demographic or financial transaction data.

- **Volume—Gigabytes is passé, Petabytes and Exabytes are the new kids on the block**
  A single human genome takes up to 100 gigabytes of storage space, and as more and more human genomes are sequenced, data storage and processing needs will go from gigabytes to petabytes to exabytes. By 2025, approximately 40 exabytes of storage capacity will be required for human genome data.[5] While storage is one challenge, the bigger challenge is the ability of the current data infrastructure to process this data for 'signal' detection.

  To come closer to the consumer world, IDC predicts the average person will have nearly 5,000 digital interactions per day by 2025, up from the average of 700 to 800 currently. Such high-volume interactions will put extreme presume on already struggling enterprise data ecosystems to process and curate the consumer data.[6]

- **Velocity—Data generation at the speed of thought**
  On a daily basis, Facebook generates 4 petabytes of data, we send 201 billion emails, 100 billion messages over WhatsApp and make 6.4 billion searches on Google.[7]

That is the mind-boggling speed of event and streaming data generated across the board—from internet, consumer, financial transactions and IoT. 'Real-time' or 'high-speed' data processing and integration is required by enterprises to interact with and service their customers. The enterprise data architecture had just achieved some degree of efficiency in processing slow-paced batch data, and now suddenly they must adapt to the need for speed.

- **Omnipresent data sources—Everything and everyone is a data source**
  In the digital ecosystem, almost every device and every human being is generating huge amounts of data. Every interaction is generating a wide array of rich data covering multitudes of behaviours, interactions, conversations.

  Every person generates an average of 2.4 GB of digital data each day, in the form of emails, messages, transactions, browsing, searches, videos, photos, health, vitals, biometrics and much more. Every device—industrial, sensors, wearables, computing—is producing data of varying forms—temperature, pressure, geolocation, biometric, logs, events, and so on.

  The sources of enterprise and external digital data have become unmanageably numerous and are ever increasing.

These digital data characteristics make handling and deriving value from it significantly more complex than what current enterprise data management systems can handle. The inherent complexity of digital data puts extreme pressure on the data ecosystem.

'Pressure points' of the data ecosystem

The good news is that the investments that enterprises have made in their data ecosystems and technology is not wasted. The enterprise data from ERPs, CRMs and other operational systems still needs to be managed, processed and curated.

The not-so-good news is that these systems are not equipped to handle the complexity of digital data. The current enterprise data ecosystem has many pressure points.

- **Inability to consume, process and integrate high-speed, complex digital data**
  The monolithic data architecture of traditional data systems lacks the ability to ingest and store data from different sources. They don't have sufficient processing capabilities to process various data forms—relational, non-relational, text, streaming, etc.

  Many organizations have taken steps to augment or migrate to big data technologies to overcome this challenge, setting up on-premise data ecosystems. It worked well for a while, but when the volumes started growing beyond the capacity they could handle, even the big data ecosystem didn't prove sufficient to fulfil the needs of the demanding digital data.

- **Limitation in curating and differentiating 'signal' from 'noise'—Enabling AI/ML-driven insights**
  The greatest value in digital data lies in its ability to enable deep insights, using artificial intelligence and machine learning, as to behaviours, patterns, recommendations, early warnings, next-best actions and much more. This allows for highly personalized, real-time actions and informed business decision support.

  However, the rigid information architecture of enterprise data systems focuses on standardization of data models and analytical tools rather than enabling dynamic business analytics demand. It is, therefore, ill-equipped to generate AI/ML-driven insights from digital data. These systems don't have the ability to curate such complex, large volume data in real-time to really differentiate and extract valuable signals for business actions and personalized customer interventions.

- **The 'golden record' is no more sufficient—Digital interactions require 'golden network' for holistic 360-degree view**

  Enterprises have lots of data, but it is siloed and disconnected. Data is spread across departments (CRM, sales, marketing, product development, customer service), product lines, platforms (web team, data warehouses, NoSQL, data lakes), locations (cloud, on-prem, edge, IoT, mobile) and systems. This complex ecosystem creates disconnected data, which leads to problems.

  A holistic or 360-degree view of its users, customers, products, accounts, partners, location and more is at the heart of leveraging value from digital for the enterprise. Most MDM systems built on an RDBMS backbone focus on creating the 'golden record' and are proving inefficient in creating a unified 360-degree view. Even with advanced computing and high-speed networks, the performance and ability of such systems continue to lag requirements. Why? Because it is no longer sufficient to build a golden record. As digital data is now an interconnected network of entities and relationships, the modern MDM system needs the ability to connect and correlate different data domains, uncovering hidden relationships and insights.

  So, while current MDM approaches continue to solve monolithic master data use cases, they have proven ineffective in serving connected data use cases.

- **Growing sophistication of cyber-attacks and data theft have redefined data security demands**

  Digital transformation is all about turning data into knowledge, and the stakes are ever higher as it brings about a data-driven and connected world. The flipside of this transformation is the increasing risk of data breaches and cyber-attacks, which can cripple even the most resilient of organizations. Additionally, new regulations, on the level of personal data protection, such as the General Data Protection Regulation, increase the costs of data breaches even more.

Digital Data Deluge - Changing profile of data in Digital age

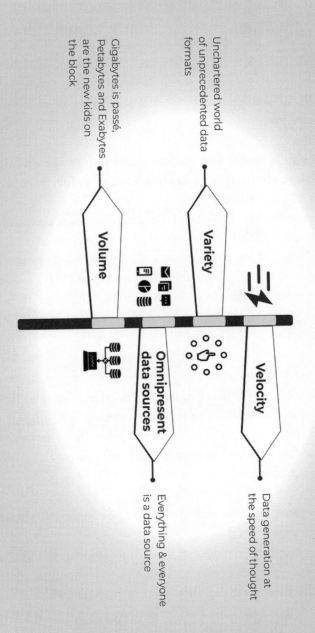

Volume

Gigabytes is passé, Petabytes and Exabytes are the new kids on the block

Variety

Unchartered world of unprecedented data formats

Omnipresent data sources

Everything & everyone is a data source

Velocity

Data generation at the speed of thought

With distribution of data across locations (cloud, on-prem, edge), managing the security and privacy of critical customer and enterprise data has become very difficult. The security frameworks which worked very well in securing data within enterprise walls will need to evolve to be secure with digital data while the enterprise also takes advantage of the business opportunity presented by it.

- **Poor data governance and quality are proving to be among the most critical challenges to truly realizing value from digital data and AI capabilities**
  Lack of data quality and enterprise data governance are proving to be the top hurdles in harnessing value from the digital data deluge. Easy and transparent access to high-quality enterprise data assets is critical to enable digital and AI/ML use cases which are worth millions (and many a times billions) of dollars. Data governance is one of the top differentiators between firms that have achieved the expected value from data and firms that have not.

  While several organizations have attempted to achieve data governance maturity, most are still struggling for a multitude of reasons, including incomplete understanding of digital data domains, inefficient or missing enterprise data architecture, poor metadata management and lack of robust data quality management processes.

- **Real-time and on-demand availability of insights whenever and wherever required**
  The enterprise data ecosystem should be able to provide 'real-time' or 'on-demand' access to insights and recommendations to make the best possible offers to the customer while they are shopping, deliver real-time alerts regarding a potential fraudulent financial transaction, or warn a machine operator about potential maintenance issues in his machine.

The insights dissemination mechanism of the existing data ecosystems is not designed to deliver such insights instantaneously or at the most appropriate times. They are designed to deliver reports and insights to business executives at a fixed frequency and at a fixed time, and not necessarily to auto-deliver them at the 'right time' and 'right place' where action is being taken.

Digital data architecture—Agility, *and not maturity,* is the new mantra for enterprise data management in the digital age

Most enterprises yearn to achieve data management maturity and keep making investments towards this end objective. The fundamental flaw in that approach is the underlying assumption that the target state (high maturity level) is static. The reality of the VUCA world of digital transformation, and hence the digital data generated by it, is diametrically opposite to that assumption.

In the uncertain and complex world of digital data, *agility (and not maturity) is a more effective fundamental design principle* to achieve the promised potential of digital transformation. As the digital wave progresses, there are several more complex data scenarios to be uncovered, even while those we already know of are being handled. Hence, the digital data architecture of enterprises has to have the capability to handle all the varied scenarios of today, but also the agility to quickly adapt to the ever-dynamic digital data landscape.

So, what are the key agile design principles enterprises should consider for digital data architecture?

1. **Data stacks don't need to be monolithic; they need to be aligned to data use cases.**
   Different stacks (traditional RDBMS, open-source big data or cloud-native) can co-exist and complement each other. The key is to identify the use cases for which different stacks are best suited.

Managing large enterprise data coming in from ERPs, CRMs and other operational systems, which is largely structured, relational and predictable, is best done by on-prem data systems leveraging well-tested data warehousing technologies. However, managing dynamic and complex digital data and leveraging artificial intelligence to derive insights from it requires modern stacks which are flexible, elastic and high-speed.

Hence, the answer to the complex question of digital data architecture lies in the complementarity of different data technology stacks in a hybrid, fit-for-purpose ecosystem.

2. **Agile data ingestion and processing capability with rich interface using external data ecosystem**

Event-streaming data is what really epitomizes digital data profiles—it is fast, complex, high-volume. Event-streaming data is far greater and faster than the standard, transaction (ERP-generated) data. In addition, the data formats are diverse. The digital data architecture should be designed with the ability to ingest such data from various sources—structured/unstructured, batch/streaming, relational/non-relational.

Not only that, the system should provision for the ability to handle data pipelines for batch, mini-batch or real-time stream processing, enabling instant availability of relevant data for a wide range of business purposes.

The agility of data ingestion and processing capability becomes a requirement of extremely high value while exploring and onboarding newly emerging data sources, making the data assets richer and AI/ML applications more effective.

3. **Data storage should be elastic and expand cost-effectively as data volumes rapidly increase**

Data is one the most important of enterprise assets, but if we don't have a cost-effective infrastructure to store and manage it, it can very quickly become a liability, resulting in either leakage of data due to lack of storage capacity or in heavy expenses and costs to store it.

An effective digital data architecture should not only be flexible, with layered architecture to store raw data, process and analytical data as it grows, but also cost-effective to ensure optimal utilization of resources. The key lies in an effective data storage framework that enables triaging of data assets into hot, warm or cold categories and defining appropriate data storage strategies, leveraging the best of cloud and on-premise storage systems.

4. **Modern master data management**

   Master data is the authoritative record of everything vital to an enterprise, including information on users, customers, products, accounts, partners, locations and much more. It is the core discipline of the entire data ecosystem. In the past, MDM required a centralized approach. It worked very well in a stable, not-so-dynamic ecosystem. However, in the digital era, that centralization and rigid schema have made changes and additions difficult and time-consuming, which limits the enterprise's ability to harness value and create dynamic 360-degree views.

   Modern MDM requires the capability to work across silos, absorb new sources of information, find hidden relationships, quickly generate insights and deliver results in real-time at scale. It should be agile enough to answer any questions that arise, not just those anticipated in advance. At the core of the modern MDM system should lie the ability to understand, identify, and manage entity networks and master *connect data.*

5. **Enable AI/ML and analytics workbench**

   The true value of digital data lies in its ability to fuel artificial intelligence and analytics algorithms and help generate insights critical for business decision-making and real-time recommendations for engaging customers, mitigating risk and enabling highly efficient operations.

The intelligence needs of businesses are very dynamic and, in most cases, cannot be solved by a standard analytics toolset. The digital data architecture should enable curated data for a diverse array of AI, ML, analytics and intelligence toolsets in form of a workbench that can truly democratize the ability to derive and use data insights across different teams in the enterprise, whichever way they want it.

An agile AI/ML and analytics workbench also provides the enterprise flexibility to onboard and leverage new, innovative AI/ML capabilities in the open-source world, hence always bringing the best-of-breed to deliver value.

6. **API-driven, real-time, on-demand data and insight dissemination**

'Real-time' and 'on-demand' are becoming synonymous with the word 'digital'. As the world of data and insights evolved into digital and artificial intelligence, the most fundamental shift was in terms of real-time generation of data and expectation of real-time availability of insights. Today, consumers require instant recommendations, businesses require instant insights, operators require instant alerts . . . and the list goes on.

Modern digital data architecture must have as one of its core design principles, the question: how do we disseminate insights to the point of action, when users want it and where users want it? A multi-modal real-time insights distribution approach leveraging Representational State Transfer (REST) APIs is critical to enable this capability, allowing end-user systems to access insights in real-time and on-demand.

7. **Robust data governance and quality management**

The growth of enterprise data makes its governance extremely important, and it cannot remain a nice-to-have topic anymore. It

Leveraging the most from Digital Data - Key design principles

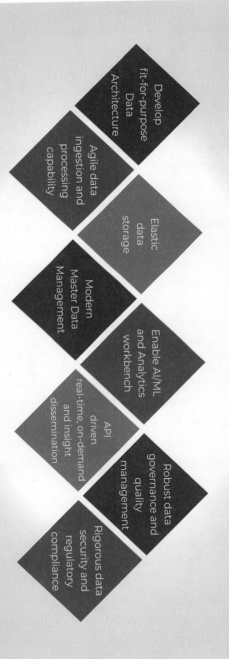

is important to have core data governance processes and policies with specific instrumentation for improving data quality across data domains and to have enabling enterprise data transparency through automated data cataloguing.

Leveraging AI/ML approaches can help automate the data quality approaches and help uncover hidden data quality issues.

8. **Well-defined and rigorously managed data security and regulatory compliance**

As the digital data architecture leverages multi-location (cloud, on-prem) and multi-stack approaches, a well-defined and rigorously implemented data security strategy is necessary. Enterprises need to implement security processes and protocols to manage data security to maintain privacy and security of critical data, network security on cloud, and connectivity to on-prem system, IAM user-group-level policies defined with limited access based on work roles and finally AI-enabled proactive monitoring of the data ecosystem.

In conclusion, the digital data deluge is unprecedented and very different from the other data challenges that enterprises have handled so far. An innovative and agile approach is needed to realize the opportunities presented by this phenomenon, while also effectively managing the risks it presents. An agile, adaptable and future-ready digital data architecture is a critical capability for enterprises to be able to ride the digital wave. As enterprises embark on or progress in their journey to achieve agile digital data architecture, they need to analyse the value and capabilities of their current data ecosystem and take iterative steps to complement it with the building blocks of digital data architecture.

The digital data architecture is the underlying foundation on which enterprises will need to build their digital journey to achieve transformational business impact and sustainable competitive advantage.

Summary

- Even enterprises that believed they had achieved data management maturity are overwhelmed by the massive amounts of data generated today. The variety, volume, and velocity of data is exploding creating an unprecedented digital data deluge.
- Current enterprise data ecosystem is facing multiple pressure points:
  - Inability to consume, process and integrate high-speed, complex digital data,
  - Limitation in curating and differentiating 'signal' from 'noise',
  - The 'golden record' is no more sufficient, we need a holistic 360-degree view,
  - Growing sophistication of cyber-attacks and data theft have redefined data security demands,
  - Poor data governance and quality,
  - Real-time and on-demand insights.

- Agility, *and not maturity*, is the new mantra for enterprise data management. This is recognizing that reality of the VUCA world of digital transformation that there is nothing like an 'end state'.
  - **Agile design principles for enterprises:** Data stacks don't need to be monolithic; they need to be aligned to data use cases,
  - Agile data ingestion and processing capability with rich interface using external data ecosystem,
  - Data storage should be elastic and expanded cost-effectively,
  - Modern master data management requires the ability to work across silos, absorb new sources of information, find

hidden relationships, quickly generate insights and deliver results in real-time at scale,

o   Enabling of AI/ML and analytics workbench,

o   API-driven, real-time, on-demand data and insight dissemination,

o   Robust data governance and quality management,

o   Well-defined and rigorously managed data security and regulatory compliance.

8

Blockchain—Going Beyond the Hype to Sustainable Value Creation

I was taught that the way of progress was neither swift nor easy

Marie Curie, Polish-French Chemist and Physicist,
Nobel Prize winner in Physics and Chemistry

Blockchain is one of the most important disruptive technologies and promises to be a key building block of the digital economy. There has been massive hype and irrational exuberance about this technology over the past two or three years, largely driven by the Bitcoin frenzy. That hype is now subsiding, which is perhaps the best thing that could have happened for blockchain, as we can now shift its focus from 'get-rich schemes' to more sustainable value creation.

In this chapter, I will deal with the following aspects of blockchain:

- The hype around blockchain is dissipating
- Opportunities with blockchain technology, why it is not curtains yet
- Challenges in implementation
- 'Two-speed' strategy for blockchain implementation.

The hype around blockchain is dissipating

Not too long back, a survey reported that advertisers believed 'blockchain' was the most overrated term of 2018. This is hardly a surprise, as many companies from fields completely unrelated to cryptocurrency claimed to have used or tested blockchain technology the year before with little to show for it.

The results of the survey seem to confirm that advertisers were aware of how companies abused the term 'blockchain' just to get free media hype. It was also reported that management consulting firm McKinsey had determined that among the 100+ supposed use cases for blockchain, the vast majority of pilots and proofs of concept were still stuck in 'pioneering mode' or were being shut down.[9]

Further, blockchain has dropped to the bottom of Gartner Inc.'s annual list of the most disruptive data and analytics capabilities for enterprise IT, having been replaced by tools that leverage artificial intelligence and machine learning.

Is this the end of blockchain? There is certainly a reality check for blockchain, but by no means is it curtains for this technology. However, we need to recognize that blockchain technology is still in a pioneering phase and it will be several years before it becomes dominant.

Opportunities with blockchain technology; why it is not curtains yet

The distributed ledger technology underpinning blockchain facilitates both record-keeping and transactions. Its fundamental value lies in enhancing trust. This it does by increasing transparency and veracity. Higher trust helps reduce multiple layers and processes for control, therefore dramatically improving speed and efficiency.

Improving trust in record-keeping and transactions is of relevance in a variety of industries and functional areas. Two areas where I see the most intensive application of blockchain technologies in the coming two or three years are financial services and e-governance.

- **Financial services:** Blockchain has wide applications in banks, especially on the payments side. Use cases range from trade finance, derivatives netting and processing of remittances. I see a number of banks now experimenting with blockchain POCs. This is similar to the nature of activity we were seeing with AI and machine learning a couple of years back. I expect some of these blockchain use cases in banks to go mainstream in the coming two or three years.
- **E-governance:** Digitization is an important objective for many governments, including in India, and blockchain has a very important role to play in this by creating more transparent and accessible public records. For example, blockchain could play a key role in land records and in most areas where certificates need to be issued.

In addition to financial services and e-governance, healthcare and supply chain are two other industries seeing significant experimentation around blockchain technology's distributed ledger applications.

The blocks to blockchain implementation

There is a big gap today between the opportunities from blockchain and their realization. A recent survey showed that out of 61 per cent of organizations that are already researching blockchain, only 28 per cent have chosen a blockchain provider. According to the survey, the majority of decision makers are still investigating the technology and comparing vendors, and have not yet defined their stance on blockchain technology.[10]

A TD Bank survey revealed that 90 per cent of treasury and finance professionals think that blockchain and distributed ledger technology (DLT) will positively affect the payments industry. However, in the survey, only 14 per cent of the respondents said their organizations had training strategies for blockchain.[11]

A survey by the Global Blockchain Business Council revealed that 63 per cent of respondents believe that senior business executives have a poor understanding of blockchain technology; 30 per cent consider their knowledge of the emerging technology as 'average'; while the remaining 7 per cent described senior executive understanding of blockchain as 'good'.[12]

The above examples highlight that blockchain is a technology still under development and that there are a number of challenges in its implementation. I believe the following six key challenges need to be addressed to derive sustainable value from blockchain implementation:

1. **Integration with existing technology:** Many of the industries where blockchain technologies are being applied are traditional industries with legacy IT infrastructure. This implies investment in integration efforts that can be time consuming and expensive.

2. **Change management:** Understanding of blockchain technologies among senior executives is often low; therefore, sustained evangelization and awareness building is required within organizations.

3. **Digitization of physical records:** Underlying records in many cases are still in physical form (e.g. land records in India) and need to be digitized for blockchain technologies to be applied.

4. **Getting blockchain technology to scale:** The blockchain infrastructure is not ready for mass adoption. It requires significant investments, and thus the costs of blockchain adoption are not competitive in some use cases compared with other technology options. This has been particularly true in the payments industry, where despite proven use cases of blockchain, they have not been commercialized at scale because of the costs, especially when compared with the value some of the fintechs have been able to bring.

Blockchain is a disruptive technology - Use this pioneering infrastructure capability to innovate

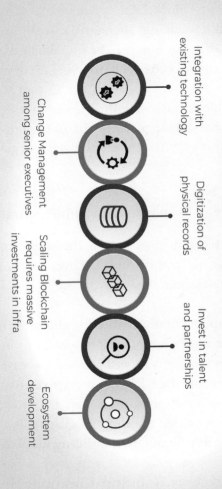

Key challenges to be addressed

Integration with existing technology

Change Management among senior executives

Digitization of physical records

Scaling Blockchain requires massive investments in infra

Invest in talent and partnerships

Ecosystem development

5.   **Talent:** There is a shortage of professionals trained in blockchain technologies, therefore, investment is required in training and in building partnerships.
6.   **Ecosystem development:** The vendor and partner ecosystem required to support blockchain technologies and their applications are still developing, therefore, it requires a reality check on use cases that can not only be implemented but also supported, and also careful consideration in choice of partners.

The challenges to blockchain described above are significant, but it is worthwhile to solve them, given the size of the prize. While the future of blockchain is still hazy, there is a way out to sensible implementation!

The 'two-speed' strategy for blockchain implementation

Given that blockchain technology is still in the early stages, and given the challenges that we have discussed above, I recommend a two-speed strategy for blockchain implementation.

*   **Speed 1: Use case implementation**—Blockchain sometimes feels like a technology searching for problems to solve! It is important to anchor blockchain programs in well-defined use cases where the business pain point and the KPI to be impacted are very clear. That will ensure engagement of business users and provide focus on end-to-end implementation to deliver tangible results.
*   **Speed 2: Progressive development of building blocks**—While use cases are the right way to focus and start a blockchain programme, they alone are not sufficient. Underlying blockchain technology infrastructure and other key building blocks (e.g. digitization of physical records) have to be developed for sustainable and scalable impact.

    Speed 2 of building blocks should run in parallel with speed 1 of use cases, with every sprint of use case implementation further helping to progressively develop the building blocks to the next level of maturity.

Blockchain is a nascent technology but one with tremendous potential, given its promise to enhance trust in both record-keeping and transactions. Blockchain got hyped well before its time because of the meteoric rise of Bitcoins. Dissipation of the hype around Bitcoins is a good thing, bringing the focus back to the underlying technology. Many challenges remain, but focused and balanced implementation approaches can help unlock the potential of this powerful technology.

Summary

- Bitcoin created a sudden hype around blockchain technology, which has now faded to an extent.
- However, the dissipation of hype is a good thing for blockchain as focus can now shift to its fundamental advantages and applications.
- The distributed ledger system underpinning blockchain brings transparency and thus improves trust. This has the opportunity to positively disrupt value chains and can find application in areas like financial services, e-governance, healthcare and supply chain.
- Blockchain technology is still in a pioneering phase, and it will take time and sustained investments for it to reach critical mass.

9

Cloud—an Enabler for Digital Transformation

The cloud has become the next-generation supercomputer, and the smartphone has provided the revolution to spur its use

Jerry Yang, Founder of Yahoo!

Most CIOs have had the cloud as one of their top priorities for several years now. Indeed, some CIOs have succeeded in leveraging the cloud as a way to change the relationship between IT and the overall business. They have enabled IT to be more flexible, efficient and adaptive to changing business dynamics than ever before. However, it is also becoming clear that to characterize the cloud as not more than an infrastructure capability to reduce costs and improve resource utilization is to sell it short. We believe that organizations should have a much more strategic view of cloud.

How can the modern cloud accelerate end-to-end digital transformation?

As part of their digital transformation journey, organizations are reimagining customer experiences, innovation, productivity and

216

data strategy (and this list is incomplete). In fact, the digital natives have demonstrated that cloud is integral to execution along all these dimensions, and can become a powerful catalyst for not just revenue growth but also for driving competitive advantage through digital transformation.

The track record of cloud usage outside of the digital natives has been less than stellar: It is estimated 32 per cent of organizations' cloud computing budget was deemed to have gone to waste in 2021.[13]

What can we learn from how the digital natives leveraged the cloud to drive competitive advantage?

We start by looking at two specific areas where the cloud can improve business performance (this is not a complete list, but two of the most high-impact areas):

- **Reimagined customer experiences:** How can the cloud enable not just faster execution of customer engagement strategies, but also help reimagine them?
- **Reduced time to market:** How can the cloud accelerate the pace of innovation to help an organization stay ahead of competition?

In addition, looking internally the cloud infrastructure is critical in driving better value from two areas where organizations have significant investments:

- **Data:** Streamlining the process for getting value from data assets
- **AI and machine learning:** Scaling AI to enable integration with operating processes

Technology for technology's sake has been the bane of organizations—and it remains one of the biggest reasons why cloud could end up not delivering on its promise. More than the cloud technology itself, driving cloud adoption in a more holistic manner is what organizations have to orient themselves towards.

We will look at some of the key factors that organizations need to keep in mind on their cloud journey.

Cloud as accelerator for business transformation

Reimagined customer experiences

Digital experience is clearly table stakes across industries. Consumers expect a complete digital self-service experience with access to their information, the facility to conduct transactions anytime, anywhere, from any device. In response, firms are having to rethink their entire customer workflows from ground up in an effort to get to an ideal digital state—one that ranges across email, mobile, website, push notifications, voice and more. In doing so, there is an opportunity to leverage cloud as a key enabler:

- *Bridging the legacy technology barrier*: Putting together a seamless digital user experience on the legacy technology backbone is not just daunting, in many cases it is plainly impossible. The cloud has provided a way for firms to put together a digital experience without having to completely upgrade their aging infrastructure. This is especially true for firms with age-old installations of core systems. Building a digital stack on that infrastructure is clearly a non-starter. The cloud provides a way to initiate a digital user experience even as the legacy technology modernization is playing the catch-up game.

- *Integration of next-generation technologies*: Delivering a seamless digital experience to customers requires integration of multiple next-generation technologies, from digital assistants (e.g. chatbots) to image recognition (e.g. digital verification). Building these technologies and integrating them into the customer workflows within the existing technology infrastructure using the in-house talent is often impossible. On the other hand, all the major cloud providers offer pre-packaged solutions, many of them with AI-cognitive technologies trained over the years to a high degree of accuracy. For instance, UPS leveraged Microsoft's cloud-based Azure bot service to deploy a chatbot in its mobile app, which enables customers to engage in text-based and voice-based conversations to get the information they need about shipments, rates and UPS locations.[14]

Reduced time to market

One common theme that runs across the digital natives which are upending markets across industries—most noticeably in retail, banking and financial services—is that they are lean, agile and 'fail fast' to reduce time to market. One consistent enabling factor at the centre of their success is their partnering with providers of point solutions. For instance, e-commerce retailers are opting to partner with cloud-native solution providers like Shopify, Stripe, Square and others to handle needs like payments, online store, fraud protection and so on. These services are cloud-native and can be consumed on a completely variable structure. And, more importantly, it gives enterprises the ability to focus on their customers, and above all, reduces the time to market new products and services.

Traditional firms would do well to take a leaf out of the e-commerce playbook and look to the cloud to reduce their time to market—both when it comes to expanding their products and services to include digital channels as well as in designing and launching digital-first services. Here are some tips from their playbook:

- *Partnering for non-core activities* and focusing on the core product development process reduces the time and cost to market. The traditional methods of discovery of product features, price points, etc., with focus groups have always been slow, expensive and often end up being hit-or-miss. Firms are increasingly transitioning this process to digital experiments as a proxy for understanding the product market fit. A leading telecom service provider adopted such a strategy to discover the market-price fit for wearable accessories as a medical assistant device for senior citizens. They ran a series of A/B experiments by partnering with a cloud-based provider, which helped them design and execute the experiments by integrating with the telecom provider's e-commerce portal. A process that would normally take several months was brought down to a few weeks before the service was launched at the national level.

- *Build versus buy versus subscribe* is an important choice that determines an enterprise's ability to onboard and offer services rapidly and seamlessly and, where possible, subscription-based solutions offered by best-in-class providers can dramatically cut the time to market. Medical providers have been on the tele-health journey for several years now. Delivering quality care through a digital channel requires integration of multiple technologies: high-fidelity video interactions in a secure manner and remote device management to measure and track medical data, to name a few. These services by themselves require sophisticated technology, not to mention putting them together to create a seamless experience for both doctor and patient. Needless to say, most medical providers have opted for cloud-based solutions to take these services to market.

- *Responding to market signals with speed*: The need and urgency for reliable digital solutions have never been as compelling as in the post-Covid world, which saw a sharp increase in digital engagement in a matter of a few weeks. A recent statistic: while the average share of customer interactions that are digital grew from 20 per cent (June 2017) to 36 per cent (December 2019), this jumped from 36 per cent (December 2019) to 72 per cent (2022), accelerated by the Covid-19 pandemic.[15] And this is not a temporary spike either—this is likely to be the 'new normal'. Companies across industries have struggled to scale their infrastructure to respond to this rapid switch to digital channels—except the ones that were already on a cloud infrastructure. If nothing else, this has led to an acceleration of cloud adoption.

It is obvious that the cloud is not just enabling scale and faster execution of existing processes, but perhaps, more importantly, also enabling new business models. Most firms have just begun to scratch the surface of the scale, speed and innovation potential that cloud has to offer in driving digital transformation.

Cloud as an enabler for organizational investments

Two key organizational assets that have always been critical to digital transformation are data and AI. And yet, most organizations have not done well in harnessing these two capabilities in a meaningful way. There are multiple reasons why they have not: organizational silos, legacy technology, lack of talent (I have dwelled on these challenges in the earlier chapters on AI and data). Many of these challenges are formidable and there is no doubt that organizations need to work hard at solving them. We believe that cloud technologies can accelerate the process for better enabling data and AI assets to power digital transformation initiatives.

Data

If there is one area where legacy technology infrastructure has created a liability, it is in enterprise data. Over the years, a patchwork of disparate applications has resulted in a smorgasbord of data—with duplications, inconsistent definitions and inadequate attention to data quality. Digital initiatives have accelerated this trend, with the explosion in unstructured data, distributed data creation and processing, to name a few. All of these have together created significant challenges for companies in extracting real value from data. While cloud cannot be the magic wand that solves all data issues, there certainly exists the potential to leverage cloud-native technologies as part of the cloud migration process to solve some of these challenges.

- **Data quality:** Several technology vendors in data integration (e.g. Talend, Informatica) offer the ability to deploy rule-based and AI/ML-based data profiling and quality methodologies that must be applied to data at the point of ingestion from the source systems. This is especially useful in cataloguing newer data sources, which tend to be unstructured (e.g. call transcripts) and high volumes of noisy data (e.g. clickstream data).

- **Data integration:** Interfaces from legacy systems to the cloud must be developed with a clear objective to integrate data from different sources based on well-established ontologies. This is easier said than done—especially when there is an accumulation of decades of historical data. This is why most firms are opting to define data integration on a forward-looking basis, without getting bogged down by historical data integration issues.

- **Cloud data governance:** Migration to the cloud brings the opportunity to redefine cloud governance—including compliance and regulatory oversight. There is a slew of firms that offer technology-based governance solutions such as data cataloguing (e.g. Alation) and metadata management (e.g. Collibra) to drive data governance at the time of data ingestion.

Scaling enterprise AI

Enterprises have—and continue to—focus on one-off AI solutions in different parts of the organization. However, many of these models struggle to scale beyond the one-off POC, often because they are trained on limited datasets. It is not possible to scale these models out. But the cloud has the potential to change all that:

- **AI model training and validation:** With data on the cloud, it becomes much more efficient and effective to train and operationalize models in production environments. The availability of cloud compute and storage is essential for training/validating the models with ever-expanding data sources.
- **AI model features store:** Creating a centralized cloud-native features store helps data science teams across the enterprise to reuse existing features. Over time, this will promote reuse.
- **AI model training at scale:** AI algorithms are usually data and compute intensive. The elastic nature of cloud can be very useful in scaling up/down of compute capacity to handle the training and validation of models in a variable cost structure.
- **AI best practices:** Most cloud AI platforms include open source algorithms that have been curated over the years. Access to a cloud AI platform enables access to these best practices.
- **AI integration with operational systems:** Most cloud AI platforms support API-based integration with most of the leading enterprise transaction systems (e.g. ERPs) and decision support systems (e.g. workflow management systems). This helps reduce the time to operationalize model recommendations for driving decision-making.

That cloud is a key component of digital transformation is no longer a question. As organizations work on truly leveraging the potential of cloud beyond infrastructure and as a key enabler of transformation, some of the key success mantras to keep in mind are:

1. **Treat cloud as more than an IT initiative—it is a joint effort with business:** For the power of cloud to be fully brought to bear, joint ownership between business and IT will help identify and prioritize programmes that directly impact business outcomes.
2. **Redesign the governance processes:** In a cloud-first world, firms will have to redefine the governance processes to handle the data security, regulatory and compliance requirements without losing

out on the flexibility and agility of a cloud infrastructure. This requires a complete redesign of the legacy governing processes to create a cloud-first data, security and infrastructure governance organization.

3. **Embrace the extended cloud technology ecosystem:** A cloud-based infrastructure opens up access to best-in-class applications at every level in the technology stack through the cloud marketplaces. Organizations must take a relook at their 'build versus buy' strategies for applications.

4. **Do not get bogged down by the 'myth of a single source of truth':** Enterprises continue to pour millions into chasing the 'golden record' as part of cloud migration efforts, which often ends up as an empty promise. It is often better to focus on forward-looking data quality and harmonization at the point of data ingestion, and let the quality of data improve over time.

5. **It is all about the people:** Over the years, firms have built large IT teams around legacy technologies. The talent and organizational model within IT and data organizations needs to be evaluated on an ongoing basis.

6. **From project to platform and program mindset:** Once the leadership team recognizes the strategic importance of cloud, it is important to orient all stakeholders towards programs and platforms rather than projects. Projects are typically one-time investments for point problems and are driven by short-term priorities. Cloud platforms, in particular, require stable, ongoing focus and sponsorship with consistent ownership over a multi-year period.

Over the last twenty-five years, IT organizations have gone through several technology hype cycles—many of them were just that. If there were any lingering doubts about cloud as just another technology fad, the pivotal role of cloud in enabling the hyper-acceleration of digital enablement across companies triggered by the Covid-19 pandemic have laid these doubts to rest. It is now clear that cloud

Cloud is the core enabler for Digital transformation

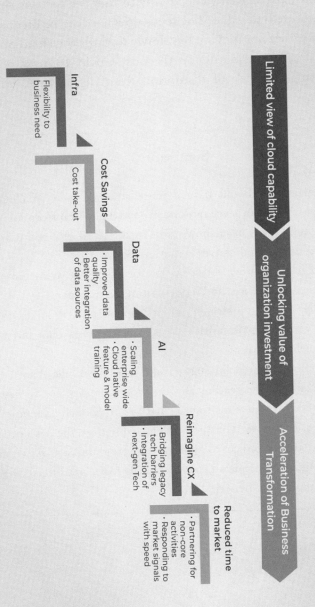

Limited view of cloud capability

Unlocking value of organization investment

Acceleration of Business Transformation

Infra
Flexibility to business need

Cost Savings
Cost take-out

Data
· Improved data quality
· Better integration of data sources

AI
· Scaling enterprise wide
· Cloud native feature & model training

Reimagine CX
· Bridging legacy tech barriers
· Integration of next-gen Tech

Reduced time to market
· Partnering for non-core activities
· Responding to market signals with speed

represents business-driven value, and with that the focus is shifting to how to capture that value. The focus now needs to be on ensuring that companies are not moving too slowly towards the cloud on their digital transformation journey in the post-Covid-19 'next normal' phase, running the risk of disruption from digital-first, nimbler competition.

Summary

- Organizations should have a more strategic view of cloud. Modern cloud can accelerate end-to-end digital transformation, as digital natives have shown, but track record of cloud usage among non-digital natives is not impressive.
- Cloud can improve business performance by reimagining customer experiences and reducing time to market.
- Equally, looking internally, cloud can be pivotal in driving better value from two critical areas for enterprises: data and AI and machine learning.
- Technology for technology's sake has been the bane of organizations, the reason why the cloud appears not to have delivered. To realize the transformative ability of cloud requires a joint effort between business and IT. Moreover, there is a need to move from a project to platform and programme mindset, as cloud initiatives require a stable, ongoing focus and sponsorship over a multi-year period.

SECTION 4

LEVERAGING THE GLOBAL ADVANTAGE

Introduction: Leveraging the Global Advantage

In section 1, we looked at VUCA, the new rules of engagement for businesses and why digital transformation matters for enterprises. As enterprises across industries embark on digital transformation, they must solve for specific challenges in their industries, as we have elaborated on in section 2, and harness the key technologies that are the building blocks of the digital stack, as outlined in section 3.

In this section, I want to propose that every enterprise in the digital age has to be a global enterprise. Introducing my eight new rules of management in chapter 1 of section 1, I had mentioned that nobody can do it alone in the VUCA world. The digital age is too complex and there are too many forces at work. It is very difficult to operate and succeed in a silo. Therefore, my rule seven was, 'Build an open organization and a web of partnerships'. One of the most important aspects of this is to have a global mindset and capitalize on global opportunities, both from the market demand and supply chain perspective.

The IT services industry is an important enabler helping enterprises leverage global advantage in delivery. This industry, which has a strong centre of gravity in India, eastern Europe and many other emerging economies allows enterprises across the world to benefit from the cost, talent and scale advantages that many emerging economies offer.

This global IT services footprint includes both service companies and global enterprises who have established their dedicated technology and operations centres in emerging economies. In this section, I have used the term Global Delivery Centre or GDC to cover both types of entities (service companies and 'in-house' centres). I have used the same term consciously for both types of entities, despite the obvious differences between the two. While the ownership structure of these entities is different and there is often a 'build versus buy' trade-off to be made between these choices, my thesis is that the operating model and mindset have to be the same for both types of companies—one of deep partnership and integration as a global enterprise.

GDCs are absolutely pivotal for enterprises to succeed in the digital age. Technology is the core foundation of digital, and GDCs are the centre of gravity for this technology execution. They provide not just the cost but also the innovation and velocity advantage necessary in this VUCA world. While GDCs have existed for many years, to meet the new expectations from technology in the digital age, the GDC's proposition and operating model have to change significantly. Historically, GDCs have been seen as cost and execution centres; this needs to change, and they have to become revenue and innovation centres. This is a fascinating opportunity. Enterprises that are able to make this transformation and leverage global delivery effectively will stand to gain a real advantage in the digital age.

I have been a participant and a leader in this industry, helping shape the evolution of the GDC over the past twenty years almost. I led McKinsey's Knowledge Centre in India from 2002 to 2010 and that was not just an opportunity to build a cutting-edge centre that was continuously defining what could be done from a GDC, but it also became a showpiece for us at McKinsey to demonstrate GDC best practices to our clients looking to set up GDCs themselves. Subsequently, I led the global delivery network for Fidelity's international business for six years. Along the way, I led the Global Inhouse Centres forum for NASSCOM (the industry body in India for IT and BPO companies) for a number of years, where I helped define the value addition framework and maturity roadmap for GDCs.

It has been a fascinating journey for me to see—and shape—how GDCs have grown from being support centres to becoming a source of competitive advantage for global enterprises. This opportunity to leverage the global advantage—the why, what and how of it—is the focus of this section.

Chapter 1: Why Enterprises Need a Global Delivery Model in the Digital Age

Here, I establish that the global delivery model is crucial for success in the digital age. Enterprises are facing the dual challenge of protecting their existing revenue streams while investing for future growth. The global delivery model is essential for reducing costs while simultaneously increasing the velocity of transformation/innovation as well as addressing the skill gaps in building world-class capabilities.

Chapter 2: Global Delivery Centres nearing Tipping Point, and Ready to Step Up

I share my observations that many GDCs are reaching tipping point and are ready to step up their role. Many GDCs are uniquely positioned to be a strategic asset for enterprises by virtue of their scale and co-location of capabilities. Additionally, the GDCs' leadership maturity can further accelerate value realization for enterprises.

Chapter 3: Global Delivery Centres Can Be Revenue and Innovation Centres

In this chapter, I highlight how best-in-class GDCs are delivering substantial value added benefits by being both innovation and revenue centres. On the one hand, they are becoming centres for change/continuous improvement for enterprises, and on the other, they are moving up the value chain in existing services. 'Cost+talent+domain expertise' is the success recipe for GDCs in the digital age. I have detailed six principles that have worked well in moving GDCs up the value chain, giving examples from my own experience in the industry.

Chapter 4: Maximizing Global Delivery Centre Potential through Changes in Organizational Approach

In this chapter, I make the observation that despite the opportunities on the horizon, many GDCs have not realized their full potential. I share my perspectives on the factors that enterprises must rethink to maximize value from their GDCs. These include structural and mindset changes with respect to the operating model, enhancing CXO-level engagement and bringing in entrepreneurial leadership at the GDC.

Chapter 5: Evolution of Global Delivery Centres and the New Ask of GDC Leaders

The call to action for GDCs is to move from execution to leadership. This is the need of the hour so that GDCs and the global enterprises can realize their opportunities in full. To make this move happen, the critical need is to develop a new generation of leaders who will be torchbearers at the GDCs on their journey from execution to leadership. Four critical shifts that are required from GDC leaders to make this happen have been discussed in detail in this chapter.

Finally, the chapter provides guidance as to how GDC managers can build a global mindset and become successful leaders.

Chapter 6: How to build a World-class Knowledge Centre

In this chapter, I lay out my perspectives on building a world-class knowledge centre. Proprietary knowledge is a key requirement in the digital age for an enterprise's long-term sustainable competitive advantage. A knowledge centre can become a source of innovation, transforming the core proposition and service model for large global firms. I describe my perspective of the journey and discuss the key building blocks necessary for a knowledge centre, based on my experiences in leading McKinsey's Knowledge Centre.

This case study provides a good example, not just for research or analytics type of capabilities, but for many other high-end, expertise-oriented capabilities that GDCs can build. I strongly believe that my learnings from building the McKinsey Knowledge Centre are still very relevant and provide a great framework for where GDCs need to now go in the digital age.

1

Why Enterprises Need a Global Delivery Model in the Digital Age

Growth can only be achieved through effective cooperation between nations. The world is a global village and global approaches to solve problems are needed

Joseph Inungu, PhD, Central Michigan University

In the digital age, as business and product cycles shrink, there is an increasing need for enterprises to develop long-term, sustainable competitive advantage. While enterprises across the globe are investing in innovation, execution requires new ways of working and collaboration. Enterprises today have **three key imperatives to win in the digital age:**

- **Address the dual challenge of protecting existing revenue and investing for future growth:** As businesses and product cycles get shorter, enterprises must defend their existing revenue streams and constantly self-fund new strategic initiatives for future growth. According to research by S&P, of twenty-five industries across the globe, almost all the industries are battling headwinds that are constraining growth and posing risks to credit quality.[1] Research by MIT Sloan on the performance of 1,200 companies in six of the most asset-heavy sectors—telecommunications, utilities, energy, materials, automotive, and industrials—revealed an equally worrying trend.[2] Traditional enterprises are facing 'industry compression', which results in a prolonged decline of both operating profits and revenues. So, they must invest in new initiatives and adjacencies so that new revenue streams garner a higher share in the mix over time. A good example of this is in telecommunications, where average revenue per user (ARPU) from voice has declined by ~19 per cent globally during 2013–15[3] and has been declining since. So, it is natural that telecoms have invested heavily in building 4G/5G infrastructure so they can increase revenues from new solutions and services.

- **Drive transformation to be ready for the cloud-first world** and not get caught in incremental and catch-up moves. This is the key to achieving hockey-stick performance. We are observing a trend of polarization and a widening gap between the performance of high-growth companies and that of the rest across industries. According to McKinsey, the gap between the top 10 per cent of the best-performing companies by economic profit and bottom 10 per cent of the worst-performing companies across sectors is increasing.[4] That gap is much wider and the polarization greater than what we witnessed in the 2008 crisis. Unless the leaders think about 'what could be' and not just focus on improving 'what is', the chances of breakthrough performance are bleak.

- **Thrive against new-age competitors** that are setting growth benchmarks across industries. According to Innosight research, in 1965, the average tenure of companies in the S&P 500 was thirty-three years. By 1990, it was twenty years. This is forecast to shrink to fourteen years by 2026. About 50 per cent of the current S&P 500 constituents are likely to be replaced over the next ten years.[5] As digital maturity increases in the industry with mainstream adoption of digital among customers, there is a higher likelihood of laggard incumbents dropping off the league tables. This has been observed in industries like traditional media, where digital agencies have outperformed them, and in retail, where e-commerce accounts for a high market share today.

In order to address these three imperatives, **enterprises must do the following to solve their key challenges**:

a. Reduce existing costs to self-fund new strategic initiatives
b. Increase the velocity of transformation and innovation
c. Address the skill-gap in building world-class capabilities with relevant domain and technology skills

a. **Reducing existing costs to self-fund new strategic initiatives**
    Long-term profitable growth requires a prudent approach towards tackling the cost structure. Enterprises are looking for ways to reduce business-as-usual costs while increasing the share of change-related costs in an overall reducing cost base. Strategic offshoring/outsourcing that rationalizes legacy high-cost teams to build nimble and efficient teams is one way. This helps enterprises reduce their costs by ~50–60 per cent. These savings help to drive key strategic capability building initiatives so that the enterprises can become stronger and drive competitive advantage. A Deloitte study has said that 84 per cent of enterprises have moved ahead towards disruptive solutions, powered by just the cost advantage of outsourcing.[6] These organizations have conducted pilots and/or implemented disruptive solutions as a result of strong relationships with the vendor and the capabilities they bring.

b. **Increasing velocity of transformation and innovation**
    As the customer needs are evolving fast and new-age competitors are emerging as a threat, enterprises are adopting the iterative 'strategy + product' mindset to stay ahead of the curve. This

defines the new way of working wherein what and how are iteratively evolved overtime, which accelerates the core value delivered to customers while addressing their fast-evolving needs. A celebrated example in this is the Spotify model of Squads and Tribes to enable alignment of teams and cross-pollination of knowledge. This generates higher velocity of engineering for new products and features that deliver better customer outcomes. This is a key consideration for enterprises, says a Deloitte survey, where 40 per cent of the respondents consider innovation as the key contract component while they go for a global delivery model.[7]

c. **Addressing skill gaps in building world-class capabilities with relevant domain and technology skills**
One of the biggest challenges for enterprises when adopting and embedding digital capabilities lies in finding the right talent with niche skills—e.g. in data science, AI and cloud, where there is a widening gap between demand and supply. All this has to be done against a backdrop of changing customer expectations too, and different skills have to come together to satisfy these customer needs. Additionally, HR, compensation and location policies have to be put in place to attract and retain the specialized talent required to operate in the cloud.

Global delivery model is the solution that will address these vital challenges

The global delivery model, over the last two decades, has been a well-known resort of enterprises that want to build a scalable operating model with lower costs. This is so for the following reasons:

- **Cost structure:** India and a number of other lower-wage-cost countries continue to offer substantial cost advantage despite

Enterprises must consider Global Delivery to succeed in Digital age

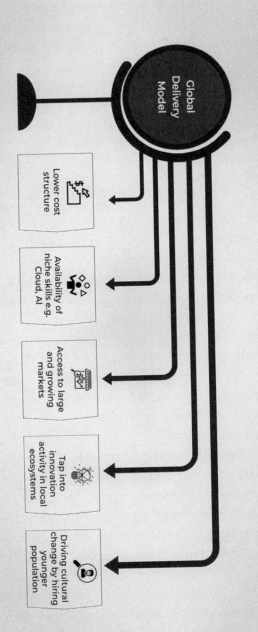

higher inflation. The US, for example, has 3–4x higher costs at entry/mid-level across functions compared to India.[8]

- **Availability of skills:** These countries also have a large and younger talent pool, which can be trained in new skills like AI and cloud. These niche skills are not in robust supply today, while demand is increasing as digital transformation is now mainstream. For example, India produces 2.8 million engineering graduates annually, a much larger number than the US, which has 0.6 million engineering graduates passing each year.[9]

- **Large and growing market:** Markets like India are among the fastest-growing and this provides enterprises the opportunity to serve the local markets. Many enterprises that have established GDCs in locations like India also open up sales operations to establish brand presence in these local markets.

- **Innovation activity in local ecosystems:** Many emerging economies are becoming hubs of innovation, given the combination of existing technology ecosystems and young talent. Many industry associations like NASSCOM (in India) are setting up incubation centres that are encouraging innovation. As enterprises are always looking for ideas that can propel their businesses ahead, tapping into such incubators and accelerators can add tremendous value.

- **A younger population makes it easier to drive cultural change:** It is much easier to drive a cultural change when the employees are younger. From my experience at McKinsey, a knowledge centre in India contributed significantly to the cultural shift in the way the research function operated and eventually became the most significant innovation hub for a global firm.

Executing the global delivery model to its full potential needs big changes in the existing mindsets and operating models. One of the most critical shifts is in setting the objective—from cost arbitrage alone to source of competitive advantage + cost arbitrage.

GDCs on journey to "world class"

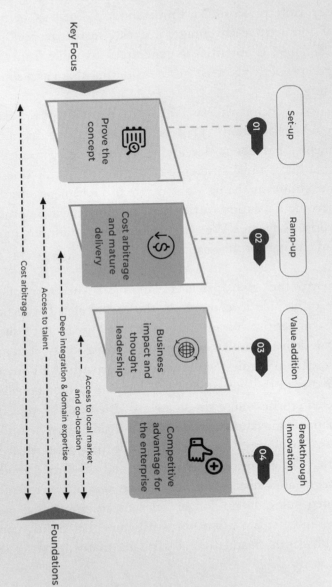

Key Focus

01	Set-up
02	Ramp-up
03	Value addition
04	Breakthrough innovation

Prove the concept

Cost arbitrage and mature delivery

Business impact and thought leadership

Competitive advantage for the enterprise

Cost arbitrage

Access to talent

Deep integration & domain expertise

Access to local market and co-location

Foundations

GDCs as a source of competitive advantage + cost arbitrage

In the introduction to this section, I mentioned the concept of GDCs. Enterprises must think about GDCs as being the source of competitive advantage, i.e., the 'secret weapon' of the enterprise. There is potential to generate 3–5x value from GDCs if leveraged properly vis-a-vis just considering them as a source of cost arbitrage.

The new benchmark for GDCs to become 'world-class' is breakthrough innovation. This is not just about incremental improvements, but about developing IP and new products and services that make a real difference to the company's top line. How do you transition from being a cost centre to a revenue centre? How do you become a solution to the most pressing business problems the enterprise is facing? We will explore these questions more in subsequent chapters of this section.

In summary, the global delivery model is necessary for an enterprise to be able to compete in the digital age. It can be the source of competitive advantage and a secret weapon of success. The global delivery model is key to reducing costs structurally while also self-funding initiatives for future growth. And one must remember that in this environment, reduction of costs alone is not sufficient; enterprises must simultaneously increase the velocity of transformation/innovation and address the skill gaps in building world-class capabilities. To make this happen, leaders must keep in mind that the traditional outsourcing and offshoring model— with its segregated team structure, onsite and offshore—and its differentiated roles, is no longer relevant in the digital world. Enterprises must create a one-team structure that tightly couples strategy with execution and must also bring a product mindset across functional teams.

Summary

Three key imperatives for enterprises to win today:

- Address the dual challenge of protecting existing revenue and investing for future growth,
- Drive transformation to be ready for a cloud-first world,
- Thrive against new-age competitors.

How to address these challenges:

- Reduce existing costs to self-fund new strategic initiatives,
- Increase velocity of transformation and innovation,
- Address skill-gap to build world-class capabilities.

Global delivery model leveraging emerging economies like India, eastern Europe and others is the solution to address these challenges:

- Continuing cost advantage
- Availability of skills
- Younger population that makes it easier to drive cultural change
- Benefit from innovation activity in local ecosystems
- Engage with and build business in a large and growing market.

2

Global Delivery Centres nearing a Tipping Point, and Ready to Step Up

You have the freedom to be yourself, your true self, here and now—and nothing can stand in your way

Richard Bach, *Jonathan Livingston Seagull*

Given that the industry has been in existence for some time in India and in a few eastern European and LatAm countries, many GDCs have reached a tipping point, when their strategic impact can be greatly enhanced for the global enterprises. Their growing maturity provides the basis by which enterprises can realize the full potential of the cost + talent offshoring proposition. There are four dimensions where this growing maturity of the GDC is especially relevant and are creating significant additional opportunities for enterprises:

1. **Domain expertise:** GDCs are going beyond functional and technical expertise and building a deep understanding of the parent company's business and the industry it operates in. This

Many GDCs have reached a tipping point and ready to add value beyond cost arbitrage

Domain expertise in addition to functional and technical expertise

Scale to drive change across the organization

GDCs emerging as strategic assets and secret weapon for enterprises success

Co-location of functions that facilitates innovation

Leadership maturity and network building

enables both higher value addition in existing roles and ability to undertake more complex, 'front-office' roles.

2. **Scale:** Some GDC centres have emerged as the largest operating sites for their parent companies, often housing a significant proportion of their total headcount. This provides enterprises the opportunity to drive change across the organization and leverage their scale to invest in innovation.

3. **Co-location of functions:** Many GDCs have become microcosms of their parent organizations, with co-location of capabilities across functions and regions. Often, a GDC is uniquely placed to offer co-location opportunities that go beyond traditional organizational structures, i.e., the only site where that co-location is possible. This helps facilitate innovation and superior delivery through collaboration.

4. **Leadership maturity and network building:** GDCs often boast a leadership that has built a deep understanding of the parent company's culture. In addition, GDCs have strengthened their delivery credibility and networks within the organization. This makes it easier for GDCs to engage in strategic discussions and get senior sponsorship.

These four factors, coupled with the global enterprises' increasing confidence in their GDCs, are strengthening the enabling environment required for the centres to deliver the next level of value addition. Moreover, the highly competitive environment that many global enterprises now operate in is creating an additional thrust for the GDCs to look at radical options to redesign their business models. Given their increasing maturity, GDCs can now emerge as a strategic option, not just for COOs/CFOs but also for CEOs and heads of businesses.

Summary

- The GDC model has been there for a while, but many GDCs are now reaching a tipping point where they are in a position to provide the next level of value addition and become a source of competitive advantage for global enterprises.
- Four factors are driving why GDCs are able to now deliver the next level of value addition:
  - Increasing domain expertise
  - Scale that makes significant investments possible
  - Co-location of functions that provides innovation opportunities
  - Leadership maturity and networks within the global enterprise.

3

Global Delivery Centres Can Be Innovation and Revenue Centres

The ladder of success is best climbed by stepping on the Rungs of Opportunities.

Ayn Rand

The increasing maturity of GDCs makes them capable of adding value that goes beyond labour-cost arbitrage on software development and back-office processes, which was what most of them started their journeys with. The framework for value addition for GDCs has four interlocking levers—innovation, expertise, customer experience and revenue growth. I call them interlocking levers as they all have an impact on each other. From an organizational perspective, I call innovation and expertise the input levers and customer experience and revenue impact the output levers.

- Many GDCs started their value-addition journey by focusing on **expertise**. We see many examples of expertise: business research, investment research, analytics, R&D and many more. While building these high-skill capabilities in itself has been a great

GDCs as Innovation and Revenue centres

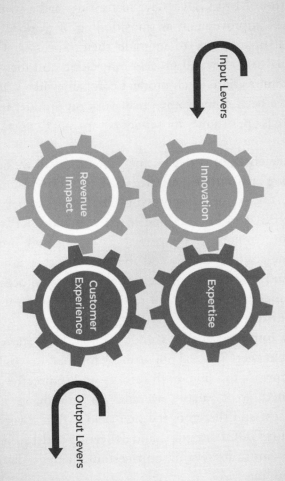

value-add, they have also helped raise the organizational DNA of the GDCs. This has helped create more opportunities for innovation and has also raised the relevance of the GDC among the senior management.

- **Innovation:** Most GDCs have historically had a strong culture of process improvement, as transitioning of work offshore was a natural opportunity to upgrade their processes. GDCs are beginning to go beyond process innovation and focus more on product innovation. Tech product companies like Cadence and SAP have been doing some great work on product innovation, and there is opportunity for service companies to now learn from them.

- In the fiercely competitive business environment we have today, **improving customer experience** is a key priority. In my ex-firm Fidelity, for example, improving our customer net promoter score (NPS) had become one of our foremost KPIs, perhaps even more important than asset gathering and profitability. Given the scale of GDCs and the fact that they are engaging deeper and deeper with the customer delivery process, GDCs have a unique opportunity for raising the bar when it comes to customer experience.

- **Revenue impact** is the holy grail. Most GDCs started as cost centres, but there is a real opportunity for them to contribute to the enterprise's top line, both directly and indirectly. Analytics has opened up so many avenues for improving marketing effectiveness and therefore revenue yield. I find it very exciting to see many GDCs designing and delivering end-to-end services that have significant revenue impact, thus making a direct impact on the top line.

In my observation, **six principles** drive end-customer and revenue-centric value addition. Also, I am sharing examples of GDCs that have driven value addition, resulting in tangible benefits for their parent organizations beyond what is typically expected.

1. *Leveraging **lower cost to serve** to **extend coverage of services** to segments that are difficult to serve using traditional models*: A significantly lower cost structure opens up opportunities that might otherwise be difficult to access. Many banking GDCs have used this principle to extend coverage of collections below ticket size that would otherwise have meant a negative ROI.

2. *Sourcing **superior talent** (given availability of high-quality talent at low cost) to dramatically **raise service quality***: Instead of aiming for 5–6x cost arbitrage, some companies go for lower arbitrage and invest the surplus into significantly raising the talent profile relative to what they have worked with in the past. This is a huge opportunity to totally redefine service quality. When the McKinsey Knowledge Centre started in 1998, it started by hiring ten MBAs. This was a significant departure from tradition as McKinsey had until then largely relied on library and information science profiles for its research function. This was a game-changer and eventually led to a significant upgradation in the scope and role of the research function globally at McKinsey. Another example has been the setting up of high-quality sales-support functions by many GDCs. This has helped frontline sales teams to focus on their customers and be a lot more productive in their sales efforts.

3. *Reducing the 'hurdle rate' for innovation, making possible initiatives that might otherwise not be feasible*: The combination of low-cost and high-quality talent is a great enabler for innovation. I call it the '**golden equation**'. Traditionally, lower costs have been leveraged for reducing the per unit cost of services. But the same can be leveraged to reduce the investment costs for innovations. This can allow an enterprise to de-risk its innovation programme and, simultaneously, significantly increase its innovation capacity. I have leveraged this principle both in McKinsey and Fidelity, where we established new, specialized analytics services

for the firms from India. Creating these new capabilities in New York or London would have been very expensive, and thus these ideas might have never seen the light of day. We were able to get going on pilots for these innovations in India with minimal investments and prove the concept. Many companies intuitively leverage this principle. There is a tremendous opportunity to use it more explicitly.

4. *Leveraging customer data for **'pattern recognition' of customer needs** to design new/refined services*: Many GDCs run customer delivery processes and are therefore close to customer requests and data. This is a tremendous opportunity to not just learn more about customers but to also leverage the insights that come along to develop new products to serve repetitive customer needs and solve pain points. At McKinsey Knowledge Centre, we analysed the research requests coming from consulting teams to develop a series of research products that not only raised analyst productivity but also significantly improved quality. These research products eventually served as the basis for new knowledge-oriented services that McKinsey introduced for its clients. Another example is the marketing analytics function that many GDCs have built; this function looks at customer data and provides rich insights to business unit heads on a regular basis.

5. *Leveraging **co-location** of functional and regional capabilities to drive **new service models and innovation***: I have pointed out that many GDCs are a complete microcosm of their parent firms. They often house multiple functions and serve different business lines and geographies. This co-location feature is a unique opportunity for collaboration, which might not be available to the firm anywhere else in the world. Innovative ideas often come not from within a box but at the intersection of many boxes. Especially powerful are the collaboration opportunities between analytics and technology in the big data space, and

Six Principles that drive revenue-centric value addition

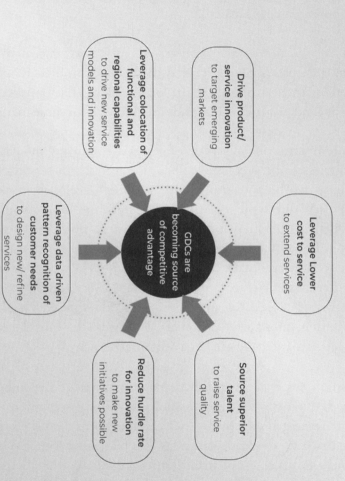

between operations and technology, given the increasing push towards automation and creation of service platforms. Another powerful opportunity here is for knowledge sharing and creation of global products/capabilities when functions serving different geographies are co-located.

6. *Driving product/service **innovation for emerging markets***: Many enterprises have leveraged their GDCs as incubators for launching their businesses in the local markets. The opportunity goes beyond just rolling out traditional services in these markets. Emerging markets like India are often very competitive and require innovations in service offerings and delivery models for enterprises to be successful. These innovations in services and products can be powerful exports to more developed markets. McKinsey did some of its most significant experiments in 'productizing' its knowledge capabilities into new client service lines in India by leveraging its knowledge centre here. Many of these services eventually developed into large global service lines. Another example is from telecom, where a very simple product that was developed for an emerging market showed very high satisfaction among new customers. This was later introduced in developed markets by the large telecom company.

Clearly, GDCs can help the global enterprises go beyond cost arbitrage. If the cost + talent proposition and the growing maturity of GDCs are leveraged effectively, they can transform the GDC from a cost centre into a revenue centre. It can become a strategic lever for business heads to solve many critical problems, thereby more profitably serving existing segments, achieving speed to market in developing new products and services, and entering new markets.

The specific value-addition opportunities for GDCs can vary widely. That will depend on the industry in which the individual GDC operates and the stage of its offshoring journey, as well as the organizational culture and capabilities. For example, organizations setting up a GDC for the first time will have the advantage of being able to embed a strategic role in the DNA of the GDC from the very beginning, which creates an opportunity for the GDC to contribute more and thereby become a source of competitive advantage for the enterprise.

Summary

- GDCs can drive end-customer and revenue-centric value addition using the following six principles:
  - Leveraging lower cost to serve to extend coverage of services to segments that are difficult to serve using traditional models
  - Sourcing superior talent (given availability of high-quality talent at low cost) to dramatically raise service quality
  - Reducing 'hurdle rate' for innovation, making possible initiatives that might otherwise not be feasible
  - Leveraging customer data for 'pattern recognition' of customer needs to design new/refined services
  - Leveraging co-location of multiple functional and regional capabilities to drive new service models and innovation
  - Driving product/service innovation for emerging markets.

4

Realizing Full Potential of Global Delivery Centres Requires Changes in Organization Approaches

You never change things by fighting the existing reality. To change something, build a new model that makes the existing model obsolete.

Buckminster Fuller, Architect, designer, systems theorist
and winner of the Presidential Medal of Freedom

While GDCs are well placed to embark on the value addition journey, successful examples, especially those with a sustained track record, are fewer than expected. Most GDCs continue to be caught in a limiting cycle. Enterprise expectations are limited to cost benefit and execution capacity, and GDCs continue to focus on meeting/exceeding operational SLAs. There is often an attitude of self-satisfaction at both ends that ends up limiting growth. Most GDCs believe their situation is unique and that they are doing an excellent job. This is not conducive to challenging the status quo; GDCs need to push hard to figure out what more can be done.

Stepping up and sustaining their value-addition journey requires a major rethink within both the GDCs and their parent organizations. Operating models, mindsets/culture and leadership that have worked so far might need to be changed to realize the new set of opportunities on the horizon. Often, there are long-held orthodoxies around governance and people models that might need to be challenged, requiring attention even at the CEO and board levels. Failure to do this might result in GDCs either not being able to gain from the opportunities in full or in promising initiatives not translating into sustainable success.

Illustrative changes in the GDC approach

- **Designing a collaborative operating model:** Typically the working relationship between 'onshore' and 'offshore' (the GDC) tends to be very directed. Onshore gives instructions and offshore acts as a compliant 'order taker'. This model ensures that the execution gets done efficiently and is quite helpful when the GDC capabilities are not mature. However, it is clear that such a directed model is not conducive to thought leadership and innovation that is so required in the digital age. For that to happen you need a relationship of equals, a partnership mindset that encourages collaboration and open thinking.

  This is a big shift that requires many design changes and has to be signalled from the top. As an example, I have seen the following two design changes work well for GDCs:

  o Aligning leadership and responsibilities by function/process rather than by geography (onshore versus offshore) leads to sharper focus on the customer. GDC leaders should consider taking up end-to-end process ownership where relevant.

  o Defining a common measure of success, e.g. CSAT scores rather than operational SLAs, that lead to much better collaboration across teams.

- **Developing an iterative loop between the what and the how:** Customer needs are continuously evolving in the digital age.

This requires an iterative process of experimentation of the 'how', which further informs the 'what' of strategy. The teams on the ground must, therefore, be regularly engaged with the bigger picture so that they can continuously inform the refining of strategy. This requires a shift in operating models. Often the 'what' has been defined 'onshore' with ownership of 'how' being with 'offshore'. Such sequential models cannot work in the digital age when iterative feedback loops are critical. It also calls for greater collaboration and even integrations between product and engineering teams, which are often segregated 'onshore' and 'offshore' respectively.

- **Deploying cross-functional teams with product mindset:** Given that digital problems are interdisciplinary, enterprises must take a relook at their teams, defining teams that are cross-functional and bringing a strong product mindset among them. Traditionally, enterprises have created functional silos that are entrusted with limiting roles. This leads to lack of ownership of execution and creates friction points in successful execution. For example, an idea once floated with the CEO PMO would be taken up by the digital PMO and the IT PMO, which would further drive the programme along with the product team. Then an Agile lead would be deployed on it; this lead will work with a development team that has a separate testing function and release function. Is this not confusing? No wonder many digital initiatives never get done or get delivered very slowly.

  The new way of deploying cross-functional teams is with a product mindset. In this, once an idea is floated it would go to a digital squad that comprises IT, digital, marketing and business leads. This would be tracked on a quarterly basis with the CXOs.

- **Developing GDC leadership that is more business-focused and entrepreneurial (versus being operationally focused 'safe**

Realizing full potential of GDCs requires changes in the organization approaches

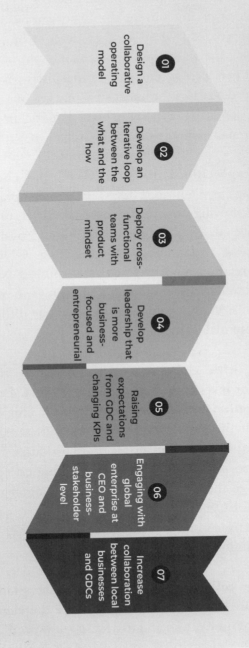

01 Design a collaborative operating model

02 Develop an iterative loop between the what and the how

03 Deploy cross-functional teams with product mindset

04 Develop leadership that is more business-focused and entrepreneurial

05 Raising expectations from GDC and changing KPIs

06 Engaging with global enterprise at CEO and business-stakeholder level

07 Increase collaboration between local businesses and GDCs

hands'): GDC leaders need to have a deep understanding of the business so they can 'join the dots' between business needs and GDC potential. In addition, they need to be entrepreneurial to challenge the status quo, move people out of their 'comfort zone' and persevere to build new capabilities. A programme of rotating leaders across business areas and regions into and out of the GDC can help in grooming high-potential talent in both the parent company and the GDC.

- **Raising expectations from the GDC and changing KPIs:** Global Capacity Centres (GCCs) need to demonstrate strategic intent by moving beyond operational SLAs to measure the value delivered. In addition, GDCs should push for ongoing value increase and external benchmarking. GDC and parent company relationships are often in a 'comfort zone', but both sides need to have the awareness and courage to raise the bar on expectations. Without this change, it will be difficult to realize the full potential of the GDC.

- **Engaging with global enterprise at CEO and business-stakeholder level (versus engaging with just the COO/CIO of organization in traditional approaches):** This is necessary to ensure that the game-changing opportunities that GDCs can provide are part of business strategy discussions. Often, given the historical positioning of the GDC as a 'support centre', it does not figure in these strategic discussions. Ongoing engagement with the CEO/head of business can make it easier to form linkages between business problems and leverage the GDC to provide solutions.

- **Increasing collaboration between local/regional business and offshore service centres to facilitate the client proximity required for innovation and to develop new products/services:** Often, GDC leadership is far removed from the eventual client and does not have a good understanding of business context. This gap needs to be bridged for the GDC to play a more significant role in product/service innovation. Linkage with the local/regional business provides the most natural opportunity to make this client connection happen. To facilitate this, both the local business and offshore centres are brought under a single leadership, of which there are emerging examples.

Illustrative changes in the global enterprise

- **Reviewing the governance model to reflect the increasing role and potential of the GDC:** For example, GDC leadership should be included in senior global management forums so they have a 'seat at the table' and are empowered to drive significant initiatives and decisions. Often, this might require going beyond traditional organizational structures and hierarchy.

- **Reviewing the people model at both GDC and the enterprise level and adapting it suitably:** As the GDC's role in the core business areas grows, it will likely have an impact on the people model in the parent organization too. The people profiles, recruitment approaches, career tracks and other aspects of the people model might need to change. These need to be fully understood so the necessary changes can be made.

Clearly, it is not easy to realize the full value-addition potential of GDCs. It will require significant changes in embedded organizational mindsets, operating models and approaches. Organizations that have the foresight and patience to make this change management effort can reap great business benefits.

Summary

- Organizational mindsets and operating models need to change significantly to realize the value-addition potential of GDCs.
- Operating models and mindsets need to shift from directed ('order taker') to a true collaboration.
- Traditional 'What-How' approaches need to change. There is a need to develop more iterative, agile and cross-functional approaches and team models that are more relevant for the digital age.
- There has to be a step change in the enterprise as well as GDC's expectations of impact to push the envelope and actualize the GDC's value-addition opportunity.
- GDCs should develop local leaders who are more business-focused and entrepreneurial and can engage key stakeholders like the CEO and business stakeholders.
- Global enterprises might need to make changes to their people and governance models to take full advantage of the GDC opportunity.

5

Evolution of Global Delivery Centres and the New Ask of GDC Leaders

Even the smallest person can change the course of the future.

Lady Galadriel, *The Lord of the Rings*

This chapter is synthesized from a number of talks I have given at NASSCOM events to GDC leaders.

In the previous chapter of the section, we have seen how global delivery models is critical for enterprises to succeed in a digital age. Further, we saw how the role of GDCs needs to evolve and they need to step up on the value addition curve. Making all of the above happen falls on the shoulders of the GDC leaders. In this chapter, I address the GDC leaders and focus on the key shifts they need to make. My insights and suggestions are structured into three parts:

- GDC evolution and priorities
- Leadership ask of GDC leaders and shifts they need to make
- Global mindset—the what and how

GDCs are maturing and poised to move to the next level

We have over 1,200 GDCs in India alone. Many of these GDCs have been in existence for more than fifteen years. GDCs are in a very different space now from where they were ten or twelve years back. Over time, they have grown not just in delivery capability and scale but also in business expertise, leadership maturity and credibility within their global organizations, who now realize the many unique advantages of this in-house model. Many GDCs have started moving to the next level, where their role grows **from one of execution to leadership** within their organizations.

There are six key aspects to the growing maturity of GDCs and their movement from execution to leadership:

1. **Value addition is now a huge opportunity:** There are tremendous opportunities for GDCs to add value beyond what derives from the traditional focus on cost and productivity in back-office processes. There is significant momentum on building high-skill capabilities like research and analytics. In addition, there are many examples of GDCs driving product/ service innovation, especially for developing markets. Finally, there are emerging examples of their contribution to revenue generation. For instance, many GDCs are leveraging the cost + talent advantage to extend services to segments and markets that were earlier not viable for the parent organization to serve. This is a transformational opportunity, not just for GDCs but also for their parent organizations. It is now not far-fetched to visualize the evolution of GDCs from cost centres to revenue centres!

2. **Cost and productivity continue to be important:** While there is a lot of interest in value addition, cost and productivity continue to be focus areas. It is still a core expectation of onshore stakeholders and GDC leaders have to continue to focus on it.
   - The good news is that the GDC model continues to deliver 40–70 per cent savings and these cost arbitrage benefits are

not going away in a hurry. They are likely to be sustained for at least fifteen or twenty years, perhaps even running up to twenty-five years.

- However, GDCs cannot rest easy. Some of the initial drivers of cost and productivity benefits might be diminishing. For example, the high growth many GDCs saw in their early years was helpful in efficient management of the talent pyramid and the per-unit infrastructure costs. With headcount growth plateauing, it becomes more challenging for GDCs to manage those costs. Therefore, GDCs have to push hard on operations excellence and talent model optimization to sustain and potentially improve benefits on cost and productivity.

3. **Development of global delivery networks:** Many GDCs have moved from a single site in India to a global network of sites. While India might continue to be the largest of their sites, organizations want to have multiple options. Location selection has become more than just a cost-arbitrage decision. It is driven by mitigation of concentration risk, access to new pools of talent and strategic business considerations. Even within India, GDCs often have multiple sites and are expanding their footprint to tier-2 cities. In addition, GDCs within the organization are beginning to be managed as an integrated global network rather than as independent sites.

4. **The sourcing model for GDCs is becoming more complex:** 'Make versus buy' has been a perennial debate. Many organizations have now moved beyond this debate, recognizing that there is a role for both and that these models can co-exist. Therefore, hybrid sourcing, where both in-house centres and vendors co-exist, is now increasingly becoming the norm. In addition, in a significant departure from the past, in-house centres are often being asked to play a lead role in managing the partner relationships for their firms, whereas earlier such relationships might have been managed directly by the head office.

5. **Governance approaches are evolving:** Historically, GDC operating models have been at two ends of the spectrum—being either shared services models or vertical integration models. Given the evolving scope of GDCs, more complex hybrid operating models are emerging. This makes their governance, especially management of the matrix, more challenging. Moreover, placement of the GDC within the organization is also evolving. From reporting into the COO or the CIO, you now often have business heads taking direct interest in the GDCs. Consequently, the roles and expectations of GDC leaders are also getting enhanced in the context of their global organizations.

6. **Workforce maturing and becoming more diverse:** Given the increasing maturity of GDCs, the workforce tenure is also increasing. This is a great opportunity but also a challenge. Many GDC staff have now acquired business expertise that can be leveraged for higher value-added roles. That is a great opportunity. However, there is also a need to provide the staff with more challenging career paths and professional development opportunities. If you don't, then there is the risk of losing your best talent. In addition, the workforce is becoming more diverse, with large numbers of the next gen joining, especially at entry level.

GDC leaders need to step up

GDCs are facing a lot of change and there are great opportunities in front of them to move to the next level of impact and relevance within their organizations. However, this journey is not easy. To realize the opportunities, GDC leaders need to step up their game significantly.

Sometimes GDC leaders are caught in a 'comfort zone'. Expectations of thought leadership and innovation are often low. The GDC leaders are able to deliver well on the execution expectations, the rewards are good and there is no urgent need to push beyond. This can limit their development as thought leaders. GDC leaders have to be conscious of this and confront the 'comfort zone' hurdle proactively. They have to ensure that they are challenging the status quo and pushing the capabilities forward. There is a critical need to develop a new generation of leaders who will be the torchbearers for the exciting GDC journey from execution to leadership.

There are great opportunities for GDCs to move to the next level, but the critical success factor lies in GDC leaders stepping up. This stepping up should not be something sporadic but one that the GDC community has to address on priority.

Based on surveys and discussions with multiple GDC leaders, I have identified four skill sets that I see as critical:

1. **A global mindset:** The expectation is for a leader to not just be effective as a team player in a global environment but to influence and lead globally. This is becoming important because of three forces. First, the change of expectations of GDCs from process execution to thought leadership and development of global delivery networks, with India often taking the lead. Second, organizations increasingly look up to emerging economies as a source of talent. Third, the fact that leadership talent in GDCs in the emerging economies is relatively inexperienced.

2. **Entrepreneurial leadership:** The next stage of growth for GDCs will not be easy. Cost arbitrage-driven growth will reach a plateau at some stage and new growth will be driven by adding value to the business. This requires leaders who are not just solid operations managers but who are also entrepreneurial and business oriented. The new generation of leaders needs to be creative and commercial, understand the business well, and engage well not just with the COO/CIO or CFO but with the CEO too. They also need to have the courage to take risks and have the resilience to navigate any opposition and setbacks that are inevitable as you build something new.

3. **Networking and influencing skills:** Managing the matrix is a reality for every GDC. With the evolving scope of GDCs and governance models, it is becoming even more complex. You often need to assert your influence without having direct authority. You need to be a diplomat to navigate through and align multiple stakeholders with different agendas. And, you need to build a coalition of supporters who will sponsor and champion development of the GDC to the next level.

4. **Managing Gen 'Y':** The GDC workforce is becoming more diverse and certainly younger. Gen Y offers great promise. They are creative, confident and have a lot more of the 'can do' attitude. However, the traditional command-and-control management style might not work with them. It is necessary to understand them well and connect with them to fully harness their substantial energies.

The shifts GDC leaders need to make

To be world-class in thought leadership and innovation calls for different mindsets and capabilities. I see four important shifts that GDC leaders need to make to get to this point.

1. **From operations managers to thought leaders and innovators:** GDC managers are very good at execution, at getting things done, whether it is project delivery or managing service quality. To be a thought leader and innovator, they will need to build strategy and critical problem-solving skills. They will need to change their mindset from a focus on 'urgent and near-term' to learning to deal with 'important-but-not-urgent', because that is the nature of a lot of thought leadership and innovation. They will also need to manage more complex conversations. Managing execution involves relatively structured and predictable conversations. Thought leadership will entail more complex conversations, carrying greater possibilities of conflict

with onshore stakeholders who might not be used to that mode of engagement from offshore managers.

2. **From functional experts to business experts:** GDCs have strong technical and process skills; however, the key success factor in the next stage of the value addition journey is business and end-customer knowledge. Managers will need to invest in this self-learning, or they will get left behind.

3. **From 'safe pair of hands' to entrepreneurial risk-takers:** Current processes and delivery models are often designed to minimize risk and ensure predictable delivery. For this we have tended to look for and encourage a 'safe pair of hands'. In an era where innovation is paramount, you need entrepreneurial risk-takers. This is not a simple change as it is deep-rooted in the culture of the organization. The senior-most leaders have to personally signal the culture change through their own actions.

4. **From local champions to global influencers:** From managing teams locally, increasingly senior management will be expected to lead and influence globally. This requires high levels of multicultural sensitivity, sophisticated communication skills and, most importantly, deep understanding of global organizational priorities.

In summary, the change requires managers to step up and become leaders. The most critical aspect of this change will be drive, 'hunger' and a relentless pursuit of excellence. If we can build and sustain that passion and energy among our managers, the rest of the required changes will follow.

Global mindset—the what and the how

The key characteristic of a successful global leader is influence. The global leader needs to go beyond boundaries to influence across geographies and culture. The other key characteristics of successful global leaders include vision, creativity, skill at resource allocation, and readiness to take risks.

So, how can GDC leaders build global mindsets and become successful global leaders? From my experience of twenty years leading in global firms, the following six lessons are important:

1. **Making an effort to understand:** The global manager should put herself/himself in the other person's shoes, be empathetic and try to understand their perspective instead of jumping to conclusions. She/he must be intellectually curious and have the urge to learn about new cultures and people.

2. **Exposure to novelty:** Going outside one's 'comfort zone' and continuously having new and varied experiences. This grows leaders and makes them more adaptable.

3. **Spending more time with global peers and clients:** Global leaders need to step out of their offices and spend more time globally. They need to go beyond operations and people management, and focus on networking and relationship building.

4. **Going beyond self-interest and building trust:** To build trust, self-interest and the manager's own agenda must be suspended to be replaced with a genuine wish to do the right thing for others. In addition, a leader must ensure open and honest communication. He must not hesitate to share bad news. Every crisis is an opportunity for building trust!

5. **Managing the matrix:** Organizational politics is a reality, so a leader must not shy away from facing conflicts in the matrix. Potential conflicts must be resolved by always bringing the focus back to what is right for the customer.

6. **Being natural and courageous:** While it is very important that the leader seeks to understand and then to adapt, it is equally important that the leader is natural and stays true to their convictions. They must trust their instincts, treasure their self-respect, and say what it is the way it is!

Four shifts that GDC leaders must undergo to champion value addition

From

	To
Operations Managers	Thought Leaders & Innovators
Functional Experts	Business Experts
Safe pair of hands	Entrepreneurial Risk Takers
Local Champions	Global Influencers

In summary, being an effective global leader is not about the cosmetics (e.g. language, fluency) but simply about the fundamentals of being a good leader. Like most things in life, it is important for a global leader to find balance between seemingly contradicting expectations. In particular, a global leader should find balance between 'cutting his/her chains' and 'staying true to his/her roots'.

It will not be an exaggeration to say that the future of GDCs depends to a large extent on how their leaders step up and drive change.

Summary

- The four critical leadership skills needed at a GDC are: global mindset, entrepreneurial leadership, networking and influencing skills, managing Gen Y.
- For a global mindset, leaders must be curious, empathetic, take risks, be authentic and develop trust-based relationships.

How to Build a World-class Knowledge Centre

An investment in knowledge always pays the best interest

Benjamin Franklin, Founding Father of the
United States of America and American Polymath

It has been my great privilege to be involved in building the McKinsey Knowledge Centre in India. Popularly known as McKC, it is a shining example of the depth and breadth of research and analytics capabilities that can be delivered from a location like India, and of how such a centre can become a force for innovation and transformation in a large, global organization. Here, I have tried to distil the key lessons I learnt in helping build McKC over eight truly wonderful years.

1. Centre required an approach different from the typical IT/BPO processes

A knowledge centre is a different beast from the typical IT/BPO Centre. There are at least three characteristics unique to a knowledge centre: its capabilities defy precise definition; they are often core to the company; and the talent required is high-skill.

Research, analytics and other knowledge-oriented capabilities that are part of a knowledge centre are not precise products or processes. They are capabilities where the deliverables can vary widely on the data-to-insights continuum. Moreover, quality and productivity too are difficult to define and measure for these capabilities. Therefore, the approach needed to transition to and build these capabilities is different from the scale IT/BPO functions that tend to have well-defined deliverables and processes.

Research and analytics are often part of the core IP, the 'secret sauce' of an organization. Therefore, there is often a high level of concern when it comes to changing the operating model for such capabilities. The risk of quality dilution is often seen as far outweighing any benefits from offshoring.

Finally, you typically require high-quality talent, often with specialized and/or pedigreed educational backgrounds for a knowledge centre. This talent profile has high aspirations and is very conscious of the opportunities before it. In addition, these hires are sensitive about their work positioning—in the 'back office'—and are often keen to move to the 'front office'. These factors make talent retention an additional challenge at a knowledge centre.

Given the three unique characteristics that I have described above, it is clear that the approach to building a knowledge centre needs to be different from the more typical IT/BPO processes. This becomes even more critical when the knowledge centre is part of a larger GDC. In such cases, the management will likely be more focused on the IT/BPO processes that are much larger in scale. They need to make a special effort to calibrate their usual approach and provide enough attention to building the knowledge centre.

2. Go slow to go fast

There are tremendous opportunities for a knowledge centre to add value and potentially be a source of competitive advantage for an organization. However, it is perhaps necessary to start small and slow to prove the concept and get the initial buy-in. As mentioned, research and analytics capabilities are not well defined and are difficult to transition. Moreover, it is easy for sceptics to brand offshore capabilities as poor in quality and as not adding value, given the lack of well-defined measures of quality. Any initial missteps can make it very difficult to progress the knowledge centre. It is therefore important to take one's time upfront to establish a very clear and strong value proposition with the primary users. Propositions need not be fancy—the focus should be on solving some real pain points for the key users. For McKC, the initial value proposition was overnight delivery of analysis for consulting teams based in the US. This helped improve the lifestyle and productivity of the consulting teams. This simple but clear proposition helped McKC establish strong support amongst consultants within McKinsey and was the foundation for McKC's subsequent meteoric rise.

To take the analogy of the hare and tortoise story, in building a knowledge centre the tortoise probably wins over the hare!

3. Ensure ownership on the part of the parent organization

Knowledge and expertise are the foundation of high-quality research and analytics capabilities. However, these are most often not well codified and lie within the minds and laptops of people. Having a close working relationship with these experts is necessary to build expertise within the offshore knowledge centre. Knowledge is transferred not through a transition process but through osmosis as onshore experts and offshore analysts in the knowledge centre work closely together. To ensure that this happens, it is important to have an organizational construct where the onshore organization feels a high level of ownership of the offshore centre. They should see the offshore centre as contributing to their success and not as competition.

At McKC, we had to make conscious efforts to get our onshore colleagues ('Practices') to take greater ownership of us. We had started McKC by building a research 'shared service' that served all offices and practices. Over a period of time, we developed teams specialized in industry and functional knowledge. However, we felt that we were not able to develop the teams beyond a level without direct ownership by the Practices. At that stage, we decided to transfer ownership of those specialized teams (including the P&L contribution) directly to the Practices. It was difficult for us in the local management to let go of teams and capabilities we had invested so much effort in to build. However, this one step was key to launching the next stage of development at McKC. Direct ownership by the Practices helped our people develop as deep subject matter experts, and this contributed to both their professional growth and the next stage of expansion of the knowledge centre.

4. Become a source of change for the global research organization

Research setups in most organizations are traditional, more art than science. The lack of legacy, and the offshore model and scale of a knowledge centre provide a good opportunity for building new processes and systems for export back to the organization. At McKC we saw this happen in multiple ways. The most significant was in the profile of talent. The research network within McKinsey was historically a support organization. However, when we set up McKC in 1998, we started by hiring top-quality MBAs. This was a significant departure from the type of talent that was hired traditionally in the research network. This raised awareness of the impact that higher-quality talent can have on research quality, and such profiles have now become the norm in large parts of McKinsey's global research network. Development of McKC also necessitated development of formal 'order taking', workflow management systems and processes for measuring customer satisfaction. All of these systems were subsequently exported back to the global network and have increasingly become the norm at other research units at McKinsey.

Perhaps the most significant contribution of McKC to McKinsey's global research network is the complete change it brought about in the architecture of research within McKinsey. Traditionally, research professionals were placed in each of McKinsey's offices. The success of McKC was not just a success of offshore delivery, but it also proved that consolidation of research in a knowledge centre and creating a well-identified home for knowledge professionals was the right configuration for building research capabilities. Subsequently, knowledge centres were set up near Brussels and Boston, later on in Shanghai, and then in Poland and Costa Rica.

5. Innovate and push the boundaries of new services

I mentioned earlier that it is important to go slow in building a knowledge centre to ensure that you are establishing a clear and unshakeable foundation. But once you have reached maturity in your core capabilities, it is important to push on innovation and explore how you can create new services for the organization. Innovation is a great opportunity but also an imperative to ensure sustainability for knowledge centres. Given the nature of the capabilities, they can play a material role in advancing the core proposition and potentially the top line of organizations. Equally, developing a new generation of capabilities can provide professional growth opportunities for the high-quality talent you have hired. In the absence of such growth, either you will see attrition or cost creep.

The true success of McKC lay in its development as an innovation hub for McKinsey. We were very successfully able to develop services beyond the initial remit of being a 'research back office', and these services have, over time, transformed how McKinsey serves clients. Well over 50 per cent of the knowledge professionals at McKC work on new services, as opposed to serving in roles that have been transitioned from other offices.

There were essentially three principles that underlay most of the innovation we drove: 1) combination of low cost + high-quality talent, making it possible to invest in capabilities that would otherwise not be viable, 2) consolidation of expertise to create new knowledge products and IP, and 3) leveraging the co-location of multiple industry, functional and regional capabilities.

A good example of the first principle was the creation of Analytics Services and Centres of Competence. McKinsey historically never had a specialized analytics capability at scale. McKC was a good opportunity to invest in building such a specialized capability, which might not have been feasible to build otherwise. Centers of Competence (CoCs) were about standardizing select modules in client engagements and leveraging high-quality experts based at McKC to deliver them. This has helped McKinsey become more competitive and expand its services to clients, leading to significant top-line contributions. This is another great example of leveraging specialized talent at low price points to drive significant innovation.

On the second principle, we made many pushes to convert the retained expertise into new knowledge products that could also be taken to clients. McKC is playing an important role in development of proprietary knowledge in McKinsey, helping the firm monetize the investments made in internal knowledge development as client offerings. A powerful example of this is the extension of industry databases into benchmarking services, making it possible to serve clients in new, useful ways.

Finally, leveraging the co-location of capabilities proved to be a massive opportunity. We saw many examples where regional practices were able to consolidate and develop a global practice utility as a result of the existing co-location of those capabilities at McKC. Even in developing many CoCs and proprietary knowledge services, co-location of different research and analytics capabilities was critical. However, I still see leveraging of co-location benefits to be an under-explored opportunity. To capture this opportunity fully, you need mechanisms to go beyond the existing governance silos. It needs senior management awareness and a strong will to make that happen.

6. Strong local capabilities are necessary to drive innovation

While the strong ownership by the Practices was necessary to build the expertise at McKC, the push for its growth as an innovation hub came from local initiatives. Having a local owned shared services capacity and strong leadership was critical in driving innovation. At McKC, in addition to the Practice-owned research capabilities, we had a shared research service called knowledge-on-call (KoC). While KoC's objective was to support all offices and practices on basic research requests, it was also, surprisingly, the nursery for many cutting-edge and specialized capabilities. Even a technically specialized capability such as analytics emerged from KoC. The vertically owned Practice research teams construct was conducive for building subject matter expertise, but the teams also worked along a well-defined and often limiting remit. The KoC construct meant lower expertise but more entrepreneurial freedom and ability to invest. The combination of the latter two factors, along with strong local management, was absolutely critical in driving McKC's outstanding innovation journey.

7. Get leadership with experience of the core business

The core success variable for a knowledge centre is not operations efficiency but the ability to integrate with the parent organization and eventually become a source of innovation. Therefore, it is necessary to get leaders who have deep experience and credibility within the core business. In the initial phases, this business experience is helpful in shaping the value proposition for the knowledge centre. In the second stage, this experience helps in integrating the GDC with the parent organization. In the later stages, to realize the innovation opportunity, it is necessary to have the full view of the core business, including the end-client needs. Innovation cannot happen in abstraction. For it to be meaningful, innovation has to link two different aspects—gaps in the eventual client service proposition and unique advantages that a knowledge centre might have. It can be a difficult bridge to make. Leaders who have the business experience and entrepreneurial ability to make the connection between the two can lead a knowledge centre to great success for the organization.

8. Create career paths for your talent

While IP is important, the core asset for a knowledge centre is talent. As mentioned earlier, given that this talent has high aspirations, it is imperative to come up with sustainable career paths for them. Money or job security alone is unlikely to retain this talent for very long. Moreover, most of this talent aspires to grow as experts and not as managers (the career path that is easier to provide in an offshore set-up). Therefore, developing and communicating career paths has to be a proactive and not passive process.

I believe there are three key aspects to developing compelling career paths for knowledge centre professionals:

- Continuous push to **develop more value-added capabilities** that allow the professionals to challenge themselves and progress. At McKC, development of analytics and CoCs provided opportunities for professionals to progress beyond the service lines of the knowledge centre that they had joined. This was critical in retaining talent within the organization for a long time.
- Opportunities to **transfer to 'front office' roles**. While it might not be possible to create this as a defined career path, even a few examples of transfers from the offshore set up to a client-serving office can act as a great motivation to the team.
- **Continuous experimentation with people profiles** to find match skills and aspirations with service lines they are aligned to. At McKC, while we continuously grew new service lines, in sync with that, we also continuously expanded our people profiles. We initially used to get MBAs for the KoC, our core research

Building blocks of a world-class Knowledge Centre

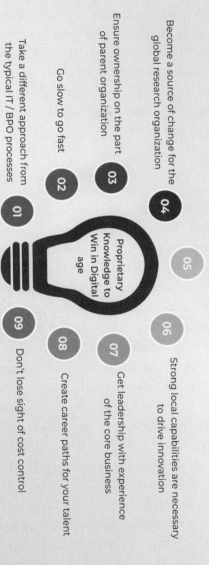

Innovate and push the boundaries on new services

Become a source of change for the global research organization

Ensure ownership on the part of parent organization

Go slow to go fast

Take a different approach from the typical IT / BPO processes

04

03

02

01

Proprietary Knowledge to Win in Digital age

05

06

07

08

09

Strong local capabilities are necessary to drive innovation

Get leadership with experience of the core business

Create career paths for your talent

Don't lose sight of cost control

service line. We then moved to hiring chartered accountants and commerce graduates. We eventually moved to hiring graduates from non-finance backgrounds. Increasing standardization and process maturity facilitated this change, and we were able to make the transition without any drop in quality (in fact, client satisfaction metrics improved!). In parallel, we were able to move the higher pedigree profiles to the newer, value-added service lines we were creating. This process of experimenting with new profiles and mapping them to service lines was critical in creating a stable talent model at McKC.

9.   Yes, it is about value-add but don't lose sight of cost control

Given the expectations from a knowledge centre, it is easy to lose sight of cost control. Hiring and retaining high-quality talent and ensuring high integration with the parent organization can drive up costs. If this is not managed well, you can go into a cost spiral that can soon erode the cost advantage of the offshore knowledge centre. It need not be so. If you are practical about talent management and administration, you can deliver high-quality capabilities without cost creep. The key lies in the combination of continuous push-on value-added capabilities and experimenting with newer talent profiles, such as the ones I have mentioned earlier.

This allows you to get in lower-cost resources at the base of the pyramid while utilizing the higher-cost resources for more value-added services. This combination of service line growth and talent model experimentation is critical. Standing still on them can lead to significant cost creep.

The other important aspect of cost control is the level of integration of your centre with the parent organization. There is a cost of integration in terms of facility standards, benefits, amount of travel, etc. Many of these aspects (especially travel) might be necessary to build a high-quality knowledge centre. However, it is important to have a reality check and question the value of your expenses. With a practical 80/20 approach, you can manage costs while not compromising on quality.

A final point on costs—cost measurement and control is often ignored and not seen as critical in a high-end capability like a knowledge centre. This is a big mistake. Reduction in the cost to serve in itself might not be a big opportunity for organizations. However, costs are a critical factor when it comes to innovation opportunity. The biggest facilitator of innovation from a knowledge centre is its low-cost structure that lowers the hurdle rate on investments. Thus, a broader range of investment opportunities become viable, which might otherwise not be so. If offshore knowledge centres are not careful about costs, they might end up sabotaging a big driver of their innovation engine.

A knowledge centre is a significant opportunity to create outstanding business value for an organization. McKC is a wonderful example of not only the breadth and depth of research and analytics capabilities that can be delivered from an offshore centre, but also of how a GDC can become a source of innovation transforming the core client service model for large global firms like McKinsey. I hope this story becomes an inspiration for many to launch even more exciting and value-creating journeys.

Summary

- A knowledge centre can multiply the IP of a firm and is a significant opportunity to create outstanding business value for a global enterprise.
- The building blocks for creating a world-class knowledge centre include:
  a. Bring in high-quality talent (well beyond what you would have for typical IT/BPO processes) who can work on unstructured situations and complex tasks,

b. Starting small and slow to prove the concept before you scale,

c. Co-ownership and co-creation with parent organizations, which ensure deep context and tacit knowledge is shared,

d. Becoming an innovation hub for the parent enterprise by leveraging the 'expertise at scale' to invest in knowledge products and IP and taking advantage of co-location of multiple capabilities,

e. Entrepreneurial freedom with the ability to invest along with strong local leadership,

f. Hiring leadership with experience of the core business,

g. Continuing to experiment with alternate talent profiles as well as move high-pedigree resources to new value-added service lines to ensure talent engagement.

• Learnings from knowledge centre provide a good framework for where GDCs need to go in the value-addition journey.

SECTION 5

TRANSFORMING THE ORGANIZATION TO WIN IN THE DIGITAL AGE

Introduction: Transforming the Organization to Win in the Digital Age

In sections one to three, I talked about the why and what of digital transformation. In section four, we shifted the discussion to the how of digital transformation, and I explained how the global delivery model is a critical aspect of execution in the digital age. In this section, I go deeper into the how of digital execution and explore the organizational elements that are necessary to support successful digital transformation.

Digital transformation cannot be successful without organizational transformation

I have made the point in the earlier sections that for digital transformation to be successful, it has to be end to end. Digital transformation is not just about technology. In fact, many digital transformation programmes fail because they are conceived and executed narrowly as just technology programmes. Moreover, digital is not just about changing the customer experience; it is also about changing business and operating models. Such a significant range of change cannot be successful and sustainable unless it is accompanied by organizational transformation.

Digital is about a new way of doing things. You need to move with speed, execute iteratively rather than sequentially, put more focus on experimentation and innovation, and take a lot more risks. In addition, technology has to become a core part of your DNA, whatever industry you are in. These changes cannot be sustained without a rewiring of the organizational culture. Change in the organizational culture is probably the most important enabler for digital transformation, allowing the enterprise to go beyond individual programmes and effect a more pervasive shift in the organizational DNA.

But culture takes a long time to develop, and it is not easy for an enterprise and its functions to change quickly. In the digital age, when the pace of change is very high, when new competitors are constantly emerging and business cycles are shrinking, the question is, what is a sustainable basis for an organization's success?

I believe there are at least seven organizational capabilities that are key to sustained success in the digital age:

1. **Proprietary knowledge:** In an era when information is so easily accessible, proprietary knowledge becomes a source of competitive advantage. In fact, I would submit that in the digital age, every enterprise has to be a knowledge company. However, the challenge is that proprietary knowledge is typically tacit. So enterprises have to be very purposeful in codifying tacit knowledge and making it accessible to the rest of the organization.

2. **Innovation:** The foundation of the digital age is innovation, and every organization has to build that as a core competence. Innovation is of four types: process, product, customer experience and business model. Often, enterprises focus more on incremental process innovation. However, to compete in the digital age, enterprises have no option but to invest in more radical business model innovations. Moreover, this calls for not a one-time effort or a stray stroke of genius. Innovation has to

become ingrained in the enterprise as a systematic process and organizational capability.

3. **Agility:** Speed is probably the most distinct attribute of the digital age. Time to market and cycle time requirements are changing dramatically. This cannot be achieved unless a fundamental shift happens in the 'way we work'. Agile is that fundamental shift. Agile began as a new way of doing software development but has expanded to cover all activities in the strategy-to-execution cycle in an enterprise.

4. **Learning:** The digital age is about constant change. So, the only way an enterprise or an individual can remain relevant is through continuous learning. The nature of learning is changing dramatically. It is becoming more self-directed, digital and byte-sized. Enterprises must harness the tremendous advancements happening in learning methods and technology, and build learning as a core competence.

5. **Diversity:** In the complex world we live in today, monolithic approaches cannot work. Diversity of thought and experience is necessary to effectively deal with complexity. Diversity in all its dimensions—gender, racial, geographic, age—is no more a good-to-have but a necessary basis for an organization to compete effectively in the digital age.

6. **Change management:** In the digital age, change is something significant and relentless. You cannot sit on your laurels. I believe companies in most industries now need to significantly transform themselves—from strategy to operating model—every three to four years. In such a scenario, change management has to become a core competency for every organization.

7. **Enabling functions:** HR and Finance are typically seen as support functions. However, in the digital age, they are assuming a more critical role. HR is a key enabler of most of the elements of organizational transformation that we have mentioned above. Given the higher risks and investment needs of an enterprise for competing in the digital age, the role of Finance also becomes

more significant. CHRO and CFO roles are becoming the most important CXO roles, apart from that of the CEO. However, these functions are often set in a legacy order-taker or control mindset and need to step up significantly to meet the new expectations.

As the digital age plays out, the question as to the future of work arises. 'Future of work' has been a topic of discussion for decades. This discussion is now becoming more real with the growth of AI. Man-versus-machine debates are occupying the popular imagination. My belief is that AI will have a very significant impact on the nature of work; it is a question of man *and* machine and not one of man *versus* machine. It is important that enterprises and leaders understand the impact of AI on their specific industries and functions and take proactive steps to redesign jobs accordingly.

In this section, I explore a number of topics I have mentioned in this introduction:

Chapter 1: Building an Organizational Culture to Succeed in the Digital Age

Across a number of world-class firms like McKinsey and Fidelity, culture has been the bedrock of their enduring success, bringing consistency and common purpose across their global footprint.

- In the VUCA world, it is critical for an enterprise to have a consistent work culture; however, it will need to go one step further and also build an entrepreneurial culture to succeed. In this chapter, I share nine aspects that are critical for success in the digital age. These are distinct attributes that enterprises will need to consciously incorporate into their culture.
- However, just articulating these attributes is not enough. We need to integrate them into the way we work to create a definitive

Transforming the organization to win in the Digital age

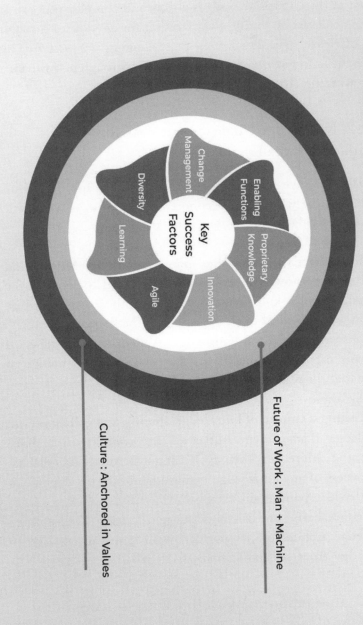

Culture : Anchored in Values

Future of Work : Man + Machine

Key Success Factors

Change Management

Enabling Functions

Diversity

Proprietary Knowledge

Learning

Innovation

Agile

culture at the enterprise. This is a slow and complex process. It can be achieved by setting the direction for employees through a set of clearly articulated *values,* encouraging *role modelling* by leadership, and *institutionalizing the culture* through performance and reward processes, to name a few ways.

Chapter 2: Knowledge Management—A Key to Differentiation in the Digital Age

In this chapter, I have covered the need for a shift in approach from vesting know-how with a small cohort of experts to a systematic method of knowledge management. This will involve:

- **Building effective knowledge management capabilities and enabling the knowledge cycle:** You will need to identify the different types of knowledge needs, as per business priorities. Second, you will need to clearly establish the knowledge experts and those who need the knowledge. And third, you will need to finally establish processes and invest in the technology to ensure that the required knowledge is available to the seekers on a timely basis.
- **Establishing a culture of knowledge-sharing and collaboration:** Knowledge management initiatives are complex and time-consuming. Moreover, their ROI cannot be easily established. The success of any knowledge management effort is dependent on leadership sponsorship, establishing a culture that encourages knowledge-sharing and collaboration, and creating a well-defined knowledge architecture supported by the right investments in knowledge processes and technology.

Chapter 3: Innovation—A Call to Action

In this chapter, I focus on innovation by taking the example of the Indian IT/BPM industry.

- The value proposition of this industry was built on high-quality, low-cost technology talent, ability to scale up at speed, customer responsiveness and a strong process orientation.
- However, due to the impact of digital transformation and the changing expectations of the customer, the ask from Indian IT/ BPM firms has changed significantly.
- The Indian IT/BPM industry needs to step up its game when it comes to innovation. It cannot afford incremental approaches anymore and needs to place bigger bets on product and business model innovation.
- To step up to the challenge, the IT industry will need to go beyond its long-standing success formula, step up its innovation budget commitments, better understand customer pain points, and explore collaboration with start-ups and acquisition of firms with niche skills.

Chapter 4: Key Insights from My First Agile Training

In this chapter, I give my key insights on Agile from my reflections following my first Agile training. I have distilled eight key points, such as: Agile is not just about project planning and software development but is applicable to all business functions including strategy and planning; to be agile, you have to simplify your processes and empower teams to drive outcomes; in a world where you cannot predict developments beyond the next six to twelve months, the 'fail fast' approach works best, and you have to get accustomed to not working and operating sequentially.

Chapter 5: Learning to Reinvent for Tomorrow

Every organization has to focus on continuous learning for its employees to adapt to the changing needs of the digital age. The Learning and Development (L&D) function, if leveraged well, can be used to build enterprise capability as well as provide it a competitive advantage. L&D priorities should help the organization meet its short-term and long-term goals by building strong technical, professional, leadership and change management capabilities. For the learning process to be effective, the content should have a degree of personalization, be byte-sized and virtual, and drive a culture of self-directed learning.

Chapter 6: Women in Leadership

Most technology companies employ a large proportion of women, varying from 25 per cent to 45 per cent of their workforce. However, as you get to mid-senior management levels, this proportion drops dramatically. Diversity in the workforce is an imperative, not only to ensure that it is a good representation of society but also so that it is a driver of innovation, has the right balance of empathy, and gives a better understanding of the buying behaviour of customers.

To drive better diversity representation, enterprises will need to create processes as well as changes in workplace design that help women employees manage maternity and their subsequent return to work, as well as help them to continue in the workforce as their responsibilities grow.

Chapter 7: Lessons in Change Management

In the digital age, organizations have no option but to adapt to the rapidly changing environment.

- Despite the inevitability of change, many organizations have been struggling to drive effective change management programmes. In this chapter, I have articulated the seven best practices that form the critical ingredients of a successful change management programme.
- Overall, enterprises have to carefully craft and monitor the transformation process and use all possible levers to capture the hearts and minds of their people.

- The transformation journey should begin with setting clear change goals, help employees understand the implications of the change process, and celebrate quick wins to build momentum. Communication is a powerful enabler which, if used well, can have a great impact in galvanizing the change process.

Chapter 8: How HR Needs to Transform to Lead in the VUCA World

HR has a historic opportunity to play a pivotal role in helping organizations navigate through these uncertain times in the VUCA world. This is because the nature of challenges organizations face in the VUCA world requires many solutions to come from HR.

- Areas where HR should take the lead in driving change include playing the role of culture champions, organizational redesign, resetting of learning and development strategies, driving new approaches to talent acquisition and engagement in the VUCA world.
- However, the HR function needs to make a number of changes to step up its impact, such as upgrading its own talent DNA, leveraging advancements in technology and data, and stepping up the positioning of its function in the enterprise.

Chapter 9: Future of Work—Unlocking the Potential of the Workforce through AI

Through this chapter, I have tried to provide a better understanding of the effects of AI on the future of work. I strongly believe that the future will be about 'man and machine' and not 'man versus machine'. If we reinvent our business processes, we will be able to take advantage of AI technologies to fundamentally reshape the nature of our work, create positive business impact and fetch benefits for our workforce. AI will not only impact the nature of jobs but can also enhance employee engagement by helping enterprises track issues more dynamically and become capable of more targeted and personalized interventions.

I strongly believe that organizational transformation is the key to successful and sustainable digital transformation. And I hope my experiences and insights in the chapters ahead will be helpful in your journey of transforming your enterprise.

1

Building Organization Culture
to Succeed in the Digital Age

Culture eats Strategy for breakfast

Peter Drucker, Author,
Management Tasks, Responsibilities, Practices

Time and again in this book, I have mentioned how culture is the critical foundation for an enterprise to succeed in the digital age. In section 1, where I introduced the new rules of management to succeed in the digital age, one of the key rules was building an entrepreneurial culture. In this chapter, I explore what are the aspects of the culture required to succeed in the digital age and how you build them.

I was very fortunate that I spent the first twenty years of my career in great firms like McKinsey and Fidelity, which showed me how culture was the bedrock of their enduring success and how it brought consistency and common purpose across sprawling global firms. Last five years, I have had the opportunity to be at the cutting edge of the digital age. My time at Flipkart, which is a true digital native, and the last three years at Incedo where I have been having the opportunity to support some of the largest companies in the world on their digital transformation journeys have given me an intimate understanding of the culture needed to succeed in the digital age.

Marshall Goldsmith's famous motto, 'What got you here won't get you there!' rings very true for enterprises making a transition to the digital age. Succeeding in the digital age requires some distinct attributes, which enterprises need to build very consciously into their culture. There are at least nine aspects of culture that I believe enterprises need to build to succeed in the digital age:

1. **Decision-making, balancing data and intuition:** The digital age is characterized by an abundance of data. Executives need to get comfortable with using the exploding volume and variety of data and make decisions using it. Data-driven decision-making is a culture that is necessary to build, especially to cut out obvious mistakes. At the same time, in the digital age when data and decision-making tools are available to everybody, how do you differentiate and make superior decisions? I believe along with data; intuition has a very important role to play. This might sound contradictory, but it is one of the many paradoxes that executives need to master in the digital age.

2. **Speed of action under ambiguity:** In section 1, I spoke about the VUCA world. Speed of action is one of the critical requirements to succeed in the VUCA world, especially as most markets are changing very fast and business and product cycles are becoming shorter. However, large organizations often have a problem in operating with speed. It is of course the complexity and additional processes that come with size. But, even more than that, sometimes a risk-averse culture can develop, which slows speed of decision-making and of actions. Accelerating speed of action is as much about simplifying processes and structure as it is about a culture change. Now the nuance is that in a VUCA world you have to operate at speed but under ambiguity; the picture is often hazy, so navigation becomes even more difficult.

Decision-making in such situations is an acquired skill, and enterprises need to create a safe space for executives to hone their skills.

3. **Audacity and intelligent risk-taking:** One of the most inspiring aspects I took away from Flipkart was a culture of audacity—of daring to dream big and to execute at scale that had rarely been seen in a large and complex market like India. In the digital age, when new opportunities are getting created at a rapid pace, entry barriers are low and incumbent positions count for less, audacity is a critical success factor. Some leaders might be intrinsically more audacious, but for most this is an acquired skill. However, like the previous point about speed of action, audacity is not a free pass. Risk-taking is essential but it has to be 'intelligent risk-taking' and not just playing the casino. This is another example of duality or paradoxes that leaders and enterprises need to master in the digital age.

4. **Innovation and creativity:** Thinking out of the box is absolutely essential to compete in the digital age, which is characterized by hyper-competition at one end and abundant new opportunities at another. Innovation and creativity have to be not just about a stroke of genius but part of the organization culture. Innovation is relevant for every part of the business and has to happen across levels. Culture of innovation and creativity has to be built systematically. It requires not just specific investments in new capabilities but often re-designing of processes and infrastructure. As an example, as innovation became a greater priority at Fidelity, we went through a major facelift of our offices—more open design, more collaboration spaces, and even a change in the colour schemes!

5. **Technology DNA:** Technology is at the heart of the digital age and building a Technology DNA is one of the most critical competencies an enterprise needs to develop. However, this is also the competency that is most difficult for traditional

enterprises to build. In many businesses, technology has been a support function focused on infrastructure provisioning and maintenance. The journey from there to building a cutting-edge technology capability is a long one. You have to bring in the right leaders. For example, in a couple of our own clients at Incedo, I have seen that CIO/CTO function (which did not exist earlier) has been established over the past three to four years and senior leaders brought in. You have to supplement the leadership by bringing the right talent. Technology is an area where the difference in output between the top quartile and median talent is very significant. This naturally leads to a war for talent and implies that you have to be not just customer-centric but also employee-centric. This calls for a shift not just in philosophy but has to be translated in processes and procedures. This is not a quick fix; it is a very substantial change that has to be persevered over a period of time.

6. **Continuous learning and humility:** The digital age is characterized by a very high velocity of change—markets, products, channels, competition, and of course technology; in fact, every possible aspect of business. With so much change, continuous learning is absolutely critical both at the enterprise and individual levels. The biggest challenge to learning is hubris, that 'you know it all' and/or 'I know best'. Successful enterprises and leaders are even more prone to hubris. This hubris can be the kiss of death! Antidote to hubris is to inculcate humility. I strongly believe humility is the necessary ingredient to ensure long-term success. Now the question is how to inculcate humility. I have seen that going 'out of your box' and getting a broad set of experiences and working with the masters in different areas gives you a 'reality check' and is a good way to inculcate humility.

7. **Inspiring, less managing:** The digital age is so complex and dynamic that no one individual, however brilliant, can manage it all. There is just too much happening; it is impossible for one

Building organization culture to succeed in the Digital age

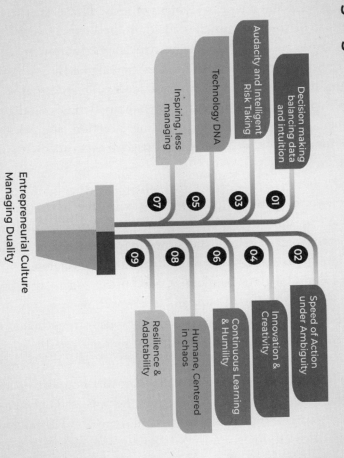

Decision making balancing data and intuition — 01

Audacity and Intelligent Risk Taking — 03

Technology DNA — 05

Inspiring, less managing — 07

02 — Speed of Action under Ambiguity

04 — Innovation & Creativity

06 — Continuous Learning & Humility

08 — Humane, Centered in chaos

09 — Resilience & Adaptability

Entrepreneurial Culture
Managing Duality

person to keep track, let alone drive execution on all the threads. This implies that not only can an individual- or 'hero'-centric culture not work but even the traditional command-and-control cultures will not work. You need teams at different levels, and they have to work in a relatively autonomous fashion so they can respond and adapt to changes quickly. However, there also needs to be some alignment and common direction across these autonomous teams. I call it the need for 'aligned autonomy'. There are multiple aspects that go into enabling aligned autonomy, but the most important is a culture and leadership style that is more inspiring than managing. It is less about defining and tightly managing, and more about providing direction, alignment to a common purpose, and then a safe space to experiment and make mistakes.

8. **Humane, centered in chaos:** The digital age is characterized by the irresistible march of technology with Artificial Intelligence (AI) as its torchbearer. When our world is dominated by machines and remote working is becoming the norm (accelerated further because of Covid-19 pandemic), the human touch is becoming even more important. Deep human connections not only enable employee loyalty and retention, but they also strengthen a sense of common purpose. One of the key reasons for the amazing success of the McKinsey Knowledge Centre were the incredibly deep human connections and team spirit that got developed. At Fidelity India, our seminal moment of the year used to be Family Day, a gala celebration where we would get families (including children) of all our employees together. Genuine engagement in community service is another powerful way I have seen that builds great human connections and loyalty for the company. Above are but a few illustrations, I am convinced that in the world dominated by machines, human connections will become even more important. This is another paradox that enterprises and leaders need to master in the digital age.

Illustrative – Incedo Mission and Values

Incedo has a dual mission

Client – Build **long-term partnerships** and deliver game-changing **business impact** by leveraging **data & emerging technologies**

People – Build a **world-class organization** that attracts, develops and retains the **best talent** and enables them to grow to their **potential**

Reinforced by 8 core values

1 Exceed Client Expectations

- **Client First** - put Client's interest always first
- **Trusted Partner** - always deliver what we commit
- **Ownership**- be Proactive, take responsibility for client success
- **Engagement**- build deep and lasting relationships
- **Value Addition**- go beyond expectations

2 Pursue Excellence

- **Problem Solving** – zone in on the right problem & solve it in a structured way
- **Expertise** – bring a knowledge spike
- **Strategy to Execution**- able to go from big picture to implementation
- **World-Class Quality** – ensure highest quality in all we do
- **Positive attitude** – be solution oriented, have drive & energy to continuously raise the bar

3 Build for the Long - Term

- **Strategic** - invest in long-term bets on clients, capabilities and people
- **Audacious** - think big and transformational, drive for growth
- **Process Orientation** - focus on right methods & structure for outcomes
- **Resilient** – stay the course
- **Two-Speed** – able to connect short and long term, manage quality

4 Embrace Change & Innovation

- **Externally Aware** – be well informed of market & technology trends
- **Entrepreneurial**- seize emerging opportunities, adapt quickly, have bias for action
- **Learning Mindset** – be curious and invest in continuous learning
- **Applied Innovation** – bring new ideas to solve client problems

5 Work as One Global Team

- **Common Purpose** – focus on team mission over self interest
- **Collaborate** - build & share knowledge, always bring the best of Incedo
- **Inclusive**- champion diversity
- **Non-Hierarchical** - respect for each other & ideas across levels
- **Fair & Transparent**- be objective & non-political, clear in communication

6 Be a Caring Meritocracy

- **Hi-Quality Talent**– bring best talent, hold high hiring standards
- **Employee First**– take an employee lens for all processes & practices
- **Grow Leaders** - provide stretch opportunities, invest in development
- **High Performance Standards**– set clear & ambitious goals, seek & provide timely feedback
- **Fun & Warmth** – build a happy, safe and family-like workplace

7 Drive Commercial Rigor

- **Price for Value** – build hi-quality, sustainable business
- **Data Driven** – define and track key metrics, use data for decision making
- **Owner Mindset**- spend like its your own money
- **Frugal but Effective** – be efficient but not hesitate to invest

8 Always act with Integrity

- **Ethical Standards**– hold the highest standards in all conduct
- **Zero Tolerance** – trust & empower but zero tolerance for breach of trust
- **Take Hard Decisions** – do the right thing, not the easy thing
- **Obligation to Dissent**– speak up if any action is not aligned with our Values

9. **Resilience and Adaptability:** Volatility and Uncertainty are a given in the digital age. Therefore, it is almost certain that you will face many headwinds and setbacks in your journey, both at the enterprise and individual levels. It is critical that you develop the resilience to bounce back and the adaptability to make the necessary adjustments. A key enabler for this is to have a long-term view, which allows you to face the ups and downs with equanimity. Another important enabler is to have support networks, both at the organizational and individual levels. For me personally, another key enabler helping me build resilience has been spirituality and the practice of meditation, which anchors me and allows me to take a broader view of life.

I have shared the above nine aspects of culture, which I believe enterprises need to build in the digital age. Now the obvious question is, how do you build or transform your culture. Building the right culture is a long and complex process. It is not a quick fix and can take years of consistent efforts. I am sharing below a few learnings from my experience on how to build culture consciously:

1. **Start with defining the values:** The foundations of culture are clearly stated values. Culture develops over a period of time and is based on the cumulative of decisions and actions. And it is values that help guide the decisions. Defining values is not easy, it takes a lot of thought and reflection. For example, when I joined Incedo, it took me less than three months to develop the company's strategy, but I took over twelve months to define our values. I saw the latter as more important and difficult to reverse, and I wanted to be sure about it. (I have shared the Incedo values in the graphic on the previous page).

2. **Role modelling by leaders:** I often see companies blaring their values and mission/vision statements across their walls, both physical and virtual. While communication is important to build awareness and embed the values and culture, it can only lead to partial success. What is even more critical are the actions of

Building organization culture to succeed in the Digital age - Guiding Principles 'how to'

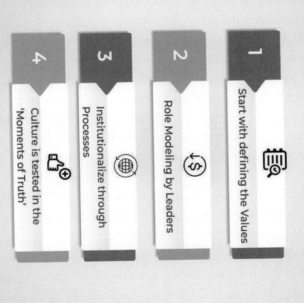

1 Start with defining the Values

2 Role Modeling by Leaders

3 Institutionalize through Processes

4 Culture is tested in the 'Moments of Truth'

leaders. 'Actions speak louder than words' is especially true here. Role modelling by leaders is thus the single most important driver of culture.

3. **Institutionalize through processes:** Culture is the way you do things. Therefore, culture is not about sporadic efforts but has to be institutionalized and thus built into all the processes. Whether it is your client service policies or internal processes like recruitment and performance management, all need to reflect your values and culture.

4. **Culture is tested in the 'moments of truth':** Crisis can bring the best or worst out of us. How enterprises and leaders act during a crisis, the 'moments of truth', truly shapes the culture of the organization. Our actions when we are tested deeply define and shape both the individual's and enterprise's character. Our actions in such 'moments of truth' carry a deep imprint for both customers and employees alike, and thus become defining points for the culture. The Covid-19 pandemic has certainly presented such an important moment of truth for enterprises and leaders.

The digital age is often seen to be about technology change. While technology is certainly a very important driver of the digital age, culture is perhaps the most important differentiator between winners and laggards in this era. It is even more so as there are many paradoxes and seemingly conflicting objectives and expectations that have to be met. A more entrepreneurial culture and managing paradoxes or 'duality' are the most unique aspects of culture in the digital age. I hope my experiences above provide you some useful perspectives both on what are some desirable culture elements to have and also how to build them.

Summary

To succeed in the digital age, enterprises need to adapt their culture to the unique characteristics and expectations of this age.

Nine key aspects that enterprises need to incorporate in their culture to succeed are:

- **Decision-making should involve a balance of data and intuition**, thereby cutting mistakes and delivering superior outcomes.
- **Speed of action under ambiguity** requires a safe space for executives to hone their decision-making skills.
- **Audacity and intelligent risk-taking** - The ability to dream big and execute at scale requires risk-taking with intelligence.
- **Innovation and creativity** need to be embedded in the organization culture and should happen across levels.
- **Technology DNA** is a critical competency in the digital age and every enterprise needs to build this, irrespective of industry. For many organizations this is a big change as this is a new competency they have to build.
- **Continuous learning and humility** are critical both at the enterprise and individual levels.
- **Inspiring, less managing** - Building a culture of 'aligned autonomy' through empowerment and inspiring leadership is important for teams to execute and respond to changes quickly.
- **Humane, centered in chaos**. The digital age is characterized by technology and AI. Human touch becomes even more important in this age of machines. It should involve employees, families, community service and engagement to drive connections and loyalty to the company.
- **Resilience and adaptability**. In the current age, setbacks at the enterprise and individual levels are expected. Aspects that help build resilience, include having an equanimous approach, support networks, spirituality and practising meditation.

To embed the above nine aspects into the culture, enterprises need to define clear and actionable values, encourage role modelling by leadership and institutionalize them through organization processes.

2

Knowledge Management—A Key to Differentiation in the Digital Age

Sharing knowledge occurs when people are genuinely interested in helping one another develop new capacities for action: it is about creating learning processes

Peter Senge, Author, *Fifth Discipline*

Digital technologies are profoundly disrupting traditional industries, offering new business model opportunities unheard of in the years before. As organizations embark on transforming their core businesses to succeed in the digital age, some questions arise: What will be our source of competitive advantage in the marketplace? What will determine our ability to demand differential pricing for our products and services? For instance, John Deere, a farm equipment manufacturer, underwent a successful transformation from a company providing equipment and machines to a precision agriculture company harnessing IoT, data and analytics to improve farmer operations and their bottom line. Transforming from a pure equipment manufacturer to a data-driven technology company requires a fundamental shift. The thinking shifts from vesting know-how with a small cohort of experts to a systemic approach where the organization reimagines how to embed processes and systems, leveraging proprietary knowledge from across all functions.

To succeed in the digital economy, where information explosion and wide availability of information are the norm, **an organization's ability to develop high-quality, contextual proprietary knowledge** to serve its customers in unique ways becomes a key source of differentiation and competitive advantage.

What is **proprietary knowledge in the digital economy**? It is an organization's unique collection of experiential knowledge and digital assets—data, algorithms, software (code), methods, techniques and processes—that a competitor will not have. It is the collective experience of individuals and teams in the organization representing its expertise. Proprietary knowledge enables a unique ability to solve problems and recognize patterns from the different functions of an organization, to connect them in ways that deliver exceptional value to customers. Often, proprietary knowledge is a collection of experiences based on work delivered by the organization to its customers and work done by individuals who develop this expertise through their career with the organization. The challenge lies in **transforming this individual expert-level tacit knowledge into a codified collection** available for use **broadly and on-demand**. In pursuing any such transformation, a common pitfall in approach is to codify all forms of tacit knowledge instead of taking a thoughtful approach to identifying sources of tacit knowledge of high value.

However, transforming an organization to succeed in the digital economy, where proprietary knowledge and expertise become a centrepiece of the business strategy, is not a trivial exercise. It requires a fundamental shift in the core business processes, including the people, the value chain functions that enable a product or service to sell (delivery capabilities) and business development (sales and marketing). It is not uncommon to find pockets of initiatives in an organization under the title of Knowledge Management, which worsens the problem in the long term by creating disconnected knowledge silos—often unusable assets—that later become part of a cost rationalization exercise. It promotes the fallacy of 'If you build it, they will come'.

An organization's approach to unlocking its full potential and capitalizing on its proprietary knowledge resides in implementing a more connected enterprise and an effective knowledge cycle—where the assets you build are the ones in demand for delivering the organization's strategic goals. When done right, it will offer better insights from existing and new data, more accurate and efficient decision-making, improved ability to conceptualize new product offerings, and differentiated positioning in the market amongst competitors. Knowledge management as a discipline then becomes an integral part of an organization's business strategy in developing and leveraging its knowledge assets to drive superior performance and impact.

Successful implementation of a knowledge management capability and supporting processes involves a two-fold approach.

The first consists of building a knowledge marketplace on the principles of supply and demand, delivering a virtuous knowledge cycle. The second entails implementation of six critical knowledge management practices to drive sustainable organizational change.

The knowledge marketplace approach

How should an organization develop an institutional knowledge management capability where the knowledge assets built are those that are in high demand to deliver differentiating value to its customers? *The answer lies in creating a knowledge marketplace.* A knowledge marketplace approach enables an organization to develop institutional capability where knowledge seekers (demand) and knowledge contributors (supply) come together in the knowledge market to build and sustain a self-creating, self-perpetuating, virtuous knowledge cycle.

For example, a leading producer of specialty chemicals for healthcare was facing bimodal workforce challenges involving:

1. A retiring R&D workforce and loss of expertise. *How does the enterprise harvest the know-how of decades of subject-matter expertise?*
2. Productivity gap among the new scientists coming onboard. *What is the best path to enable institutional knowledge?*

By implementing a knowledge marketplace approach that codifies individual expert knowledge into documented institutional know-how, while simultaneously connecting the new scientists as consumers of the proprietary knowledge to become productive, the organization protected and improved its competitive advantage.

The essential components of a marketplace should include:

1. **Knowledge objects (data and knowledge):** Types of knowledge that an organization cares about and focuses on while building the knowledge base, emphasizing the proprietary knowledge assets of:
   - **Explicit content** representing codified knowledge in the form of artifacts, algorithms, data, industry domain models, software and code libraries.
   - **Tacit knowledge** representing the expertise, intuitive know-how and pattern recognition rooted in experience and context.
   - **Structured data** generally consisting of the data found in databases, associated with 'rows and columns'. This data usually comprises about 20 per cent of an enterprise's total data.
   - **Unstructured data** representing the knowledge assets in the form of text, diagrams, audio, video, streaming data, and more.

2. **Supply (knowledge contributors) and demand (knowledge seekers):** Knowledge supply in the marketplace is the combination of experts and the different knowledge objects that

are most valuable for the organization's broader use. Knowledge seekers ensure that knowledge supply is in response to demand.

3. **The knowledge market:** This enables interplay and connection between supply and demand through knowledge brokers, who are knowledge professionals facilitating the best use of knowledge supply and demand in the marketplace; they are enabled by knowledge systems, in the form of the knowledge repository and search as the underlying technology infrastructure.

Why knowledge management initiatives fail

As organizations embrace the knowledge economy and develop strategies and programmes to win in the digital age, it is not uncommon to find knowledge management initiatives underway in many organizations. However, many such initiatives still fail, for the following reasons:

1. **Organizational culture:** Peter Drucker's famous phrase, 'Culture eats Strategy for breakfast', applies well to knowledge management. An organizational culture where the majority thinks 'this is how we have always done things' becomes a significant roadblock for the organization in shifting the mindset from 'knowledge is mine, why should I share?' to 'I will openly share and consume knowledge'. Incorporating knowledge management as a catalyst to an organization's digital strategy drives cultural change from the top and makes it systemic.
2. **Knowledge-specificity:** Viewing knowledge assets as general-purpose and abstract constructs invariably leads to a situation where they are available, but no one wants to use them. Useful and actionable knowledge assets are industry-specific, domain-rich, and should help improve in work performance.
3. **Knowledge cycle design and implementation:** A poorly designed and implemented knowledge cycle will result in

Vision for Knowledge Marketplace

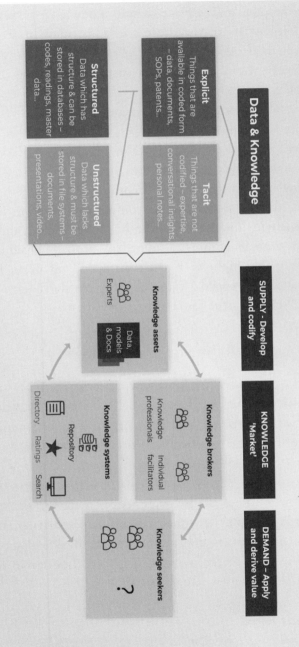

Data & Knowledge

Explicit
Things that are available in coded form – data, documents, SOPs, patents...

Tacit
Things that are not codified – expertise, conversational insights, personal notes...

Structured
Data which has structure & can be stored in databases – codes, readings, master data...

Unstructured
Data which lacks structure & must be stored in file systems – documents, presentations, video...

SUPPLY - Develop and codify

KNOWLEDGE 'Market'

DEMAND – Apply and derive value

Knowledge assets
Experts
Data, models & Docs

Knowledge brokers
Knowledge professionals
Individual facilitators

Knowledge systems
Repository
Directory · Ratings · Search

Knowledge seekers
?

a knowledge marketplace where knowledge assets become available but are of very little use. This points to a disconnect between demand and supply, or a disconnect in the processes that implement them. Methods for sustained adoption, continuous feedback for improvements, and a focus on those assets that deliver value and differentiation require effective governance and audit mechanisms.

4. **Return on investment (ROI) is elusive:** Expecting to immediately reap benefits from a short-term investment in a knowledge initiative and becoming disillusioned when the returns do not materialize is common. ROI from knowledge management initiatives is often hard to measure and can take a long time in coming, leading to executive disillusionment. A sustainable high-ROI programme will involve a two-speed approach, with speed 1 targeting tangible short-term goals and speed 2 building the foundation to scale up.

Six best practices for organizational success

A focus on what matters most, what represents proprietary knowledge, and a knowledge marketplace approach is essential, but these three elements by themselves cannot drive organizational change.

I have had the opportunity to be intimately involved in developing the knowledge management capability within McKinsey and also engaging with many clients on their knowledge management journeys. In my experience, there are six knowledge management best practices that are critical for driving sustainable change and momentum and in shifting the day-to-day operations in an organization where individuals are conditioned to having an attitude of 'this is how we do our work'.

1. **Strategic levers**
   a. *Leadership commitment and explicit embedding of the strategic importance of knowledge aspirations in the strategy and values*

of the organization: A top-tier global consultancy embraces a knowledge culture through its leadership commitment: 'Knowledge is the lifeblood of the firm. We have easily doubled our investment in Knowledge over the past couple of years. If that means that we do 10–15 per cent less client work today, we are willing to pay that price to invest in the future.'

b. ***An organizational culture that promotes sharing of knowledge and design of incentives*** *for long-term career growth and promotions*: An organization must have role models in the shape of leaders driving thought leadership and encouraging others to engage. Role-modelling on the part of leaders drives thought leadership and enables leveraging of in-house expertise rather than reinventing the wheel each time. It demonstrates organizational commitment by moving high-quality professionals to lead knowledge initiatives, making them visible to the organization through consistent communication of the financial benefits and increased productivity. Successful knowledge initiatives must be profiled with the same enthusiasm as business success stories are. Additionally, incentives are aligned to encouraging a culture of knowledge development and sharing.

c. ***Organizational design*** *or incorporation of knowledge management deliverables and output into individual roles and responsibilities and performance measures*: A best-in-class organizational design incorporates the enablers for knowledge management functions—research, knowledge-development support, knowledge systems as centralized functions for economies of scale—anchored by experienced practitioners. It decentralizes practices in the functional areas of the organization that encompass dissemination of knowledge, sharing of best practices and learning agendas to develop new perspectives.

2. Operational levers

d. ***Knowledge architecture****: Specificity of the knowledge domain is a crucial principle behind an effective knowledge architecture.* Specificity results when the design principles of taxonomy and its structure are industry-specific. A knowledge map brings it together by mapping the domain-specific areas and the assets under its scope. A well-designed knowledge architecture enables knowledge discovery, powered by search capabilities that can go beyond the classic keyword search to a cognitive search that can bring a variety of knowledge sources together, interpret the search's intent and personalize the results for relevance. Through policies and quality indicators, governance ensures that the knowledge assets in the knowledge marketplace are of high quality and will go through an editorial review process before publication.

e. ***Knowledge processes****: Processes and prescriptive methods for content creation and curation are critical enablers for codification of tacit knowledge from existing bodies of work and enforce a discipline for knowledge capture, standardization and availability.* It sometimes involves special projects, such as building the right processes and methods for curating a knowledge base of AI algorithms across an organization. Key supporting processes covering taxonomy management and audit mechanisms for ensuring relevance and high quality of content in the knowledge base at all times are critical to avoid the risk of the knowledge assets becoming stale and of diminished value to the users. A customized taxonomy organized by a functional area of a given industry or function and breaking it down to its next levels of subject matter, topics and assets, ensures a continuous cycle of methodical identification of knowledge gaps and the nature of knowledge demand in the organization.

Six best practices for organizational success in Knowledge Management

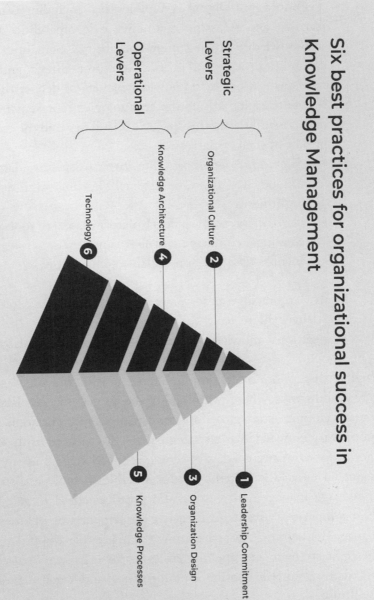

Strategic Levers

Operational Levers

Organizational Culture 2

Knowledge Architecture 4

Technology 6

1 Leadership Commitment

3 Organization Design

5 Knowledge Processes

f. **Technology**: Digital technologies, including machine learning and AI, offer distinctive new capabilities for use in knowledge management platforms. Semantic search capabilities using NLP can interpret intent and draw relationships between knowledge assets to deliver the most relevant results. While the technologies represent multiple new possibilities in this space, it is vital to avoid the common pitfalls of such initiatives:

- *fragmented technology initiatives* (disparate data sets, unique classification systems), leading to integration nightmares
- *multiplicity of access points* (microsites, search tools), often creating a confusing end-user experience
- Inconsistent and non-scalable architectures

By embracing best practices, focusing on initiatives that deliver high RoI, technology can effectively enable an organization's knowledge management vision and goals.

Digital disruption offers unique opportunities for organizations across industries where winning in the global marketplace calls for developing strategies for competitive differentiation using proprietary knowledge as a strategic asset. To succeed in the digital age, every company needs to become a knowledge company. This is not an easy task, but those who are able to build a distinctive knowledge management culture and practices stand to gain long-term competitive advantage. Effective implementation of knowledge management approaches, combining the marketplace approach with the right strategic and operational levers for organizational change will deliver superior business performance and value creation in the future.

Summary

- Proprietary knowledge is a key differentiator in the digital age. It will not be an exaggeration to say that every company needs to become a knowledge company in the digital age.
- Knowledge management involves transforming individual expert-level tacit knowledge into a codified collection available for use broadly and on-demand.
- Knowledge management initiatives are notoriously difficult to get right. They are not a quick fix. ROI is unclear and can take long. Changing the organizational culture is a tough process and designing self-sustaining knowledge cycles is not easy.
- Getting knowledge management right is a sustained, long-term effort. It requires leadership commitment and signalling, building a knowledge-sharing culture, building supportive organization structure and knowledge processes, and investing in the right knowledge and technology infrastructure.

3

Innovation—A Call to Action

Every block of stone has a statue inside it and it is the task of the sculptor to discover it

Michelangelo

In this chapter, I have focused on the Indian IT/BPM industry, its innovation challenges and priorities.

Innovation is an imperative for the Indian IT/BPM industry

The Indian IT/BPM industry is at a crucial juncture. This industry has been the crown jewel of the India Shining story and one of the few areas where India is truly a global leader. However, the industry's growth trajectory has hit a few speed bumps in recent years. An industry that was growing consistently at over 20 per cent in the 1990s and 2000s is now growing in the single digits. The economic environment has been challenging, customer needs are becoming more complex, competition is increasing, and, most importantly, technology megatrends like cloud, AI, big data and automation are changing the rules of the game. Clearly, **given the combination of**

these forces, India's IT/BPM industry needs to innovate, not just to drive the next stage of growth but perhaps also to stay competitive.

In many ways, the Indian IT/BPM industry is well placed to drive innovation and become a great example of what needs to happen more broadly in the country. It has scale and global penetration; it has built domain and business knowledge; most of the companies in this industry are resource-rich, sitting on piles of cash; and most importantly, it has great talent. The young talent in particular has great potential. India's young are ready and itching to do something creative and impactful with their lives.

However, as an industry, IT/BPM is perhaps **lagging in both quantum and quality of innovation**. It is ironic that the Indian IT/BPM industry, which has itself been a huge, disruptive innovation over the past twenty years, has not stepped up its own innovation engine enough to lead in the digital age. There is minimal differentiation in processes and service offerings across these companies in India. There is not enough IP creation and brand building, either at the company level or at the industry level, and this is in a scenario where many companies are sitting pretty with a lot of cash on their balance sheets! There are, of course, many examples of incremental innovation and of the famous Indian *jugaad* at work. However, there is little to suggest that widespread systematic innovation is happening. It is precisely this challenge—the upgrade **from** *jugaad* **to systematic innovation**—that we need to address.

Why the Indian IT/BPM industry has not realized its innovation potential

There are four types of innovation: process, product, customer experience and business model. The Indian IT/BPM industry has done well in the first type of innovation (process) but has struggled to be innovative in the other three. That raises the question as to why the industry has not realized its innovation potential, despite the market imperative for innovation being so strong and the industry having so many of the required ingredients in place.

I believe there are five key issues that have hampered progress on this front:

1. **It is difficult to change a success formula:** It is undeniable that the Indian IT/BPM industry has been a spectacular success story over the past couple of decades—showing steady revenue growth, dominating market share and high profitability. It has been built on a business model based on the availability of high-quality, low-cost technology talent, ability to scale up at speed, customer responsiveness and a strong process orientation. It has led to the creation of world-class mega companies like TCS, Infosys, Wipro and HCL, and also a host of successful mid-tier companies.

   However, digital is changing customer expectations. There is a greater need for design thinking, change management, agile delivery and a number of new technology and management competencies. These changing expectations call for a more intense engagement model, a broader range of skills, more product depth and an iterative operating model. This runs counter to the scale-based efficient service factory model that the IT/BPM industry has executed so well all these years. It is not easy to change a success formula that has worked well for so long. The relatively steady growth and good financial performance of the Indian IT/BPM industry perhaps do not result in a 'burning platform' for driving innovation as a priority.

2. **Driving product innovation in a services business model is tough:** As both time-to-market expectations and technology cycles keep getting shorter in the digital age, companies are changing their 'build versus buy' criterion and shifting more towards buying products and IP. This trend means that Indian IT/BPM companies need to step up on product innovation.

WINNING IN THE DIGITAL AGE 323

Driving product innovation in a services business model is a big challenge. The organizational DNA is very customer-delivery focused, where expectations are clear and typically set by the client. A product mindset, which requires more thought leadership, tolerance for ambiguity and self-direction, is difficult to build and have co-exist within a services model organizational culture. Moreover, the financial and operating KPIs and frameworks of services companies do not support the requirements of product innovation.

3. **Lack of deep understanding of customer pain points:** Indian IT/BPM companies typically have good technology and process skills but lack in domain depth and end-customer understanding. The starting point of any product, customer experience or business model innovation is a deep understanding of customer pain points. Often, I see a lot of enthusiasm about innovation in Global Delivery Centres (GDCs) in India and many well-intentioned efforts, but lack of deep understanding of customer pain points means that these efforts often end up missing the mark. Deep end-customer understanding is not easy to build. It is not about general knowledge or theoretical knowledge but about a direct set of experiences that leads to a deep and intuitive understanding of the end customer.

4. **Short-term orientation:** Perhaps it is a natural outcome of the services-oriented business model or perhaps it is a broader cultural issue, the short-term orientation you often see in Indian IT/BPM companies is not conducive to driving substantial product or business model innovation. Such innovation calls for long investment cycles and extended payback period expectations. I see many well-intentioned innovation initiatives getting off the ground, but many are not able to stay the course as their executives run out of patience or move on to the next big thing!

5. **Lack of deep tech and problem-solving skills:** While the entire basis of the IT industry in India is access to abundant tech talent, paradoxically, there is a shortage of deep tech talent in the country. One of the characteristics of the digital age is the rise of emerging technologies like AI, cloud and automation. These technologies are still evolving and offer tremendous opportunities for development and innovation, which the Indian industry is not fully capitalizing on. The other shortcoming in talent lies in its problem-solving skills. The service factory model that the Indian industry has focused on does not allow for the development of problem-solving skills of the nature needed to drive significant innovation.

What the Indian IT/BPM industry needs to do to unlock its innovation potential

Stepping up the game on innovation is not a quick fix. Sustained action is needed in multiple areas. I believe the following ten action areas are important for the Indian IT/BPM industry to unlock its innovation potential:

1. **Continuous innovation:** We search for game-changing ideas, but we must never forget the small ideas. They can add up to significant impact. Ideation platforms that allow employees to share their ideas on different problem statements can be very powerful. Regular hackathons can also be very effective. However, just generating ideas is not enough. Processes must be established to follow up on these ideas and track their implementation.
2. **Investment budget:** It is important to carve out a specific budget for innovation. Innovation does not arise from mere good intentions; hard dollars need to be committed to innovation initiatives.
3. **Centres of excellence:** It is helpful to build specialized capabilities separately from your core service lines. They can

provide you the flexibility to experiment with different talent profiles and not be limited by the operating models of your core capabilities. They can allow you to do contained experiments at high speed. Such centres of excellence (CoEs) played a critical role in the breakthrough innovation we were able to achieve at the McKinsey Knowledge Centre (McKC). (Case study shared in chapter 6 of section 4.)

4. **Culture of innovation:** You need to reinforce the 'creative confidence' of the staff. You must build a culture where risk-taking is encouraged and new ideas supported. Moreover, it is important to create a buzz in the organization around innovation. Clear signalling from senior management and sustained employee engagement are needed to build innovation momentum.

5. **Collaboration with start-ups:** There is now a vibrant ecosystem of start-ups in India. They are also being supported by NASSCOM and a host of other incubators. It is likely that breakthrough innovation happens not in large companies but in start-ups. Therefore, it is imperative that larger companies stay engaged with the start-up ecosystem and keep scouting for partnership opportunities.

6. **Serving the domestic market:** One of the challenges in driving innovation for Indian IT/BPM companies is getting to understand customer pain points deeply when the customer is on a different continent. Engaging with the domestic market can provide you with the proximity and market content for experimentation. For example, partnership with the India office was a critical enabler of the experimentation we were able to drive at the McKinsey Knowledge Centre, which had a global remit.

7. **Leveraging the global model:** Most Indian IT firms now have global delivery models. 'Onshore-offshore' collaboration can be a win-win. Onshore can bring a deeper understanding of customer pain points and offshore can provide a scale advantage.

8. **Acquisitions:** Indian IT/BPM firms have typically approached M&A with the objective of expanding their market coverage. They need to look at M&A as a way of acquiring niche capabilities and IP, which can give them a time-to-market advantage.

9. **Investment in learning and development:** Deep tech talent and problem-solving skills are key gaps for Indian IT companies, and these are also the foundational skills required for innovation in the digital age. Sustained investment in learning and development needs to happen to build these skills to the right quality.

10. **Partnership with academic institutions:** Talent is the foundation for innovation in the IT industry, and to acquire it companies need to look beyond their boundaries and to the broader supply chain. Companies need to consider partnering with select universities to ensure that the curriculum and teaching reflect their needs. This requires not just investment in internships and industry projects, but also active engagement in the teaching process.

Clearly, innovation is an imperative for the Indian IT/BPM industry in the digital age, whether it is for the larger companies, start-ups or product companies. There needs to be a call to action to leaders and companies to spark and sustain significant innovation journeys in their organizations. Equally, it is a challenge and responsibility for industry bodies like NASSCOM to help create an ecosystem that ignites a culture of innovation.

Conclusion

This chapter is about innovation imperatives and challenges of the Indian IT/BPM industry. However, innovation is a critical requirement for every industry in the digital age. In fact, technology, customer experience and business model innovation constitute the entire foundation of the digital age. I believe lessons from this chapter are widely applicable in other industries too.

Ten action areas to unlock Innovation potential

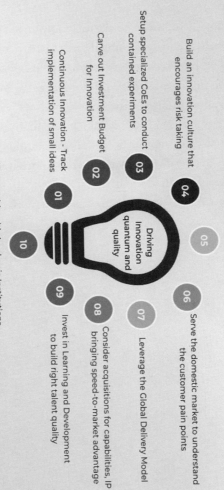

Build an innovation culture that encourages risk taking

Setup specialized CoEs to conduct contained experiments

Carve out Investment Budget for Innovation

Continuous Innovation - Track implementation of small ideas

Tap into the startup ecosystem

Driving Innovation quantum and quality

04

05

03

02

01

10

09

08

07

06

Partnership with Academic Institutions

Serve the domestic market to understand the customer pain points

Leverage the Global Delivery Model

Consider acquisitions for capabilities, IP bringing speed-to-market advantage

Invest in Learning and Development to build right talent quality

Summary

- Innovation is a key driver and imperative for every industry in the digital age.
- The Indian IT industry needs to innovate to drive the next stage of growth and stay competitive. In particular, they need to step up on product and business model innovation.
- Innovation does not happen by chance. It needs to be a structured and sustained effort.
- Some of the action areas to unlock the innovation potential are: methods for capturing and implementing small ideas, committed budget for innovation, collaboration with start-ups and partnership with academia.

4

Key Insights from My First Agile Training

Speed is the new currency of business

Marc Benihoff, Chairman and CEO, Sales Force

The need for Speed and therefore a move to Agile in everything we do is a fundamental shift in the digital age. In this chapter, I share some of my key learnings about Agile from a training programme I went through a few years back.

When I went through my first Agile training course, I was initially not looking forward to spending a couple of hours on a training programme where the topic was something, I felt I had a fair idea of. I had heard a fair bit about Agile from the tech leaders in my team and had read a few articles too. So, I was not sure what more I would get from the training. I was wrong! The Agile training was a good opportunity for reflection and for some key concepts to sink in.

I want to share eight key insights that I took away from the training:

1. **The business world is changing at an unprecedented pace and with that, the traditional rules of management (structured and stable are passé):** The combination of technology innovation, shortening business cycles, hypercompetition and shifting of

traditional markets in the digital age is creating unprecedented uncertainty and a high velocity of change. This implies that the management rules developed for a more structured, stable environment will almost certainly not work. This is a great challenge for managers (especially those of us above the age of forty!) as we probably need to unlearn what has made us successful so far. {I have shared perspectives on the new rules of business in detail in section 1 of this book.}

2. **Speed is king ('Fail fast' and move on is the new mantra):** One of the stark insights from the training was that a typical business requirement has a life of six months. This makes any long-drawn plans and execution cycles totally irrelevant! Therefore, the focus on short delivery sprints to deliver working software over comprehensive documentation. I also loved the concept of 'fail fast'—trying something, getting fast feedback, and then adapting or terminating it before more money is spent. It also reinforces the virtues of 80/20 thinking, something all of us know but don't always practise!

3. **Dealing with uncertainty (Build for today, design for tomorrow):** Given the unprecedented velocity of change, there is little point trying to predict the future. I loved the mantra 'build for today, design for tomorrow'; instead of solving for the very long term, we should handle present requirements efficiently (and quickly) but keep the design open/extensible for future requirements (which are not yet clear). I also liked the concept of 'cone of uncertainty', which says the only way to reduce variability in the estimate is to reduce variability in the project itself. This implies that the focus needs to be on smart decisions and actions that will help reduce variability.

4. **Customer collaboration is key (Getting close to the customer and building trust):** Given the combination of uncertainty and need for speed, to achieve success, it is paramount to be very close to the customer. You have to get the customer requirements/pain

Insights from Agile Training

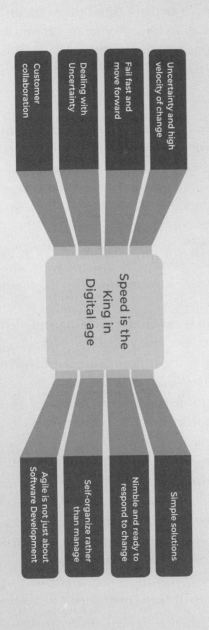

points spot-on and be very connected to understand any changes in real-time. This requires significant change in mindsets and operating models, from delivering to a contract over a period of time to real-time customer collaboration, frequent deliverables where you get feedback and, most importantly, building strong trust.

5. **Keep it simple (Turn to the most important needs of your most important customers):** Complexity is the antithesis of Agile. The key to meeting expectations of speed from the enterprise is to have simple solutions. This means that instead of trying to do everything afresh, one must use standard platforms and reuse components where possible. This also means that we should avoid customizing and attempting to solve every possible customer need but focus instead on addressing the most important customer needs of our most important customers.

6. **Linear thinking is out (From thinking and planning to doing):** You do not have the time to develop a nice sequential plan and almost certainly will not have the opportunity to follow it in a structured fashion. You have to be nimble and ready to respond to change. This also calls for a shift in managerial focus, from thinking and planning to doing. As the instructor said, 'to understand, do!' It is only by being very connected to the action that managers pick up the changes quickly enough and respond to them decisively without getting into long 'analyse-plan-approve-do' cycles.

7. **Self-organize rather than manage (Empower people, tolerate failure):** A key mantra of the agile approach is the focus on individuals and interactions over processes and tools. This requires a significant shift in our approach to people. Instead of trying to manage teams, we need to empower people. We need to break our hierarchical mindsets and processes. Very importantly, we will also need higher tolerance towards failure.

8. **Agile is not just about software development (It applies across the business):** Agile is clearly a significant and necessary shift in our approach to software development. However, it is not just about that. For example, I can see how the fundamental principles of Agile are equally relevant for strategy development and business planning work. The underlying driver of high-velocity change is common across business areas and functions, and thus the agile concepts are something that can and need to be applied across business/project situations.

This training triggered self-reflection; the world is changing fast and therefore the need to revisit mental models and approaches. I will conclude this chapter with one of the opening comments the Agile instructor made, 'There are no best practices, only good practices.' The time for hubris is over; the time for learning is now!

Summary

1. **The business world is changing at an unprecedented pace,** and with that the traditional rules of management.
2. **Speed is king:** a 'fail fast' or 'lose early' philosophy helps one to move quickly to areas with higher chances of success.
3. **Dealing with uncertainty:** the focus needs to be on smart decisions and actions that will help reduce variability
4. **Customer collaboration is key:** develop real-time collaboration and frequent feedback on deliverables to achieve success.
5. **Keep it simple:** the key to meeting expectations of speed is to have simple solutions and processes.
6. **Linear thinking is out:** be nimble, pick up changes quickly and act decisively.
7. **Self-organize rather than manage:** Empower teams to be self-directed.
8. **Agile is not just about software development:** Agile concepts can be applied across business and project situations.

5

Learning to Reinvent for Tomorrow

We cannot teach people anything, we can only help them discover it within themselves

Galileo

The velocity of technology and business change is unprecedented; product and technology cycles are becoming shorter and customer expectations are changing rapidly. Additionally, the Covid-19 pandemic has catalyzed digitization. As a result, firms have started recasting enterprise-wide processes to adapt to the needs of their internal target audience—the employee, who is digitally savvy, demands high-quality solutions and is not ready to wait. Additionally, everything has gone virtual and prior degrees of separation with respect to distance, geographies and time zones have been eliminated.

All these forces at work have made learning a strategic priority for organizations across industries and across the globe. Every organization has to focus on continuous learning for its employees and on building a learning culture to meet the changing expectations to stay competitive in this digital age. The way I see it is, these

334

transformational forces are resulting in a complete reimagination of every aspect of the learning and development (L&D) function, and potentially the L&D industry.

In this chapter, I will be covering the following aspects of learning and development:

- Five key shifts that are being witnessed in the Learning and Development space
- What are the Learning and Development action areas enterprises should focus on
- The challenges that will need to be addressed to actualize the Learning and Development promise

Five key shifts are being witnessed in the learning and development space

1. A shift from **one-size-fits-all learning** to **a high degree of personalization.** Technology is now a mature industry and there are diverse sets of needs. While there is a growing demand for new, digital skills (AI, data science, cloud, etc.), a large volume of demand is still there for legacy skills. This calls for a segmented approach.

2. There has been a shift from **standard predetermined push-based sessions** to **byte-sized self-directed learning sessions.** The classic delivery model was a classroom-based model with standard full-day training sessions, which involved dedicated time away from work. The new ask from trainees involves:

   - **Byte-sized learning** that can be consumed by the learners at their own pace.
   - They want to do this **virtually and quickly,** embedding it in their day-to-day work schedules.

3. As a result of the above two shifts, **learning is becoming multi-dimensional and channel-agnostic** which involves innovative

approaches so that millennials are engaged. This includes but is not only limited to:

- **On-the-job learning** aided by mentors on critical projects.
- **Blended learning, through videos, etc.,** on digital channels accessible through various devices.
- **Group social learning** where the learners can converge around common topics of interest and share notes and projects.

4. Another interesting shift is **from technologies to focus on core competencies** like problem solving, communication and leadership skills. Select IT companies have already recognized the need for these core competencies at scale and begun different programs to train the workforce.

5. The final shift includes moving away from **physical certificates** to **learning passports** and **creation of a digital reputation for the learner** on social media that is verifiable.

What should learning and development action areas be?

Most organizations have defined the following four key action areas for learning and development:

1. **Developing organizational capability to deal with the VUCA world:** Every organization has to focus on continuous learning for its employees to meet changing expectations and stay competitive in the future. This entails:
   - **Empowering employees by building core competencies:** In this rapidly evolving environment, it is important to empower employees by helping them build key competencies such as problem solving, business communication, stakeholder management, time management and project management through byte-sized training and video sessions.

Five shifts that are being witnessed in Learning & Development

From	To
One-size-fits-all learning	High degree of personalization
Standard predetermined push-based sessions	Byte-sized self-directed learning sessions
Classroom channel primarily	Omni-channel delivery
Hard skills focused	Soft skills focused
Physical certificates	Learning passports and digitally-certified

- **Building business acumen to better understand customer context:** It is very critical to have deep functional domain or business/vertical specializations to deliver high-quality customer-centric solutions. It is important for employees to build business acumen and align their learning priorities to a domain. This can help them understand the client context and pain points better.

- **Creating leaders who build high-performing teams:** This involves developing leaders who are no longer the command and control type but will influence, inspire and enable innovation within teams. The new breed of leaders consists of those who will be successful in building high-performing teams, who are resilient to change and are able to drive high-quality outcomes for team members who are geographically dispersed and working virtually.

- **Change management training:** Change is a given in these turbulent times. It is important to not just help build the change management expertise of the enterprise leadership team but also to help them stay connected and navigate changes.

- **Opportunistic technical skill upgrades aligned to projects and initiatives:** This involves two levels of development efforts:
  o *Drive to multi-skill employees*—Businesses will continue to work on projects with legacy skill requirements. While we should train employees in legacy skills, investment in multi-skilling is necessary to ensure that the workforce is fungible and can be rotated across projects. This is not just about 'resource utilization' but helps the workforce stay engaged and relevant.
  o *Building future-ready skills* to ensure businesses have a workforce trained in emerging technologies and ready to be deployed on new projects.

2. **Building fit-for-purpose infrastructure and technology that delivers content, tracks progress effectively:** In the digital age, the ability to position curated content in small consumable byte-sized modules is the most effective way to enable learning. The delivery of this content is needed to be increasingly virtual and accessible across devices. A fit-for-purpose technology infrastructure is critical to monitor learning journey maps that records progress against individual development plans. Further, enterprises need platforms or channels to attract learners and engage in group learning, creating processes that involve a seamless handshake between self-directed and social learning. This enhances the overall user experience as boundaries are blurring between these two distinct styles.

3. **Build a learning culture:** Drive focus on learning by making it part of performance appraisal while ensuring organization-wide access to learning programmes and platforms. Additionally, partnerships with learning organizations and institutions that are centres of excellence, academia and other institutions of excellence to keep up with emerging technologies is key to driving a learning culture.

4. **Tracking the impact of learning:** This is an evolving area of the L&D function. Organizations have been trying to define metrics that go beyond tracking learning activities to understanding the impact and return on investment. The key drivers for it are:

   - L&D is now mission critical for many enterprises and they are depending on it to develop capabilities that are enabling them to compete and/or differentiators in business performance. Therefore, it is natural that there is an expectation to measure the impact of L&D in terms of business metrics.
   - For example, reduction in cycle time to make a new hire effective on the job is fundamental to revenue recognition for technology services companies.

The costs of not getting L&D right or falling behind in this race have serious implications for business readiness. The workforce of tomorrow as well as the jobs of tomorrow will likely be very different from what they are now. This talent is not 'off-the-shelf' and has to be developed. Therefore, L&D has to step up and deliver on the talent and capabilities necessary for enterprises to compete.

The challenges that will need to be addressed to actualize the learning and development promise

In this chapter, I have shared how expectations from L&D are changing and what shifts enterprises need to make in their L&D approach. It is important to recognize that the L&D space is continuously evolving, and nobody has all the answers. Therefore, leaders need to have an open perspective, I would say a 'learner's mindset' as they approach the topic of L&D for their organizations. I would like to leave you with four key challenges that enterprises will need to address on L&D. Continued reflection on these will help you realize the full promise of L&D:

- How do we build a consistent learning culture, aligning workforce from different regions, backgrounds and time zones?
- How do people develop empathy and contextual intelligence to seamlessly work with others?
- How do we address technology infrastructure challenges to deliver high-quality training, personalize it and create enriching virtual experiences?
- How do we build problem-solving, leadership skills and other soft skills at scale, which are typically best learned through an apprentice model? Furthermore, how do we build these competencies through a digital medium to a dispersed and virtual workforce?

Summary

Every organization has to focus on continuous learning and build a learning culture to meet the changing expectations and to stay competitive in the digital age.

- **Key shifts are being witnessed in the L&D space**
  - One-size-fits-all to increased personalization.
  - Standard full day push-based sessions to byte-sized self-directed learning.
  - Multidimensional and channel agnostic.
  - Focusing on core competencies like problem solving.
  - Creating a digital record of learning.

- **The action areas for L&D include**
  - Developing organizational capability to deal with VUCA world by building business acumen, leadership skills and ability to navigate change.
  - Building fit-for-purpose infrastructure to create a platform to deliver content and manage individual learning journeys.
  - Building a learning culture and partnering with learning organizations, technical CoEs.
  - Tracking the impact of learning efforts.

- **L&D is rapidly evolving and there are multiple challenges that will need to be continually addressed,** including how to build a consistent learning culture; how to keep investing and stepping up the technology infrastructure, and how to build at scale soft skills like problem solving, leadership and collaboration that are the defining competencies required to succeed in the digital age.

6

Women in Leadership

Diversity is the engine of invention. It generates creativity that enriches the world

Justin Trudeau, Prime Minister of Canada

This chapter is based on insights from a panel discussion I had moderated on 'women in leadership' at a CEO meet organized by the NASSCOM Regional Council, Haryana, India.

Most IT/BPM companies employ a large proportion of women—varying from 25 per cent to 45 per cent of the workforce. However, as you get to mid-senior management levels, this proportion drops dramatically, to as low as 5–10 per cent. This is a challenge that we need to understand and address as an industry.

In this chapter, I will discuss the following topics:

1. Why diversity is important
2. Why there are not enough women at mid-senior management levels
3. What companies should do to bridge this gap

Why is diversity important?

It is now beyond debating that diversity is not just a 'nice-to-have' but a very important senior management imperative:

- It is not just a gender diversity agenda but a business agenda
- Men and women have different viewpoints and market insights, which enables better problem solving and different solutions, ultimately leading to better organizational performance. Statistically, 80 per cent of consumer buying is influenced by women. A gender-diverse team better aggregates industry knowledge and allows the company to serve an increasingly diverse customer base.
- Diversity is natural and reflects the composition of the population. Just visualize a male-only organization or a female-only organization. Neither is likely to be an effective or interesting place to work in!
- Women who reach the top are less conventional and bring high empathy, creativity and innovation to the enterprise.
- The impact of diversity is backed by many research studies showing that organizations with higher diversity in senior roles deliver superior business results.
- In the digital age, when there is a lot more complexity and volatility, and collaboration is a key success factor, diversity becomes even more important.

Why are there not enough women at mid-senior management levels?

The drop in the proportion of women in mid-senior management roles is striking. Many leaders have shared that they often did not find women candidates for senior positions even when they specifically went looking for them. There seem to be four sets of reasons behind this situation:

1. **Career losing momentum for women after maternity:** There seems to be an 'invisible cliff' on the path from junior- to mid-management where we lose a large proportion of women. This often coincides with women having their first or second child. The initial couple of years after childbirth are very challenging for women, most of whom find it difficult to balance the multiple responsibilities at work and at home, and their career loses momentum.

2. **Unintentional prejudices of the majority:** Men who are typically the majority in an organization often carry gender stereotypes or 'unintentional prejudices' from their homes to the workplace. There is often a typecasting of what jobs women would prefer and what they would not.

3. **Women carry subconscious biases:** Women often carry subconscious biases where they put limits and barriers on themselves. They often lack the self-belief and/or the aggression needed to push to the next level.

4. **Societal inequalities:** The root cause behind many of the issues we have observed above lies in the structure of the society in India and its deeply embedded expectations from the respective genders. If we go beyond the relatively privileged middle class in the big cities, education and growth opportunities for women are often limited. Even in the cities, while many women work, the expectations society has of the woman versus of the man, have not changed. Societal change will not happen overnight. However, unless we do something about it, we might not be able to move the needle significantly on gender diversity.

What should companies do to bridge this gap?

Improving diversity at senior management levels is a multi-dimensional and deep-rooted problem that needs action at multiple levels. I believe there are six areas where positive action needs to happen:

Women in leadership

Reasons for not enough women at mid-senior management levels

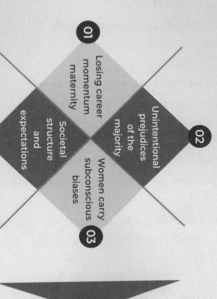

01 Losing career momentum maternity

02 Unintentional prejudices of the majority

03 Women carry subconscious biases

04 Societal structure and expectations

Positive steps companies can take to bridge this gap

< Support for women after maternity

< Career support at mid-management level

< Catch them young

< Rethink practices and workplace design

< Change majority mindsets

< Steps to change the society

- **Support for women after maternity**
  - o Give women the power of career choice—don't impose your prejudices on them
  - o Provide flex-working opportunities
  - o Provide crèche facilities in or near office

- **Career support at mid-management level**
  - o Identify sponsors who will champion a high-potential woman manager's case and help create opportunities for her.
  - o Provide mentorship—this need not be just women mentoring women. Man-to-woman mentorship can sometimes work even better.
  - o Create networks of women for not just sharing best practices and for peer networking but also for exposure to senior management.

- **Catch them young**
  - o Reach out to young women passing out of college to shape mindsets early.
  - o Provide mentorship to women even at junior levels in the organization.
  - o Raise awareness about role models.

- **Rethink practices and workplace design**
  - o Address possible intake bias through mixed gender panels—otherwise, 'men hire men'!
  - o Bring gender sensitization to workplace design—most offices are of men, designed by men, for men!

- **Change the majority mindset**
  - o Build the understanding that the discussion is not just about diversity but about inclusion too. This moves the discussion from 'form to substance'!

    o Raise awareness of 'unintentional prejudices'. Unless the majority mindset changes, inclusion will not happen.

- **Steps to change society**
  - o It is a difficult process, but corporate leaders need to step up and consider how they can make a difference.
  - o Focus Corporate Social Responsibility (CSR) spend towards initiatives like education and care of the girl child.
  - o Consider women-focused business initiatives—for example, Vodafone (Vi now) has opened all-women staffed 'Angel stores' since 2018.

In conclusion, we as an industry do have a problem today when it comes to inclusion of women at senior management levels, and we need to address it. Fortunately, most companies seem to be very aware of the issue and are taking a number of positive steps to address the situation. This raises hope for improvement in female inclusion in management in the coming years. That will not just be very positive for our businesses and potentially a competitive advantage in the digital age but would also be a good contribution we can make towards a positive change in our society.

Summary

- In the Indian IT/BPM industry, as you progress from junior to mid-senior levels, the proportion of women employees drops dramatically, to as low as 5–10 per cent.
- Diversity is important; it provides multi-faceted approaches to problem solving, builds greater empathy, creativity and innovation, and delivers superior outcomes for businesses and customers.

- There are not enough women at senior levels because of reasons like loss of career momentum after maternity; unintentional prejudices and subconscious biases carried by both men and women; and societal challenges and expectations.
- Efforts that need to be taken by firms to bridge the gender gap include career guidance, mentorship and support provided after a career break on account of maternity and during the woman's journey to mid-management level, rethinking of policies, processes and workplace design, changing of mindsets and driving efforts to influence society.

7

Lessons in Change Management

It had long since come to my attention that people of accomplishment rarely sat back and let things happen to them. They went out and happened to things

Leonardo Da Vinci, Italian polymath and Renaissance Painter

Change, for any organization, is inevitable. And the velocity of change in the business environment is now higher than ever before. The global economic outlook continues to be uncertain; business cycles are becoming shorter, existing markets are declining and new ones becoming significant, customer needs are changing, technology is continuing to evolve at a dazzling pace, and there is a lot of opportunity for innovation. Organizations have no option but to adapt to the many changes happening in their environment in the digital age. **Those who step up and capture the opportunities can become world beaters.** Equally, those who fail to adapt can see surprising decline. Despite the inevitability of change, many organizations struggle to get going with meaningful change, and even those who do, often find it difficult to implement their change management programmes and derive the desired results from them.

Clearly, **change management is a story of many paradoxes. Change is inevitable, but very difficult to initiate and implement.** Get it right, and you become a world-beater; get it wrong, and you can destroy a business built over many decades. It can be a source of energy for people or destroy their morale. And, when it comes to HR, change can even make you a hero or a villain!

I have had the opportunity to be centrally involved in change management across multiple organizations. It started in McKinsey, where I had the opportunity to transform the McKinsey Knowledge Centre from a back-office research centre into a cutting-end innovation centre. My change management journey continued at Fidelity International, then Flipkart, and now at Incedo. While the industry focus and the change management objectives have been different across the organizations I have been involved in, there have been some common lessons.

Best practices in change management

Change management is a fascinating but complex topic. Even after my engagement with change management for over twenty years as a manager and consultant, I still see myself as a keen student of this topic, and I am continuing to learn. And from what I have learned over the years so far, here are the seven best change management practices, according to me:

1. **Focusing on the right type and amount of change:** While change is inevitable, leaders need to make a conscious choice to change those things that will produce the most impactful results. Change is inherently difficult, so it is important to focus one's efforts and not dissipate one's energy. **Change for the sake of change does not help.** For example, there is often an over-reliance on changing organizational structures as a way of driving performance change. In my experience, such changes cause a lot of heartburn while rarely fulfilling their promise. In addition,

it is important to recognize that any **organization has only a certain capacity to absorb change.** Therefore, it is **critical to prioritize and sequence change initiatives,** so managers have clarity on what to focus on and equally the capacity to execute the changes. This is an area where my perspective, as a manager, has changed significantly from when I was a consultant. As a consultant, I was focused on getting all possible smart ideas on the table. As a manager, I realized that if you put too much on the table it will confuse your people. To ensure successful execution, you have to **focus on a few, not many, ideas.**

2. **Establishing 'why change?', clearly and persistently:** The biggest challenge in change management is to move people out of their 'comfort zones' and get them to truly accept the need for change. Inertia is inherent in human beings. We like predictability and certainty. We convince ourselves that what we are doing is the right thing. Moreover, it is hard for people to achieve the objectivity needed to question and change their daily routine while they are actively immersed in it. Therefore, **it is critical that you establish the need for change clearly and persistently.**

    It is important to go beyond the corporate logic and **see the change from the perspective of the individual—why should he or she change, what can he or she do differently, and what will be the impact.** In doing this, you have to appeal to both the head and the heart. Moreover, you need to be **persistent in establishing the need** for change. Rarely do people accept significant change at one go even if they say they do. You have to keep at it! If you are persistent, you can reach a tipping point when people finally get convinced about the need for change. That is perhaps the most important milestone in your change journey.

3. **Identifying change agents:** It is critical to have a core team of committed and inspiring change agents at the centre of the

change programme. **No leader, however inspiring, can drive significant change alone**. You need to have **force multipliers** who will not only embrace the change themselves but **evangelize it** across the organization, those who will stay through the journey through its ups and downs. There are certain types of individuals who are more open to change—those who have **high levels of personal confidence and a broader outlook.** They are analogous to the 'early adopters' in marketing! In my experience, I have often found more change agents in the second line of management than in the first. The latter are often too vested in the status quo, while the former can see opportunities in the change.

4. **Focusing on some early wins:** Driving change is not just about strategy but also about tactics. You need to ensure some early wins. **This will build credibility for your change agenda** so that it is no longer merely conceptual but also tangible. It is not easy for people to agree to change when the status quo is disturbed. Moreover, people have an inherent distrust of words and **respond much better to actions or outcomes** that are concrete and visible. Early wins will work as compelling reference cases and help you gather momentum. They will help build an understanding among the team about what you are trying to accomplish and encourage people to embrace the change.

5. **Going slow to go far:** While I have talked about early wins, it is important to recognize that organizations have a lot of inertia, and change, especially in mindset and behaviours, takes time. You have to be patient and persistent. Often, new managers rush to declare all that was done before them as rubbish in their frenzy to change everything. This is a recipe for failure. You have to take the time to fully understand the situation, especially the history and culture of the organization, and build trust with the people. The 'Hare and Tortoise' story is very relevant in change

Best Practices in Change Management

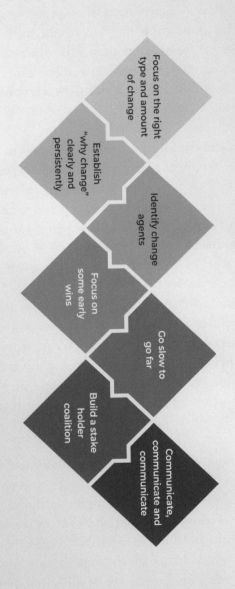

- Focus on the right type and amount of change
- Establish "why change" clearly and persistently
- Identify change agents
- Focus on some early wins
- Go slow to go far
- Build a stake holder coalition
- Communicate, communicate and communicate

management. You need to take not a one or two-year view but a three-to-five-year view for achieving substantial change outcomes. I have experienced that progress at the two-year mark can be underwhelming, but if you are persistent, results in the three-to-five-year period can be outstanding. Therefore, you need to pace yourself and set realistic expectations. Do not lose heart. It is OK to lose or not fight a few battles. If you are persistent, results will come.

6. **Building a stakeholder coalition:** You need to understand the organizational politics and recognize the power centres and learn to work with them to achieve your change objectives. One of the key aspects of my corporate education has been recognition of the reality of organizational politics. Self-interest is an inherent aspect of human nature, so politics exists in all organizations and you have to be prepared for it. Moreover, organizational politics is not always bad; you can also use it for good (Lord Krishna from Indian mythology provides an excellent role model for using politics for good!). Any organization will have power centres, and people are very sensitive to cues from them. You can give your change programme a big boost if you can understand the motivations of the key stakeholders and find alignment and visible support from them. If you don't, your change programme can get derailed very quickly.

7. **Communication, communication, communication:** Communication is absolutely critical. There are four aspects important in communication—keeping it simple, coverage of all levels, frequency and consistency, and openness and honesty. You need to articulate the need for change (why), your vision (what), and the benefits of the change for the organization and its individuals in a simple manner. Employees at all levels should be able to understand the messages and what they mean for them. Often, the messages remain limited to the top levels and do not reach

down the line; and if they do, they are articulated in ways that are not relevant for the majority of the staff. Moreover, you need to communicate often and be consistent in your messaging. When you are going through change, people feel insecure and have a high need to know. Repetition helps in such cases! Finally, you need to treat your people like mature adults and be open and honest with them, even if it is bad news you are bringing them. That works much better than trying to hide or soft-pedal any difficult messages.

I hope these best practices help you play a positive leadership role in transforming your organization in this digital age. Please remember, change management is not just about the CEOs, HR or the senior management, but something that professionals at all levels can and need to play a role in. Change needs to happen across the organization. This presents opportunities for professionals at every level of the organization to step up and make a difference. If you aspire to develop as a leader, then be proactive and take ownership of the change opportunities around you. Don't let the size of the challenge weigh you down. Just be positive and focus on your karma. You will be surprised how much power your individual actions can have!

Summary

Change for organizations is inevitable and the velocity of change in the business environment is higher than ever before in the digital age. The seven best practices in change management include:

1. **Focusing on the right type and amount of change:** Any organization has a limited capacity to absorb change, so it is critical to prioritize and sequence the change initiatives.

2. **Establishing 'why change?', clearly and persistently:** See the change from an individual's perspective and how it will impact them. You have to persist to establish the case for change till it reaches a tipping point.

3. **Identifying change agents:** Force multipliers are needed to embrace change and evangelize it. Select leaders who have high levels of personal confidence and a broad outlook.

4. **Focusing on some early wins:** Builds credibility for the change agenda; employees respond much better to actions than to words.

5. **Going slow to go far involves:** You need to be patient and persistent in the change journey especially when you want to achieve substantial change.

6. **Building a stakeholder coalition:** You can give your change programme a big boost if you can understand the motivations of the key stakeholders and find alignment and visible support from them.

7. **Communication, communication, communication:** To achieve success, you need to understand four aspects of communication—simplicity, comprehensiveness of coverage, frequency and consistency, and openness and honesty.

8

How HR Needs to Transform Itself to Lead in the VUCA World

There is at least one time in the history of any company when you have to change dramatically to rise to the next level of performance. Miss that moment and you start to decline

Andy Grove, ex-Chairman, Intel Corp

During my tenure at Flipkart, India's largest e-commerce company, I had direct responsibility for the HR function, and this was a tremendous learning opportunity, providing me with an intimate understanding of the powerful role HR can play in helping organizations cope during these uncertain times in this digital age.

As underscored across this book, firms are undergoing transformative changes, the future is ambiguous, and business models, organizational structures, technology requirements, expertise requirements—and therefore, skill development efforts—will continue to evolve rapidly. I believe this situation presents a historic opportunity for HR to play a pivotal role in helping organizations navigate through these uncertain times in the VUCA world. This is because the nature of challenges organizations are faced with in the

VUCA world require many solutions to come from HR. However, HR is currently not able to keep pace with this demand and would need to significantly step up its game. If HR leaders don't see the writing on the wall and move quickly, their failure to transform will result in the relegation of their function to a less relevant support role at the enterprise.

Historic opportunity for HR to lead

HR has a key role to play across the eight 'new rules of business' I had introduced in the first chapter of section 1 of the book. HR is also the key driver of most of the building blocks of organizational transformation that we have talked about in this section, pushing it to a key leadership position in the digital age.

Here are some of the key areas where HR needs to play its part:

1. **Culture champions:** Building a more entrepreneurial and agile culture is a key requirement for enterprises to succeed in the digital age. HR needs to play the role of culture champions, working closely with the CEO to define the underlying values, embed them in all the processes, and ensure they are followed consistently, especially in times of crisis ('moments of truth').

2. **Organization redesign:** There are many forces at work impacting organizational design in the digital age. There is the pressure to move towards simplification to drive speed, the need to develop and manage a global delivery model, to create an extended enterprise that includes a variety of partners and stakeholders, and finally, to manage an increasing proportion of work done virtually (accelerated dramatically by the Covid-19 pandemic). HR has to bring science and method to this organizational design process, balancing the often-conflicting requirements.

3. **Learning reboot:** The scope and importance of learning have manifold dimensions in this digital age. In addition, the methods and technologies involved in learning are going

through a complete transformation. At the same time, it is not easy to establish ROI for learning initiatives. HR leaders need to drive an upgrade of the learning function while ensuring it is well anchored to the organizational and business objectives.

4. **New talent acquisition:** One of the key requirements of the digital age is for every organization to build a technology DNA. This, coupled with the fast pace of technology changes, means that acquisition of high-quality tech talent is a priority for most enterprises. The increasing requirements of diversity add another dimension to talent acquisition. Talent sourcing, which has historically been an execution-oriented function, is now a strategic, mission-critical capability.

5. **Employee engagement:** Historically, enterprises have talked about being 'customer-centric'. My view is that in the digital age, enterprises need to have a dual mission—to become both 'customer-centric' and 'employee-centric'. The expectations, the new workforce—millennials, technology talent, knowledge workers—have of the organization are also very different from before. Plus, many digital natives have set the bar very high in the matter of employee engagement. This means HR needs to be very creative and purposeful in engaging employees across their life cycle.

6. **Leadership development:** The VUCA world we are living in puts immense pressure on enterprise leaders. They need to navigate the enterprise through immense change; they have to step up their own game on many fronts; and they have to be resilient to absorb the knocks they will inevitably face in such an uncertain environment. HR needs to play counsellor to the leaders and also be a connector, helping the team come together.

The complication—HR not able to keep pace

As things stand, HR works with multiple handicaps and is struggling to keep pace with developments in the environment. It is on the back foot on many fronts. There is a negative cycle of mindsets/ processes/capabilities falling short, leading to perception issues, which makes it even more difficult for the enterprise to attract top-notch talent.

- **Legacy mindsets:** The traditional orientation in HR is a command-and-control model; it tries to exercise control and focuses on compliance of organizational processes. This might not appeal to the knowledge worker who is looking for greater autonomy and flexibility.
- **Heavy processes and systems:** HR systems and processes face a couple of unique problems:
  - *Traditional models and frameworks that are inflexible and clunky and difficult to apply seamlessly in the rapidly pivoting business environment:* For example, annual goals and KPIs may not make sense when priorities are shifting every few months. There is an urgent need to recast performance management systems (PMS) and HR systems because their current construct is limiting for fast-moving organizations.
  - *Regulatory limitations, which require manual interventions, coupled with archaic labour laws:* These need to be adapted to the changing needs of businesses.
  - *Most organizations haven't even started to review their processes to address contract worker experience.*

- **Limited leverage of analytics and technology:** Employees are the most valuable and critical of resources of the enterprise. Most HR functions don't spend sufficient time and resources on talent analytics. Even if they do, the effort is sub-par, for the following reasons:
  - *Shift in mindset required:* The reporting metrics need to shift from proving that the function is working efficiently to focusing on information that will be relevant to help the business/function perform better or take better decisions.

o *Better technologies and models are required to help consolidate the data flowing in from various employee touchpoints:* Many HR-focused start-ups have been coming up, especially in sentiment analysis and virtual chatbots. However, there is a long way to go for these technologies to be leveraged properly.

o *Finally, HR must develop the skills to go beyond reporting data to using analytics for forward-looking projections:* For example, they can make projections on attrition or use data to identify employee issues, or interpret data for pattern-recognition for other purposes, for which business context is required.

- **HR talent DNA and capabilities falling short:** For this reason, HR talent is often not able to connect with business leaders as peers. Relationships often regress into order-taking on the part of HR. Currently, there are three key gaps in HR capabilities:

  o *Follower-versus-change agent orientation:* Historically viewed as a support function, HR is something many firms choose to compromise on when it comes to costs and hiring high-quality talent. As a result, the typical HR team consists of individuals who are probably good doers but will not demonstrate a contrarian point of view, instead tending to execute without questioning.

  o *Limited investment:* Some firms go half-way, with a view to spending the necessary dollars on hiring the right HR leaders, but make cost trade-offs at junior levels, which again delivers limited results because the leaders' impact will come to a grinding halt over time because of their inability to delegate.

  o *Lack of deep business and customer understanding:* HR is often so tightly caught in a tactical activity loop that they are not able to spend time understanding the business. Therefore, their ability to engage with the business leaders at a strategic level remains limited.

- **Poor speed and bias for action:** HR teams often do not keep pace with the business expectations. To address this, the HR team has to step out of the mindset of measuring impact in terms of the effort put in rather than from the perspective of actual business outcomes.

- **HR often taken for granted:** This is an issue of perception. Often, the HR function is taken for granted. A lot of good work done by the function is not fully appreciated. Even if it has a 'seat at the table', HR is treated as a support function. This leads to lack of motivation among the team, making it difficult for the function to attract top-notch talent.

HR needs to step up in the following five areas:

Significant transformation is required in mindsets and capabilities across areas for HR to realize the opportunities in front of it. Some of the aspects that need overhaul are:

1. **HR talent profile**
   - HR leaders have the opportunity to be coach, sounding board and change guides for CXOs. This must be planned.
   - For this to happen, HR leaders need to evolve from being SMEs (Subject Matter Experts) with HR functional skills and become leaders with deep business understanding and agility.
   - The current skill gap is significant. The function needs a new generation of business-oriented Chief Human Resource Officers (CHROs).
   - Movement of line leaders into the CHRO role must be encouraged. Stepping up the importance of the role to bring it on par with CFO and a stepping stone to CEO/other CXO roles, would be a good idea.
   - Strengthening of business understanding of the next line of HR leaders through stretch projects in business, co-

ownership of business results, and cross-pollination of talent between HR and business, must be encouraged.

2. **Use of data and technology**
   - In line with the movement on the business side towards customer segmentation and now to individual-level personalization, similar opportunities exist on the employee side.
   - The new mantra for employee engagement is EVP to IVP (employee value proposition to individual value proposition)!
   - Analytics and technology can facilitate individual-level understanding of employee needs and customization of interventions accordingly, e.g. a flexible rewards mix, learning and development.
   - Analytics can also play a crucial role in talent retention, e.g. through pulse tracking, predictive models and early warning systems.
   - The technology focus has to move from back-end systems to omni-channel employee engagement

3. **Learning and development**
   - The key challenge—how to make L&D relevant to the business, especially when it is moving very fast. (L&D actions are covered in detail in chapter 5 of this section.)
   - Actions to enable key needs:
     o Enabling rapid re-skilling to adapt to changing business needs
     o Developing leaders internally, with a focus on soft skills

   - Finding a way to leverage the rapid changes that are happening in education delivery for internal L&D using external networks, content curation, MOOCs, and internal wikis/leader blogs.

4. **Managing deep tech talent/high-end knowledge workers**
   - HR processes are typically designed to manage scale.
   - With rapidly evolving technologies all around us, HR needs to learn to manage deep tech talent.
   - Due to the aggressive job market, there is a consistent war for high-quality talent. Therefore, both recruitment and retention are a challenge.
   - Expectations of deep product/tech talent are different from those of regular talent, and therefore HR would need to customize its approach business-wise.
   - High expectations—in the current scenario there is a high premium on differentiated career development and rewards, based on impact/potential and individual motivations. HR needs to change its one-shoe-fits-all approach and adopt targeted approaches.
   - Emotional connect—we need to build passionate, inspiring leadership that can embrace and evangelize the new culture.
   - Fairness and transparency—this result from building inclusive HR processes that are fair.

5. **Building a distinctive culture**
   - A distinctive culture is key to building a sustainable organization in the VUCA world. Culture is a common theme across the eight paradigms I have shared earlier.
   - HR has to play the role of culture champion, helping define, then uphold, the culture at the firm.
   - It is important that culture initiatives go beyond the buzzwords and address the key tensions in behaviours.
   - Upholding the culture that has been decided upon can bring HR into conflict with business functions. Alignment with the CEO here is very necessary.
   - HR processes from recruitment to performance management to employee engagement are important 'culture carriers'. It is critical that the key values for the enterprise are embedded

HR has a significant role to help enterprises realize digital ambition

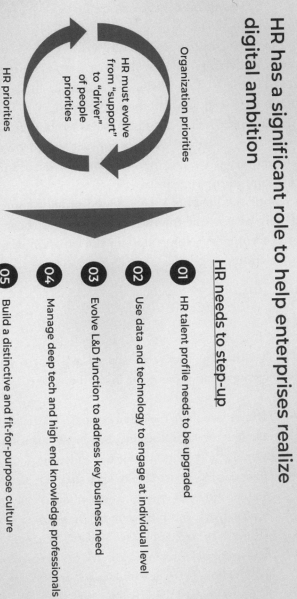

Organization priorities

HR must evolve from "support" to "driver" of people priorities

HR priorities

HR needs to step-up

01 HR talent profile needs to be upgraded

02 Use data and technology to engage at individual level

03 Evolve L&D function to address key business need

04 Manage deep tech and high end knowledge professionals

05 Build a distinctive and fit-for-purpose culture

into all the HR processes. Employee experience with these processes makes the culture real!

There is a historic opportunity for HR to step up and play a critical leadership role in helping organizations transform and succeed in the VUCA world. The nature of challenges organizations (both legacy and new) face in the VUCA world is such that a significant proportion of solutions has to come from HR. If HR can step up and provide these solutions, it would be a great service to organizations as well to the HR function itself, uplifting its impact and stature in the enterprise.

I hope the insights I have shared provide some helpful pointers and help spark constructive debate among boards and executive teams, eventually helping step up the capabilities and impact of the HR function.

Summary

HR has the opportunity to step up and play a powerful role in helping organizations navigate in the digital age.

- HR needs to drive the culture change, take lead in organization redesign, reboot of learning, build new talent models, and be a counselor and connector for the leadership.
- However, HR is not able to keep pace due to legacy mindsets, complex processes and systems, limited leverage of Technology and Analytics, and HR talent falling short.
- HR needs to step up to play its role as a change agent. For this, there needs to be an upgrade in the talent and capabilities of the HR function, better use of data and technology and step up of the positioning of the HR function.

9

Future of Work—Unlocking the Potential of Your Workforce through AI

Some people call [it] artificial intelligence, but the reality is this technology will enhance us. So, instead of artificial intelligence, I think we'll augment our intelligence.

Ginni Rometty, CEO and Chairperson of IBM from 2012-2020

Artificial intelligence, machine learning, deep learning and automation are no longer future technologies; they have already found traction in enterprises as well as our daily lives. Amazon Alexa's answers, Google Maps' directions, Netflix's movie recommendations, tailored emails in our inboxes—AI is already pervasive in the consumer world. It is no longer a question of if we let AI into our lives, the AI 'or' humanity consideration, but how AI 'and' humanity can work together to improve all aspects of life.

Recently, I have seen a more dramatic and aggressive shift in the deployment of AI in enterprises. When the first edition of this book was being written, clients were talking about POCs in AI and getting the data infrastructure sorted out to support the projects. Today, I see many of our clients investing significant dollars in 'at scale' AI implementations. Personalization of customer journeys, process automation and decision science are the areas where I am seeing the highest application of AI.

It is certain that there is going to be a lot of disruption over the next five to ten years as AI technologies work their way through companies and across industries and geographies. It will be a time of accelerated change and painful uncertainty for many people across the globe as industries and their occupations are modified or consumed by the implementation of AI and other technologies. But if we get a better understanding of the effects of AI and reinvent our organizational processes, we will be able to take advantage of these technologies to fundamentally reshape the nature of work, help individuals to be better prepared for the changes, create tremendous wealth opportunities and increase benefits for the global workforce.

I see three dimensions of the impact AI has on the workforce:

1. Impact of AI on the nature of jobs
2. Need for retraining and upskilling
3. AI as an enabler of employee engagement

I will discuss these in more detail in the rest of the chapter.

1. Impact of AI on the Nature of Jobs

Jobs as they exist today will certainly be impacted by AI. But it is not a situation of human-versus-machine (as is often portrayed in the media) but one of human-*with*-machine or human-complementing-machine. Robots posing a threat to humankind is something way too futuristic. The sooner we realize this and understand the underlying nature of AI technologies, the more we will be able to harness them and benefit from them.

Here are some simple facts about AI technology and its impact on the nature of jobs:

A. Ever since the advent of technology, there has been a fear that jobs will be lost because of the arrival of new technology. This is true. Some jobs are eliminated due to new technology, but we also end up creating new jobs in other areas because of the efficiency effects of technology. For example, just a short time ago, we had to physically go to a bank to deposit cheques, get cash and carry out other types of transactions. Many of these activities performed by humans physically and on paper have been replaced by digital applications on a mobile device. This has allowed us (customers) to conduct business directly. Banking jobs that were inefficient were eliminated, but thousands (I could argue millions) of new jobs and companies were created to support the new processes and technology just in the banking industry. So, it can be said that because of AI, **some jobs will certainly be lost, but new jobs and industries will also be created.**

B. The debate needs to move from **'general AI'** (the type we see in movies with robots outwitting humans on all fronts), which is a long time away, to more **specific applications of AI**. Today, AI is being used in very narrow domains where there are specific problems and data is available such as Natural Language Processing (NLP), image and speech recognition and prescriptive analytics. The number of these domains needs to be expanded.

C. The debate should focus on **reorganization of tasks rather than replacement of jobs.** All jobs (even highly paid ones, like those of a financial analyst and financial advisor) will undergo transformation because of AI. However, jobs are very unlikely to be entirely disrupted or replaced by machines. The more likely scenario is that specific tasks will be performed by AI, and even so, some jobs are likely to have more of their tasks automated than others (for example, customer service or operations-related jobs).

D. Therefore, the question is, what are the relative strengths and weaknesses of humans and machines, and **how do we redesign**

current jobs to benefit from their complementarity? Humans are good at asking the right questions, while machine learning is good at ingesting massive amounts of information, often more than a human could look at in a lifetime, to arrive at the right answers. Together, they can have a massive business impact. AI can take away the stress of manual and tedious work by making such tasks automatic, freeing up humans to do the things we are inherently well suited to do. However, we need to make sure that we are asking the right questions first and not setting the cart before the horse.

E. The future of artificial intelligence isn't exactly clear, but it will definitely have an impact on the workplace and society. I believe, on the whole, it will be a positive impact. McKinsey estimates that only 5 per cent of current occupations can be fully automated, which will result in about 15 per cent of workers being potentially displaced and 3 per cent being required to change occupational categories by 2030.[9] But McKinsey also predicts that most workers will be able to continue in their current roles, **augmented by machines**. Moreover, McKinsey foresees the creation of up to 890 million new jobs by the same time, thanks to rising incomes and consumption and the need for more skilled workers amid technological advances. Positioning workers for success in the workforce of the future will require ongoing education and training to ensure that their skills and experience match the needs of the labour market and integrate optimally with advances in AI technologies.

AI should, therefore, not be looked upon as a job killer. It should instead be **embraced as a job enabler**, one that promises to create several new employment opportunities even as it redefines employees' roles and increases productivity several fold.

The need of the hour, more importantly, is to **shift the current debate from replacement of jobs to reorganization of tasks**. The focus should be on how existing jobs can be redesigned to leverage the synergies of human and machine, which would then lead to a major beneficial impact on society, governance and business.

2. Need for retraining and upskilling

The debate above makes it clear that the advent of AI does not spell doomsday for the workforce but could be seen as a great opportunity to make jobs more meaningful and rewarding. However, to realize AI as an opportunity would require massive investments into relearning and upskilling.

Relearning and upskilling need to factor two dimensions:

- Training the workforce in AI technologies
- Upgrading skills so that they are relevant when jobs get redesigned

I see a lot of debate and action in enterprises on the first dimension—**training employees at scale on AI technologies.** This is extremely relevant for employees in technology roles and in IT companies, whose job it is to develop and/or use AI applications. However, for the majority of the workforce, this **basic training in AI is more like 'general knowledge'**—good to have, but something that will not fundamentally change their approach to their jobs.

For the bulk of the workforce, what is a lot more relevant is an **assessment of how their job is likely to change because of AI** and what skills they need to upgrade to be relevant in an AI-centric future. For example, a customer service associate's job will be less about the process (that smart bots will increasingly do) but more about the ability to pick up on customer emotions and make decisions accordingly. For a financial analyst, it will be less about data analysis and more about the ability to identify patterns and develop intuition. For a financial advisor, it will be less about the knowledge of financial products and more about the ability to elicit and understand customer needs and build deeper client relationships.

Ironically, in a technology-intensive and an AI-centric world, relationships and emotions will become even more crucial. The current AI has two major drawbacks—it lacks any capacity whatsoever for love or compassion and has zero creativity.

With the explosion of data and AI technologies, the ability to work with data and make decisions based on data, supported by AI technologies, will be important. However, I believe the most critical skills that will be needed in the future lie somewhere else. They will be:

- **Problem solving:** creating the ability to ask questions and discover and frame problems
- **Pattern recognition:** honing intuition and ability to identify complex patterns (though there is a debate as to whether in the long term, big data and AI will make human 'intuition' less relevant)
- **Improving emotional intelligence (EQ):** developing the ability to understand emotions and build empathy and relationships.

We should make no mistake that AI will impact every job in some way. This can be an opportunity but would require us to rethink how a job would look in the future and call for upgradation of skills in order to stay relevant and effective in that future.

Organizations can play their part by giving employees incentives and time to improve their skills. This is the age of accessible information, which means employees have the opportunity to upskill themselves when they feel their present skills are not up to the task.

However, though the organization can formally encourage and assist employees, the responsibility for this relearning and upgradation of skills lies fundamentally with the individual themselves. The impending change is so significant that one must take charge of their future. Moreover, the explosion of e-learning has now democratized access to knowledge, placing learning within the individual's reach. Eventually, the changes that AI will bring over a period of time are so far reaching that skill building for the new era of jobs will need to start in schools and colleges, where curricula will need to be substantially rethought and upgraded.

3. AI as an enabler for employee engagement

To clear the air around AI further, I wanted to highlight one area in which I have deep experience due to my years at the global powerhouse Fidelity as well as India's largest e-commerce company, Flipkart, and my current company Incedo—AI applications in the area of employee engagement. One of the fast-emerging applications of AI is its support employee engagement, which can contribute to a happier, healthier and more productive workforce. There are many emerging tools with applications such as sentiment analysis (which helps in attrition management), HR support, learning and development, performance management and even job design. Let me elaborate on each of these applications:

- **Sentiment analysis:** A host of AI tools now help assess employee engagement and predict risk of employee attrition dynamically. Significantly, they can also help identify mental health and depression triggers, which are increasingly a problem in the workplace. Mental health issues have become even more acute in the extended work from home triggered by the Covid-19 pandemic and the post-event return to offices or business travel through crowded public spaces.
- **HR support:** This includes 'virtual assistants' or conversational smart bots that improve the efficiency and responsiveness of internal HR support processes, e.g. payroll help desk. In fact, many enterprises are trying to use AI to raise the quality of their internal processes as a part of, or even as a prelude to, using AI to improve their customer engagement.
- **Learning and development:** These tools help identify skill gaps and develop customized and targeted learning interventions.

- **Performance management:** AI tools can help make performance management an ongoing process and provide real-time feedback.
- **Job design:** These tools can assess employee performance and capabilities and align them to appropriate jobs (and to tasks within a job), which maximizes employee effectiveness and satisfaction.

AI can enable dynamic assessments and more personalized and targeted employee interventions. Therefore, it has the potential to be a significant enabler of employee engagement, productivity and satisfaction in the digital age. However, like most things with AI, there is an 'other side' to consider here too. AI-based employee engagement can lead to a 'Big-Brother-is-always-watching' type of environment, which is not only intrusive but potentially dangerous.

Privacy guidelines and data access are important considerations that must be taken into account to ensure that the vast amount of employee data available to the enterprise is not misused.

So, the bottom line is that **AI has its place, as do humans,** and we are NOT headed for a zero-sum showdown between humans and machines! AI will certainly have a significant impact on jobs, and more fundamentally, on the nature of work. It should develop as a force of good and have a net positive effect, both on jobs and workforce productivity and engagement. However, for that to happen, considerable effort needs to be made on the design of jobs, significant upgrading of skills and alignment of skills to the emerging needs.

Foundational to this discussion on the AI framework is the reality of human existence and our need to connect with others. Let us take one small example. AI has contributed to the dramatic reduction in time we spend interacting with others during economic transactions, evidenced by the rapid increase in online shopping. That will only accelerate as more advanced, personalized and predictive AI offers us exactly what we want before we know we want it and ships it safely to our home. One less trip to the store, and one less human

AI is a key enabler for enhancing workforce productivity and engagement

"AI + Human" is the future of workforce

Nature of jobs will change to more value-add roles

Re-training and upskilling will be key to work with AI

AI will enable a better employee engagement

interaction. Additionally, in the new, post-Covid-19 accelerated, hybrid work world where people are working from home or remotely, with limited time in a company office, the power of human interaction has become profoundly more important. With reduced time together in an office, school, or other human organizations, those few hours in the office, classroom or meeting hall connecting via face-to-face socialization will become even more important for building connections and culture.

In this new world, being human and having a high level of empathy to connect is beyond the AI's capability and is a critical and unrivalled skill that will remain unique to humanity.

Summary

- AI will have a significant impact on the nature of all jobs. It will be a 'human with machine' not 'human versus machine' scenario.
- AI will create new job opportunities but also call for redesigning of jobs, processes and tasks.
- The workforce must be trained in AI technologies and their skills upgraded, so that they can stay relevant in an AI-centric world.
- AI will be an enabler for employee engagement as it will help understand employee sentiments more dynamically and enable personalized, targeted interventions.
- In a hybrid work world, with remote working and work from home, due to limited time in a company office, the power of human interaction has become profoundly more important.
- Empathy and the ability to connect are key and unrivalled skills that will remain unique to humanity.

SECTION 6

LEADERSHIP IN THE DIGITAL AGE

Introduction: Leadership in the Digital Age

In section 1, we had discussed the fact that digital transformation is a lot more than incremental technology change and it has to be end to end. In section 5, we further built on this theme and emphasized that digital transformation cannot happen without organizational transformation. We also explored the various elements of organizational transformation. In this section, we will focus on the role of leaders in the digital age.

Digital age and this VUCA world are a great test for leaders. They have the responsibility for navigating their business through uncertain times while making sure that they are driving innovation and a growth agenda and are being cheerleaders and role models for the employees. Clearly, leadership in the digital age in the VUCA world is not for the fainthearted.

From managers to leaders

'Manager to Leader' sounds like a cliché, but it is very true in the digital age. In an era of unprecedented uncertainty and change, traditional tools of management like structure, strategy, planning and policies not just lose their effectiveness but can become a roadblock.

Instead you need vision, inspiration, intuition, collaboration, and ability to constantly adapt. This requires a shift in the expectations of executives from being efficient managers to entrepreneurial leaders.

Fundamentals of leadership do not change

Even though this is the VUCA world, the fundamentals of leadership do not change. The most important aspects of leadership remain: the focus on giving rather than getting, the ability to inspire others, and the courage to do the right thing. However, building these leadership fundamentals is easier said than done. A key challenge for enterprises and leaders is how to inspire and develop the next generation of leaders.

Managing duality becomes more important

Digital age poses many contradictions that leaders need to respond to—vision/strategy versus execution, growth versus profitability, short-term versus long-term, customers versus employees, data versus intuition, man versus machine, and many more. It is not enough to find the trade-odds on these complementary values, but leaders need to find win-win solutions. This increased need to manage duality is an important expectation of leaders in the digital age.

Balance and Sustainability are also critical

The breath-taking pace of activity is a defining feature of the digital age, but it is also one of its biggest challenges. The pace, the frenzy, the growth obsession, have significant repercussions at all levels—the individual, the organization, and the society. Individuals are at a greater risk of burnout, anxiety and depression. At society-level, the obsession with growth is resulting in irreparable damage to the environment and is creating grave socio-economic issues. All of this is leading to a world that is increasingly volatile, violent and unsustainable. I strongly believe that leaders in the digital age have a responsibility not just to their enterprises, but to the society as a whole. First, they need to find balance within themselves. I believe spiritual practices and meditation can be very helpful for leaders to centre themselves and find peace within. In addition, they need to consider how they can build an ethical foundation for their organizations and make a broader contribution to the society.

I have explored these themes across the chapters of this section.

Chapter 1: My Leadership Beliefs

In this chapter, I have shared the core leadership principles that I believe in and try to live by. The leadership fundamentals for me are helping others realize their full potential, making a difference, building a compelling view of the future, courage, trust-building, connecting, integrity, balancing the head and heart, humility and being true to yourself. Leadership beliefs act as a compass pointing us in the right direction. They act as the beacon that lights the way and enables the team to navigate uncertain times.

Chapter 2: How Great Leaders Inspire Others: The '5 Cs' Formula!

In this chapter, I have tried to cover why inspiring the team is important and what is the best way to do it. Across the previous sections, we covered the fact that an organization's ability to win in the VUCA world depends not just on the leader but also on the readiness and ability of the team. Whether it's through role modelling, creating a compelling vision or effective storytelling the role of the leader is pivotal in inspiring others. Getting others to sign up for a higher purpose, go beyond the call of duty, beyond their ordinary limits and achieve great results. To be able to do so, the leader has to care, connect and inspire them from within.

Chapter 3: How to Create Great Leaders

For enterprises to succeed, it is important for the leader to not have the sole responsibility to drive change and deliver on enterprise growth targets but build a team of next-level leaders who are driven, empowered, customer-centric and have the right level of expertise to own and deliver outcomes. To be able to build a team of great leaders, first we have to believe that everybody has leadership potential within them. Second, we need the right trigger of experiences to **unlock it** like providing stretch assignments and teaching through role modelling. Before you ask others to follow suit, you have to live the values you want them to demonstrate.

Chapter 4: Mastering Duality: A Key Skill for Leaders to Succeed in the Digital Age

Among the challenges the VUCA world throws at leaders, most of which have been dealt with in the previous chapters, this one is particularly unique. It is a very critical need for leaders to manage contradictions or seemingly conflicting objectives at the same time. Because of the level of volatility, leaders will need to be agile, consistently evaluate scenarios and go beyond making trade-offs to mastering operating with duality to succeed. Those who are able to master this skill will grow to a different level of professional maturity and impact.

Chapter 5: Spiritual Balance—A Necessity in Today's Digital Age

In this chapter, I cover a topic you might not expect to find in a book on digital transformation: the need for spiritual balance! The unprecedented pace of change has increased expectations from leaders and their teams on various fronts—to lead the firm through this period of uncertainty, stay on top of the digital transformation implications for their firms and build their own capabilities. While this has led to its own share of stress, what adds to it is the constant stimuli and distractions provided by the extraordinarily digitized and interconnected world, consisting of multiple gadgets, 24x7 connectivity and social media. All of this does not provide us with an opportunity to take a breather and reflect. As a consequence, stress levels are increasing, and people are developing serious health problems. I feel it is imperative to develop spiritual balance to centre ourselves, prioritize, clear our minds and focus on things which are most important.

Chapter 6: Sustainable Development—Rethinking Consumption

In this chapter, I wanted to take a moment to pause and recognize the fact that we are, by nature, competitive and will constantly strive for growth and challenge the status quo. Our current mental and economic models—individual, corporate, societal—are driven by growth. We are driven by ever-increasing needs and desires and the constant race to fulfill them. However, if left unchecked, it can spiral out of control and lead us down an unrecoverable path. My recommendations are to drive a set of prudent actions for sustainable development. At an individual level, it is to balance spirituality and materialism; at the corporate level, we should put customers before profits; and, for our society, it is for all of us as citizens to take the initiative and drive positive change.

1

My Leadership Beliefs

If your actions inspire others to dream more, learn more, do more and become more, you are a leader

John Quincy Adams, President of the United States

One question that I often get asked is: What are the traits of an effective leader in the digital age? My view is it is important to first find anchors on the leadership fundamentals that stay constant. In this chapter, I share my personal beliefs on the timeless principles of leadership. These are by no means the last word on leadership, but they are perspectives that I feel are important and which I try to live by.

*Leadership is about **helping others realize their full potential**. Every person has unique and abundant potential. A leader helps people realize their potential by challenging and stretching them.*

*Leadership is about **making a difference**. It is about striving to create a positive and lasting impact in all aspects of your work and life. In any situation, ask not what you are getting but what you are giving.*

*Leadership is about **building a compelling view of the future**. A leader must have an inspiring vision that will benefit the organization and will provide a sense of common purpose and direction to the team.*

*Leadership is about **courage**. A leader must take risks and not be afraid of treading a new path. Leadership means saying what you mean and having the spine to stand up for your beliefs.*

*Leadership is about **trust building**. Trust is a force multiplier. Building it means suspending your own agenda, walking the talk and delivering on promises.*

*Leadership is about **connecting**, about touching both the hearts and minds of people. It is about communicating and connecting with warmth and openness at all levels. People need to see and hear you for themselves.*

*Leadership is about **integrity**, about striving to do the right thing so you have a clear conscience and can hold your head high.*

*Leadership is about the **balance of head and heart**. It is about both delivering excellent business results and being an empathetic and caring people leader. A leader must consciously find that balance.*

*Leadership is about **humility**. About not letting success or position go to your head. It is about staying humble and grounded, which will earn you the love and respect of people. It is about listening better and avoiding making big mistakes.*

*Finally, leadership is about **being yourself**. Each one of us has unique strengths. So leadership means being authentic, digging within yourself, introspecting and defining your own leadership mantra and style.*

Leadership fundamentals do not change. I believe it is important for any leader to stay anchored to the fundamentals. I hope these principles provide you with helpful guidance for your leadership journeys.

Leadership beliefs

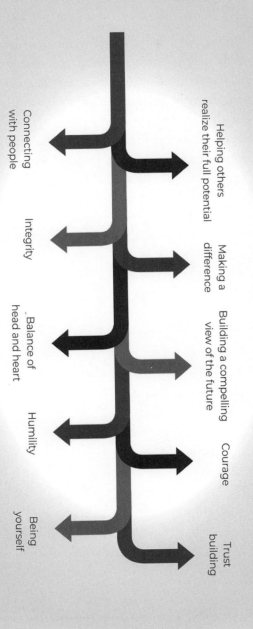

Helping others
realize their full potential

Making a
difference

Building a compelling
view of the future

Courage

Trust
building

Connecting
with people

Integrity

Balance of
head and heart

Humility

Being
yourself

Summary

- Leadership is guided by the following factors—helping others realize their full potential, making a difference, building a compelling view of the future, courage, trust building, connecting, integrity, balance of head and heart, humility and being yourself.
- These are by no means the last word on leadership, but the fundamentals that I feel are important and try to live by.

2

How Great Leaders Inspire Others: The '5 Cs' Formula!

The greatest leader is not necessarily the one who does the greatest things.
He is the one who gets the people to do the greatest things

Ronald Reagan, President of the United States.

The ability to inspire others is a critical test of a leader. To achieve outstanding results in an increasingly complex world in the digital age, you need to go beyond just managing the organization and its people efficiently. You need to touch people at a deeper level where they get inspired from within. Inspiration is the elixir that helps individuals go beyond their ordinary limits and achieve great results. And, it is not just about results and performance. Inspiration is also the spark that helps people rise and realize their full potential. This aspect is very precious. I believe that helping others realize their full potential is one of the biggest contributions that any human can make. Truly, the ability to inspire is a necessary requirement for a leader to go from good to great!

So, how do great leaders inspire others? I am sharing below the '5 Cs'—Cause, Care, Courage, Communication and Character—that I have seen great leaders use to inspire:

1. **Cause:** Identify and champion a cause or vision that makes a real difference. A cause that goes beyond the routine and touches an emotional chord. A cause that is meaningful today and will lead to a better tomorrow. Great leaders focus on the 'why', the purpose. Once the purpose is clear, the means follow. A powerful purpose can help bring disparate individuals together as a team and galvanize them to go beyond their ordinary limits.

2. **Care:** Leadership is not about the leader but about leading. It is not about your own dreams but about touching and bringing to life the silent dreams of others. Develop a genuine interest and empathy for others, understand their goals and aspirations, and look to contribute to their progress. Suspend your self-interest; ask not what you are getting from any situation but what you are giving to it. As you give, you get a lot more in return. When you go beyond your self-interest and tap into what matters to others, you will build their trust and they will willingly go the extra mile for you.

3. **Courage:** You can inspire others only when you are inspired yourself. Walk the talk and have passion for the cause at hand. Take risks and say what you mean. Any worthwhile cause will face some roadblocks. Opposition and challenges are the real tests for a leader, his or her moment of truth. You need to have the spine to stand up for your beliefs and your people. You have to persevere in the face of difficulties and not give up. That is crucial for your credibility. People will observe your approach, and your personal example of courage and commitment will ignite those around you.

4. **Communication:** Connect directly with people and get your message across yourself. Don't depend only on formal channels (which are often impersonal) or on others to carry your message.

Great leaders '5 Cs Formula' to inspire others

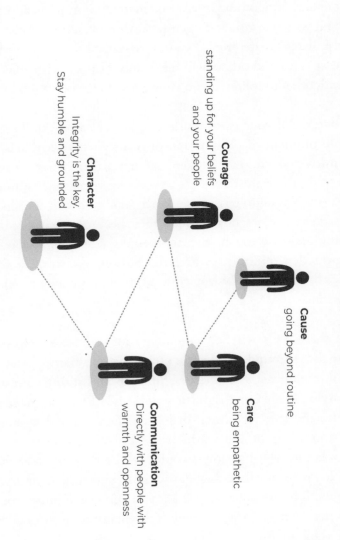

Courage
standing up for your beliefs
and your people

Character
Integrity is the key.
Stay humble and grounded

Cause
going beyond routine

Care
being empathetic

Communication
Directly with people with
warmth and openness

People need to see and hear you for themselves. You need to touch both hearts and minds. For that to happen, it is not your polish but your authenticity and intent that matter. Communicate often and do it with warmth and openness. Moreover, do not just talk but also listen. Listening is even more critical for a leader. You will learn a lot and others will feel valued. Listen with sincerity and patience and follow up on your conversations.

5. **Character:** All your great work as a leader can be undone by a single moment of indiscretion on your part. Integrity is the glass mirror which, once broken, can never be repaired. Always strive to do the right thing. However, recognize that as human beings, we are fallible; there is both good and bad within us. Many great leaders fall because they become arrogant, stop listening and lose touch with the people. Always stay humble and grounded. Humility will earn you love and respect from people. It will also allow you to listen better and avoid making big mistakes.

I hope these '5 Cs' will help you hone your own leadership skills and inspire those around you. While I have shared a framework with you, I want to emphasize that leadership is about **finding your own personal style.** There is no right or wrong style. A leader needs to be authentic and true to himself or herself. Each of us has unique strengths and views of the world based on our life experiences. Your formula for inspiring others could well be very different from mine. So, learn from others but dig within yourself and find your own formula. That is your best chance of success. Finally, please remember that leadership is a journey. You are not born a leader, but you realize the leader within you with your actions. So, just focus on your karma as a leader and you will find yourself continuing to grow as an inspiring one.

Summary

- Inspiration is the spark that helps people rise and realize their full potential. Helping others realize their full potential is one of the biggest human contributions that any one of us can make.
- 5 C's that great leaders use to inspire others: Cause, Care, Courage, Communication and Character.
- Leadership is about finding your own personal style. Your formula for inspiring could well be very different from others'. So, learn from others but dig within yourself and find your own formula.
- You are not born a leader, but you realize the leader within you with your actions. So, just focus on your karma as a leader and you will find yourself continuing to grow as an inspiring one.

3

How to Create Great Leaders

The role of a leader is not to come up with great ideas, the role of a leader is to create an environment where great ideas can happen.

Simon Sinek, Author and Motivational speaker

In this chapter, I want to share insights with you on a topic very close to my heart—'How to Create Great Leaders'.

Leadership can be viewed from many levels—corporate, individual, national, global.

At any level, a true leader must be inclined towards:

1. **Doing the right thing rather than the easy thing:** This means a leader is fearless and makes clear and courageous decisions even in ambiguous situations.
2. **Focusing on the larger goal versus personal goals:** This calls for selflessness. Leaders help their teams grow by aligning towards a common purpose and cohesively working towards the larger goal.
3. **Inspiring people to go beyond the direction set by himself:** This asks for long-term vision on the part of the leader but also

trust in the team and providing them the freedom to surpass his vision.

So, how should we create leaders who are fearless, selfless, and visionaries? Here's my take:

All of us have the potential to be leaders

To start with an example from my own life, I was an introvert as a child and an average sportsperson in school. When I came to IIT Delhi and was elected as the sports secretary—which was a huge responsibility—my fears and inhibitions gradually started to fade away. This opportunity unleashed tremendous energy and passion in me, unlocking the leader inside me.

So, my first important realization about leadership was that a 'born leader' is a myth. All of us have the seeds of leadership within us. It just needs the right trigger and context to **unlock our leadership potential**. This, to me, has to be the starting point for any leader. You have to believe in the vastness of human potential and constantly be on the lookout for opportunities to unlock the leadership potential in yourself and your colleagues.

The second important realization was about the importance of **creating stretch opportunities**—the tasks which challenge you to overcome your fears and inhibitions, force you to go beyond your comfort zone, and make you accomplish much more than what you think you can! I've personally experienced this during my initial days at McKinsey. I was just a fresher when, one day, a senior partner asked me to join a meeting with the CEO of a reputed financial institution. I was initially hesitant, but it forced me to step up, and I still thank him for that stretch opportunity. This has eventually become my signature leadership style, to push my team to go beyond what they think they can do!

My third understanding was about **giving before getting**. I joined McKinsey as a consultant and later on headed their knowledge centre (McKC), which at that time didn't seem as exciting as consulting. Apprehensive about my new role, I soon realized that my team was also looking up to me with similar concerns. It was then that I decided to consider my team's development as the priority instead of obsessing about my personal professional growth. This shift in focus from 'short term and self' to 'long term and others' led to many young colleagues in the team stepping up as leaders and to the phenomenal growth of our knowledge centre. It became a hub of innovation and a source of multiple new services that revolutionized McKinsey's business model. This success also enabled me to grow into a senior leadership position, which otherwise would not have been possible.

My last takeaway was that to create leaders, you must start with yourself and be **an inspiring role model**. To inspire others, you have to be inspired yourself. Our personal values and actions are the most potent way of influencing those around us. Leadership is not something you can fake; it is **who you are**. If you are in a position of influence, people are always observing you. It is important to be authentic and stay consistent with your espoused values even in moments of stress. How leaders handle 'moments of truth' constitutes the making of a great leader. I have been fortunate to observe some great leaders both at IIT and then throughout my career, and to work with them. They have had a deep impact on me and have massively shaped my development as a leader.

As leaders, it is our responsibility to create more leaders. However, this journey is not smooth. There are many problems that pull us down, and we can lose our way. Often, our tendency is to criticize the system and focus only on the problems. I believe with the youth today, we have a huge amount of human energy in store, waiting to find expression. We need to channelize this energy with a bottom-up approach instead of just waiting for top-down actions. Start taking initiatives at the ground level and keep trying to 'be the change' you want to see. Small actions, when persisted with over

Five mantras to create great leaders

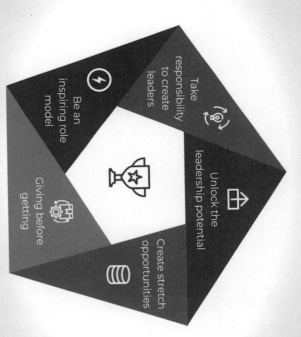

- Take responsibility to create leaders
- Unlock the leadership potential
- Create stretch opportunities
- Giving before getting
- Be an inspiring role model

a period of time, can snowball and gain visibility and momentum. With this, the people sitting at the top are more likely to be shaken up too and will be forced to change the status quo.

I am very excited about the energy and potential I see in the youth. If our generation can do our bit to spark their talent, I am confident we will see many more leaders from this young generation stepping forward in all walks of life.

Summary

- A true leader must possess three crucial traits—Doing the right thing over the easy thing (fearlessness), focusing on larger goals versus personal goals (selflessness), inspiring the team to go beyond one's own direction (vision).
- Five beliefs and actions that will enable you to develop leaders:
  - Belief in the vastness of human potential and constantly being on the lookout for opportunities to unlock the leadership potential of your colleagues.
  - Creating stretch opportunities for those around you, challenging them to overcome your fears and inhibitions, forcing them to go beyond their comfort zone.
  - Learning the approach of giving before getting. A shift in focus from short term and self to long term and selfless service will lead to phenomenal growth.
  - Lastly, to create leaders, start with yourself and be an inspiring role model.

- Youth today have a huge amount of untapped potential. We need to channelize this energy with a bottom-up approach instead of just waiting for top-down actions.

4

Mastering Duality: A Key Skill for Leaders to Succeed in the Digital Age

Just as we have two eyes and two feet, duality is a part of life

Carlos Santana, Musician

Among the challenges the VUCA world throws at leaders, most of which have been dealt with in the previous chapters, there is one particularly unique. It is the most significant, in my experience, and it is the need for leaders to manage contradictions or seemingly conflicting objectives at the same time.

Opposite values are complementary and coexistent in nature—day/night, heat/cold, male/female—and it is no different in business. Leaders in the digital age face many conflicting objectives, or what I like to call 'duality'. While opposite values are complementary, they are certainly not easy to deal with. As leaders, we tend to develop preferences, get stuck in a particular mode of working, and thus tend to focus on only one aspect of the complementary values. In some cases, our way of dealing with complementarity is to make tradeoffs between the opposing values. My submission is that complementary values or conflicting objectives are such an intrinsic feature of the digital age that leaders need to go beyond tradeoffs and master operating with duality—create win-win on both values.

Here are some examples of conflicting objectives that are often difficult for leaders to balance:

- **Short-term versus long-term:** High velocity of change and shrinking business and product cycles call for intense short-term focus. However, in parallel, if you do not invest in the long-term, you will not have a future. Moreover, short-term and long-term are not parallel tracks; they need to connect with each other. Many leaders get stuck in either short-term or long-term frames and find it difficult to toggle between the two.
- **Execution versus strategy:** We saw earlier in the book that traditional strategy-to-execution cycles have got reversed in the VUCA world and there is even more focus on execution today. However, it is important to connect the dots from execution and develop clarity on strategy. Strategy to execution is no more linear but iterative, so it becomes even more important to toggle seamlessly between the two.
- **Growth versus profitability:** This a classic conundrum—one that is becoming even more difficult to balance in the digital age. Revenue growth and profitability are the twin pillars of enterprise-value creation. However, it is not easy to manage both at the same time. Revenue growth typically requires investments, which hit your profitability. This becomes even more challenging when profitability is already under threat in many areas because of pricing pressures and rising costs. So it is a great challenge for business leaders to develop a win-win formula that can drive growth and profitability at the same time.
- **Customers versus employees:** Customers are the bedrock of any business, and in the digital age, which is characterized by hypercompetition and abundant choices, customer-centricity becomes even more important. Driving for customer delight will likely require employees to go the extra mile. But if you are not

careful, this might compromise your employee mission. I believe that in the digital age it is important to have a dual mission— keeping both customer and employee in mind. You have to be both customer-centric and employee-centric at the same time. And, if you balance the two axes (customers and employees) well that can create a virtuous cycle for your business.

- **Sales versus delivery:** Sales and delivery require different mindsets. Sales is often about selling a promise, while delivery is about making it happen. Sales often tends to be aggressive, and delivery conservative. If you oversell, you will falter in delivery. At the same time, if your promise is too conservative you might not be able to sell anything either!

- **Quality versus speed:** While driving at speed, your chances of accidents increase. Similarly, in business, pushing for speed can result in compromising quality. A good example of this is in recruitment: pushing for scale-up can end up compromising both candidate quality and experience. Speed is one of the defining features of the digital age; but it is imperative to find the formula to ensure high quality while operating at speed.

- **Data versus intuition:** We have talked at many points in the book about how data is exploding in volume, variety and velocity. This, coupled with the rise of data science and AI, enables more fact-based decision-making. However, the role of intuition does not go away. It becomes even more important. Intuition is a source of creativity and competitive advantage. The question is, how do you develop both the faculties of logic and intuition at the same time?

- **Man versus machine:** The relentless march of technology, led by artificial intelligence as its torchbearer, is leading to the redesign of many jobs and processes. The question is, how best can leaders designing the jobs and processes of tomorrow understand and incorporate the complementary capabilities of both machine (technology) and man (human capabilities)? I strongly believe it is an AND, not an OR opportunity.

- **Products versus services:** In technology, there has been a divide between products and services. These are typically different business models and require different mindsets and are typically delivered by different types of companies. However, the boundary between products and services has been blurring. Many services companies are developing product/intellectual property capabilities, while product companies are realizing the need for client-specific customization.

- **Input versus output:** Business leaders, especially those running public companies, are measured on the basis of their output—for example, financial results and stock market performance—and this tends to take a lot of their attention. However, if there isn't focus on the right inputs—for example, investment in capabilities, talent and culture—it will be difficult to sustain high-quality output. At the same time, if your efforts (input) are not anchored by a clear end in mind (output), you might lose your way.

- **'Knowing something' versus 'knowing someone':** Most business leaders tend to have a dominant style, either relationship-driven, or content-driven. I believe this is no more a choice. In the digital age, it becomes important for leaders to have both skills.

- **Autonomy versus governance:** The fast pace of the digital age means that traditional command-and-control structures cannot work. To ensure the speed of decision-making and action, you require autonomy at various levels of an organization. At the same time, the need for governance and risk management does not go away. How do you balance autonomy and governance at the same time?

- **Learning versus doing:** The dynamic nature and high velocity of change in the digital age make continuous learning imperative. At the same time, it is critical to have a bias for action. Learning and doing can take time away from each other, but it is important to find the right balance between the two.

- **Innovation versus delivery:** Innovation is one of the key success factors in the digital age. However, innovation by definition

Mastering duality - A key skill for leaders to succeed in the Digital age

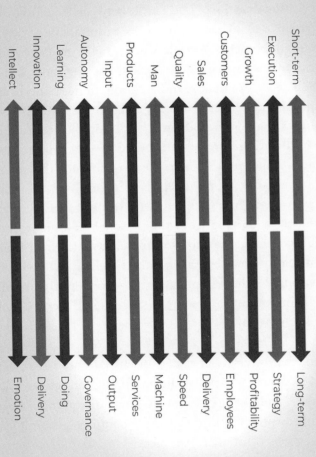

implies creativity, experimentation and risk-taking. On the other hand, high-quality delivery typically requires predictability and consistency. Often, innovation and delivery call for two different mindsets. It is more important than ever before to manage both at the same time.

- **Intellect versus emotion:** The battle between head and heart is a perennial one. Most of us have a dominant style. The conflicting requirements of leadership in the digital age implies that all executives need to develop and use their IQ and EQ equally. A balance of intellect and emotion, of head and heart, is more important than ever before for a leader.

- **Spirituality versus materialism:** In a highly frenzied and volatile world, being able to find peace in the midst of chaos is extremely important. When there is so much happening outside, being able to go deep within and anchor oneself becomes even more important. It is no wonder that meditation or mindfulness is moving from the personal realm and finding increasing acceptance at the workplace, even in boardrooms. While spirituality and materialism might seem at odds with each other, I strongly believe that having a strong spiritual core is increasingly important for leaders to succeed in the crazy VUCA world we live in today.

The complementary sets of values discussed above make for a long list. And it is but a sample of the conflicting objectives leaders face in the digital age! Duality is a given. Now, the question is, how can leaders improve their ability to handle conflicting objectives? I have five suggestions from my experience:

1. Build **awareness and understanding of the complementary values**, and the realization that you have to master both. You don't need to settle for trade-offs, win-win solutions are possible.
2. Get a **range of experiences**, which broaden your worldview and give you an understanding of different aspects of reality.

Five ways to address the duality and handle conflicting objectives

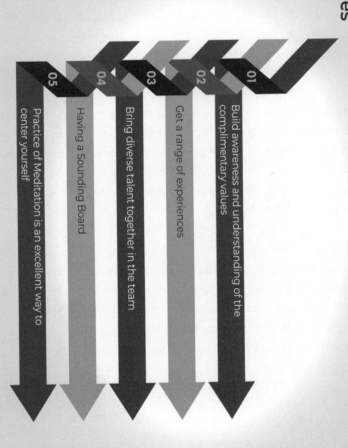

01 Build awareness and understanding of the complimentary values

02 Get a range of experiences

03 Bring diverse talent together in the team

04 Having a Sounding Board

05 Practice of Meditation is an excellent way to center yourself

3. Bring **diverse talents** together in the team. While it is desirable for a leader to master a range of complementary values, it might not be easy to do so. Bringing together talent with diverse backgrounds and experiences can help bring the complementary values together as a team.

4. Have a **sounding board**. In our personal lives, our spouse complements us. He/she is not just a sounding board but also often holds a mirror to us, helping us see the bigger picture of life. Similarly, in our professional life, it is very important to have a trusted sounding board, whether it is a mentor or a colleague, who can help us go beyond our biases and see the bigger picture.

5. **Practise meditation.** This is an excellent way to centre yourself. The challenge with complementary values is that we tend to get stuck in extremes. Meditation is a great way of centering yourself. I have seen in my personal experience that the practice of meditation brings clarity to any complex situation and helps you get to win-win solutions.

Complexity is a defining feature of the digital age, confounding leaders by laying in front of them many conflicting objectives. Therefore, mastering duality is a key skill for leaders to succeed in the digital age. It makes leadership a more difficult task, but those who are able to master different aspects of duality will grow to a different level of maturity, both as professionals and as human beings.

Summary

Managing duality in the form of contradictions or seemingly conflicting objectives is the most significant challenge that leaders need to manage in the digital age. Leaders will have to learn to go beyond trade-offs and develop win-win solutions.

- **Some examples of contradictions include**—Short-term versus long-term, execution versus strategy, growth versus profitability, customers versus employees, sales versus delivery, quality versus speed, data versus intuition, man versus machine, products versus services, input versus output.
- **Leaders have to strike a balance between various leadership skills** which include—'Knowing something' versus 'knowing someone', autonomy versus governance, learning versus doing, innovation versus delivery, intellect versus emotion, spirituality versus materialism.
- Finally, five approaches that will help the leader handle conflicts arising out of duality, these include:
  - Building **awareness and understanding of complementary values**.
  - Getting a **range of experiences**, which broaden worldview and understanding.
  - Bringing **diverse talents** together in the team to manage duality.
  - Having a trusted mentor or colleague who can be a sounding board and help you go beyond biases and see the bigger picture.
  - **Practising meditation to centre yourself.**

5

Spiritual Balance—a Necessity in Today's Digital Age

Most of us feel stress and get overwhelmed not because we are taking on too much, but because we are spending too little on what really strengthens us.

Marcus Buckingham, Author, *First Break All Rules*

We are in the age of digital deluge and hyper-consumerism, where there are many attractions and temptations. We are always running after the outer trappings of success—money, possessions, power and position. However, this is a trap. We are on an ever-running treadmill of desires and expectations. The faster we run and the more success we get, the more our desires keep rising and the treadmill runs faster. We can never find true peace and happiness as long as we are on the expectation's treadmill. As we run faster and faster to catch up, it leads to more and more stress. Eventually, we get fatigued and lose our spirit, and then start going through the motions of life like a mechanical robot.

This situation of stress and fatigue is further worsened by the extraordinarily digitized and interconnected world we live in. In this era of multiple gadgets, 24*7 connectivity and social media

(Facebook, Twitter etc.), we face constant stimuli and distractions. We are always switched on and in constant response mode; the barrage of information we get and the demand on us for response further aggravates our stress. Having to be in constant action mode also does not allow us time for reflection and rumination. As a result, the quality of our decisions and actions suffers.

Stress levels are increasing, and people are developing serious health problems sooner than ever before. Tolerance and empathy are on the downswing, leading to relationships of strife and conflict. Our moral fabric and integrity are weakening, resulting in a massive increase in corruption and crime.

If the current situation continues to spiral downwards, it will be disastrous for both individuals and society. If we want to reverse this trend and move into a virtuous cycle, we have to find a balance between spirituality and materialism.

Spirituality is the process of connecting with our inner self. To find true peace and happiness in today's fast-paced digital age, it is imperative that we discover spirituality and connect with our inner self. There is a great power that lies deep within all of us—a universal force that also connects all of us. We look for solutions to our problems outside of ourselves, whereas all solutions lie within us. We just have to connect with the divine and abundant energy within us. As we do that, it removes the haze and brings us clarity of thought and action—to discern between right and wrong, between what is important and what is not. Our fears and concerns dissipate; we come into the present moment and find the positive energy to achieve great outcomes that we might have never thought possible.

I have seen these benefits of spiritual balance in my own life. I have always led a very busy life juggling many balls at the same time. When I was in engineering college and later, during my MBA, it was academics, sports and extra-curricular all at the same time. Throughout my professional life I have continuously taken on multiple challenging responsibilities together, which have often gone well beyond my job scope. I have done this while staying true to my responsibilities towards my family and society.

Many people have asked me the secret of my 'multi-tasking'. Regular practice of meditation has been my 'secret weapon'. It has helped me manage the enormous stress, pressures as well as progress in my life with strength and integrity. Life is not all rosy; it is inevitable that some failures and disappointments will come. A big disappointment in my life was the failure of a business venture I had set up with a few close friends in 2000. I had to close it down two years later. Discovering 'Art of Living' at that stage of life and regular practice of Pranayama (breathing exercises) and the Sudarshan Kriya were undoubtedly the turnaround for me, helping me recover from the disappointment and enabling me to rededicate myself to my professional career with renewed energy and inspiration.

Clearly, finding spiritual balance is a necessity for coping successfully in today's material world. However, finding this balance is not easy. The daily stresses of our material world keep taking us away from our inner self. As children, we are born free and natural. However, as we grow, we build layers of protection that take us far away from our greatest asset, our inner self. That is where we need to build knowledge and discipline of spiritual practices that will take us ahead on the path of self-realization. There are many spiritual paths: yoga, pranayam, reiki, meditation, chanting, prayer, to name a few. However, their end objective is the same—self-discovery and connecting with our inner self.

I feel strongly that finding spiritual balance and learning the techniques to centre oneself is important for every leader to cope with the crazy VUCA world we are operating in. More is noise outside and more is the need for activity, greater is the silence and the rest you need to prepare yourself. I am happy that this awareness is now increasing amongst corporate leaders, and topics like spirituality and meditation are becoming mainstream in the corporate world.

Spiritual Balance is a necessity in Digital age

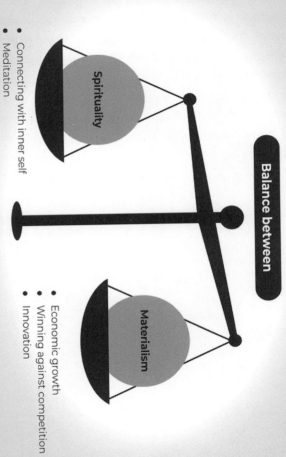

Summary

- We are in the age of digital deluge and hyper-consumerism, where we are caught on a never-stopping treadmill of desires and expectations. Running faster only leads to more stress.
- If we want to reverse the trend and move into a virtuous cycle, we have to find a balance between spirituality and materialism.
- There is a great power that lies deep within each of us and also connects all of us. We should not look for solutions to our problems outside, when all solutions lie within us.
- Practices like meditation can help reduce stress, increase work capacity and creativity, and improve mental and emotional well-being.

6

Sustainable Development—Rethinking Consumption

The things you own end up owning you

Tyler Durden, *Fight Club*

This chapter is adapted from the talk I gave at the IILM Second International Conference on sustainable development, in Delhi, India.

Sustainability at all levels—individual, corporate, societal—is an important challenge in the VUCA world we are operating in. Fast pace in everything we do and a relentless drive for growth is making sustainability a real question mark. Ever-increasing desires and search for growth are the cause of stress at the individual level, lack of judgement and unethical behaviour among corporations, and increasing crime, pollution and a variety of disasters in our societies. Corporate leaders in today's age cannot ignore these issues, they have to step up and address them directly.

Now, for sustainable development, it is critical to rethink our current mindsets and approach to consumption. Mahatma Gandhi captured the problem beautifully when he said: 'There is enough for everyone's need but not for everyone's greed.' However, solving this problem is easier said than done. Our current mental and economic models at all levels—individual, corporate, societal—are driven by growth. They are about ever-increasing needs and desires and the constant race to fulfil them. The desire for growth is a source of motivation for and a driver of human endeavour. It is this desire for growth that has helped human civilization develop over many millennia. However, mankind's ever-increasing desires and search for growth are also the cause of stress at the individual level, lack of judgement and unethical behaviour among corporations, and increasing crime, pollution and other disasters in our societies.

This is a complex issue, and I do not have any 'silver bullet' answers. However, I would like to share with you some of my practical attempts to address this challenge in my different roles—as an individual, a corporate leader, a citizen and society leader.

1. Individual

The root cause of the consumption debate lies at the individual level. It is ever-increasing individual desires that eventually reflect in our collective behaviours as a society. We work hard towards meeting our desires, which, however, keep growing. As soon as we fulfil one cherished desire, a new one seizes us. It becomes very difficult to break this cycle. This leads to increasing stress and loss of peace of mind. Stress does not just mean loss of mental peace; it is also one of the key root causes of diseases like hypertension and diabetes.

Yoga and meditation have been of great help to me in finding balance in my life. I have been following 'Art of Living' practices for almost twenty years now, and in the recent years have started reading the ancient Indian spiritual texts, especially the *Bhagavad Gita*. All this has helped me understand life better and go deeper within myself. As you do all this, the feverishness of desires in you reduces and you feel content and at peace with yourself.

We live in a material world and it is not possible for most of us to withdraw and become hermits. However, it is possible and desirable to find a balance between spirituality and materialism in our daily lives. I would encourage all of you to explore spirituality and adopt some spiritual practices in your daily lives.

2. **Corporate leader**

Many economic models have been experimented with in the recent centuries, but eventually capitalism has emerged as the most effective model. The entire basis of this model is free markets and growth. If you look at how capital markets value companies, growth expectation is clearly the biggest driver of value. This focus on constant growth leads to many problems. The over-leveraging of companies, the high levels of debt in financial institutions and the resultant (and frequent) financial crises are all outcomes of this obsession with growth. At the same time, we do not have an alternate economic model yet. Despite its many ills, capitalism, with its growth focus, makes for the most tenable economic model today.

I am sure that over a period of time, our thinking will evolve, and newer economic models will emerge. The question is, what can corporate leaders do *today*? We can perhaps differentiate between *good growth* and *bad growth*. The former benefits many, while the latter is self-centred and often leads to disastrous consequences.

The way many companies are trying to focus on 'good growth' is by putting the customer above profit. Companies that are truly customer-centred focus on identifying and serving the genuine needs of their customers. They place customer interest above their own interests. They ignore short-term profit considerations, knowing that if you do the right things for the customer, profits will follow in the long term. In my corporate experience, the customer-centric approach is the most important mantra for ensuring 'good growth' and building a high-quality business. Most companies that have been consistently successful over a long period of time (including the two that I have had the privilege of working with—Fidelity and McKinsey) have customer-centricity as their guiding mantra.

3. **Citizen and society leader**

Over the past decade, I have had the opportunity to co-chair and then chair the NASSCOM Regional Council (industry body for IT/BPM companies) for Haryana in India. Given that the IT-BPM industry has over 3 lakh employees in Gurgaon, the future of the industry there is closely tied to the health of the city. This has given me a great opportunity to understand the challenges of a new city like Gurgaon, among the most prominent being traffic congestion and air pollution. The city is choking with traffic; there is a high rate of accidents, and air pollution levels are among the highest in the world.

This situation is an outcome of our obsession with cars and the car-oriented planning we have today. Cars are an important status symbol, and everyone wants to own bigger cars. The rate at which cars are increasing significantly outstrips the building of new roads in many Indian cities.

The more advanced cities in the world (especially European cities, like Copenhagen, Amsterdam) have adopted a very different planning paradigm. They have focused on provision of public transportation and on encouraging walking and cycling. Over time, this focus has shown dramatic results—not just changing behaviours, but eventually improving pollution levels and even reclaiming roads and converting them into public parks.

At NASSCOM, we have been championing this cause of 'active commuting' (walking, cycling, use of public transportation) for the past few years. This required a number of interventions from the government. We struggled to get action from them, and this was a source of much frustration to us. Over the past few years, we changed our approach from just trying to influence the government to focusing on raising awareness about 'active commuting' and getting people to change their habits. We walked the talk by getting many CEOs from our industry to walk, cycle and use public transportation. This has now become a significant movement in Gurgaon, one that has also resulted in outstanding citizen initiatives like the 'Raahgiri Day', when many roads are reclaimed/blocked on Sunday mornings for pedestrians. All of this has forced the local administration to take notice, and they are beginning to make some steps to encourage walking, cycling and use of public transportation.

The reason I share this example is not just to show why 'active commuting' is so important for our cities to be sustainable, but to also bring out the value of citizen initiative. Often, as citizens, we are held back by the seemingly large and daunting effort that is required to bring changes in a large and seemingly unresponsive system. However, there is great value in individual actions. Our individual actions add up and have the power of making a significant difference in our society.

Rethinking our consumption models is a very complex question, to which there are no easy answers. However, I am delighted that these discussions are now taking place and becoming more mainstream. In the end, I would like to reiterate my three learnings on how to 'rethink consumption' as a driver of sustainable development. At the individual level, it is to balance spirituality and materialism; at the corporate level, it puts customers before profits; and for our society, it is for all of us as citizens to focus on our individual actions and behavioural changes. On all of these fronts, leaders need to lead by example.

Summary

- Sustainability at all levels—individual, corporate, societal—is an important challenge in the fast-paced, growth-obsessed digital age we live in.
- It is this desire for growth that has helped human civilization develop over many millennia. However, ever-increasing desires and search for growth are also the cause of stress at the individual level, lack of judgement and unethical behaviour among corporations, and increasing crime, pollution and a variety of disasters in our societies.
- For sustainable development, it is important to rethink our mental models and approach to consumption and to growth
- At the individual level, it is to balance spirituality and materialism; at the corporate level, it puts customers before profits; and for our society, it is for all of us as citizens to focus on our individual actions and behavioural changes.

SECTION 7

ADVICE TO YOUNG PROFESSIONALS

Introduction: Advice to Young Professionals

In this book, we have so far looked at digital transformation from the perspective of the enterprise. We have looked at the impact of digital on various industries, understood the technology implications, looked at organizational change elements, and then finally at how leaders need to step up and drive this change. In this last section, I want to change track and take the perspective of a young professional looking to build a career in the digital age.

If the digital age is a big change for the enterprise, then it is a big change also for the individual. If enterprises need to understand the fundamentals of the change and develop new rules to win in the digital age, the same is also true for the individual. If winning in the digital age is important for the enterprise, it equally so for the individual.

I believe the unprecedented disruption we are seeing in the digital age offers amazing opportunities to young professionals. This technology-based disruption is a great equalizer. Prior experience and successful track records are less relevant than before because you need to unlearn and learn the new rules of the game. In fact, the fresh perspective that young professionals bring to the enterprise is an advantage. They are 'digital natives', more intuitively able to understand new technologies and how new businesses can be built using digital technologies.

So how should a young professional prepare to win in the digital age? Many of the desirable competencies and mindsets for enterprises and leaders that we have talked about in the earlier sections are also relevant for young professionals. Prominent among these requirements are continuous learning, creativity and innovation, tech DNA, agility, management of duality, and spiritual and ethical balance. In addition to these six competencies and mindsets, there are six more points of advice I have for young professionals to win in the digital age:

1. **Find and live the unique purpose of your life:** In a period of constrained career opportunities, you have a limited set of choices. However, in this digital age there are vast opportunities for young professionals. That should release the pressure on them to conform to a narrow set of choices. It should liberate them to explore, find and live the unique purpose of their own lives. The discovery of one's unique purpose of life is a powerful source of energy. It helps you achieve your full potential and achieve lasting happiness.

2. **Be an entrepreneur:** Digital disruption is creating a host of new business opportunities. A supportive ecosystem makes it easier for entrepreneurs to get started. The risks are relatively low and the returns high. Being an entrepreneur in the digital age is a very attractive proposition. All you need is passion for an idea and risk-taking ability.

3. **Be a maverick:** The digital age is fast evolving and is multi-dimensional. To succeed, you need to go beyond straight-line conventional thinking. Do not be afraid to challenge the norms and accepted ways of doing things. Being unorthodox and independent is a good thing. Mavericks like Steve Jobs and Elon Musk are the role models of the digital age.

4. **Stay the course:** While the digital age is all about fast pace of change and speed of action, staying the course is also important.

Mantras for young professionals to win in the Digital age

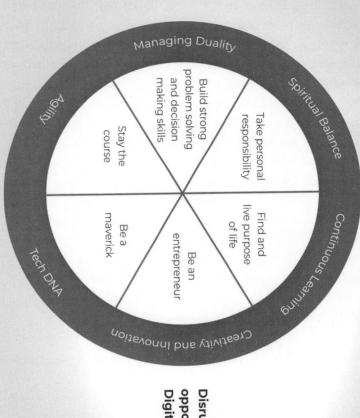

Managing Duality

Spiritual Balance

Continuous Learning

Creativity and Innovation

Tech DNA

Agility

Build strong problem solving and decision making skills

Take personal responsibility

Stay the course

Find and live purpose of life

Be a maverick

Be an entrepreneur

Disruption and opportunities in the Digital world

Longevity and steady progress (compounding) are key for success. Staying the course is difficult in an environment where there is a lot of frenzy around you. So patience and steadfastness are important qualities to build in the digital age.

5. **Build strong problem-solving and decision-making skills:** The VUCA world we are living in is characterized by high volatility and complexity. So, problem-solving and effective decision-making skills have become more important than ever before. These are foundational skills that every young professional should build in the digital age, irrespective of his or her choice of career.

6. **Take personal responsibility and drive change around you:** There are many challenges in the world around us—whether they are at the level of community, country or world. These range from pollution to socio-economic inequality to conflict, and at multiple levels. Young professionals need to take up the responsibility of tackling these challenges and driving change. Moreover, as you take personal responsibility, your zone of influence increases and you grow as a leader. In today's world, leadership is not about a position assigned to you but about the responsibilities you take on proactively.

I have expanded on these points of advice for young professionals across the chapters of this section.

Chapter 1: Seven Success Mantras

In the VUCA world, we live life at such a fast pace that we rarely get a chance to pause. We keep running mechanically, sometimes losing sight of where we are going. This can lead to fatigue, boredom and, eventually, burnout. Therefore, it is important once in a while to reflect on what is important to you and your plans for getting it, so you can anchor yourself. In this chapter, I propose a simple framework, based on my experiences, which will help you define what success means. I give you seven principles for achieving the success you want. It is important for any young professional to reflect on what success means to them and revisit it every couple of years.

Chapter 2: Finding your 'Sweet Spot'—The Powerful Purpose of Your Life!

In this chapter, I move the dialogue one step further—from the framework advocated in the previous chapter to define success—to talk about how we can identify our unique purpose in life. Having a powerful and sustained life purpose is the key to both achieving your full potential and finding lasting happiness in life. It can spark the leader within you and lift you and your world to a different level. I believe our purpose lies in the 'sweet spot', or at the intersection of three forces: our passions, our unique talents and the important and ethical needs we have to serve. Finding your 'sweet spot' is not an easy journey, but one you must embark on and persist with.

Chapter 3: Your Time is Now!—Ten Mantras for Young Entrepreneurs

The exciting part of the digital age consists of the availability of opportunities, funding, technology, and an active entrepreneurial ecosystem, making the launch of an entrepreneurial journey much easier than before. This is an opportunity every young professional should consider grabbing. In this chapter, I have shared ten mantras for individuals who aspire to become entrepreneurs. I believe these mantras can improve their chances of success.

Chapter 4: Lessons from the Incredible Life Story of Steve Jobs

The previous chapters have been about leadership, professional success, and the frameworks that can be followed to achieve them. My dialogue would not be complete if I didn't talk about one of the most visionary leaders and entrepreneurs of our time, Steve Jobs. In this chapter, we look at the various lessons his incredible life holds for us, and which we can learn and take inspiration from. Some of the learnings that stand out for me include driving with passion; finding innovation at the intersection of engineering and arts, end-to-end ownership and simplicity. Steve Jobs was a maverick who broke many rules in his drive to create amazing products. This maverick spirit, of being unorthodox and independent, is becoming so relevant in the digital age we are in.

Chapter 5: Five Lessons in Longevity and Greatness from the Giant Sequoias

In the previous chapter, I wanted to bring out Steve Job's spirit of being a maverick and how that led him to greatness. However, there are many paths to greatness, and longevity and staying the course are among them. In this chapter, I bring some inspiring lessons from the giant sequoias, amongst the oldest and largest living organisms on earth. The giant sequoia is a classic example of adaptation of an organism to survive adversity, of innovating to live and grow, of making the most of every situation presented to it, and of using the collective strength of the community to survive. I find the giant sequoia one of the most inspiring metaphors in nature for success.

Chapter 6: Ten Things I Wish I Learnt in Business School

As many of you step into the professional world from universities or start moving up the enterprise hierarchy, you discover that what you learned in college can potentially be applied at work and to your projects, but only up to a point. You will come across situations where you are stuck at the crossroads of decision-making, wishing there was something that could come to your aid. In this chapter, I present ten powerful frameworks that I have distilled from my own professional journey. These frameworks will help the reader in problem structuring and more effective decision-making, both critical skills for the digital age.

Chapter 7: Take Personal Responsibility and Change the World!

In this chapter, I encourage you to expand your concept of self and start taking broader responsibility. In our professional and personal lives, we will come across many situations that need fixing, gaps in processes, services, products, etc., and this can get frustrating. Whilst we spend a lot of time focusing on what other people are doing wrong and what they should do differently, we rarely look inside to see what *we* could do differently. This is a negative cycle; you land up changing nothing and only get frustrated. All of us have the potential to make a difference in the world around us, and we should start by taking small steps. If you simply act on what is within your zone of influence, that zone will keep expanding. As you take personal responsibility for the problems immediately around you, the leader within you grows. Taking greater responsibility is the surest way to your growth as a professional and human being.

1

Seven Success Mantras

Success is knowing your purpose in life, growing to reach your maximum potential and sowing seeds that benefit others

John C. Maxwell, Author, *21 Irrefutable laws of Leadership*

This chapter is a synthesis of the talks I have given on this topic at a number of MBA colleges in India. Of course, it applies to anyone from any discipline entering the enterprise world, even non-MBA students.

I would like to talk to you about building a successful career. When you are in the early stages of your professional journey, the main thing on your mind is career success—what type of job should I aim for, what I should focus on during the MBA programme, how to ensure I get my dream job, and so on. Having been through this stage of life and thought myself, I share some perspectives on career success, now that I have more experience in life and some sense of what works and what doesn't.

To help spark your thinking, I would like to share with you my beliefs about success. I don't have any magic formula for success. However, based on my experiences, I would like to propose some ideas as to what success is and my seven principles for achieving it.

What is success?

When I was graduating from the MBA programme in IIM Lucknow in 1996, success for me was about getting the best job. And, how did I define 'best job'?—one in the company that had the best brand, offered the best compensation, and where I saw my peer group joining or wanting to join. More than twenty years after my graduation, do I think those were wrong objectives? I don't think they were wrong, but in hindsight, they were not sufficient. Career is not a sprint; it is a multi-stage obstacle course. When you take a longer-term view of your career, additional perspectives start becoming important.

Many of my friends are at mid-career, in their forties and fifties, with at least twenty years of work experience under their belt and perhaps another twenty years to go. Most of them are very successful by any conventional yardstick—in senior positions in great companies, earning more money than anyone would ever need. However, I often sense emptiness and boredom in many of them. They are searching for something more. Some have even started talking about retirement in a few years' time! Why is that? Money and position are important. However, if you are just focused on them, you will be stuck in a 'rat race'. Whatever you achieve will never be enough, you will always want more. This never-ending cycle can become very stressful.

For sustained happiness and fulfilment, you need to meet some deeper objectives in life. To me, true success has three dimensions:

- **Making a difference:** Human life is a precious gift and with it, comes a big responsibility. It is to leave the world a better place than we found it. It is to make a positive impact and create lasting change around you. You could make a difference at many levels. It could be in your family, organization, community, industry, nation or the entire world. It is not important whether the difference you are making is big or small; what matters is that you are progressing on that journey. The positive legacy you leave behind is an important measure of your success.

- **Realizing your full potential:** All of us have abundant and unique potential. There are very few absolute truths in life, but among the ones I believe in strongly is that we are all operating at only a fraction of our potential and could do a lot more. We have very big opportunities, both as individuals and collectively as a society. So, success is about discovering and realizing your full potential. Success is not about winning a race against others. Success is progressing on your own personal development journey and winning the battles within.

- **Being happy:** That is the most obvious one, isn't it? Happiness is our basic nature and we are constantly seeking it. Success is when you stop searching for happiness in the past or the future and find it in your present moment. You accept your present situation; you live it fully and find joy and contentment in it. However, it is important to recognize the difference between happiness and pleasure. Happiness is stable, while pleasures are momentary. Pleasure can vanish, sometimes even leading to negative long-term consequences.

Seven success mantras

So, how do you achieve true success? I am not sure if there is a simple, linear formula to achieve the life objectives I have mentioned above. However, I believe in seven principles that I have found to be very useful, which I share here with you.

1. **Think big and take risks:** Often in your career, you get caught in a 'comfort zone'. You get some success; you are satisfied with that and want to protect it. That is when you miss the bus. You have no option but to take risks. My experience is that the downside of taking risks is often less harmful than what you fear and the upside, a lot more rewarding than you imagine. Even if you fail, it will not be a catastrophe, and you will probably learn a lot from it. For me, leaving McKinsey early in my career and

setting up my venture ActiveKarma was a big risk. The venture failed, but I was able to recover and get going again very quickly. Moreover, I grew tremendously from the experience. I thought I was a 'hot shot' consultant before I did the venture, but my lessons in building a business really came from my ActiveKarma experience. Whatever I achieved subsequently at McKinsey Knowledge Centre (McKC), Fidelity, Flipkart and now Incedo, I owe to those lessons. I am convinced that the risk I took with ActiveKarma and the experiences I had in running it have helped me do better as a manager and leader than I might have otherwise.

2. **Persist in search of excellence:** Friends, let me tell you that there are no shortcuts to excellence. Look at any successful person, and you will find they have some distinctive competence and that they have worked hard to build it. So, go through the grind, overcome short-term pains and distractions, and commit yourself to your mission. The fruits of your persistence will be sweet. As you build distinctive competence, your work will become easier, more enjoyable, and the rewards will be exponential.

    Moreover, the business world is full of uncertainties. You will rise but you will also certainly see some setbacks. Therefore, you have to be resilient and persist in your search of excellence. If you give up too quickly, you will likely miss out on the pot of gold. I learnt this the hard way. Having started my career as a consultant I was used to rapid career progression. But when I did my venture, I was taken aback by the lack of progress and ended up shutting it down in two years. In hindsight, I realize that it takes much longer than two years to build anything meaningful and that I should probably have given my venture more time. That lesson has stood me in good stead subsequently in my career. I spent eight years at McKC and six in Fidelity. It is this perseverance that has helped me realize the visions and achieve the business impacts that would have appeared fanciful in the early part of the journey.

3. **Build lasting relationships:** When I joined McKinsey in 1996, one of the senior partners during our induction journey said that to succeed, you either need to know something or know someone. At that time, I felt I was the 'know something' type and that success that came from knowing someone was a bit superficial. As I have gained more experience, I now realize better the tremendous value of relationships. People respond more to trust and emotions than to knowledge and logic. Whether it is achieving difficult targets as a team, resolving conflicts, or finding your next job, relationships are the key to success. They are a force multiplier, helping you achieve outcomes that you could never get on your own. Moreover, relationships are not just a means to an end. They are an end in themselves. Man is a social animal. We crave for trust and togetherness. Deep relationships bring joy and warmth to life, making it more meaningful. So, build trust-based relationships and nurture them with care. They will be your most important asset in life, the best investment you can ever make.

4. **Be proactive and take responsibility:** Whether it is the organization you work for or the society at large, you will see many chronic problems that can create a sense of helplessness about the 'system'. If you aspire to develop as a leader, then be proactive and take ownership of the problems around you. Don't let the problems weigh you down. Just be positive and focus on your karma. You will be surprised at the power your individual actions can have. As you take action, your zone of influence expands and the leader within you grows. Slowly, the change you started with your actions can come to a tipping point, when the 'system' also starts changing. Yes, there are limits to human action and you have to accept some situations. However, the power of individual action and influence is a lot more than we realize. So, do step up and take responsibility for the situations around you.

5. **Focus on giving, not getting:** In the early stages of our career we are often obsessed about value addition to self—'what is

in it for me'. This is a narrow perspective and might lead to disappointment. Let go of your self-interest and seek to give and to add value to people and situations around you. Focus on 'we', not 'I'. That will grow you as a leader and as a human being, and eventually more success will come to you. I learnt this at the McKinsey Knowledge Centre (McKC). While I was consulting in McKinsey, the value addition for me was very tangible. However, during my early years as a manager at McKC, I began to feel very frustrated at the seeming lack of value addition for myself. At that time, I fortunately asked myself the question, 'what value was I adding to others?' I then started focusing on developing the people around me. As I did that something magical happened. My team members flowered; McKC grew tremendously, from a research back-office to an innovation hub; and as a result, I gained success as a leader. Truly, letting go of the obsession with what you are getting and focusing on what you are giving can work wonders.

6. **Stay humble and true to your values:** One of the negative consequences of success is arrogance. Sometimes successful people become too full of themselves, stop listening and eventually lose touch with reality. That is the beginning of their end. So, do not let success or position go to your head. Always stay humble, grounded, natural and spontaneous. It will help you connect with people and earn you their love and respect. It will also keep you from making big mistakes. In addition to being humble, always uphold high ethical standards and strive to do the right thing. Have a clear conscience and ensure you can always hold your head high. This is critical. Integrity, once broken, can never be repaired. All your work can be undone in a single moment of indiscretion.

7. **Keep your balance and pursue interests beyond work:** In the early phase of one's life, one tends to be obsessed about career. I would encourage you to find a balance in your life. Life is not

Seven Success Mantras

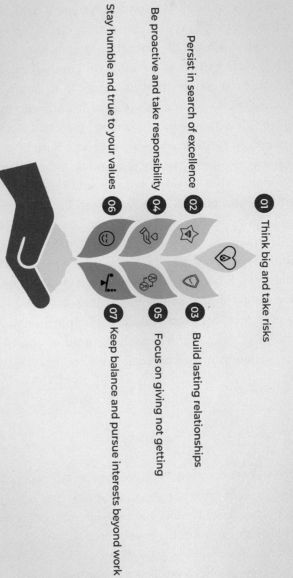

01 Think big and take risks

Persist in search of excellence **02**

03 Build lasting relationships

Be proactive and take responsibility **04**

05 Focus on giving not getting

Stay humble and true to your values **06**

07 Keep balance and pursue interests beyond work

a sprint; it is more like a marathon. You need to learn how to sustain yourself in the long run. For that, cultivate interests and passions outside of work. They will give you a fresh and deeper perspective of life. They will also recharge and rejuvenate you, ensuring that you have the energy to play a long innings. For me, my big anchor in life is my family. I am married, have three beautiful children and am part of a large joint family. They are an enormous source of strength in my life and keep me centred. In addition, I have many passions that I pursue. I am passionate about sports and play squash twice a week. I have been following Art of Living for almost twenty years now, and religiously attend yoga and meditation sessions every Sunday morning. Finally, I love to travel and take at least two vacations every year. These passions help rejuvenate me and keep my energy levels high.

In conclusion, I would say that you are in a very privileged position. The digital age we are living in offers wonderful growth opportunities. You can have a good shot at achieving great professional success and earning lots of money. So, please do use this opportunity to ask some bigger questions of your life. My wish is for all of you to flower as great leaders, realize your full potential and make a positive impact around you.

Summary

- Success is more than money or possessions. The material gains from success can often trap you in a 'rat race'.
- Being truly successful means making a difference while realizing your full potential and being happy about it.
- Seven principles to achieve true success: think big and take risks, persist in the search of excellence, build lasting relationships, be proactive and take responsibility, focus on giving and not getting, stay humble and true to your values, keep your balance and pursue interests beyond work.

2

Finding your 'Sweet Spot'—The Powerful Purpose of Your Life!

Purpose is the reason you journey, Passion is the fire that lights your way.

Will Craig, US Major League baseball player

Achieving your full potential

Every human being has abundant potential. Everybody is blessed with some unique talents, which if discovered and nurtured can lift the person and the world around him to a higher level. However, very few achieve their full potential. In fact, most of us are perhaps operating at a tiny fraction of our full potential. This is perhaps one of the greatest challenges and opportunities we have as individuals, collectively as society, and at some level as mankind.

Why is this? Why are we not operating at our full potential?

The reason is, it was not meant to be so easy. Life is a voyage of discovery. Nature expects us to progress from one level to the next. At each level, we discover something new and powerful about ourselves and the world around us. This moves us towards awareness of our true calling. However, progressing from one level to another is not easy. Our life situations condition us and exert a strong gravitational pull that does not allow us to break free. The laws of physics seem to apply here! Gravity keeps us rooted. To launch a rocket into orbit you need a turbo booster. Once the rocket moves into orbit, it can stay there with little additional energy. Similarly, we need a push, a trigger, to lift ourselves from our current situation and move to the next level.

This sounds difficult. So, how do we progress on the journey to unlocking our potential?

I believe the key to unlocking our potential is to have a **positive and sustained purpose,** a cause to which we can dedicate our lives. This purpose will be the positive force that creates focus and commitment and can inspire extraordinary effort. It is the magnet that will create means where none seem to exist and align the forces of nature in a mysterious yet powerful way. It is indeed the turbo booster that can lift us from one level to another and in the process help us realize our full potential. History gives us abundant examples. M.K. Gandhi was a simple man, but he had a powerful purpose. This lifted him to the level of a Mahatma and ended up shaking the foundations of a mighty empire. Tulsidas was a village simpleton. His love of Rama helped him create the epic Ramcharitamanas and made him a saint. Joan of Arc was a young and frail peasant girl. However, her convictions helped rouse a beaten people to defeat a powerful enemy. She is revered to this day as one of the patron saints of France. This clearly shows that there is incredible power even in the meekest amongst us. A powerful purpose can unlock the amazing energies within us, not just uplifting our own selves but the world around us too.

So, how do we find a positive and sustained purpose?

Finding the purpose of your life

Some might be fortunate to find a guru who helps them find their path, while some might go through dramatic events that make their life purpose clear. India's freedom fighters are an illustration of the latter. The fight for the nation's freedom inspired a generation to lift themselves up and force a change that was not seen as possible. However, most of us might not be in either of the above situations and defining our purpose might call for conscious effort.

In the daily pulls and pressures of life, this question of finding our life purpose often gets lost. You float through life driven by the forces around you. You do not seem to be in control of your own destiny. The purpose of one's life seems like a difficult puzzle. It is sometimes difficult even to find the starting point from where you can begin unravelling this puzzle. However, it is necessary that we attempt to solve this puzzle of life. Having a powerful and sustained purpose in life is the key to not only achieving your full potential but also finding lasting happiness in life. It brings you the energy and focus that can unlock your potential, spark the leader within you, and lift you and your world to a different level. In addition, having clarity of purpose and being able to live it brings alignment in life, which leads to lasting happiness and inner peace.

I believe our purpose lies in the **'sweet spot', or the intersection of three forces**—our passions, our unique talents and serving important and ethical needs. Finding your 'sweet spot' is a journey. Passions are the likely starting point, but they are not enough. They need to be coupled with talent. Finally, and most importantly, you need to channelize your passions into meeting some important needs or solving some important problems around you. Magic happens when you find the 'sweet spot' at the intersection of the three forces I have mentioned. You realize the powerful and sustained purpose of your life. However, there is no predictable formula for finding this 'sweet spot'. It is a voyage, a patient journey, an exciting adventure.

Here are some thoughts on finding your 'sweet spot', your powerful, sustained purpose:

Start with your passions

Passions are a gift. They are a source of energy. They light up your life and bring you joy and vitality. A life devoid of passions is not a full life. Passions are also the foundation of excellence. You are likely to give your best in what interests you and brings you happiness. Passions are like a luminous compass that lights up the way to your purpose. Follow your passions and you will have begun your journey of life well.

However, we often do not follow our passions because of our fears and conditioning. As children, we have few fears. As we grow up, we keep building fears inside ourselves and it becomes progressively more difficult to overcome them. Fears stop you from connecting with your true self. They limit your enjoyment of life. Let go of your fears and take more risks. The downside is less damaging and the upside, a lot more gainful than you imagine. So, take that initial leap of courage and go after your passions. Be like a child, live your life freely!

The other big factor stopping us from following our passions are the external expectations of us. As we grow up, we start accumulating the expectations of family, friends and society. We often look at the world from another's lens. We are conscious of what we are expected to do and how we are expected to behave. Success has a narrow and rigid definition. We often end up living our lives for others or as others expect of us. This is very limiting. You need to challenge this conditioning and live your own life. It is important to be conscious of one's responsibilities towards others and to discharge them fully. However, in that process do not forget yourself. You need to find a balance between living your life and living it for others.

So, break free from your fears and conditioning and follow your passions. That is a happy and energizing way to begin the beautiful journey of life!

Seek opportunities to serve important needs

Passion is a very important ingredient in the journey to finding your purpose, but it is not sufficient. Passion will spark the initial momentum, which may not sustain. Your passions need to be aligned with serving an important need so that the sparks of inspiration become a bright and sustainable fire. Life is not to be lived in isolation. We live in an interdependent world. One of the fundamental objectives of life is to make a positive difference in the world around us. We need to translate that into our personal purpose. Moreover, this is not just about nobility of purpose. At a more practical level, any effort needs to create value for others for it to be sustainable. You create value not just by pursuing your own self-actualization but also by solving problems or serving the needs of others. Therefore, we need to figure out how our passions and/or skills (which are internal) can be made relevant for the world around us. How can our interests and talents create value or solve problems for others? You need to link the internal with the external or, to put it in more commercial terms, you need to link supply with demand!

Solving other people's problems and creating value is not easy. We are naturally wired to be self-oriented. Therefore, it is easier for us to have an understanding of our own needs, our aspirations, our strengths and our passions first. To create value, you need to have an outside-in orientation, where you have the empathy to understand the world around you. You need to go out of your cocoon and relate to others. That allows you to understand the needs of people around you. This is necessary to spark the thought process on how you can solve their problems and create value.

You also have to open yourself up to different experiences. Finding out where and how you can create value is not easy. You are unlikely to uncover significant opportunities if you look at the world through a narrow lens. Therefore, exploration and allowing oneself a range of experiences is very helpful. As you do this, you discover more about yourself and the world around you. This process can help uncover where and how you can add value.

Persist to build unique skills

Once you have identified your passion and/or the needs you want to serve, you need to practise deeply to develop the required unique skills or competencies. They are necessary to provide depth to your purpose, taking you from the ordinary to something that has a significant and lasting impact on the world around. Equally, unique skills can also be a starting point to figure out opportunities for you to add value. You are likely to more easily find opportunities where you have unique skills.

However, building unique skills and competence is not easy. It requires hard work, patience and discipline. Even if you are blessed with natural talents, you have to practise hard and long to build distinctive competencies. There are no shortcuts. It takes time and you have to keep at it. The devil will test you in this process. You will face pain and feel like giving up. But you have to persevere, bite through the pain and not give up. As you build the habit of not giving up, of not taking the easy course, you will discover hidden reserves of energy within you. You will find that you are able to go on for much longer. However, even upon reaching higher and higher levels, you cannot rest on your laurels. You have to keep practising; the aim at any point is to move to the next level. The fruits of your persistence will be sweet. Once you build distinctive skills, you will find that future activities become effortless and actually pleasurable.

There is a synergistic relationship between your passions, serving important needs and your unique skills. Passion can lead to the building of distinctive skills. Passion and skills can point you to opportunities where you are most likely to create value. However, this flow is not necessarily sequential or linear. The three can connect with each other in different ways. What is important is that you are

Finding your sweet spot

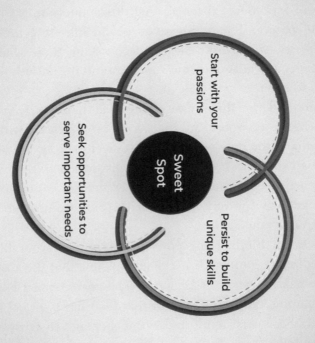

able to link them well. This can lead to a virtuous cycle where they can feed into each other, each becoming stronger in the process. The 'sweet spot' that emerges will be powerful and can create magic!

I want to leave you with three final thoughts on how to proceed on this magical journey of discovering your 'sweet spot'—the powerful purpose of your life:

1. **Ask the question:** The starting point is to question the unique purpose of your existence. Ask that question of yourself and of nature. The answers you get in life are a function of the questions you ask. As you keep asking these challenging questions, the mist of confusion clears and the answers you seek begin to emerge.
2. **Understand the flow:** Everything that happens in your life happens for a purpose. All the answers you seek are within you, so 'connect the dots of your life'. Reflect on your life and your various experiences. Whatever has happened in your life has happened for a purpose. As you piece the jigsaw puzzle of your life together, it is very likely that the purpose of your life will jump out at you.
3. **Keep faith:** Finding the powerful purpose of your life is an unpredictable journey. It is equally possible that the answer lies at the next corner or is far away. The answers may take some time coming but keep the faith that God has a special purpose for you. Seek persistently and with belief, and the answers shall start to follow.

Finding the powerful purpose of life is one of the most profound quests of mankind. It is a quest that you must attempt. If you can find your 'sweet spot', it will lift you and the world around you to a higher level. Mahatma Gandhi put it beautifully when he said, 'Find purpose, the means will follow.' However, this process of finding your purpose is a patient journey. Take it as an exciting adventure and do embark on it!

Summary

- Striving to achieve your full potential is what will keep you ever inspired and moving up in life.
- A powerful and sustained purpose can help you achieve your full potential and find lasting happiness.
- Finding that 'sweet spot' is one of the most profound quests of human life—your passions, your unique skills and the opportunities around you to serve important needs, will lead you to this spot.

3

Your Time Is Now!—Ten Mantras for Young Entrepreneurs

In a world that changes really quickly, the only strategy that is guaranteed to fail is not taking risks

Mark Zuckerberg, Co-Founder and CEO, Facebook

Excerpts from my talk on entrepreneurship at an engineering college in India.

In this chapter, I want to tell you why I think digital age is the right time for young professionals to consider entrepreneurship. I will also share with you ten mantras for success, gained from my own experiences as an entrepreneur. My insights are based on four sets of experiences— starting and failing in my own startup (ActiveKarma 2000–02); working for many years as an intrapreneur in McKinsey and Fidelity; my leadership role at Flipkart, India's largest and most successful startup; and leading Incedo, a high-growth technology services firm.

Why should young professionals become entrepreneurs?

I strongly believe it is a great time to be an entrepreneur today in India and all of you should consider this path. There are at least five reasons why I believe so:

A. **Technology disruption is creating unprecedented new opportunities:** The velocity of technology change and business disruption we are witnessing is perhaps unprecedented in human history. Mobile, e-commerce, cloud, big data, have changed consumer behaviors and business models dramatically, and yet these trends are barely fifteen years old. We are now into the next phase of technology, with artificial intelligence, machine learning and the internet of things dominating. Technology change is a great equalizer. Big companies don't have an advantage at leveraging technology change, often they are at a disadvantage. Smart entrepreneurs are best placed to experiment and leverage new technology. We have seen with the example of Flipkart, Paytm, MakeMyTrip and Ola how you can leverage new technology (e-commerce) to create a huge business in less than ten years. And this is just the tip of the iceberg.

B. **It accelerates personal growth:** If you are ambitious and want to change the world, then entrepreneurship is the path for you. Pursuing your own idea provides a great sense of ownership and independence, which is difficult to find in a job. It creates a sense of purpose and energy that helps you grow as a person and achieve things that will be impossible in a standard job. I meet many young entrepreneurs and always get amazed at how much they have grown and matured in a short period of time. In addition to personal growth there is off course the opportunity for life-changing wealth creation. Jobs today pay well but nothing compared to the wealth you can create through a successful venture.

C. **There is availability of risk capital and an entrepreneurial ecosystem:** A positive development in India over the past 15 years is the development of the venture capital industry and entrepreneurial ecosystem. Capital is now available for each step of the entrepreneurial journey, even for very early-stage ideas. This makes it easier for young professionals to pursue their ideas without betting on the hard-earned money of their parents.

Capital also helps them scale up their ideas rapidly. Most importantly, there is development of an active entrepreneurial ecosystem where experienced entrepreneurs and professionals are themselves investing into ventures and are available for mentoring and support.

D. **The cost of failure is not high:** My parents' generation saw a lot of hardship and was very risk-averse. These conservative mindsets have historically permeated in our society and acted as a deterrent for taking risks. However, the India of today is very different. The cost of failure is low. I have already mentioned the availability of risk capital. Even more importantly, there are abundant opportunities and company mindsets have changed. An individual whose start-up has failed is not frowned upon. In fact, failure is increasingly seen as a positive experience. I have seen it in my own example. I did my venture ActiveKarma in 2000-02. The venture failed but I was able to bounce back very quickly. In fact, a lot of what I have achieved in my corporate career is because of the invaluable learnings from ActiveKarma.

E. **You can make a contribution to the country:** India's biggest asset is its age pyramid. Almost half the population of 1.35 billion is below the age of twenty-five. However, this also presents a massive challenge of job creation. Government and the public sector will never be able to create the required number of jobs. Massive entrepreneurial activity is needed to create jobs. Moreover, entrepreneurs can create world-beating, successful ideas and companies and put India on the world map. IT and BPM industry, which was driven by first-generation entrepreneurs has done that very successfully over the past twenty years. Opportunity is there for Indian entrepreneurs to rise and dominate in many more sectors.

So hopefully I have convinced all of you to become entrepreneurs! Let me now share some insights based on my experiences that can help you succeed as an entrepreneur.

Ten success mantras for young entrepreneurs

Exceptionally successful entrepreneurs are often mavericks, they have an X Factor, which is difficult to replicate. However, I will still attempt to share ten mantras based on my experiences that should improve your chances of entrepreneurial success.

1. **Passion for your idea:** This has to be the starting point of your entrepreneurial journey, a core idea and/or purpose that is really driving you. Entrepreneurship is a tough journey and there will be many moments when you might feel like giving up. It is this passion for your idea, a sense of mission that will keep you going. Moreover, entrepreneurship is a journey into the unknown. When you are creating something new it is difficult to be clear about your strategy and plans at all stages. Your passion and mission will give you direction in moments of uncertainty. For example, Flipkart has a clear and strong mission, 'transforming lives of a billion Indians through technology'. While the Flipkart strategy might have kept changing over the past ten years, this mission has provided a strong anchor and inspiration for the organization.

2. **Route to clients:** Customers are the lifeline of any business and this is even more critical for a startup. You might have a great concept or product, but if you can't get clients, your business will never take off. That is why you really need to think back from a client perspective on what real needs you are looking to solve and will the client pay for it versus thinking about a business idea just from your perspective. For a B2B business, your first few clients might come based on your relationships. While for a B2C business, the key consideration is customer segmentation and targeting. You will not be able to be everything to everyone, certainly not in the early stages of your business.

3. **Audacity:** Audacity is the willingness to take bold risks. This is a core aspect of the culture I saw at Flipkart and one that inspired me a lot. To build something new, especially in a new or changing industry, you cannot be incremental. You have to think big, take bold risks and believe you can change the world. The great Steve Jobs famously said, 'those who are crazy enough to believe they can change the world are the ones who actually do so'. This is a key success factor for successful entrepreneurs across generations. This is certainly true for this generation's superstars like Jeff Bezos, Elon Musk and Jack Ma and a key factor behind their companies astounding success. This is also the quality that makes companies like Flipkart and Ola dream big and take on giants like Amazon and Uber.

4. **Innovation:** Innovation is the foundation of a start-up, the key value an entrepreneur brings. To drive innovation, deep customer understanding is key. You need to have an intimate understanding of their pain points. This will not happen sitting in a room. So, go out and have a range of life experiences.

   Most powerful innovation often happens by connecting the dots across different areas. This was the unique strength of the great Steve Jobs. He was able to connect the dots across his many life experiences and passions to create many market defining innovations. iPod was a celebrated example where his passion for music, technology and design all came together. The other key requirement for innovation is deep product-tech expertise. As we have discussed earlier, technology disruption is the most defining feature of the world we are living in and at the heart of breakthrough opportunities for entrepreneurs. So, I encourage you to learn and build deep engineering expertise.

5. **Your team:** We are in an increasingly complex environment where it is almost impossible for any individual, however talented,

to have all the skills required to build a successful business on his own. Therefore, it is very important for an entrepreneur to build an effective team. While building a team, we often seek people like us (I did that when I built my venture ActiveKarma, all three of us from IIT Delhi!). While it is critical that you work with people who have similar values, it is important that from a skills perspective you bring together people who have complementary skills. Most successful partnerships have been of leaders who had such complementary skills. For example, Bill Gates–Paul Allen at Microsoft, Steve Jobs–Steve Wozniak at Apple, Larry Page–Sergey Brin at Google, and nearer home, the team of Infosys founders.

6. **Funding:** It is critical that you secure adequate funding sooner than later for your venture. While the power of your idea and team are the most important determinants of success of your venture, lack of funding is the factor that can take you to failure immediately and irreversibly. Many entrepreneurs try to time the market or to delay funding to maximize value. Don't delay raising funding; secure the future of your venture first. If your venture survives and thrives, you will create enough personal value for yourself. If it gets strangled for funds and dies, your high ownership of the venture will not help. Another point of funding is that the questioning you face in the process also helps you sharpen your idea, improving your chances of success. A final point on funding, while raising too much capital can be a problem (can lead to inefficient use of funds), make sure you raise adequate capital required to scale up and fight the competition.

7. **Patience and resilience:** Entrepreneurial journey can be a roller-coaster with many ups and downs. I have not yet come across any successful startup that has not gone through a near-death experience at some point in their journey. Therefore, you

need to have the patience to play for the long term and resilience to bounce back. As mentioned in the first point, deep passion for the idea and a sense of purpose inspire you to see the long term and help you ride through the short-term challenges. It helps you value and enjoy the daily journey and not be obsessed with outcomes. In addition to this, I believe it is important to have anchors in life outside of work. They give you strength, help you see the big picture of life and bounce back from disappointments. For example, my anchors are my family, spirituality (meditation + *Bhagavad Gita*) and sports. These anchors have made me resilient and helped bounce back from the many challenges I have faced.

8. **Communication and networking:** It is very important that you as an entrepreneur are able to tell your story passionately, clearly and repetitively. You need to do so to sell your idea to investors, to attract talent to join your team, and most importantly to convince customers. And, you have to do so multiple times over because you will not succeed in any of the above three tasks the first time around. Nobody else can tell your story with the authenticity and power that you can do so yourself. You cannot delegate this to anybody else.

   You will also need to become a master networker. In today's interconnected world, you will have to build a web of partnerships—with customers, suppliers, investors, advisors and mentors. For this, you have to be proactive and learn to reach out. Sometimes entrepreneurs, especially technologists, can be introverts. You have to get out of that and build both your willingness and skills to network. The future of your venture depends on it!

9. **Humility:** World is changing so fast that you can never sit back on your laurels and allow hubris to settle in. Arrogance is a sure shot recipe for failure. A strong trait of a successful entrepreneur

Ten mantras for young entrepreneurs

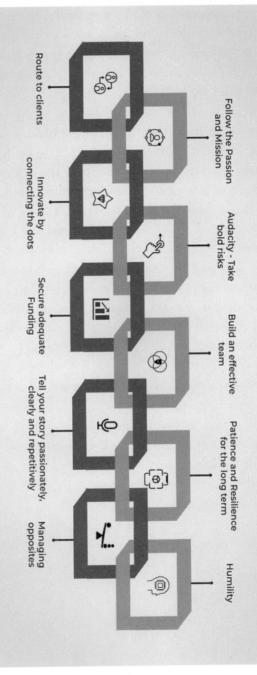

Route to clients

Follow the Passion and Mission

Innovate by connecting the dots

Audacity - Take bold risks

Secure adequate Funding

Build an effective team

Tell your story passionately, clearly and repetitively

Patience and Resilience for the long term

Managing opposites

Humility

is that he/she approaches life as a student. We meet people, we learn, we read something, we learn, we watch a movie, we learn, we have any experience, we learn. If one is not humble, one will not learn. One who does not learn will not succeed. This has never been truer.

10. **Managing opposites:** This is a philosophical point but a very important one. In the complex and fast-evolving business environment today, you need to build the ability to manage many opposites. You need to have very sharp execution focus; at the same time, you need to be strategic. You need to survive in the short term while also need to build for the long term. You need to ensure outstanding customer experience and growth while also ensuring profitability. These opposites can become difficult to manage; however, they are inevitable. It is important that you recognize this and build your mental ability to balance these opposites. Ability to manage this duality will be one of the most important skills in the twenty-first century.

I hope the above insights inspire you to pursue your entrepreneurial journey with even more passion and clarity. The time to start your journey is now, so go forth with hope and energy and let a thousand flowers bloom. This is the best possible journey you can take for yourself and for the country.

So, go forth and shine on, you crazy diamonds!

Summary

- Young professionals nowadays should choose the path of entrepreneurship as technology disruption is creating many opportunities for startups.
- Moreover, an active entrepreneurial ecosystem is developing in the country, with experienced entrepreneurs and professionals personally investing in these ventures. Additionally, a number of industry forums also provide infrastructure as well as mentoring support for startups.
- Ten success mantras for young entrepreneurs to follow in their life-
  o Passion and Mission
  o Route to clients
  o Audacity
  o Innovation
  o Patience and Resilience
  o Team
  o Funding
  o Communication
  o Humility
  o Managing opposites

4

Lessons from the Incredible Life Story of Steve Jobs

Taking risks, breaking rules and being a maverick have always been important but today they are more crucial than ever

Gary Hamel, Management Consultant, Author of
Leading the Revolution and Competing for the future

Steve Jobs was one of the most fascinating icons of our age. He had revolutionary impact across multiple industries—personal computers, mobile phones, music, movies, retailing. His record of innovation and transformation is unbelievable; in this respect he is perhaps the tallest amongst business leaders in recent history. Recently, I read Walter Isaacson's biography of Steve Jobs.[5] It is a detailed life story of a complex and fascinating personality. The book surprised me as Jobs came across as a lot more complex than what I earlier understood him to be. I was also rather taken aback and disappointed by the many imperfections in his personality. However, as I read on through Isaacson's book, there developed a better understanding and even deeper respect for Jobs and Apple's remarkable achievements. I thought I would synthesize and share the eleven key lessons I have taken away from Jobs' extraordinary life story.

1. **Passion:** The defining characteristic of Jobs was his sheer intensity. And that intensity came from his three primary passions—to build great products, to build Apple into an enduring company, and to make a 'dent into the universe'. The most visible of his passions was for products. He prioritized products over profits and strove for perfectionism in his products. This passion for products clearly paid rich dividends, as Apple ended up creating a series of industry-shaping innovative products that also led to great financial success for the company. Jobs believed that life does not just happen to you but that you can shape the future. His philosophy is well captured by Apple's famous 1997 'Think Different' commercial: 'The people who are crazy enough to think they can change the world are the ones who do.' This great passion for making a real difference was the force that led him to incredible feats.

2. **Intersection of engineering and arts:** For me, one of the most unique aspects of Steve Jobs's talents was his ability to straddle and assimilate the seemingly contrasting worlds of engineering and arts. He had a range of eclectic interests, from music to calligraphy to Hindu philosophy to Zen Buddhism. He was able to bring intuition and empathy from the world of humanities into the staid world of engineering and technology. That was perhaps the distinguishing feature of Apple that separated its products so much from other technology companies. Jobs put it nicely, 'I'm one of the few people who understands how producing technology requires intuition and creativity, and how producing something artistic takes real discipline.' This concept of intersection of disciplines has many lessons for both new-age professionals and for industries in need of transformation. Significant innovation happens not within a box but at the

intersection of different fields. This will increasingly become a formula for the future, especially so in the digital age.

3. **End-to-end ownership:** Jobs' quest for perfection led to his insistence that Apple have end-to-end control of every product it made. He doggedly pursued vertical integration across design, hardware, software and content. This approach could be attributed to Steve Jobs' obsession with control. However, there is a positive basis to this approach. Steve believed that he had to take responsibility for ensuring that the customer got a superb product, and for that end-to-end ownership was necessary. Apple's ability to integrate hardware, software and content into one unified system enabled it to impose simplicity and avoid the fragmentation that an 'open architecture' approach could lead to. This 'closed loop' approach was a key secret behind Apple's success. It led to great products, helped Apple achieve high profit margins even with small market share, and was the foundation for new innovative products like the iPod, iPhone and iPad. *The Jobs example explains better to me why some entrepreneurs who have a long-term orientation look to have end-to-end control over all aspects of the value chain.*

4. **Simplicity:** Steve Jobs had a strong belief in simplicity and minimalism, likely influenced by his interest in Zen Buddhism. His maxim was that 'Simplicity is the ultimate sophistication'. This mantra is reflected both in his products and in his personal life. The intuitive usability of Apple products, which has been one of the keys to their success, was driven by the focus on reducing clutter and ensuring that interfaces were as simple as possible. This simplicity was achieved not by avoiding but by mastering complexity. It took a lot of thought and detailing to get to those simple designs that would be most intuitive for users. Jony Ive, Apple's design chief, captures this philosophy well, *'You have to deeply understand the essence of a product in order to be able to get rid of the parts that are not essential.'* Simplicity is reflected in Jobs'

personal life as well—in his trademark black turtleneck shirt and denim trousers or his relatively spartan home. He believed that material possessions often cluttered life rather than enriched it. Jobs' example brings out both the value of simplicity and also the depth that goes into achieving simplicity.

5. **Reality distortion:** One of the more surprising discoveries from Isaacson's book was about Jobs' 'reality distortion field', or simply put, bending reality. Jobs would envision seemingly impossible outcomes. However, he had the ability to get others to trust him and then see reality the way he wanted them to, often against their judgement. This led them to achieving outcomes that appeared impossible to them earlier. One of Jobs' friends put it well, *'If he's decided that something should happen, then he's just going to make it happen. If you trust him, you can do things.'* At some level, this seems delusional, and even manipulative. However, it does prove that extraordinary results can be achieved by having a very clear picture of the outcomes you want, a strong will and conviction to achieve them, and the confidence and charisma to focus and align others on achieving that vision.

6. **Perfectionism:** Jobs was a perfectionist. He was not just a great visionary but had an incredible eye for detail. Isaacson's book has many examples of Jobs picking up mistakes that the entire product team had missed. Jobs had also imbibed the philosophy that people do judge a book by its cover. He would spend an incredible amount of time on the product packaging and its initial look and feel for the customer. However, it was not just about his products' look and feel for Jobs. He was equally obsessed about getting the internals of all his products perfect. He had learnt early in his life from his father that a good carpenter uses good wood and finish even for the insides of a cupboard. He carried this lesson throughout his life. There is a fascinating story about how he insisted that the rows in the circuit of Apple computers

be lined perfectly. Jobs' perfectionism is a great lesson in 'God is in the detail', especially for senior executives often obsessed with grand strategy.

7. **Focus:** Jobs was able to channelize his intensity and perfectionism through sharp focus. On his return to Apple in 1997, he saved the company from bankruptcy by reducing the number of products and focusing on single products in each of the four well-defined segments. There are many stories of how he would take charge of the whiteboard at business meetings, slashing down the many ideas presented to just three priorities. His focus extended to the choice of people he would work with. He wanted to work only with A-players and was brutal in weeding out B-players. He did not want to waste his time and dilute the organizational quality with B-players. His obsessive focus did sometimes have negative effects, most notably in his personal life. He would filter out whatever he did not want to focus on or did not have the time for. This resulted in his indifference towards his first daughter when she was very young, and perhaps even to the delay in focusing on treating his cancer. However, in the net, *his focus helped him channelize his intensity and achieve extraordinary outcomes that might otherwise not have been possible.*

8. **Resilience:** Jobs' life story is one of amazing resilience and rebound from adversity. Jobs was kicked out of Apple, a company he had founded with a lot of passion, at the age of thirty. For most people, that would have been a knockout blow. However, Jobs was able to pick himself up and keep going. He faced more failures, notably at NeXT Computers, but he persevered. And in a remarkable reversal of fortune, he came back to Apple and led it to unprecedented glory. This resilience is apparent also in his battle with cancer. He did lose his third battle with cancer, but he came back from his first two battles, each time leading Apple to major product breakthroughs. Jobs' life story is a great example

of a man 'never giving up', a lesson that if you persevere you can achieve a better future, whatever the challenges in your present.

9. **Connecting the dots:** Jobs' impact grew exponentially over the course of his career. This was because of his ability to 'connect the dots' across his many life experiences and to learn from his mistakes. Jobs was a rebel in his youth—experimenting with drugs, dropping out of college (but learning calligraphy in the process) and making a self-exploration trip to India. This was not a standard recipe for greatness in the business world. However, Jobs was able to connect these experiences into a unique success formula. Jobs also had more than his share of failures—getting kicked out of Apple, the struggles to build a successful business at NeXT, and the misplaced focus at Pixar on hardware. Again, Jobs was able to learn and grow from these failures. This comes out clearly as you compare his two stints at Apple. Act 1 at Apple was successful, but patchy. His contribution in setting up the company was secondary to that of Steve Wozniak, the technical genius who created the personal computer. Moreover, the negative aspects of his personality began to emerge and overshadow his contributions, resulting in his unceremonious ouster from the company in 1985. In Act 2, back at Apple, he was unbelievably successful, bringing in revolutionary thought leadership and creativity to the company. The series of industry-shaping products he created—iMac, iPod, iTunes, iPhone, iPad—were unprecedented, and Apple became the most valuable company in the world.

Jobs' story illustrates the power of the learning curve. Jobs might not have started out as a technical genius, but he was able to evolve into a creative giant by 'connecting the dots' in his life. He didn't invent many things outright, but he was a master at putting together ideas, art and technology in ways that invented the future. *Jobs' life story is a great lesson in the value of having varied life experiences. Moreover, it shows that if we look within and reflect deeply on our experiences and intuitions, we will find answers to our most difficult questions.*

10. **Nobody is perfect:** Jobs was a complex person with many contradictions and imperfections. I found his interpersonal style to be particularly disappointing. He was brutal with his colleagues, bullying them and publicly humiliating them. He was manipulative, not taking no for an answer. He seemed to take credit for ideas that often came from others. He also seemed to lack integrity and consistency in some of his dealings. Most sad for me was his lack of loyalty—he was mean and ungrateful to some of his close friends. Yet, despite these failings, most colleagues loved working with him and, of course, he achieved phenomenal results.

    There are three important lessons in this: a) Nobody is perfect, not even a great and highly acclaimed genius like Jobs; b) We should not focus too much on an individual's imperfections but look at the whole c) We should not be too judgemental about what works and what does not—Jobs' style was not 'copybook', but achieved tremendous results.

11. **Different paths are possible:** Jobs' life and work are in great contrast with those of other geniuses and phenomenal business leader, Bill Gates, who interestingly, was also born in 1955 (the same year as Jobs). Two individuals and their life and work philosophies could not be more different. Jobs was the eternal rebel; temperamental and charismatic. Gates is more the establishment-types, more balanced and orthodox in his approach. The two adopted very different philosophies towards technology and product development. Jobs had a strong belief in end-to-end integration and 'closed' systems, while Gates has been one of the strongest votaries of the 'open architecture' approach. Despite their different personalities and approaches, both created tremendously successful companies and are amongst

Lessons from Steve Jobs' life

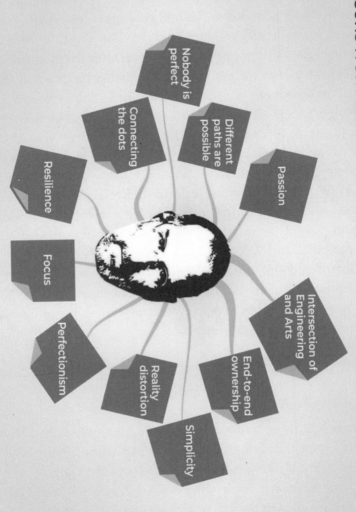

the most admired role models of our times. Their intersecting life stories prove that there is no one path to success.

Different paths are possible and can be equally successful, both at work and in life. Therefore, we should choose our own path, based on our own strengths and situation.

Reading Isaacson's biography of Steve was both an emotional and intellectual experience for me. Jobs had a fascinating life and there is so much to learn from it. His life achievements are so tremendous that he almost seems like a 'superman' who was transported from an alien planet to earth for a period of time! I am not sure if Jobs as a leader can be replicated in entirety or if that's even a desirable thing to do. However, there are certainly many lessons from his incredible life that all of us could learn and take inspiration from. If we could imbibe and consistently live even a few of these lessons, they would possibly help us progress on our path towards realizing our full potential.

I want to end this note with one of Jobs' favorite comments, which he used in his famous Stanford commencement address: 'Stay hungry, stay foolish'. This, in many ways sums up his life philosophy and is a great message to take away!

Summary

- Steve Jobs is one of the most fascinating icons of our age. He had a revolutionary impact across multiple industries—personal computers, mobile phones, music, movies and retailing.
- There are eleven inspirational lessons I gathered from his incredible life and his style as a leader—passion, intersection of engineering and arts, end-to-end ownership, simplicity, reality distortion, perfectionism, focus, resilience, connecting the dots, nobody is perfect, different paths are possible.
- *Stay hungry, stay foolish* sums up his life philosophy.

5

Five Lessons in Longevity and Greatness from the Giant Sequoias

Obstacles don't have to stop you. If you run into a wall don't turn around and give up. Figure out how to climb over it, go through it or work around it.

Michael Jordan, American professional basketball player

In this chapter, I have synthesized some fascinating insights in longevity and greatness from my visit to the Sequoia National Park in California.

It was a most remarkable experience for me to stand in the midst of the giant sequoias at the Sequoia National Park in California. Giant Sequoias are special. They are like gentle giants. They are not just the largest trees in the world, they are also the largest and amongst the oldest living organisms on earth. They are on average 200–300 feet tall, and have a diameter of twenty-five feet, with the oldest growing up to 3,000 years. The largest tree in the world, General Sherman, has a volume of 52,508 cubic feet, weights over 2.7 million pounds, has a circumference of 102 feet at the base, branches 7 feet in diameter, and a height of 275 feet (equivalent to a twenty-six storeyed building. It is 2,500 years old.

Phew! That is simply awe-inspiring. Spending time amongst the Giant Sequoias was a deeply moving experience for me. As was my time spent with their cousins, the Coastal Redwoods, in Muir Woods outside San Francisco. They were really special experiences. It is of course natural to be awestruck and humbled by the sheer size of these giants. But it is more than that. It was a meditative experience. These 'immortals' have a tranquil presence that touches your core. You feel that within them lie the secrets of all creation and eternity.

I was reflecting on what we learn from these giants, these immortals. There are five lessons that I took away, that I want to share them here.

Lesson 1: The smallest of seeds can produce the tallest of trees

The Giant Sequoia comes from a tiny cone. The Sequoia cone is the size of a chicken egg with seeds smaller than oat flakes. This is such a powerful reminder of the infinite potential of life. Within the smallest of us lies the potential for greatness. This is a great lesson in hope, respect and humility. Hope and respect that amazing potential lies in every being. And humility to not dismiss any person or situation lightly, because great depth and potential might lie within them, which we might not see today.

Lesson 2: Power of positioning and luck

The Giant Sequoias grow in a fairly small region. There are only sixty-five groves found in an area of a mere 144 sq km in the Sierra Nevada ranges in California. The trees need a humid climate, characterized by dry summers and snowy winters, and granitic-based residual and alluvial soils, which this region has. Even within a grove,

Five life lessons from The Giant Sequoias

- Smallest of seeds can produce tallest of trees
- Power of positioning and luck
- Growing bigger and taller with age
- Strength through community
- Growth through fires

not all Sequoias end up being giants. Their positioning in the grove, access to sunlight, surroundings and other factors play a key role in the eventual size they will attain. This is a powerful life lesson: many might have the same intrinsic potential but being at the right place at the right time can make all the difference in eventual success.

Lesson 3: Growing bigger and taller with age

The hardiness, age and size of the Giant Sequoias are all connected. They keep growing in size and strength as they get older, and therefore are even more difficult to be blown over by winds. They seem to have conquered diseases and natural death and die only by accident. The older Sequoias are therefore, even more magnificent. That is a powerful inspiration for us humans in so many ways. The big lesson for me was to never stop growing and that our best days are ahead of us. Moreover, the value of longevity. If you can stay the course, you can achieve great impact.

Lesson 4: Strength through community

Giant Sequoias have surprisingly small roots, only six feet to twenty feet deep. Yet these shallow roots support these giants for thousands of years. The answer lies in the fact that Sequoias grow close to each other and their roots are intertwined. It is this matting of their roots, the network effect, that gives Sequoias the incredible strength and stability they have. It is a powerful reminder of the strength of the community and that no leader can stand tall without the support of many.

Lesson 5: Growth through fires

Perhaps the biggest secret of the Giant Sequoias' longevity is how they survive fires. The Sierra Nevada region, the habitat of the Giant Sequoias, is dry and prone to lightning. This is a deadly combination that results in many fires, resulting in a big survival challenge for the Sequoias. We found many Sequoias in the park with large fire scars.

However, Sequoias have a great mechanism in their bark to overcome fires. Their bark is very thick (~ 3 feet) and has tannin, which protects it from fire. Giant Sequoias are able to not just survive fire but also use it for both regeneration and growth. Fire clears the undergrowth and opens their cones, allowing the seeds to germinate. Moreover, fire removes the competing thin-barked species around, promoting growth of these ancient giants. In fact, fires are typically followed by a growth spurt in the Giant Sequoias.

Their mastery of fire is such a powerful lesson for us. Life throws many challenges our way. The way we tackle them determines how we grow in life. We need to develop our own unique coping mechanisms (thick bark and tannin for the Giant Sequoias). The most successful are able to not just survive the challenges but use it as an opportunity for fuelling further growth. That is such a beautiful and powerful life lesson. This lesson has been so true during the Covid-19 pandemic, where the high-quality resilient companies have outperformed during these difficult times.

I hope these life lessons of hope, courage, excellence, resilience and longevity are as inspiring for you as they were for me. However, mere words cannot do justice to these magnificent, immortal giants. I strongly encourage you to go and see the Sequoias and absorb for yourself the mystery and wonder of these incomparable giants!

Summary

- Giant Sequoias are not just the largest trees in the world, they are also the largest (and amongst the oldest) living organisms on earth. These immortals have a tranquil presence that touches your core.

- Five lessons that I took away from them:
  - Infinite potential of life—even the smallest of seeds can produce the greatest of trees
  - Being at the right place at the right time can make all the difference in the eventual success of a person.
  - Longevity is a key driver of greatness. We should never stop growing as our best days may lie ahead of you.
  - No leader can stand tall without the support of many.
  - We need to develop our own unique coping mechanisms to not just survive challenges but use them as opportunities for fuelling further growth.

6

Ten Things I Wish I Learnt in Business School

The value of a college education is not the learning of many facts but the training of the mind to think critically

Albert Einstein, Nobel Prize winner in
Physics and Theoretical Physicist

Problem solving and effective decision-making skills are more important than ever before, given the VUCA world we are living in. You need to make sense of the volatility and complexity of this new world and operate at high speed, that too in an environment of uncertainty. To be effective in such a scenario, you need decision-making skills of a very high standard. I have found frameworks to be very helpful in providing a structure for problem solving and thus in making better decisions.

I was very fortunate that I started my professional career in an outstanding firm like McKinsey, which had an intense focus on building problem-solving skills. It is there that I got exposed to the power of frameworks. For any problem, we were trained to use frameworks; moreover, we were encouraged to create new frameworks for repeatable problem situations. Those habits have stayed with me, and I very naturally think of frameworks for any situation that asks for problem solving.

In this chapter, I share with you some of the most important management concepts and frameworks I have learnt over the past twenty years. These concepts and frameworks can be applied in both life and business situations to improve the quality of decision-making and actions. I have used them in numerous situations and have found them to be tremendously beneficial. I thought they would be helpful to you, especially those of you in the early stages of your life and career, to learn these frameworks.

Here are the ten frameworks I use most often. The first five are more about the 'what', and the latter five more about the 'how'.

1. Sweet spot

One of the biggest questions that confronts all of us is, 'how we can better realize our full potential?' I have already described how one can find this 'sweet spot' and how its discovery releases tremendous energy in you, making your activities easy, bringing high quality to your work and happiness in your life, thereby helping you plumb your full potential.

This concept is relevant for businesses too. Business leaders are constantly having to prioritize across multiple options—for example, where to invest? Where to focus? One of the simplest but most powerful frameworks for such business situations is 'opportunity versus ability to compete', which is really an application of the 'sweet spot' concept.

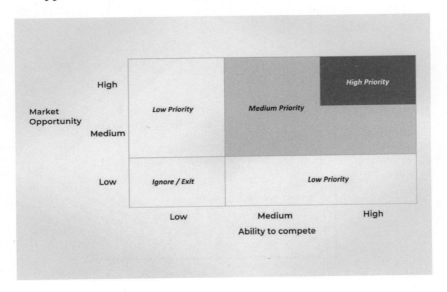

2. Risk-return tradeoff

As you make decisions, one of the most important things to understand is the risk-return profile. There is no free lunch. If you want higher returns, you will typically need to take higher levels of risk. This is one of the most fundamental concepts in finance but is relevant in personal life too. It is important that we understand our risk propensity. For the same risk-return curve, the point to play might be different for different individuals. A good example of this is a question I'm often asked by students— should I do a start-up right after MBA or work for a couple of years before becoming an entrepreneur? Clearly, there can be no one right answer to this, the answer lies in understanding your risk profile!

To play at the optimal point in the risk-return curve, it is important to define and understand risk better. If you keep risk at an amorphous level, it will paralyse you. When you define risk clearly you can differentiate between what is real and what is imaginary. That will allow you to make bigger bets and play at higher levels on the risk-return curve. Defining your risks clearly becomes even more important in the VUCA world we are operating in.

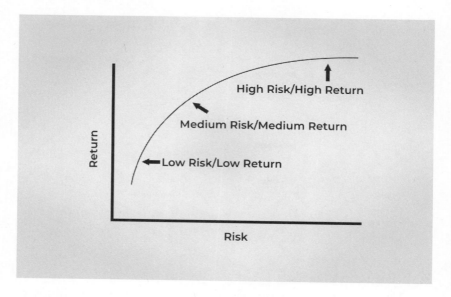

3. The 80-20 rule

The Pareto principle, or the concept that a few vital tasks drive the majority of results, is a well-known concept. However, not many are able to apply it practically in their daily lives. The reason is, while the 80-20 principle is evident in hindsight, it is difficult to see it with foresight. To improve your 80-20 ability, it is important to make the time to think about it. This is easier said than done, as most of us are so caught up in the flow of routine events that we don't make enough time to think through our options and approaches. In addition, it is imperative that we make time for reflection. Writing a diary can be very helpful. This practice of reflection can improve the intuition one requires to make the right 80-20 decisions.

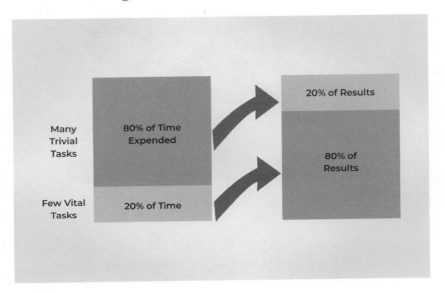

4. The one thing

There is a Russian proverb that says: 'If you try to catch two rabbits, you will not catch either one'. The One Thing is an extension of the 80-20 rule. During the early stages of our career, we are often obsessed with multi-tasking. However, multi-tasking dissipates energy. You will maximize your chances of success if you focus on one thing at a time. We have finite will power. We need to focus it on where we need it most.

The concept of The One Thing[8] can be applied in any situation. The question to ask in any situation is 'what's The One Thing I can do, such that by doing it everything else will be easier or unnecessary?' This concept has been brilliantly illustrated by Eli Goldratt in his book *The Goal*,[9] where he demonstrates how a chain is no stronger than its weakest link. Goldratt makes the point that any situation is a system, and that system output is

Any situation will have a constraint that is limiting achievement of your goals

limited by a constraint or a bottleneck. Unless you identify and act on the bottleneck, you will not make meaningful progress. So, a very important skill that you need to develop is to identify and zone down on the most critical problem to be solved.

5. Urgent-important matrix

Talking of books, another of my favourites is *The Seven Habits of Highly Effective People* by Stephen Covey[10]. In this book, Covey introduces the 'Urgent-Important Matrix', which is an invaluable tool for time management.

Our natural instinct is to do the urgent tasks first. Instead, we need to shift focus to the important tasks first. If we focus only on the important-urgent quadrant, it keeps getting bigger and bigger until it dominates us. The important-not urgent quadrant is the heart of effective personal management and the key to long-term success. It takes discipline to work on the important-not-urgent tasks. that is why the 80-20 rule is so important. it is only if we have a few well-chosen priorities in this quadrant that we can focus and make progress on them.

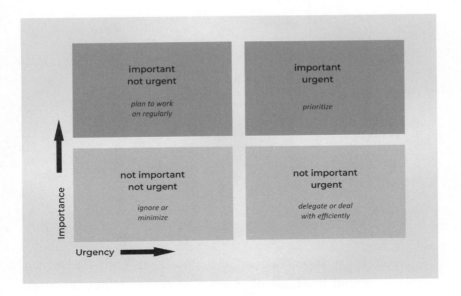

This urgent-important matrix is very important in business too. Most enterprises are very focused on short-term actions and are thus caught in endless firefighting. An important task for leaders is to identify a few high-impact important-not-urgent priorities and get their teams to focus on them.

6. Trust equation

Trust is the foundation of relationships and a key to success, both in our personal and professional lives. It is like a super-powerful lubricant that makes interactions and working together easy and effective. Trust can take time to build. However, once you build trust in a relationship, it moves to a totally different level of effectiveness. Trust Equation is a great framework to understand how to build trust. Your trustworthiness is driven by your credibility (expertise, knowledge), reliability (consistency of actions) and intimacy (personal connect). However, the most important driver is self-orientation in the denominator. All the great work resulting from the earlier three factors can be undone by a perception of self-centredness in you.

$$T = \frac{C \times R \times I}{S}$$

T trustworthiness
C credibility
R reliability
I intimacy
S self-orientation

Trust Equation is a good reflection of the human balance of the head and heart. Credibility and reliability reflect the head, and intimacy and self-orientation the heart.

7. Virtuous-vicious cycle

No situation is as good or as bad as it seems. Most times, we find ourselves in either a virtuous cycle (positive feedback loop) or a vicious cycle (negative feedback loop). This shows how emotions play a big role in our decisions. We see this in markets, industries and companies.

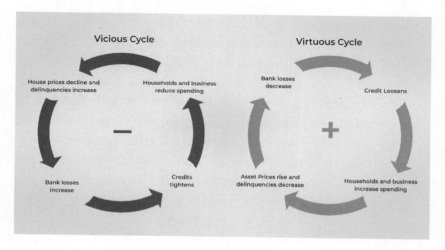

Equally, we see this in team and individual situations.

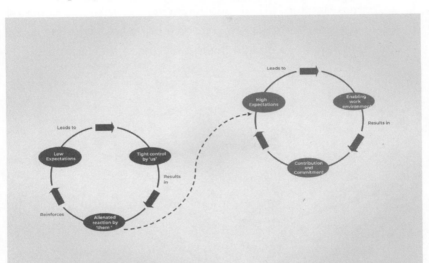

The question is, how to break out of a vicious cycle and move to a virtuous cycle. It is difficult to have perspective when you are in the midst of a cycle. Those who are around you may see it sooner. Seeking advice and help from others will lead you to make the changes required to break out of a negative cycle. Turning a vicious cycle into a virtuous cycle is a critical skill that any business leader needs to have, and especially so in this digital age. In the digital age, cycles are becoming shorter and it is easy to flip from a positive cycle to a negative one. Thus, a leader's ability to quickly identify cycle shifts and turn them around becomes even more important.

8. **Pain barrier**

In most tasks, you will have to cross a pain barrier to make progress. You go through a period of great pain when you feel like giving up. However, if you battle through the pain barrier, the pain diminishes, and you can go on more smoothly. Every athlete is keenly aware of the pain barrier. This is very true of entrepreneurs too. Most entrepreneurs go through a period when it seems to make sense to give up. Those who persevere are often able to go on and make a success of their ventures.

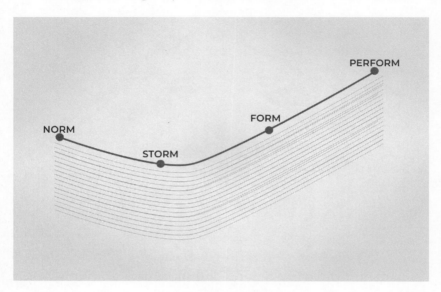

The pain barrier is present in most team and project situations. You often start on a high but then very quickly hit a low. As you battle through the low phase, you can then move on to a steady growth phase. Understanding the existence of the pain barrier should give us the strength and perseverance to build our ability to crest any learning curve. It is a very simple but important concept— 'no pain, no gain', or 'short-term pain leads to long-term gain'!

9. S curve

The Sigmoid curve (or the S Curve) is an extension of the learning curve where, after the growth phase, you see a period of maturation and then eventual decline. The S curve represents many business and life situations and has profound implications for both companies and individuals.

To ensure sustained growth, you have to move from one S curve to another. The only option for shifting from one curve to another is when you are on your way up. This is because you can never predict the top, and when you are in the decline phase, you lose energy. It may be that the first curve is longer than anticipated, in which case you can keep cruising along until you are indeed nearer to the peak. But preparing for the second curve too early is far better than waiting until it is too late, and decline has set in. However, making a shift when you are in a growth phase and things are going well is not easy. You have to break out of your comfort zone. Moreover, when you transition between S curves, you will go through a period when the rewards are lower (as you have to battle through the learning phase of the next S curve).

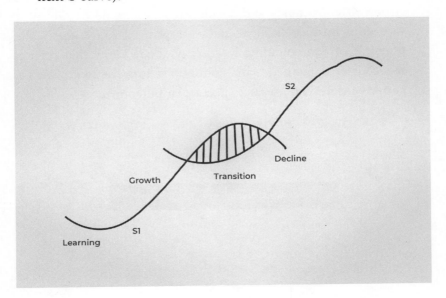

Successful individuals and organizations are self-reflective and constantly monitor their own positions on the S curve. Riding the first curve while cultivating the second is always the best option. Clinging to the first and trying to prolong it is a pointless waste of energy. When all is well and you are at the top of your game, then you know it is time to plan your next move.

Clearly, being able to identify the nature of the S curve you are operating in, being able to transition from one S curve to the next and then stitch them together, would be key to continued growth.

10. Compounding

One of the most powerful laws or frameworks relevant in both life and business is compounding. There is great power in tiny but consistent improvements. We all understand the principle of compounding, but it is surprising how few apply it consistently. We are often attracted by the big, bold moves, which certainly are important in the digital age, but we can easily overlook the virtues of consistency and steady progress. Some of the most successful business leaders and enterprises I know apply the principle of compounding religiously. They know that staying the course, combined with continuous improvements over a period of time, can produce spectacular outcomes.

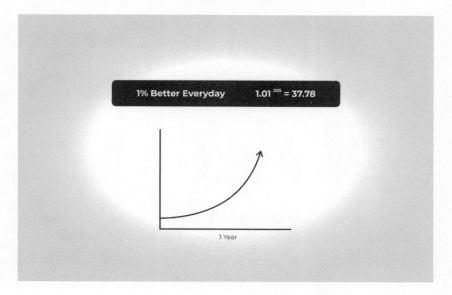

Ten things I wish I learnt in Business school

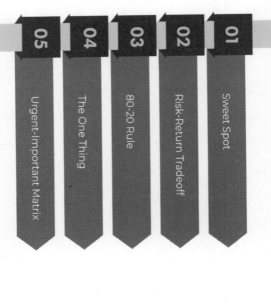

- 01 Sweet Spot
- 02 Risk-Return Tradeoff
- 03 80-20 Rule
- 04 The One Thing
- 05 Urgent-Important Matrix

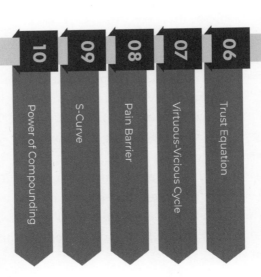

- 06 Trust Equation
- 07 Virtuous-Vicious Cycle
- 08 Pain Barrier
- 09 S-Curve
- 10 Power of Compounding

In the end, I want to mention another very important factor. That is LUCK.

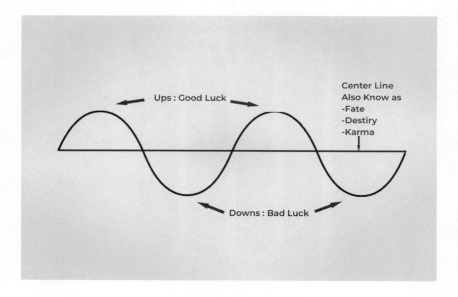

As I go through life, I realize that success is not a predictable formula. Sometimes your best efforts go to waste and sometimes you get success that you never anticipated. That is the nature of life; it is not linear and deterministic. It is uncertain, with many unpredictable ups and downs. That is why it is very important to have a broad and relaxed perspective of life. This means neither becoming arrogant with success or nor too depressed at failure.

The *Bhagavad Gita*, talking about karma, says, '***Karmanye Vadhikaraste, Ma phaleshou kada chana*** (do your duty but do not worry about the results).' There is deep truth in this. If we realize this truth, both our individual lives and the world around us will improve so much!

Summary

- Frameworks can be very helpful in better structuring problem situations and improving the quality of decisions.
- My ten frameworks applicable in life and business: Finding your 'sweet spot'; risk-taking, the 80-20 principle; focusing on one thing at a time; emphasizing Important-Not Urgent; trustworthiness; mastering the vicious-virtuous cycle; crossing the pain barrier; transitioning from one S curve to another; and understanding the power of compounding.
- Finally, a relaxed and philosophical perspective on life will help you cope, as life is unpredictable.

7

Take Personal Responsibility and Change the World!

Be the change you wish to see in the world

Mahatma Gandhi, Father of
the Indian Nation, nationalist and lawyer.

We often cry about the 'system' and find faults in the situations and people around us. We blame the 'system' for the various problems we face on a day-to-day basis, whether it is corruption, traffic or pollution. We are perennially disappointed with the companies we work in, whether it is with their policies, their politics or the company itself not recognizing our worth. Even in our personal lives, we have ready explanations for what other people are doing wrong and what they should do differently. However, we rarely look inside to see what *we* could do differently. This is a negative cycle. You change nothing and keep living in frustration and disappointment.

Why does this happen? Why do we see others as the problem and not take responsibility for our problems ourselves?

It is human nature to excuse or rationalize one's own shortcomings while focusing on the obvious improvement needs of others. Our ego is the big culprit. It creates a sense of separateness and also a defensive shield. It makes us stand apart from the 'system', as opposed to being part of it. It makes us separate from other people, as opposed to being connected with them. It also creates a defensive shield that refuses to accept that we could be part of the problem. It leads to the 'I am OK, you are not OK' posture. All of this results in the rationalization that 'if I did not create the problem or I am not part of it, then it is not my responsibility to fix it'.

Even when we recognize the problem for what it is, there is often a sense of helplessness about any one individual's ability to change the 'system'. The 'system' often appears like an unshakable giant, impossible for an individual to move. Therefore, you end up rationalizing that it is pointless to make the effort!

The other challenge is inertia and fear of the unknown, which makes it difficult to move out of the status quo. We certainly crib about the status quo, but often find it difficult to rouse ourselves to action to change it. Inertia makes it difficult to leave the safe harbours of our daily existence. It requires additional effort and risk-taking to break away and set sail for the open seas. Fear of uncertain storms often overpowers the excitement of opportunities.

Why is it important to take more personal responsibility?

We can keep crying about the 'system'. We can keep explaining how we are in the right or how little influence we have on the 'system'. That is futile. Your frustrations and self-pity will make no difference. Any 'system' is nameless and faceless. You cannot hold it accountable. It cannot change on its own. Clearly, you cannot leave it to divine intervention! So, what choice do you have? If you are suffering, then it is in your interest to do something about the 'system'. Given that the most control you have is over your own actions, it is best to start by taking personal responsibility. Your efforts will not be wasted. Any 'system' is made up of individuals. When enough individuals change, there comes a tipping point when the 'system' also starts changing.

We often feel that our influence on the 'system' is limited. The funny thing about influence is that if you act on what is in your zone of influence, that zone keeps expanding. This leads to growing confidence and broader impact. Conversely, if you keep focusing on what is not in your zone of influence, the boundaries keep pushing in, further limiting what you control. This only leads to further despair and frustration. Clearly, it is better to act and grow your zone of influence, as opposed to it continuing to push into you.

Finally, if you aspire to develop and be recognized as a leader, you have no option but to take broader ownership. Leadership is about going beyond the self and creating broader impact. As you take personal responsibility for the problems around you, the leader within you grows. We see numerous examples of this. Many leaders might have been spurred on their leadership journey by a personal hurt (e.g. Mahatma Gandhi, George Washington, Nelson Mandela), but they gained success because they took ownership of problems on behalf of others and created wide-ranging impact.

How do we make the change?

The starting point is self-awareness. You must realize that there is no option but to take personal accountability. The only thing you can control is your actions. You can keep floating through life, frustrated and beaten by the system and the circumstances. On the other hand, you can stop, take personal responsibility, and do something about your circumstances. If you are not completely satisfied with a situation, ask yourself, 'What can I do about it? If I can't control it, how can I positively influence it?'

It is perhaps best to start small and focus on issues most in your control. They could be as simple as not wrongly overtaking on the roads, not throwing litter in public spaces, or not bribing the traffic cop when you can. At work, it could be giving your 100 per cent to your job, reaching out to a colleague who needs help, reaching out to the company to point out a wrong policy or two and suggesting solutions. If you see problems in your industry or local community,

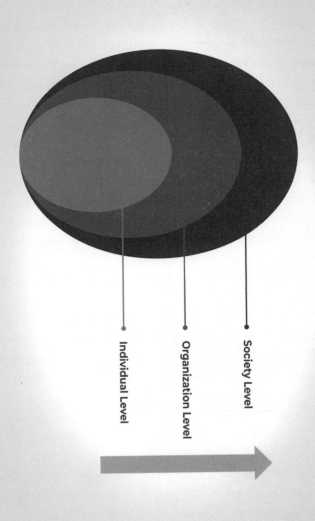

Evolution as a Leader

Individual Level

Organization Level

Society Level

then you could create a forum to get people together to discuss the matter and take common action on it. In personal life, it could be about being more empathetic and seeing issues from the other's perspective. As you log in the small personal victories, your self-confidence grows, you gain more clarity on how to make broader change, and eventually your zone of influence grows.

There are, of course, limits to human action and what you can influence at a given point in time. Therefore, it is important to be able to understand and discriminate between what you can change and what you cannot at any point. However, the limits to human action and influence are a lot more than what we realize. Moreover, as I have said earlier, as we focus on action our zone of influence expands to include what earlier might not have been within our control.

The world around us is complex and has many problems. It is important that we move away from blaming others and take personal responsibility to tackle the problems that bother us. When we blame others, we give up our own power to change. When we take personal responsibility and action, we can create more positive change than we imagine.

I leave you with these beautiful words from Mahatma Gandhi, **'You must be the change you want to see in the world'**. If more of us could live this, our personal lives would improve immeasurably, and the world would be a more beautiful place to live in!

Summary

- It is human nature to rationalize one's own shortcomings, thus creating a sense of helplessness about any one individual's ability to change the 'system'.
- As you act on what is in your zone of influence, that zone keeps expanding. As you take personal responsibility for problems around you, the leader within you grows.
- When we take personal responsibility and act, we can create more positive change than we imagine.

India: A New Digital Superpower and Your Opportunity

If I had to bet on one country in Asia, it's India; if I had to bet on two countries, it would be India twice. There's no better place to invest than India.

John Chambers, Chairman Emeritus
and CEO of Cisco from 1995–2016

We live in an amazing time. It has already been defined by the World Economic Forum as the Fourth Industrial Revolution— the digital age. The digital age is changing everything—what we consume, how we live our lives, every business both large and small, how industries operate, the growth of countries and our relationship with the world.

As shared earlier in the book, I have been fortunate to have my career coincide with the emergence of the digital age and experience it at every level while uncovering and recognizing the emerging patterns. As an ex-McKinsey consultant and student of history, analysing data and recognizing patterns has been an important part of my training. Post Covid-19, the pattern has become very clear—there are many fundamental shifts happening in business and technology, creating new opportunities (new challenges too, but I believe that opportunities far outweigh the challenges). Thus, an exciting future is possible for the world in the digital age.

History has demonstrated over and over again that in every Industrial Revolution, there is a reshuffling of the deck as new countries emerge and take the lead in technology, culture and economics. Focusing on the recent past, the first modern Industrial Revolution—the age of steam power and mechanization of production together with colonialism—shifted economic power from the East to the West, with Europe emerging as the leader. In the Second Industrial Revolution, the age of machines, industrialization and electricity, the United States emerged as a leader. During the Third Industrial Revolution, the Information Age, the US surged ahead as the primary superpower. Other countries also appeared to rise, such as Japan (for a brief period), and more recently, China, but the US continues to be the central power of the third age. I believe with the Fourth Industrial Revolution, the digital age, we could see another shift and the rise of one or more new superpowers.

The age of abundance

Let me preface this section by stating that the digital age is not about the emergence of one single superpower. Digital really is an age of abundance; it is about multiple opportunities, high velocity change and balancing multidimensional factors. In this Volatile, Uncertain, Complex and Ambiguous (VUCA) environment, there are frequently many winners. Let me explain with a practical example that we are witnessing first-hand. Facebook was once a preeminent social media platform—the undisputed world champion. Now, TikTok is growing faster and aggregating key younger population segments better than Facebook.[12] This change was brought about by the same digital age that allowed Facebook to supplant Myspace in the span of a few years. Is Facebook still the leader? Yes, but others are also benefitting quickly from the expanding abundance of the digital age. In the digital age, there is room for more than one leader.

If we examine where we are at on a global level through the lens of the Fourth Industrial Revolution, China is well placed based on the phenomenal economic growth they have achieved, their strong technology base, leading manufacturing base and huge investments in key advancements such as AI. However, India is a powerful force in this global race and likely to be a dominant leader in the churn happening in the digital age due to its inherent democratic DNA.

The most fundamental aspect of the digital is its democratization of access to information, knowledge and technology. This is an amazing enabler for a large, yet relatively poor country such as India. Historically, hundreds of millions of people did not have access to high-quality education and infrastructure, and that limited their opportunities. *In the digital age, that changes—access is democratized. It becomes very easy to share knowledge and information with low-cost widespread technology.*

For India, this is a chance for a second independence. India's first independence occurred in 1947, yet, despite political freedom, hundreds of millions of Indian citizens have been left economically and socially disadvantaged. The digital age opens the door for these disadvantaged individuals (which includes a large powerhouse cohort of young population), and all of us, by offering education, low-cost access, technology and the power of opportunity. The human plus economic potential of this equation is mind-boggling! How many new entrepreneurs will be created? How many new enterprises will be established? How many global leaders will find their voice? What new innovations will emerge? What exciting new creative minds will be unlocked? The possibilities are truly endless.

India: A new digital superpower

What are the facts that support the emergence of India as a digital superpower in this post-Covid-19 world? First, underpinning everything is democracy, which is embedded into the DNA of India. With the foundation of freedom via democracy, India can naturally embrace and take advantage of the VUCA nature of the digital age. Built on this foundation of democracy, I surmise that there are five key factors unique to India. Let me elaborate:

1. **Smartphone penetration:** India has over 1.17 billion wireless subscribers, and is among the largest base of population with internet access at over 830 million people due to low cost and wide mobile network availability.

2. **Low-cost data:** In India, the average revenue per user is below $2, whereas in developed markets, it is around $20. This dramatic cost advantage has propelled access to information across the large population base of India. Data is truly the fuel that is powering the digital age, and the relatively low cost of data is a major advantage for India.

3. **UID JAM:** The Unique Identification (UID) and Jan Dhan-Aadhaar-Mobile (JAM) trinity is a leapfrog digital transformation for public services combining a unique ID with online services, a physical ID and a mobile phone. With over 1.35 billion citizens enrolled in this digital service, India is leading globally by investing in the technology that enables Indian citizens to access modern and protected online transactions and services, which can support unprecedented growth in the public/private sector. This has already enabled India to become the global leader in digital payments *with 48.6 billion real-time digital transactions in 2021. To put this in perspective, this is significantly higher than the nearest challenger, China, that was at 18 billion, and incredibly, India's activity is 6.5x higher than the US, Canada, France and Germany combined.*[13]

4. **Global IT services hub:** India is the Information Technology engine of the world, *supplying over 50 per cent share of the global IT services headcount in 2022, up from 35 per cent in 2013.* Simply put, India fuels innovation and is at the leading edge of information technology for the globe.

5. **Abundant young talent:** Over 40 per cent of India's population is under the age of twenty-five, and 60 per cent under the age of thirty-five—with over 800 million people. By 2047, India will have 20 per cent of the world's working inhabitants. This will also be the world's largest cohort of digital natives. Indians below the age of thirty-five, who have been born in the digital age, can easily adapt to technological changes.

These powerful factors combined are quite unique to India and critical for realizing the benefit of the democratization of access and data brought about by the digital age. Widespread penetration of mobile devices, low-cost data, a modern public tech infrastructure, leading IT knowledge hub and a young, digital native population is the formula for explosive growth and dramatic innovation in the digital age resulting in India's high potential to be a digital age leader.

'Digital first' success for India

As the facts show us, India is well placed to achieve the status of a digital leader, but it is not assured in this VUCA world. To improve India's growth and trajectory for success, there are four important areas for differentiation that need attention. A concept I call 'Digital First' needs focused attention to establish a firm foundation of digital technology and the new business rules put forward in this book. To achieve digital superpower status, India should pursue the following:

1. **Global IT services leadership:** Continue to nurture, fuel and grow leadership in IT services. This is a complex formula involving education, technology access, capital, industry and other factors. Leading from the front is critical—industry associations, educational institutions, government and enterprises need to push continually for tech hub growth, improved infrastructure and high quality knowledge access across India.

2. **Innovative global businesses from India:** Create the next generation of new, innovative digital age businesses and 'unicorns' like Google, Facebook and Alibaba in India. To do this, start-ups and enterprises in India will need to develop deeper end customer understanding, spur higher levels of innovation, move from a country to a global vision and invest for scale. All of these factors can be driven by the forcing factor of innovating *from* India.

3. **Digital transformation in conventional industries:** Modernize existing conventional industries and enterprises such as pharmaceuticals, steel production and the automotive industry based on digital transformation and the new rules of business. India has lagged behind other countries and especially China in manufacturing and other similar traditional segments. If India can digitally transform these traditional industries, it will be a great opportunity to both catch-up and then leapfrog ahead of competition.

4. **'Digital First' public services:** Increasing technology investment in public services to leapfrog ahead of other more economically advanced countries by using digital technology to offer more effective and available services to the Indian population. All aspects of central, state or local government as well as education should go 'Digital First' to provide easy-to-access, high-quality and rapid-response assistance and administration to citizens.

All of these factors have to be supported and driven by unleashing a tsunami of entrepreneurship in India. The groundswell of entrepreneurs with innovative new ideas and business models, added to the rapid digital conversion of older industries, will create a virtuous cycle, fuelling the next wave of entrepreneurs. Each entrepreneur will reach a higher level of success and drive the next cycle of innovation and growth—success creates its own success! *Starting from the first unicorn in 2011, India is now home to 107 unicorns today, and is the third largest unicorn producer in the world after the US and China. Typically, start-ups founded before 2011 took an average of 9.3 years from the date of inception to enter the unicorn club, whereas in 2021, it takes 6.6 years on average to become a unicorn.*[14]

I find it very encouraging that the key elements are in place for the next set of leading global technology powerhouses to emerge from India. By focusing on Digital First, we can quickly unleash John Maynard Keynes's famous economic 'animal spirits' and the economic prospects of a billion plus people.

What is your part in the digital age?

So, I have discussed the possible future for India, but what is your part in this digital age regardless of where you reside? I believe the single greatest opportunity in the digital age is to be an entrepreneur. I do not just define an entrepreneur as someone who starts their own company, though it is a large part of the traditional definition; I expand this definition dramatically—you should approach any job with an entrepreneurial mindset. Being an entrepreneur is about taking ownership, creating and innovating and taking on risk. Applying the entrepreneurial mindset to any job you do can result in positive benefits for any company and your career. Walking this path will unlock your potential as well as that of millions of others.

Let me also state that the next generation of entrepreneurs is not just emerging from big metros and major universities, but also from smaller towns and rural areas all over the world. The composition of the next generation of entrepreneurs is going to change significantly over the next fifteen years, just like that of the Indian cricket team and American Major League Baseball. After drawing talent from bigger cities for years, the Indian cricket scene is now dotted with talent from smaller towns as opportunities, competition and pursuit of talent has expanded. In the US, professional baseball teams are scouring the world for athletic talent and a competitive advantage over their rivals. Given the new global field, opportunity is greater and more abundant, however, so is the competition. You need to be well prepared for the VUCA nature of your career.

Six key skills for future-proofing your career

In the competitive digital age, with its new business rules that I have discussed earlier, it is important that you are well prepared for what can happen. Here are the six key skills for young and young-at-heart professionals to focus on that which will not only help them future-proof themselves but also give them innate advantages over the full course of their career:

1. **Problem solving:** The ability to look at any situation and distil it down to the real issues so that they can be comprehended and solved.
2. **Learnability:** It refers to deliberate learning, which implies not just learning the basics but learning how to master a topic and know it in-depth and to be able to understand and build on that knowledge.
3. **Leadership:** The ability to connect and inspire others in a complex and ambiguous world and provide direction and clarity to shape the future——much like shining a light in a dark room and leading the way.
4. **Communication:** The ability to truly connect with others in an empathetic way, putting oneself in other's shoes and conveying one's ideas in impactful, meaningful ways.
5. **Creativity:** A close relative of learnability, creativity refers to out of the box thinking and the ability to go beyond what already exists. Often, one must learn or know something so well that they can expand beyond it.
6. **Mindfulness:** It refers to connecting to one's inner spiritual nature. The digital age is so complex that it's critical to have

this anchor. India is the home of mindfulness with practices such as meditation and yoga rooted in the culture. With even the West rapidly adopting them, it is time young Indians fully understand and embrace the abundant wisdom and potential of their heritage.

Most see these six skills as 'soft skills' as opposed to 'hard skills'. There is a need to shift from a pure focus on hard skills, the 'technical skills', and bolster these six critical 'soft skills'. However, none of these six soft skills are a quick fix—one cannot develop or acquire these skills during a three-month class. These are fundamental skills that take time and long-term foundational effort to build and refine.

When discussing India, the opportunity and how to emerge as a winner in the digital age, reviving the approach to education is crucial. India needs to focus on embracing 'soft skills' education to supplement the existing strong emphasis on mathematics, science and the traditional hard skills. In addition, it needs to pursue programs and make adjustments in the educational system that encourage and help develop entrepreneurs at the grassroot level. If the young professionals of today acquire these six skills and leverage them along with the entrepreneurial spirit of the digital age, there is little doubt that they and India will emerge as visionary, twenty-first-century leaders.

Conclusion

I am deeply encouraged that there are key enablers in place for many twenty-first century global technology enterprises to be born in India. How powerful is it to know that we are on the cusp of unleashing the potential of a billion people via the power of the digital age. Perhaps with our active participation, history will look back on the digital age as India's second independence and the momentous pivot to becoming a digital superpower.

Summary

- In every Industrial Revolution, there has been a reshuffling of the deck as new countries emerge and take the lead in technology, culture and economics.
- Digital is a phenomenal opportunity for India to leapfrog. The democratization of access to information, knowledge and technology are unique enablers that position India as a leading superpower contender in the digital age.
- India is well placed to achieve digital leader status, but there are four important areas for differentiation built on a concept I identify as 'Digital First':
  1) Global IT services leadership
  2) Innovative global business in India
  3) Digital transformation for conventional industries and enterprises
  4) Public services and enterprises

- There is a need to unleash an entrepreneurial wave and create millions of entrepreneurs. Creating the right role models and building ecosystems at the micro-level for different industries will play a key role in this.
- There are six key skills for professionals to focus on that will not only help them future-proof themselves but also give them innate advantages.
- Properly fostered India is on the cusp of unleashing the potential of a billion plus people via the power of the digital age. This can be the second independence moment for India.

Conclusion: Carpe Diem

The journey of a thousand miles begins beneath one's feet.

Lao Tzu, Chinese philosopher

In life and in business, we find ourselves often caught in the inertia of the status quo and limited to incremental steps. We simply go through the motions and are not able to discover our best selves, our full potential.

In the digital age, status quo is just not possible. Digital disruption, due to its scale and scope, is too significant to avoid. The digital age is inevitable, it is a pervasive reality. Covid-19 pandemic has further accelerated the irreversible march of digital age in many ways.

Whoever you are, wherever you are, you will need to make changes to adapt and survive in the digital age. Old rules, methods and mindsets will not work. There is no option but to rouse yourself to make fundamental changes.

When change is inevitable, you might as well set your sights high. Play to win, not just to survive. Any change will involve some pain. When you have to go through the pain, make it count and aim to get the best out of it.

Across the seven sections and more than fifty chapters of this book, we have talked about the multi-dimensional nature of digital disruption and the challenges and opportunities it presents at various levels—of overall business, technology, organization, leaders and young professionals. On balance, I strongly believe the opportunities the digital age presents far outweigh the challenges. Digital is a great equalizer, legacy and past history do not count for much. It provides a level playing field for new ideas, creativity, drive and perseverance. The digital age is an opportune time for those wishing to be entrepreneurs to build new businesses, for visionaries to leapfrog the traditional stages of growth in their markets, for managers to step up as leaders and be change agents, and professionals across levels to realize their full potential in business and in life.

Therefore, do not wait. Get up and seize the day. Do not let the uncertainty of change weigh you down. Commit to taking action, be proactive and make the most of the opportunities around you in the digital age.

I hope the **seven building blocks** I have shared in this book provide you clarity and a helpful framework to realize for yourself the opportunities from digital transformation and create your own action plan. To conclude, I would like to remind you of the need to manage duality, the complementary objectives that we have talked about multiple times in the book. The digital age abounds in these seeming contradictions—growth/profitability, strategy/execution, customers/employees, and many more. In my experience, the complexity arising from the seemingly contradictory objectives of the digital age is one of the biggest reasons for confusion and tentativeness in action, and that is why I am emphasizing this point in the conclusion.

Therefore, as you develop your action plan for digital transformation, you need to consider and execute on both short-term and long-term objectives at the same time. This **'two-speed implementation'** approach is the way to manage the complex and often contradictory objectives that abound in the digital age. The two speeds are:

- **Speed 1:** This involves short-term actions, where you solve specific problems and can get quick wins. Any change is difficult, you need to break the hold of inertia and lack of conviction. Therefore, quick wins are absolutely essential. They provide the positivity and the momentum to trigger a positive cycle of change.
- **Speed 2:** Speed 1 actions are the necessary starting point of your change journey, but they are not enough. Opportunities in the digital age are very significant and you will not realize them by taking just incremental steps. In parallel to speed 1 actions, you also need to work on speed 2 actions—which are bigger, more strategic and longer-term steps. Moreover, your speed 1 (short-term, focused) actions and speed 2 (longer-term, bigger picture) actions need to connect with and reinforce each other.

The structure and the clarity that the seven building blocks provide combined with the discipline of two-speed implementation will help you successfully realize the amazing potential of digital transformation. This is the core mantra of this book, one which will certainly help you win in the digital age.

I have found my own journey in the digital age to be full of fun and adventure, one that has allowed me to learn and grow continually, and to create impact at the business level and even beyond, which I could not have imagined possible. I encourage you to embark on your own journey of transformation and of winning in the digital age. I promise you it will be a fascinating journey. So, please seize the day and take the first steps **now**!

All the best!

Let's continue the discussion

ask me your questions, discuss
best practices and learn about
latest trends in all things digital !!

www.winninginthedigitalage.com

Acknowledgements

It takes a village to raise a child.

African proverb

It is not just the family that determines a child's development—that is what the African proverb above means. There are many persons in the child's surroundings who influence his or her personality. This is true for this book too! So, there are many people I need to thank for this book.

First and foremost, I want to thank my wife Arpna and my children Karmishtha, Devishi and Pragun for their encouragement, for weighing in on the many aspects related to the book and for patiently supporting me over the past few months as I worked to bring this book to fruition.

I would especially like to thank all of our clients at Incedo, who have given us the opportunity to partner in their digital transformation journeys. It is a real privilege for me to have a ringside view of digital transformation at so many amazing world-class companies and understand its patterns and nuances across many industries.

I would like to give a big thanks to my core team consisting of Manit Seth, Apurv Bhatnagar, Prerna Chaurasia and Shailaja Iyer for doggedly working through nights of Zoom call reviews over cups of coffee. Your constructive criticism and ideas on a host of topics and your collaboration on research have helped make the content so much better. And, you shared my belief that we had something valuable, determinedly pushing through our periods of self-doubt. Thank you for working with me as a team and for collectively ensuring that we held ourselves to the deadline.

Many of my leadership team members at Incedo contributed their perspectives on how digital transformation is playing out across industry segments and horizontals in their areas of focus. My gratitude to Krishna Rupanagunta for generously sharing insights and real-time examples from the banking industry, payments and operations transformation space; to Krishna and Shashank for contributing to the cloud story; to Gaurav Sehgal for being a source of ideas on wealth management; to Pratul Chopra for articulating best practices around customer design experience; to Pratul and Anupam Wahi for highlighting transformation challenges of the telecom sector; to Anupam for sharing his views on the game-changing shifts in product engineering; to Ashish Gupta for defining opportunities and challenges around data and AI; to Manit Seth for his contribution to bringing the global advantage story to life; to Aravind Ramamurthy for giving colour to the life sciences journey as well as the knowledge management roadmap; and to Shailaja Iyer for sharing her perspective on the overall shifts that learning and development and HR need to make. I thank all of you for your thought leadership, suggestions and advice. The book is the richer for you.

I would also like to thank my many ex-colleagues across McKinsey, Fidelity, Flipkart and ActiveKarma for the amazing learnings I've had with them over the years. My experiences across these firms have deeply shaped my understanding of the various aspects of digital transformation and of life.

I would like to end by thanking the editors Ankita Poddar from Penguin Random House and Kripa Raman for their guidance and support, their willingness to call it as they see it, making them great partners in this endeavour.

Glossary

3 D	Three-Dimensional
ACH	Automated Clearing House
AHT	Average Handling Time
AI	Artificial Intelligence
ANN	Artificial Neural Network
API	Application Programming Interface
AR	Augmented Reality
ARPU	Average Revenue Per User
ATO	Account Takeover
AWS	Amazon Web Services
B2B	Business to Business
B2C	Business to Customer
BCG	Boston Consulting Group
BPM	Business Process Management
BPO	Business Process Outsourcing
BSS	Business Support System
BU	Business Unit
CEO	Chief Executive Officer
CFO	Chief Financial Officer
CIO	Chief Information Officer

CLV	Customer Lifetime Value
CHRO	Chief Human Resource Officer
CMO	Chief Marketing Officer
CoC	Centres of Competence
CoE	Centres of Excellence
COO	Chief Operating Officer
CRM	Customer Relationship Managers
CSAT	Customer Satisfaction
CSR	Corporate Social Responsibility
CTO	Chief Technology Officer
CX	Customer Experience
CXO	Chief Experience Officer
D2C	Direct-to-Consumer
DIY	Do It Yourself
DLT	Distributed Ledger Technology
DNA	Deoxyribonucleic Acid
EQ	Emotional Quotient
ERP	Enterprise Resource Planning
EVP	Employee Value Proposition
FAANG	Facebook, Amazon, Apple, Netflix and Alphabet
FDA	US Food and Drug Administration
FP & A	Financial Planning and Analysis
GDC	Global Delivery Centre
GCP	Google Cloud Platform
GDPR	General Data Protection Regulation
GIGO	Garbage In Garbage Out
GPS	Global Positioning Systems
GST	Goods and Services Tax
GTM	Go-to-market; Google Tag Manager
GUI	Graphical User Interface
HCP	Health Care Personnel
HR	Human Resources
IAM	Identity and Access Management
ICT	Information and Communications Technology

IIM	Indian Institute of Management
IIT	Indian Institute of Technology
IoT	Internet of Things
IP	Intellectual Property
IQ	Intelligence Quotient
IT	Information Technology
IVP	Individual Value Proposition
IVR	Interactive Voice Response
KoC	Knowledge on Call
KPI	Key Performance Indicator
L & D	Learning and Development
LTV	Life Time Value
M2M	Machine to Machine
M & A	Mergers and Acquisitions
MBA	Master of Business Administration
McKC	McKinsey Knowledge Centre
MDM	Master Data Management
ML	Machine Learning
MNC	Multinational Company
MOOC	Massive Open Online Course
NIGO	Not In Good Order
NLP	Natural Language Processing
NCR	National Capital Region
NPS	Net Promoter Score
OCR	Optical Character Recognition
OEM	Original Equipment Manufacturer
OSS	Operations Support System
OT	Operations Transformation
OTT	Over the Top
P&L	Profit and Loss
PaaS	Platform as a Service
PMO	Programme Management Office
PMS	Performance Management System
PO	Purchase Order

PoC	Proof of Concept
POS	Point of Sale
PSD2	Payment Services Directive 2
QoE	Quality of Experience
R&D	Research and Development
RDBMS	Relational Database Management System
RE	Recommendation Engines
REST	Representational State Transfer
RFID	Radio Frequency Identification
RIA	Registered Investment Advisor
ROE	Return on Equity
ROI	Return on Investment
RPA	Robotic Process Automation
RWE	Real World Evidence
SLA	Service Level Agreement
SON	Self Organizing Networks
TQM	Total Quality Management
UX	User Experience
VA	Virtual Assistant
VoIP	Voice over Internet Protocol
VR	Virtual Reality
VUCA	Volatile, Uncertain, Complex, Ambiguous
WMS	Warehouse Management System

Bibliography

Section 1

Chapter 1

1. **Nitin Seth. (Jun 2017).** *Winning in the VUCA World—key priorities and transformation priorities for enterprises. http://nseth71.blogspot.com/2017/06/winning-in-vuca-world-key-principles.html*
2. **Accenture Interactive. (2018).** Pulse Check 2018. *Moving from Communication to Conversation https://www.accenture.com/_acnmedia/PDF-77/Accenture-Pulse-Survey.pdf*
3. **Boston Consulting Group. (2019).** *Global Wealth 2019. Reigniting Radical Growth. https://image-src.bcg.com/Images/BCG-Reigniting-Radical-Growth-June-2019_tcm9-222638.pdf*

Chapter 2

4. **Nitin Seth. (April 2020).** *What is digital transformation in business: everything you need to know.* Information-age. *https://www.information-age.com/what-is-digital-transformation-in-business-123477523/?fbclid=IwAR*

511

28RMsrNqkNhAcCsOuDpIneirtHHMBzzpbVYUr-kfJ5a3XbmQDhYlwIgR8

Chapter 3

5. **Nitin Seth. (Oct 2018).** *Six Reasons Why Digital Demands A New Business Paradigm.* Forbes. *https://www.forbes.com/sites/forbestechcouncil/2018/10/19/six-reason-why-digital-demands-a-new-business-paradigm/#71a2643d3aeb*

6. **Emily A. Vogels. (Sept 2019).** *Millennials stand out for their technology use, but older generations also embrace digital life.* Pew Research Center. *https://www.pewresearch.org/fact-tank/2019/09/09/us-generations-technology-use/*

7. **DATAREPORTAL. (July 2020).** *Digital 2020: July Global Statshot. https://datareportal.com/reports/digital-2020-july-global-statshot*

Chapter 4

8. **Nitin Seth. (Dec 2018).** *Five Rules For Successful Digital Transformation. Forbes. https://www.forbes.com/sites/forbestechcouncil/2018/12/26/5-rules-for-successful-digital-transformation/#37026e3a1dcd*

9. **Gartner. (March 2019).** *Why Data and Analytics Are Key to Digital Transformation. https://emtemp.gcom.cloud/ngw/globalassets/en/doc/documents/744238-100-data-analytics-predictions-2025.pdf*

Chapter 7

19. **Nitin Seth (Sept 2019).** *Digital Strategy for building scalable models in VUCA World. http://nseth71.blogspot.com/2019/09/digital-strategy-for-building-scalable.html*

20. **The Digital CIO. (April 2019).** *Digital transformation initiatives underway, but companies need help.* https://www.cio.com/article/3390137/digital-transformation-initiatives-underway-but-companies-need-help.html

Section 2

Introduction

1. **Mckinsey & Company. (Jan 2020).** *On the cusp of change: North American wealth management in 2030.* https://www.mckinsey.com/industries/financial-services/our-insights/on-the-cusp-of-change-north-american-wealth-management-in-2030
2. **Diffusion.** *2020 Direct- to-Consumer Purchase Intent.* https://www.diffusionpr.com/us/news/130/diffusions-2020-direct-to-consumer-purchase-intent-inde
3. **Innosight.** *2018 Corporate Longevity Forecast: Creative Destruction is Accelerating.* https://www.innosight.com/wp-content/uploads/2017/11/Innosight-Corporate-Longevity-2018.pdf
4. **Mckinsey & Company. MIT Sloan Management review. (May 2017).** *The Best Response to Digital Disruption.* https://www.mckinsey.com/mgi/overview/in-the-news/the-right-response-to-digital-disruption

Chapter 1

5. **Federal Reserve Bank of St. Louis (Aug 2020).** *Return on Average Equity for all U.S. Banks (USROE).* https://fred.stlouisfed.org/series/USROE
6. **Forbes. (Jun 2020).** *The World's Best Banks 2020.* https://www.forbes.com/worlds-best-banks/#30c0fcd71295
7. **CBS News. (Jun 2016).** *12 ways Amazon gets you to spend more.* https://www.cbsnews.com/media/12-ways-amazon-gets-you-to-spend-more/

8. **Oliver Wyman.** *The State of the Financial Services Industry 2020. https://www.oliverwyman.com/content/dam/oliver-wyman/ v2/publications/2020/January/Oliver-Wyman-State-of-the-Financial-Services-Industry-2020.pdf*

9. **Forbes. (April 2019).** *How much do Banks spend on Technology. https://www.forbes.com/sites/ronshevlin/2019/04/01/how-much-do-banks-spend-on-technology-hint-chase-spends-more-than-all-credit-unions-combined/#387b2bf4683a*

Chapter 2

10. **Nitin Seth. (Oct 2020).** *Digital Transformation: A Key Enabler For Wealth Management Firms In Post-Pandemic Times. Forbes. https://www.forbes.com/sites/forbestechcouncil/2020/10/26/ digital-transformation-a-key-enabler-for-wealth-management-firms-in-post-pandemic-times/?sh=91cf913856e3*

Chapter 3

11. **McKinsey & Company. (Sept 2019).** *Global Payments Report 2019. Amid sustained growth, accelerating challenges demand bold actions. https://www.mckinsey.com/~/media/mckinsey/ industries/financial%20services/our%20insights/the%202021%20 mckinsey%20global%20payments%20report/2021-mckinsey-global-payments-report.pdf*

12. **McMinsey & Company. (Oct 2020).** *The 2020 McKinsey Global Payments Report. https://www.mckinsey.com/~/media/McKinsey/ Industries/Financial%20Services/Our%20Insights/Accelerating%20 winds%20of%20change%20in%20global%20payments/2020-McKinsey-Global-Payments-Report.pdf*

Chapter 4

13. **GSMA. (Dec 2019).** *IoT Connections Forecast: The Rise of Enterprise. https://iot.eetimes.com/gsma-forecasts-slight-short-term-iot-market-disruption/*
14. **tmforum. (July 2018).** *Monetizing 5G depends heavily on OSS/BSS transformation. https://inform.tmforum.org/research-reports-cat/2018/07/monetizing-5g-depends-heavily-ossbss-transformation/*

Chapter 5

15. **BCG. (Nov 2019).** *How software companies can get more bang for their R&D Buck. https://www.bcg.com/publications/2019/software-companies-using-research-and-development-more*

Chapter 6

16. **Harvard Business Review. (2006).** *What Business Are You In?: Classic Advice From Theodore Levitt. https://hbr.org/2006/10/what-business-are-you-in-classic-advice-from-theodore-levitt*
17. **Deloitte. (Jan 2019***). Deloitte/MIT Study finds only 20% of Biopharma companies are digitally mature. https://www2.deloitte. com/be/en/pages/life-sciences-and-healthcare/articles/biopharma-press-release.html#*

Section 3

Chapter 1

1. **Nitin Seth. (Jan 2020).** *Maximizing Returns From Digital Investments: Part One—Why The Problems Persist. Forbes. https://www.forbes.com/sites/forbestechcouncil/2020/01/14/maximizing-*

returns-from-digital-investments-part-one-why-the-problems-persist/#5f82d59ecc95

2. **Harvard Business Review. (2019).** *Digital Transformation is not about Technology https://hbr.org/2019/03/digital-transformation-is-not-about-technology*

3. **The Financial Brand. (March 2019).** *Omnichannel Banking: Essential Capability? Or Unrealistic Fantasy? https://thefinancialbrand.com/81484/omnichannel-banking-mobile-branch/*

4. **Redpoint Global. (March 2019).** *Addressing the Gaps in Customer Experience. A Benchmark Study Exploring The Ever Evolving Customer Experience And How Marketers And Consumers Are Adapting. https://www.redpointglobal.com/wp-content/uploads/2019/03/RedPoint-Gaps-in-CX-White-Paper_3.20.19.pdf?_ga=2.60626541.1914644966.1579181242-50309445.1579181242*

5. **Boston Consulting Group. (Aug 2017).** *Profiting from Personalization. https://www.bcg.com/en-ma/publications/2017/retail-marketing-sales-profiting-personalization*

6. **McKinsey Digital. (Oct 2016).** *Straight talk about big data. https://www.mckinsey.com/business-functions/mckinsey-digital/our-insights/straight-talk-about-big-data*

7. **Forbes. (Jul 2018).** *How To Improve Customer Experiences With Real-Time Analytics. https://www.forbes.com/sites/louiscolumbus/2018/07/08/how-to-improve-customer-experiences-with-real-time-analytics/#6dd2e9ad6e82*

Chapter 2

8. **Nitin Seth. (Jan 2020).** *Maximizing Returns From Digital Investments, Part Two : Play Offense, Not Defense. Forbes. https://www.forbes.com/sites/forbestechcouncil/2020/01/31/maximizing-returns-from-digital-investments-part-two-play-offense-not-defense/#76e2d9c67ba7*

9. **Gartner. (Jul 2019).** *Gartner Says the Future of the Database Market Is the Cloud. On-Premises DBMS Revenue Continues to Decrease as DBMS Market Shifts to the Cloud. https:// www.gartner.com/en/doc/100-data-and-analytics-predictions-through-2025*

Chapter 3

10. **Siegel+Gale. (2019).** *The world's simplest brands 2018-2019. https://simplicityindex.com/*

Chapter 4

11. **Nitin Seth. (Jul 2018).** *Analytics Are A Source Of Competitive Advantage, If Used Properly. Forbes. https://www.forbes.com/ sites/forbestechcouncil/2018/07/18/analytics-are-a-source-of-competitive-advantage-if-used-properly/#21f30ad31894*
12. **Nitin Seth.(April 2018).** *Analytics Is Still At 10% Of Its Maturity, https://analyticsindiamag.com/analytics-is-still-at-10-of-its-maturity-says-nitin-seth-ceo-incedo/*

Chapter 5

13. **McKinsey & Company. (Jun 2019).** *Banking Operations for a customer centric world. https://www.mckinsey.com/industries/ financial-services/our-insights/banking-matters/banking-operations-for-a-customer-centric-world*

Chapter 7

14. **The Medical Futurist (TMF). (Oct 2018).** *The Genomic Data Challenges of the Future. https://medicalfuturist.com/the-genomic-data-challenges-of-the-future/*

15. **IDC. (Nov 2018).** *The Digitization of the World from Edge to Core.* *https://www.seagate.com/files/www-content/our-story/ trends/files/idc-seagate-dataage-whitepaper.pdf*

16. **Forbes.** *How Much Data is Created on the Internet Each Day?. How Much Data Do We Create Every Day? The Mind-Blowing Stats Everyone Should Read.* *https://www.forbes. com/sites/bernardmarr/2018/05/21/how-much-data-do-we-create-every-day-the-mind-blowing-stats-everyone-should-read/#7813003360ba; https://techcrunch.com/2020/10/29/ whatsapp-is-now-delivering-roughly-100-billion-messages-a-day/; https://www.internetlivestats.com/*

Chapter 8

17. **Nitin Seth. (Mar 2019).** *Blockchain—going beyond the hype to sustainable value creation.* *http://nseth71.blogspot.com/2019/03/ blockchain-going-beyond-hype-to.html*

18. **McKinsey & Company. (2018).** *Despite Billions of Dollars, Corporate Blockchains Have Achieved Little. FIAKS.* *https://fiaks.com/mckinsey-despite-billions-of-dollars-corporate-blockchains-have-achieved-little/*

19. **Globant. (2019).** *The 2019 Blockchain Technology Business Guide.* *https://blog.modex.tech/more-and-more-organizations-intend-to-invest-in-blockchain-5aac7795c835. https://mkt.globant.com/ Blockchain2019*

20. **TD Bank. (2019).** *America's Most Convenient Bank, at the 2018 Association for Financial Professionals Annual Conference. Ledger Insights.* *https://www.ledgerinsights.com/google-public-blockchains-searchable-bigquery/*

21. **Global Blockchain Business Council (GBBC). (Jan 2019).** *A Survey of Institutional Investors. International Finance.* *https://internationalfinance.com/poor-understanding-of-blockchain-among-senior-executives-gbbc-research/*

Chapter 9

22. **RightScale. (2019).** *State of the Cloud Report from Flexera™. https://resources.flexera.com/web/pdf/Flexera-State-of-the-Cloud-Report-2022.pdf*

23. **Microsoft. (Sept 2017).** *UPS paves the way for better service with faster development and artificial intelligence. https://customers.microsoft.com/en-us/story/ups*

24. **McKinsey & Company. (Oct 2020).** *How Covid-19 has pushed companies over the technology tipping point—and transformed business forever. http://www.mckinsey.com/business-functions/strategy-and-corporate-finance/our-insights/how-covid-19-has-pushed-companies-over-the-technology-tipping-point-and-transformed-business-forever?cid=eml-web; https://www.mulesoft.com/lp/reports/connectivity-benchmark*

Section 4

Chapter 1

1. **S&P. (Dec 2019).** *S&P Global Ratings. Industry Top Trends 2020. https://www.spglobal.com/_assets/documents/ratings/research/industry-top-trends-2020.pdf*

2. **MIT Sloan. (Mar 2017).** *MIT Sloan Management Review. The Big Squeeze-How compression threatens Old Industries. https://www.spglobal.com/_assets/documents/ratings/research/industry-top-trends-2020.pdf*

3. **S&P. (Dec 2019).** *S&P Global Ratings. Industry Top Trends 2020. https://www.spglobal.com/_assets/documents/ratings/research/industry-top-trends-2020.pdf*

4. **McKinsey & Company. (Jul 2020).** *Polarization between best and worst performers greater than in 2008. The Economic Times. https://economictimes.indiatimes.com/markets/expert-view/polarisation-between-best-and-worst-performers-greater-than-in-2008-mckinsey-co/articleshow/76942515.cms?from=mdr*

5. **Innosight**. *2018 Corpory Forecast: Creativate Longevite Destruction is Accelerating. https://www.innosight.com/insight/creative-destruction/;* **Inc. (Mar 2016).** *Why half of the S&P companies will be replaced in the next decade. https://www.inc.com/ilan-mochari/innosight-sp-500-new-companies.html*

6. **Deloitte. The Deloitte Global Outsourcing survey 2018.** *Traditional outsourcing is dead Long live disruptive outsourcing. https://www2.deloitte.com/content/dam/Deloitte/us/Documents/process-and-operations/us-cons-global-outsourcing-survey.pdf*

7. **Deloitte. The Deloitte Global Outsourcing survey 2018.** *Traditional outsourcing is dead Long live disruptive outsourcing. https://www2.deloitte.com/content/dam/Deloitte/us/Documents/process-and-operations/us-cons-global-outsourcing-survey.pdf*

8. **Everest Group. (Oct 2017).** *Labour arbitrage. https://www.everestgrp.com/tag/labor-arbitrage/*

9. **Forbes.(Feb2017).** *The Countries With The Most STEM Graduates. https://www.forbes.com/sites/niallmccarthy/2017/02/02/the-countries-with-the-most-stem-graduates-infographic/#1f4f38e2268a*

Chapter 2

10. **Nitin Seth.** *GICs can help transform the core business—Part 1: GICs reaching a Tipping Point. http://bpoinsights.blogspot.com/2011/11/transforming-your-core-business.html*

Chapter 3

11. **Nitin Seth.** *Transforming your core business http://bpoinsights.blogspot.in/2011/11/transforming-your-core-business_20.html*

Chapter 4

12. **Nitin Seth.** *GICs can help transform the core business—Part 4: Realizing Full Potential of GICs requires many changes in Organization Approaches http://nseth71.blogspot.com/2011/11/gics-can-help-transform-core-business_20.html*

Chapter 5

13. **Nitin Seth.** *Evolution of Global In-house Centers (GICs) and the new ask of GIC leaders. http://nseth71.blogspot.com/2013/05/some-reflections-on-global-in-house.html*

Chapter 6

14. **Nitin Seth.** *How to build a world-class Knowledge Centre?. http://nseth71.blogspot.com/2012/03/how-to-build-world-class-knowledge.html?q=knowledge*

Section 5

Chapter 3

1. **Nitin Seth.** *Innovation—a call for action for the Indian IT/BPM industry. http://nseth71.blogspot.com/2013/05/innovation-call-for-action-for-indian.html?q=innovation*

Chapter 4

2. **Nitin Seth.** *Key insights from my first Agile Training. http://nseth71.blogspot.com/2015/11/key-insights-from-my-first-agile.html?q=innovation*

Chapter 5

3. **Nitin Seth.** *Learning to Reinvent for Tomorrow.*
    http://nseth71.blogspot.com/2020/02/learning-to-reinvent-for-tomorrow.html?q=innovation

Chapter 6

4. **Nitin Seth.** *Women in Leadership.*
    http://nseth71.blogspot.com/2014/06/women-in-leadership.html?q=innovation

Chapter 7

5. **Nitin Seth.** *Change Management—Organization Dream or HR Nightmare?.*
    http://nseth71.blogspot.com/2012/09/change-management-organization-dream-or.html
6. **Nitin Seth.** *Lessons in Organisation Transformation.*
    http://nseth71.blogspot.com/2012/07/lessons-in-organization-transformation.html?q=transforming

Chapter 8

7. **Nitin Seth.** *How HR needs to transform itself to lead in the VUCA world.* *http://nseth71.blogspot.com/2017/05/how-hr-needs-to-transform-itself-to.html?q=innovation*

Chapter 9

8. **Nitin Seth.** *Unlocking the Potential of Your Workforce through AI.*
    http://nseth71.blogspot.com/2019/03/unlocking-potential-of-your-workforce.html?q=innovation

9. **McKinsey & Company. (Nov 2017).** *Jobs lost, jobs gained: What the future of work will mean for jobs, skills, and wages. https://www. mckinsey.com/featured-insights/future-of-work/jobs-lost-jobs-gained-what-the-future-of-work-will-mean-for-jobs-skills-and-wages*

Section 6

Chapter 1

1. **Nitin Seth.** *My Leadership Beliefs. http://nseth71.blogspot.com/2011/02/my-leadership-beliefs.html?q=knowledge*

Chapter 2

2. **Nitin Seth.** *How Great Leaders Inspire Others—The "5 Cs" Formula!. http://nseth71.blogspot.com/2011/11/how-great-leaders-inspire-others-5-cs.html?q=knowledge*

Chapter 3

3. **Nitin Seth**. *How to Create Great Leaders. http://nseth71.blogspot.com/2018/10/how-to-create-leaders.html?q=innovation*

Chapter 5

4. **Nitin Seth.** *Spiritual Balance—a necessity in today's material world. http://nseth71.blogspot.com/2013/08/spiritual-balance-necessity-in-todays.html*

Chapter 6

5. **Nitin Seth.** *Sustainable Development—Rethinking Consumption* *http://nseth71.blogspot.com/2015/01/sustainable-development-rethinking.html*

Section 7

Chapter 1

1. **Nitin Seth.** *Seven Success Mantras. Seven Passions for Young Indians, Building blocks for a successful career.* *http://nseth71.blogspot.com/2012/05/seven-success-mantras-convocation.html* *http://nseth71.blogspot.com/2015/02/7-passions-for-young-indians.html* *http://nseth71.blogspot.com/2013/07/building-blocks-for-successful-career.html*

Chapter 2

2. **Nitin Seth.** *Finding your "Sweet Spot"—the powerful purpose of your life!. Achieving your full potential.* *http://nseth71.blogspot.com/2012/02/finding-your-sweet-spot-powerful.html.* *http://nseth71.blogspot.com/2011/02/achieving-your-full-potential.html*

Chapter 3

3. **Nitin Seth.** *Your time is now!—8 mantras for young entrepreneurs. Launching a successful entrepreneurial journey.* *http://nseth71.blogspot.com/2017/05/your-time-is-now-8-mantras-for-young.html.* *http://nseth71.blogspot.com/2017/09/launching-successful-entrepreneurial.html*

Chapter 4

4. **Nitin Seth.** *Lessons from Steve Jobs incredible life story http://nseth71.blogspot.com/2013/06/lessons-from-steve-jobs-life-story.html*
5. **Isaacson Walter.** *Steve Jobs. Simon & Schuster (U.S.), 2011*

Chapter 5

6. **Nitin Seth.** *5 life lessons from The Giant Sequoias. http://nseth71.blogspot.com/2017/08/5-life-lessons-from-giant-sequoias.html*

Chapter 6

7. **Nitin Seth.** *9 things I wish I knew in Business School http://nseth71.blogspot.com/2014/08/9-things-i-wish-i-knew-in-business.html*
8. **Keller Gary, Papasan Jay.** The One Thing. *Bard Press, 2013*
9. **Goldratt.** *M. Eliyahu.* The Goal. *North River Press,1984*
10. **Covey Stephen.** *The Seven Habits of Highly Effective People. Free Press, 1989*

Chapter 7

11. **Nitin Seth.** *Take personal responsibility and change the world! http://nseth71.blogspot.com/2012/01/i-am-ok-you-are-not-ok.html*

India: A New Digital Superpower and Your Opportunity

12. *Teens, Social Media and Technology 2022. Pew Research Center.* 'TikTok has established itself as one of the top online platforms for US teens, while the share of teens who use Facebook has fallen

sharply'. *https://www.pewresearch.org/internet/2022/08/10/teens-social-media-and-technology-2022/#:~:text=YouTube%20tops%20the%202022%20teen,six%2Din%2Dten%20teens.*

13. *https://www.thehindubusinessline.com/money-and-banking/with-digital-ecosystem-india-can-cast-its-net-wide/article66160326.ece*

14. *https://www.investindia.gov.in/indian-unicorn-landscape*

About the Author

Nitin is an accomplished industry leader with a unique combination of experiences as a global manager, entrepreneur, and management consultant. Nitin is the Co-Founder & CEO of Incedo Inc., a high-growth Technology services firm focused on digital transformation and analytics. Prior to Incedo, Nitin has held several top management positions. He was the Chief Operating Officer of Flipkart, India's largest e-commerce company; Managing Director and Country Head for Fidelity International in India, where he also led Global Offshore Operations and Business Strategy for Fidelity's International business; and Director of McKinsey's Global Knowledge Centre in India, where he developed many new knowledge and analytics-based capabilities that have had far reaching industry impact.

Nitin has been elected twice to the NASSCOM Executive Council, was a Founder & Chairperson of NASSCOM's Global Capability Centers (GCC) Council and was the Chairperson of the NASSCOM Regional Council (NRC) in Haryana, India. He is as an avid speaker in the areas of leadership, entrepreneurship, business transformation, technology and spirituality, and writes a blog called 'Nitin's Fundas'.

Nitin holds an MBA from the Indian Institute of Management, Lucknow, where he was awarded Chairman's Gold Medal for standing first in the MBA programme, and a degree in engineering (B.Tech) from the Indian Institute of Technology, Delhi.

He lives in New Jersey, USA with his wife and three beautiful children.